THE ENGLISH COMMONWEALTH
1547–1640

PROFESSOR JOEL HURSTFIELD

THE ENGLISH COMMONWEALTH

1547–1640

ESSAYS IN POLITICS AND SOCIETY

EDITED BY PETER CLARK,
ALAN G. R. SMITH
AND NICHOLAS TYACKE

BARNES & NOBLE

BOOKS

10 East 53d St., New York 10022
(a division of Harper & Row Publishers, Inc.)

1979

Published in the U.S.A. 1979 by
Harper and Row Publishers, Inc.
Barnes & Noble Import Division
Copyright © Leicester University Press 1979

Designed by Douglas Martin
Set in 'Monotype' Van Dijck
Printed in Great Britain
by W & J Mackay Limited, Chatham

Library of Congress Cataloging in Publication Data
The English Commonwealth, 1547–1640.
Festschrift in honor of Joel Hurstfield.
Includes bibliographical references and index.
CONTENTS: Dickens, A. G. Joel Hurstfield, a memoir. –
Fuidge, N. M. Joel Hurstfield and the Tudor seminar. –
Elton, G. R. Reform of the 'commonwealth men' of Edward
VI's reign. (etc.)
1. Great Britain – History – Edward VI and Mary, 1547–1558 –
Addresses, essays, lectures. 2. Great Britain –
History – Elizabeth, 1558–1603 – Addresses, essays,
lectures. 3. Great Britain – History – Early Stuarts, 1603–
1649 – Addresses, essays, lectures.
4. Hurstfield, Joel – Addresses, essays, lectures.
I. Clark, Peter. II. Smith, Alan, G. R.
III. Tyacke, Nicholas. IV. Hurstfield, Joel.
DA340.E53 1979 942.05 78-32060
ISBN 0-06-491171-3

CONTENTS

CONTENTS

TABLES

MAP

NOTES ON CONTRIBUTORS

PETER CLARK is a Lecturer in Economic and Social History at the University of Leicester. His publications include *English Towns in Transition 1500–1700* (with P. Slack, 1976); *English Provincial Society from the Reformation to the Revolution* (1977); *Crisis and Order in English Towns 1500–1700* (edited with P. Slack, 1972); *The Early Modern Town* (edited 1976). He is currently writing a book on alehouses.

PATRICK COLLINSON is a graduate of Cambridge and London. He has taught at the University of Khartoum and at King's College, London. He has been Professor of History at the University of Sydney and is at present Professor of History at the University of Kent at Canterbury. He is the author of *The Elizabethan Puritan Movement* (1967) and was Ford's Lecturer in the University of Oxford in 1979.

A. G. DICKENS was successively a Fellow of Keble College, Oxford, and head of the History Departments at Hull and at King's College, London. During the last decade he has served as Director of the Institute of Historical Research, as Foreign Secretary of the British Academy, and as Chairman of the British National Committee of Historians. He has published some 15 books and 60 articles, chiefly on the Reformation in its local, national and international aspects.

G. R. ELTON, Fellow of Clare College and Professor of English Constitutional History in the University of Cambridge; Fellow of the British Academy; President of the Royal Historical Society 1972–6. At one time a fellow member with Joel Hurstfield of Sir John Neale's seminar at the Institute of Historical Research, his numerous publications include *The Tudor Revolution in Government* (1953), *England under the Tudors* (1955, revised edn 1974), *Policy and Police* (1972), *Reform and Renewal* (1973), *Reform and Reformation: England 1509–58* (1977).

ELIZABETH READ FOSTER is Professor of History at Bryn Mawr College, where she also formerly served as Dean of the Graduate School of Arts and Sciences. She has long been associated with the Yale Center for Parliamentary History. Her published work includes *Proceedings in Parliament 1610* (1966) and *The Painful Labour of Mr. Elsyng* (1972). She is married and the mother of four sons.

NOTES ON CONTRIBUTORS

NORAH M. FUIDGE, Research Assistant, History of Parliament Trust, was educated at King's College, London, and in 1968 and 1970 worked at the Yale Center for Parliamentary History. She has contributed to the *History of Congleton*, ed. W. B. Stephens (1970), and has written various articles. She is a Fellow of the Royal Historical Society.

JOAN HENDERSON has been a member of the Tudor seminar in London held both by Sir John Neale and Professor Joel Hurstfield.

W. J. JONES is a graduate of the University of London and is now Professor of History at the University of Alberta. He has written *The Elizabethan Court of Chancery* (1967), *Politics and the Bench* (1971), and numerous articles.

WALLACE T. MACCAFFREY took his Ph.D. from Harvard in 1950. He taught at the University of California, Los Angeles, and Haverford College, and since 1968 has been Professor of History at Harvard University. He has published *Exeter 1540–1640* (1958) and *The Shaping of the Elizabethan Régime* (1968).

CONRAD RUSSELL was an undergraduate and subsequently a Domus Senior Scholar at Merton College, Oxford. Since then he has been in the History Department, Bedford College, London, where he is now Reader in Modern History. Among his publications are *The Crisis of Parliaments* (1971), and *The Origins of the English Civil War* (edited 1973). He has just completed a study of *Parliaments and English Politics 1621–9*, to be published by Oxford University Press, and is at present working on a biography of John Pym.

ALAN G. R. SMITH was an undergraduate at Glasgow University and undertook postgraduate work at University College, London. Since 1962 he has taught at Glasgow University where he is now Senior Lecturer in History. He has written a number of books on early modern English and European history. His latest work, *Servant of the Cecils*, was published in 1977.

A. HASSELL SMITH is Reader in History at the School of English and American Studies at the University of East Anglia, where for six years he has directed the Centre of East Anglian Studies. Previously he taught at Homerton College, Cambridge, and Woolverstone Hall School, Ipswich. He is author of *County and Court: Government and Politics in Norfolk 1558–1603* (1974) and editor of *The Papers of Nathaniel Bacon 1569–1622*, volume I (1977).

NICHOLAS TYACKE was an undergraduate and research student at Balliol College, Oxford. Since 1965 he has been Lecturer in History at University College, London. He has written several articles and is currently completing a large-scale study of Arminianism in early Stuart England.

PREFACE

In editing this Festschrift we have had the happy task of paying tribute to a man and a scholar whom we admire and respect. We have also been responsible for gathering together the other historians who have contributed to the volume. That was not an easy task. Those whose names appear here were delighted to accept our invitation but we are very conscious that there are many on both sides of the Atlantic whose names do not appear but who would have been eager to contribute and who had a claim to inclusion in our list. We can only say that the resulting volume would have been an inordinately large one, not a practicable proposition in the current publishing climate.

The contributors who do appear range from Professor Hurstfield's contemporaries to his pupils, from close colleagues at London University to teachers in other universities in Britain and North America. All are professional workers in the field of early modern English history and many of them have been, at different times during the past two decades, regular members of the famous seminar which Hurstfield has conducted on Monday evenings at the Institute of Historical Research.

The contributions themselves can be related closely to both the time-span and the theme of Hurstfield's own work. With the notable exception of his studies of aspects of government policy during the Second World War his major publications cover the period from Edward VI's reign to the Revolution - exactly the years considered in this volume. The principal overall theme of our essays might not unfairly be described as discussion of the interrelationship between politics and society at both national and local level. That interrelationship, so splendidly described in Hurstfield's major work on *The Queen's Wards,* has arguably been the dominant theme in his whole corpus of writings. He has never tired of reminding us of the need to see government not simply in terms of institutions but chiefly in its effects on the men and women of the time. We all hope that these articles will add something to knowledge of that theme and of others which are important in sixteenth- and early seventeenth-century history. If no general consensus about the period emerges that will doubtless evoke no regrets in one who has written that 'the study of history flourishes best amidst diversity of opinion.'[1]

P.A.C.
A.G.R.S.
N.R.N.T.

1. J. Hurstfield, *Freedom, Corruption and Government in Elizabethan England* (1973), 19.

JOEL HURSTFIELD

A. G. Dickens

People acquainted with Joel Hurstfield's clear-cut address, his confident personality, his organized way of life, his steady devotion to teaching and scholarship, are apt to be surprised when he tells them that he came to his career only after years of uncertainty and heart-searching. Early life is by no means simple for those with multiple interests and talents. In fact he had reached his mid-thirties by the time he finally decided where his future should lie. On the other hand, he had never done anything by halves. Coming up in 1931 from Owen's School to University College London, he worked his way to a First, was awarded the Pollard and Gladstone Prizes, did two years research under J. E. Neale and from 1937 to 1940 held a lectureship at University College, Southampton. But alongside the academic ascent there ran a profound fascination with politics: it was based not only upon social and international idealism but upon the discovery of a remarkable talent for debate. Soon after taking his degree in 1934 he visited the United States as a member of the British Universities debating team, an event which started his enduring love-affair with that absorbing and provocative country. At Southampton he combined his university appointment with serious political activities, and he was due to be adopted as a parliamentary candidate in the very week that Hitler invaded Poland.

The resultant six years as a wartime civil servant gave Hurstfield the chance to reconsider his plans. The experience of the late 1930s and early 1940s did not, of course, blunt his political sensitivities. In particular the rise of Fascism and Nazism, together with the arrival of so many émigré scholars, bred in him a loathing for authoritarianism in all its forms, whether expressed in the adulation of governmental triumphs, in the crushing of dissent or in the manipulation of scholarship for party purposes. The attempt to define liberty in its historical context was destined to become a prominent theme of his writings. The civil service episode had a more unexpected influence in store when he came to work for four years as a historian in the offices of the War Cabinet. In this capacity he contributed a volume to the civil section of the official history of the war, later published as *The Control of Raw Materials*. He still claims that this experience taught him a great deal about the handling of Tudor source-materials. Having seen government documents and official handouts in process of concoction, he returned to the Tudor scene with what he has described as 'an instructed scepticism about statutes, preambles and inspired records of officialdom'.

By the end of hostilities Hurstfield fully realized the superior force of his own academic motivation. In 1946 he accepted a lectureship at Queen Mary College, London, from whence five years later he moved on to University College, being promoted to a readership in 1953 and to a chair in 1959. His important role in the postgraduate seminar, at first alongside Neale, is admirably described by Miss Fuidge in the essay which follows. Naturally enough, with his transfer to University College his relationship with his former mentor became ever closer. During the last 30 years of Neale's long life few weeks passed without a visit, a conversation or at least some exchanges on the telephone. Unlike too many scholars enjoying similar privileged relationships, Hurstfield has always acknowledged his debt to Neale in the frankest and most generous terms. For him it came to involve a merging of functions: those of pupil, colleague and friend. In his British Academy account of Neale he has written:

> I admired him greatly for his achievements, for his single-minded devotion to his chosen cause, for his capacity to inspire others, for his warmth in readily making available to successive generations of scholars the fruits of his learning and reflection, for his wit (which could sometimes be scathing) and for his humour which was always infectious.

All the same, as time passed Hurstfield was far from being the sole beneficiary of this friendship. And while drawing from it the palpable advantages, he avoided the possible dangers, for he was in no sense swallowed by the great man. He developed different concepts of Elizabeth and the politics of her reign. He operated in important fields not directly touched by Neale, while his skill in writing informally on current issues enabled him to contact a wide readership well outside the orbit of Neale's magisterial pronouncements. In so many respects he belonged to a more relaxed academic world and to a new stage of early modern historiography. Moreover Neale was not the only London historian whose influence he felt deeply, since Tawney had always captivated Hurstfield by his bold vision and range of analysis, by his toleration and courtesy to his critics and above all by his compassion and humanity.

While competent specialists in early modern English history cannot overlook the close interdependence of state and society, in practice most of them incline quite strongly toward the one theme or the other. Though primarily a historian of government, Hurstfield has held the balance more evenly than most, and it was not merely by following Tawney's example that he came to investigate the Tudor social and cultural scene. From an early stage he stood convinced of the need for historians to draw closer toward literary scholars. He has accordingly written several articles linking Shakespeare studies and Elizabethan historiography, together with at least one book which extends across both fields: *The Elizabethan Nation* (1964). That in addition he could as easily have become a major figure in local and regional history is shown by his chapter on county government 1530-1660 in the *Victoria County History* of Wiltshire, in which he reveals a fresh vista of provincial politics and of their relation to national affairs. Yet again, he has edited individually or jointly several important collections of studies covering diverse aspects of the period: *Elizabethan Government and Society* (1961); *Shakespeare's World* (1964); *The Reformation Crisis* (1965). A persuasive editor, he improves work submitted to his judgment while yet leaving the author's self-regard unimpaired. One ends by half believing one has done the job unaided! The same tact, based upon a deep respect for other personalities and viewpoints, has enabled him to collaborate most effectively with his able juniors – for example with Alan Smith in choosing and editing that admirable documentary collection, *Elizabethan People: State and Society* (1972). Alongside all this adaptability he has nevertheless preserved the strong ethical impulse which motivated his earlier political aspirations. This has disposed him, for example, to probe deeply into the nature of political corruption, especially as it appeared in the world of Burghley and his son Robert Cecil, on whose immensely significant careers he has become the leading authority.

One need hardly add that Hurstfield came to the Cecils largely through his pioneering study of the Court of Wards, which eventually led to the publication of *The Queen's Wards* (1958), a work which might still be regarded as his most erudite and massive single contribution to scholarship. On its technicalia I cannot here embark, but I may perhaps be permitted to cite a correspondent – one not given to hero-worship – who has called it 'a masterly work by any standards: on the one hand a pioneering study of social attitudes and behaviour, ... on the other, a major political analysis of Elizabethan England, examining not just the administrative anatomy but also the political muscle and sinews which made it work'. In this book and other writings Hurstfield also drew attention to the vital importance of the 1590s in the breakdown of the Tudor political order, the breakdown which did so much to shape the history of Stuart England. More responsive than Neale to this factor of disintegration, he has helped to stimulate the wave of realistic research by younger scholars who are by no means in love with Gloriana. At all events, when in 1962 Hurstfield succeeded Neale as Astor Professor of English History, one sensed not only continuity but development.

As soon as it became generally known that I was secretly writing this brief sketch, a number of Joel's friends and pupils sent me suggestions, praising not only his published works and his formal teaching but also the ease and naturalness of his exchanges, his modesty and avoidance of pomp. Sixth-formers, run-of-the-mill undergraduates, American research students beginning the Tudors from square one, they had all emerged from his presence not only better informed but with a heightened confidence in their own powers. One writer describes him as a major pillar of Anglo-American co-operation in the study of early modern history. Another remarks that 'he combined the rigour and humility of the true scholar with a real sense of the best way to help his pupils'. For my own part, I must record gratitude for his help as a pillar of the Institute of Historical Research. In addition, as a colleague in the undergraduate seminar held at King's College – it included also Bindoff, Dugmore and Collinson – I had ample opportunities to observe his unfailing adroitness and humanity as a teacher. Having known so many of the best performers in the game, I have naturally encountered several with equally well-stocked minds and even longer bibliographies, yet few if any with sharper cutting edges. How damaging he could have been had he not been furnished with a kind heart!

These things said, there remain several other Hurstfields, for he is nothing if not versatile. The bright young debater re-emerged in later years as the effervescent occasional commentator of *Don's Diary* in the *Times Higher Education Supplement*, as a frequent and ever-lively broadcaster, and again as the witty Public Orator of the University of London. In this latter capacity he somehow managed to be even better on zoologists than on historians: the less he knew of the subject, the more easily and civilly did he impale the eminent victim. He never forgot that the honorary graduand must appear not just a little larger than life, but also distinctly more amusing. Yet in the last resort, one cannot doubt that – even for this optimist – the job of being a senior London professor has had its asperities as well as its pleasures and privileges. More than other men, we are *servi servorum*. Moreover we are toothless spiders, ever visible and vulnerable at the centre of the webb, ever attacked by aggressive flies, each duly conscious of his uniqueness. At the eye of this whirlwind, there is no circle of calm, unless it be the domestic circle. Here I think we have the first clue to Hurstfield's achievements. In his family life he acknowledges himself to have been singularly fortunate, since the *lares* and *penates* have awarded him household blessings to match those gifts he has ever sought to bestow upon his wider academic family.

JOEL HURSTFIELD AND THE TUDOR SEMINAR

Norah M. Fuidge

A postgraduate seminar in history is first recorded at University College London in 1906; one of the earliest members was Rachel Reid. However, the immediate ancestor of the Tudor seminar at the Institute of Historical Research was the one led by Professor A. F. Pollard and entitled 'English Constitutional History from the fourteenth to the sixteenth centuries', which met on Tuesday afternoons or early evenings at University College. Gradually the period covered became shorter, until by 1931 it was only the sixteenth century; in this year the word 'Constitutional' disappeared from the title and it became simply 'Tudor History'. By this date it had been registered for some years at the Institute instead of the college and, apart from a break during the Second World War, it has met there ever since, from 1949 on Monday instead of Tuesday evenings.[1] Pollard, full-time director of the Institute from 1927 to 1931, insisted that it should be held in the large 'England' room so as to ensure ready access to appropriate books of reference during the discussions – a policy still adhered to, and sometimes a source of complaint from medievalists and students of post-seventeenth-century history who find themselves displaced for up to two hours a week. If anyone had the temerity to voice such objections in Pollard's day he or she probably received short shrift from the director, who was ruthlessly singleminded about the value of the seminar, to which his international reputation attracted postgraduate students from overseas, notably from the United States and Canada.

Those who attended Pollard's seminars included Professor (later Sir John) Neale, Elfreda Skelton (now Lady Neale), Professor S. T. Bindoff and Marjorie Blatcher (Mrs Bindoff). They and other members have borne witness to the rigorous standards of scholarship which Pollard demanded. The stimulating effect of this on first-class minds was unfortunately offset by his unconcealed impatience with less able students; a member of the Institute who has since done valuable work on sixteenth-century English history remembers once being physically led into the seminar by a friend who had found her downstairs, too nervous to force herself to attend it.

1. For details of the changes in siting of the Institute buildings, including the 'Tudor Cottages' and Tavistock House, see the articles by C. G. Parsloe and A. T. Milne in the *Bulletin of the Institute of Historical Research* for 1971.

The Institute possesses attendance registers from 1927 to 1939 (the last session before the Second World War) and from 1946 onwards, and for the first of these periods a set of 'minutes', i.e. lists of subjects raised with the names of those who introduced them, and occasionally brief accounts of the discussions. In 1927 the joint leaders were given as Pollard, Neale and Miss Eliza Jeffries Davis; from October 1931 to June 1933 Neale and Miss Davis with Mr C. H. Williams; from 1933-4 Neale and Williams; and from 1934 (the year in which Hurstfield's name first appears on the register) to 1939 Neale alone. The 'minutes' make fascinating reading. Some subjects raised would be considered outside the scope of the present seminar. Early in 1928 Neale asked, 'What was the authority of the court that offered Joan of Arc the alternatives of death or perpetual imprisonment?', while Pollard was concerned to find conclusive evidence that the Lancastrian rose was red. No answer to either question is recorded, nor to two others raised in 1933 and the following year: 'How many people could the Court of Star Chamber hold?' and 'Where was Henry VIII on the day of Anne Boleyn's execution?'

Other entries are humbling to a later generation of scholars, not only becouse they show that 'new' subjects currently exercising historians were already in debate almost 50 years ago, but because with all our modern aids to research we have still failed to answer many of the questions raised. The much discussed and often misunderstood 'biographical method' appears in 1928, when Neale reported on Colonel Josiah Wedgwood's proposal for a biographical list of Members of Parliament; in the following years Elfreda Skelton led a discussion on the giving of votes or voices by judges in the Star Chamber; while at various sessions before 1939 Pollard fulminated against the 'evil' indexing of *Letters and Papers of Henry VIII* and the 'mendacity' of J. A. Manning's *Lives of the Speakers of the House of Commons*. R. B. Wernham spoke on the alleged treason of Sir Edward Stafford, Jean Wilson asked what kind of credentials ambassadors carried with them, and Marjorie Blatcher discussed John Doe and Richard Roe and led a later debate on the Bill of Middlesex. One meeting concentrated on the propaganda value of sermons, with special reference to those at Paul's Cross organized by the government in 1601 at the time of the Essex rebellion. As early as 1933 Neale raised one of the most difficult problems still facing the editors of the *History of Parliament* – the significance of 'blanks' in parliamentary indentures and the insertion of names of Members in different hands.

The atmosphere of the seminar must have changed considerably when Neale succeeded Pollard. No one could be more severe than the new leader on work that he considered (in his favourite phrase) 'sloppy', but his infectious enthusiasm and sense of humour could make even diffident, inexperienced students feel that they had something useful to contribute. Neale once described the seminar as a 'workshop', a place where people concerned with different aspects of the sixteenth and early seventeenth centuries could find material, tools and skilled help. For this reason he disliked the reading of set papers and preferred that all members of the group should feel free to report discoveries or raise problems arising from their work since the last meeting. This policy was not always successful, since there were inevitably 'dead' weeks when few or no interesting questions were produced; but Neale felt that at such times he or other experienced scholars such as Professors Bindoff and Hurstfield who often attended the seminar would be ready to share their knowledge and insights with the less well-equipped.

During the post-war period, when Neale was the sole leader, and the subsequent years from 1956 when he and Hurstfield conducted the seminars together, the attendance registers contain such well-known names as Patrick Collinson, Geoffrey Elton, W. J. Jones and Jack Scarisbrick, with distinguished visitors from the United States – Elizabeth Read Foster, Basil Henning, Wallace MacCaffrey, Walter Richardson and, among a group of eminent clerical scholars, J. F. Larkin and A. J. Loomie. Neale's confidence in the quality of help available to beginners was well-founded. None of those who worked with him could fail to appreciate his own contribution to their understanding of the period, and many can bear witness to the lasting effect of the seminars in the 1950s and 1960s on the scope and standard of the group's research. This applies with especial force to scholars concerned with political and constitutional history. The interests of the director are necessarily reflected in a seminar's discussions, and one objection raised not altogether unjustly to Neale's leadership was that parliamentary and religious questions tended to receive a disproportionate amount of the time available. But nothing can detract from the stimulating effect of group work under his guidance.

There followed some years during which, as a result of Neale's increasing physical infirmity, Hurstfield became in effect sole leader, and when Neale died in the autumn of 1975 the seminar (now styled 'English History c.1500– 1650') continued in the form which Hurstfield had already introduced. The main innovation since the Neale days has been the reading of prepared papers, often lasting no more than half to three-quarters of an hour, preceded by a few minutes during which members can raise urgent questions; once or twice a term there is a reversion to the earlier system with no planned topic of discussion. Within this framework there is room for plenty of variety; especially as more time is now given to social and economic subjects. The apparently irresistible temptation for contemporary historians to find alliterative titles might lead one to label Neale's seminars 'Parliament and Puritanism' and Hurstfield's 'Consent, Consistency and Corruption'; but this would be unfair to the multifarious interests of both men.

Hurstfield's own high standard of scholarship is one factor in the stimulating effect of his seminars; another is his intellectual humility and readiness to share leadership with younger university teachers. Recently he has made the seminar a joint venture by enlisting as co-directors Mr Conrad Russell of Bedford College, with his detailed knowledge of early Stuart parliaments, and Dr Nicholas Tyacke from University College, an expert on the Elizabethan and Jacobean Church. This innovation should ensure a constant influx of new postgraduate students of all three leaders, with a further widening of the scope of discussions. In the present session members are working, *inter alia,* on county society in Hertfordshire; Lincolnshire Crown lands; the Exchequer under Edward VI; Tudor opinion on the status of women; the impact of Scottish armies in Northumberland and Durham during the 1640s; and early seventeenth-century figures such as Dr Robert Flood, Henry Parker, and General Thomas Fairfax. The seamy side of life under the Tudors and early Stuarts is strongly represented, with research into the duties and tribulations of parish constables, 'notorious English murderers 1580–1620', and 'professional crime in Elizabethan London'. Neale's two specialities are not neglected: one student is studying the moderate puritan tradition from 1580–1610; while Miss Joan Henderson's imminent completion of her study of the House of Commons in 1589 will mark the end of the team work on English parliaments begun when Neale was preparing his *Elizabethan House of Commons* and the two subsequent volumes.

Over this veritable minefield of potential danger for unwary researchers Hurstfield moves competently and cheerfully; he shows unfailing judgment as to when to urge on or to recommend caution. After a busy day at University College he hurries in smiling, and (with a reminder of Neale) contriving to look as if he expects to be stimulated, even excited, by the forthcoming discussion. The seminar grins back affectionately. We know that he will have lost the paper on which he meant to make notes; that he will fight a losing battle with the names on the register; that he will promise not to interrupt the speaker, and then feel that a knotty point or an ambiguous term cannot be allowed to pass without comment; that at the end of the paper, having insisted that he will listen to questions from others before raising his own, he will add, 'But there is one small point . . .'; and that a chance reference to the sixteenth-century meaning of 'consent' or to the prevalence of corruption in Elizabethan and Jacobean England will prove an irresistible challenge. But we know also that he will generate an atmosphere of courtesy and friendliness; that he will find something to praise in even the most tedious or inadequate paper; that he will keep the discussion on useful and productive lines; and that not only will his own contribution to the debate be invaluable but that he will know where to find and draw out the expertise of others so that the current topic, however apparently limited in scope, can be fitted into the wider context of Tudor and early Stuart history. At the end of the session comes the inevitable invitation, 'Does anyone want to see me before next week?' The hours which Hurstfield has given to private interviews with members of the seminar – often with students for whom he has technically no responsibility

– must run into hundreds, and many scholars on both sides of the Atlantic can bear witness to the spontaneous generosity with which he sets aside time to help and encourage them.

As long ago as 1956, Mr (now Professor) W. J. Jones wrote that in the seminar 'everything seems relevant. A recent inquisition began somewhere in the Chancery, moved out into Chester, back into the Privy Council and the sphere of executive authority, across the waters to Ireland picking up Sir Thomas Smith on the way, and so through administrative problems of that many-sided man to the failings – or virtues – of Queen Elizabeth'.[1] The scope of discussion has become even wider now, but under Hurstfield and his fellow leaders the seminar, often attended by as many as 30 students, lives up to its longstanding reputation as 'a joint committee dedicated both to research and evaluation'.[2]

1. *The Pollardian* (student magazine of the History Department, University College London); special edition in honour of Professor Sir John Neale, 9.
2. *Ibid.*, 10.

I

REFORM AND THE 'COMMONWEALTH-MEN' OF EDWARD VI'S REIGN

G. R. Elton

Amongst the received truths of Tudor history, the existence in the reign of Edward VI of a group of reformers called the commonwealth-men occupies an apparently secure place. I have myself before this called them a party,[1] as has W. K. Jordan even more firmly.[2] That party stands at the centre of the standard work on the Tudor common weal.[3] Others, though less persuaded of quite such a formal coherence, still accept that a body of people, likeminded and active, surrounded Somerset's government, offering criticism and advice on the problems of the day and their solution. A collection of concerned and vocal individuals are supposed to have been working inside government circles in the age of Somerset, more articulate and influential even than their predecessors in the age of Cromwell whose existence has more recently been demonstrated.[4] Only Michael Bush, casting a critical eye on all the traditional views of Somerset's régime, finds that if there were commonwealth-men they did not work together, formulated no agreed programme, and constituted no 'group or party'.[5] He comes very close to discovering this particular emperor totally devoid of clothes.

Where, indeed, did the notion originate? If we look to the nineteenth-century historians we find no mention of commonwealth or commonwealth-men. Dixon managed to discuss John Hales and the movement against enclosures at some length without ever using the shibboleth, and Froude, recognizing that what he calls the 'sincere and upright among the Reformers' concentrated on the social evils produced by human greed rather than on theological dispute, also had never heard of this party.[6] But as the twentieth century opened the whole concept sprang fully armed from one man's head. 'Under Edward VI,' said Pollard, 'a small but able party, including divines and politicians, began to form.' What is more, 'it was called the "Commonwealth" party'; and he cited among its followers the threesome who have dominated that scene ever since – Latimer, Lever and Hales.[7] Such a categoric description, alleging even a contemporary use of the term party, must

G. R. ELTON

surely have rested on solid evidence. In fact, Pollard had only one quotation to offer: a letter from Sir Anthony Auchar to William Cecil, written on 10 September 1549 to complain of those who by their critical attacks on the practices of the upper classes had helped to stir up the commons.[8] Auchar did not use the word party, but he did refer to 'these men called common-wealths' and 'that commonwealth called Latimer'. Though we may, therefore, believe that some critics of society had been nicknamed after one of their favourite catchwords, Pollard would seem to have erected his party structure on somewhat narrow foundations. He certainly made that letter work hard for himself, citing it again and again in his book on Somerset so as to create an impression of multiple support.[9] When some years later he came to write his general history of the period, Auchar had suffered multiplication or subdivision, and his men 'called commonwealths' had become the fully fledged concept: 'staid officials', we are told, 'wrote in alarm about the new commonwealth party'.[10] It is necessary to remember that we still depend solely on that one letter with its brief reference to undefined possessors of a soubriquet and its mention of only one name. In due course Tawney (who in *The Agrarian Problem in the Sixteenth Century*, published in 1912, appeared never to have heard of these people whose concerns were so very close to his own) added his authority to the story when he spoke of a group 'known to their enemies as the "Commonwealth men"' whose prophet was Latimer and whose man of action was Hales.[11]

Thus, blessed by the twin stars of the Tudor heaven, the commonwealth party of Edward VI's reign entered the general consciousness of historians: a body of likeminded men, including preachers and administrators, devoted to a programme of social reform, and attached to the Protector Somerset who espoused their policies and attempted to put them into effect. As we have seen, not everybody since then has accepted this view in every detail, but the historiography of the reign has nevertheless been marked by their alleged existence (with the maverick and honourable exception of Dr Bush). And yet, anything like a closer look must at once call up doubt. The very name 'commonwealth men' is nowhere vouched in the record: Pollard's sole piece of evidence does not use it but instead gives us the much more attractive, if contemptuous, term 'the commonwealths'. If the concept of the common-wealth – which, as is now well accepted, did not originate in the 1540s and in any case meant no more than 'the common good'[12] – had really been such a hallmark of reform one would expect to see it freely used in the reforming legislation of the day; but it occurs there much more rarely than in the statutes of Thomas Cromwell's time. I have found only nine mentions of it. On five occasions it is used to advocate a measure beneficial to the common weal;[13] three Acts attack vagabondage and such like as dangerous to the common weal;[14] once only does it seem to carry the meaning of 'body politic' which has generally been regarded as its primary significance.[15] Of

24

Somerset's proclamations only six contain the word, four of them using it to mean the state;[16] why, even the famous enclosure proclamation of 1 June 1548 has no hint of it.[17] Similarly it rates no mention in Acts which one might think would call for it, such as those against price-fixing arrangements, or the codifying Acts for tillage, cloth manufacture and usury.[18] What is more, of those nine statutory occurrences only four could conceivably be associated with Somerset's administration; the rest came too late. (Northumberland's proclamations use the word nine times.)[19] Of course, the term may have been more freely used in the many failed bills of the reign, but at any rate it has left no convincing signs of being any sort of party slogan.

Worse doubts arise as one looks at the people whose pronouncements and actions have been used to define the programme of this 'party' and who were active in 1548–9, until the rebellions of the latter year provoked a reaction which allegedly swallowed up Somerset and commonwealth alike. Four names recur with convincing regularity: Hugh Latimer, Thomas Lever, Robert Crowley and John Hales. Professor Bindoff almost alone draws attention to Thomas Smith, the most remarkable economic theorist of the day, while Dr Jones adds a list of eminent divines (Bradford, Ridley, Becon and Hooper) who, however, cannot really be said to have written seriously about the social ills of the common weal. That first quartet deserve a closer look: they all unquestionably addressed themselves to such problems, they left behind plenty of evidence for their views, and it need not be denied that they approached the issues with much the same preconceived convictions touching the miseries of the poor. However, even a first glance, before the look becomes closer, raises a striking fundamental difficulty. If these 'commonwealth-men' influenced the policy of 1548–9, one must surely find them expressing their views in those years, not later. Yet there survives no sermon of Lever's from before 1550, and most of Crowley's relevant writings – including that cited most often – belong to that year and the next. Pollard's treatment of Latimer reinforces apprehensions first raised by his treatment of Auchar. Latimer did preach two series of sermons before Somerset's fall – one before Edward VI in Lent 1549, and one at Paul's Cross ('On the Plough') a few months earlier. It is this second series on which Pollard relies in claiming that Latimer attacked enclosure.[20] Since there is not one word on enclosure in the one sermon extant from the series, one must suppose that Pollard had intuitive knowledge of what was in the three that are lost. Only Hales unquestionably and entirely devoted himself to these commonwealth matters at the right time, in the years 1548–9, and only Hales can be proved to have established direct contact with Somerset; the rest, no doubt at times in favour at Court, never entered the inner circles of government.

This analysis has so far been entirely negative, to clear the ground. It has really become manifest that there was no such thing as a commonwealth movement or party in the days of Somerset; those that have failed to find a programme devised by thinkers and applied by government (the sort of thing that happened in the 1530s) are quite right. But that does not necessarily dispose of certain other aspects of that mistaken interpretation. Doing away with the commonwealth-men does not deny the existence of the economic crisis – inflation and destitution – or the antisocial practices of landlords and middlemen. No one would wish to shut his eye to the crisis; and while the alleged malpractices deserve rather more searching discussion than they usually receive from those for whom the sermons of the day contain the whole truth, they cannot here be considered at length. This essay will confine itself to an examination of the actual views expressed by those who, whether a party or not, have so strongly influenced posterity's notions of that age. Now that we have disposed of the commonwealth party it does not matter whether Lever preached and Crowley wrote before or after the upheavals of 1549; it matters greatly that we should be sure we know what in fact they said if we are to understand them and their age correctly. Here again, it seems to me, the established consensus of historians rests on at best a partial reading of their works, and a reading moreover blinkered by the sort of convictions which Pollard and Tawney brought to their investigations.

Hugh Latimer deserves his place of primacy as a champion of the poor: age, authority and the passion of his discourse make him a leader. Even Auchar, as we have seen, singled him out as a chief instigator of discontent and also a protector at court for others who thought like him. It is not certain that we really know what he said in his preaching: he worked without scripts, and we possess no texts written or passed for printing by himself, but only reports taken down at the time and printed without his assistance. In all public addresses, the best bits are always likely to survive such treatment; duller passages will vanish from the memory. Still, what we have looks sufficiently of one piece and the product of one voice to overcome nihilist scepticism: it is very probable that Latimer said approximately what has been preserved as his sermons. What then did he say?[21] Of the four Paul's Cross sermons on the plough only the last survives,[22] but it sufficiently indicates the burden of his message, especially as it begins by recalling the preacher's theme for the series. The traditional title easily misleads one into thinking that he was preoccupied with the agrarian problems of the nation, but his plough was a metaphor and had nothing to do with husbandry. He was talking of preparing the ground for the sowing of true religion, and the main targets for his displeasure were not the enclosing landlords but the inadequate clergy, especially the bishops. The prelates, he charged, were neglecting their duty to preach the word: 'They are otherwise occupied, some in the king's matters, some are ambassadors, some of the privy council, some to furnish the court, some are lords of the parliament, some are presidents and controllers of mints.'[23] The last especially seems to have rankled: 'The saying is, that since priests have been minters, money hath been worse than it was before. And they say that the evilness of money hath made all things dearer.'[24] In this sermon, this is really the only reference to the economic problems of the day, and while what 'they' said rightly pointed to debasement as the cause of inflation it was hardly sensible to lay the blame exclusively on the Durham mint. What we really hear in these charges are Latimer's reasons for refusing to resume the episcopal office he had held in the 1530s: preaching, not government service, he regarded as the first duty of the clergy, and this is the overriding burden of his sermon. A secondary line called for educational reforms, to make all the laity more useful to the community, a commonplace inherited from the reformers (humanist as well as protestant) of Latimer's old acquaintance. He also observed the rules of popular preaching by attacking a decline in charity: Londoners, especially, were blamed for no longer supporting learning with bequests for scholarships.[25] In this address to a public audience, the preacher said nothing at all about the miseries of the peasantry or the wickedness of landlords – and this even though it was only a few months since the enclosure commissions had gone forth to do battle with those alleged abuses. There is no sign here that such things interested him.

On the other hand, they did on occasion engage him in the seven sermons he preached at Court between 3 March and 19 April 1549. The first of them contained those famous passages which have been quoted over and over again to prove the depravity of the Edwardian régime – his splendid threnody on the yeomen of Old England and his crack about the 'pretty little shilling' which he had nearly mistaken for a groat. It also included some brief references to the agrarian problem. He spoke of 'graziers, enclosers and rent-rearers' who were causing depopulation;[26] covetous landlords, he cried, by their enhancing of rents had produced 'this monstrous and portentous dearth made by man' at a time of plentiful harvests (what had become of the Durham mint?). Throughout, of course, he showed himself concerned for the poor who, he repeatedly said, could get no justice: he urged the Protector to hear their suits in person and charged the Lord Chancellor with needlessly delaying poor men's causes by refusing to attend every day to his sealing duties.[27] However, it would be quite wrong to treat those Lent sermons as primarily directed against the oppressors of the poor. For one thing, all the really stinging things were said in the first, which caused offence; in the third, Latimer defended himself and others against charges of preaching sedition but thereafter noticeably avoided such contentious themes. His famous lament on the decline of the yeomanry reveals what his real grievance was. He was not primarily concerned with bettering the peasant's lot: what troubled him was that impoverishing that rank of society would bar them from educating their sons and marrying their daughters: the universities would collapse and whoredom increase. 'I say, ye pluck salvation from the people and utterly destroy the realm.' The remark about the new shilling,

which reads very much like an impromptu preacher's joke, will hardly bear
the burden of economic criticism so often placed upon it by historians,
though at the time some of his hearers, against whose pompous resentment
Latimer unleashed some of his best irony, displayed the same humourlessness
at the other end of the spectrum.[28] Other themes certainly got far more
thorough treatment than economic grievances: insufficient preaching by the
clergy, the general decline of university studies, the prevalence of pro-
stitution in no way arrested by the closing of the stews in 1546. He gave
almost more time to his advocacy of archery as a cure for lechery than to
enclosing landlords.[29] Above all, the last three of those seven sermons are
astonishingly dominated by the preacher's defence of the destruction in-
flicted upon Thomas Seymour, the Protector's brother, a defence which
gradually drove all other matters from his mind. Interesting though his
words are, and important in that they reveal some of the activities of court
faction, they gravely call in doubt his genuine independence and his real
role. To me at least, these quite intemperate, even hysterical, attacks on a
man already lost deprive Latimer of a claim to which his preaching otherwise
entitles him – the claim to have bravely confronted the mighty with the
immorality of their worldly dealings. But even if a more charitable view is
taken of one who thus used the pulpit for the benefit of faction, it must be
plain that the confused heaping up of delinquencies seen in the body politic
constitutes at best only a general outburst of grieved spleen, devoid of either
a reforming programme or any rational understanding of what had gone
wrong. As one might expect, Latimer was not analysing the ills of the common weal but denouncing sin and blaming those who permitted it to flourish.

This truth is brought out more clearly still in the last of his court sermons,
delivered in the Lent of 1550. After the upheavals of the previous year one
might have expected him to devote his time to the causes of unrest, and we
do indeed hear scathing remarks touching those who rob the ploughman
of his pasture – almost the only passage surviving from Latimer which shows
a positive understanding of peasant life.[30] Latimer also once more defended
his preaching against the charge that it caused sedition. But the real subject
of the sermon is once again sin, the sin of covetousness, and he charges
everybody with it, the rebellious peasantry as much as the exploiting lords:
'both parties had covetousness, as well the gentlemen as the commons.'[31] His
insistence that the greed of the supposedly dispossessed, and not the misdeeds
of the possessioners, had led to rebellion is worth remembering; Latimer
gives no comfort to those who would regard an uprising as a legitimate
response to misery. What really must startle the reader, however, is the
manner in which he leads into the subject of greed. He begins by demanding
the death penalty for adultery and involves himself at length in a diatribe
against lechery, a diatribe which clearly amused his hearers so that, indig-
nantly, he was forced to cry out that it was no laughing matter. Lechery, he

argues, leads to covetousness because lechers need cash.[32] So that was what was wrong with England. And what is Latimer's proposed remedy? The sermon ends with a passionate appeal to the king to use all means to enforce the law against all who take profit at other people's expense: 'For God's sake, make some promoters. There lack promoters, such as were in king Henry the Seventh's day, your grandfather.'[33] Promoters – professional informers – had been among Henry VII's most disliked expedients. In this appeal Latimer fully demonstrated his inability to think constructively rather than emotionally about the common weal. Harking back to a strangely glorified past, he stuck to that past's sole conviction about the human condition: that man's covetousness caused all his troubles. That had been the message of Colet's preaching;[34] it had been the message of More's *Utopia*; and it was no doubt valid enough in any display of virtuous indignation. But what was the practical use of such declaiming? If all, poor and rich alike, were sinful greedy men, what did Latimer propose to do about it? He proposed to hang some and fine the rest, searching them out by means of entrepreneurs who made a profit out of prosecuting breaches of the law.

Latimer, of course, was an old man, an old man with memories though still full of passion. Thomas Lever, on the other hand, was only 29 in 1550 when he preached three powerful sermons about the evils of the commonwealth, and from him we might expect a much more direct involvement in the problems of the day. Since we have these sermons in a printed version published under the preacher's own oversight, we can be sure that we hear his authentic voice. We also, in consequence, have magnificently composed and tightly structured discourses in splendid prose, in place of the run-about and knock-about flood which Latimer was recorded as delivering.[35] Lever's three relevant sermons were preached early in 1550 in the shrouds at St Paul's, on 16 March 1550 before the king and privy council, and on 1 December 1550 at Paul's Cross: all, therefore, after the rebellions of 1549, which in fact constitute the main theme of his discourses. We have not one word of Lever's from before those troubles, and since all he has left us was said after Somerset's fall it is not possible to associate him with the reforming activities of the duke's régime.

However, though Lever cannot be supposed to have had any influence on the policies of the so-called commonwealth-men, his preaching fits the conventional notions of that group a little better than does Latimer's. At least he did attack the behaviour of the upper classes in some detail, and to their faces, crying out at landlords who forced tenants to surrender their leases by sharp practices, thus increasing the numbers of the starving and homeless poor who earned his special compassion, at traders who were more anxious to make money than to provide cheap goods, at impropriators of livings and those who bought offices for money. It has, however, to be said that he sounds most convincing when he weighs in with complaints against the clergy[36] and about the decline of education. Nothing in his sermons exeeds in sincerity his bitter conviction that the English nation, rescued so lately from the darkness of popery, has utterly failed to benefit from that reformation: 'it is not virtue and honesty but very vice and hypocrisy whereof England at this day doth most glory'.[37] 'Papistry is not banished out of England by pure religion, but overrun, suppressed and kept under within this realm by covetous ambition.'[38] Lever, predictably, was a Christian preacher, concerned with the wrath that God has in store for the reprobate; he too is more concerned with reproving sin than with improving the economy. This is not to overlook the positive suggestions he makes – more and better schools financed from the monastic lands, as was first intended, or the use of the profits enjoyed by unfaithful office-holders in state and Church for the relief of the poor – but it is to put the emphasis where he thought it belonged.

To treat Lever's concern for the poor as though he had been a premature Fabian pamphleteer is to misjudge both him and his century. In the first place, he is quite as much concerned to denounce rebellion as he is to condemn oppression, and his words on this point sound fully as sincere as anything he says: he was assuredly not just pandering to his audience. That 'generation of vipers, the ungracious rebels' who in his opinion had been treated much too mercifully the previous year,[39] get an equal share of his anger with the gentlemen whose practices impoverish the realm for private gain. Almost in one breath he upbraids his noble audience for abusing the gifts of the reform ('the fault is not in the things to be set forth but in you that have set them forth') and calls for the destruction of all rebellion.[40] The tenets of communism – he is thinking of Anabaptists and similar sectaries – get very short shrift: they encourage only greed. He agrees that no one should be left in need and that the rich must use their surplus to relieve the poor, but that, he says, is a very different thing from demanding that all things should be owned in common.[41] Like Colet, Latimer and all good moral preachers since the dawn of time, he identifies covetousness as the ultimate cause of all trouble, 'the root of all evil', and wants to see it pulled from everybody's heart – not only from those of gentlemen who exact high rents and fines but also from those of husbandmen only too willing to pay what was demanded in order to take other men's lands.[42] The one thing he denies to the oppressed without any qualification at all is the right to help themselves even against unjust treatment: 'As the people can have no remedy against evil rulers by rebellion, so can the rulers have no redress of rebellious people by oppression.'[43] And while it is assuredly wrong for rich men to 'make strait laws to save their own goods', it is worse to rebel and thus wreak greater havoc than that produced by the most tyrannical of laws.[44] How very serious he could wax about the duties of subjects: they must even pay all taxes as demanded – though the government should demand only what is just – 'and not to be curious to know for what cause it is asked'.[45] The

doctrine of obedience could go no further. After all that convincing denunciation of exploiting gentlemen and corrupt clergy, the commons are left
with no chance of redress except through the voluntary amendment of the
upper classes instructed by the preacher's moral exhortation.

Those who have seen in Lever a social reformer and a fiery champion of
the poor should really have noticed what lies at the heart of his system: not
the redistribution of wealth to relieve poverty, but the exercise of voluntary
charity. While communism is evil, it is the duty of the rich to distribute
largesse. If they, too, fall on hard times and have no surplus to give away
they must liquidate resources to fill the coffers of charity: 'yea, if there be
great necessity he must sell both lands and goods to maintain charity.'[46]
This is not a prescription that displays much understanding of economic
problems or was likely to lead to a better maintained common weal. When
all is said and done, Lever's complaint against the gentry may be summed
up in his own words:

> For a gentleman will say that he loveth his tenants as well as his father
> did, but he keepeth not so good house to make them cheer as his father
> did, and yet he taketh more fines and greater rents to make them needy
> than his father had.[47]

The good gentleman will not only avoid squeezing his tenants but he will
in particular provide them with hot dinners.

Of course, Lever denounced the covetousness which ruined the peasantry
and had diverted the wealth of the secularized estates from the good social
and educational purposes at first intended. But his remedies remain uncon-
structive, backward-looking and moralistic, and through all his sermons
his devotion to a conservative, hierarchic society in which active protest
equals foul rebellion shines through. Lever was a very powerful and very
attractive preacher, readily angered by the doings of sinful men, but he was
neither a liberal nor a socialist. Nor was he a commonwealth-man, and the
court at which he preached was dominated by the duke of Northumberland
who willingly let him have his say.

Latimer and Lever were divines, in holy orders and closely tied to the
universities: Latimer's repeated complaint of the lack and poor quality of
matriculands shows this as plainly as does Lever's affecting description of
the frugal life led by Cambridge scholars. With Robert Crowley, even though
he took a degree at Oxford and in 1551 got ordained, we are in a different
company – that of the London-based printers and pamphleteers who put
forth books of topical concern. He assuredly belongs to the long tradition
of social protest, and it is no wonder that those who believe in the 'commonwealth party' are likely to mention the two preachers with respect but to
cite from Crowley. True, such quotations are not always as well considered
as they might be. Crowley's splendid invective against the rich – 'men that

31

have no name because they are doers in all things that any gain hangeth upon; men without conscience; men utterly void of God's fear; yea, men that live as though there was no God at all,' and so on – naturally attracted Tawney's attention, and his use of it has firmly established this diatribe in the reservoir of useful quotations.[48] But what Tawney failed to say, and what those who take their Crowley at second hand do not know, is that Crowley does not here profess to speak for himself: this is the sort of thing, he explains, which a poor man will say if asked for the cause of his troubles. Later on he similarly puts picturesque abuse of the commons into the mouth of a notional rich man. On the whole Crowley was certainly on the side of the poor, but he did not assert that he personally endorsed all that colourful abuse.

Two works of Crowley's are relevant here, one written in 1548 and as part of a campaign to get action from Somerset in aid of the distressed (*An Information and Petition against the Oppressors of the Poor Commons of this Realm*), and one written in 1550, after the experience of rebellion (*The Way to Wealth*).[49] They display interesting differences arising from circumstances as well as a reasonably coherent standpoint. The first was addressed to the Lords and Commons of the Parliament then sitting; it was 'compiled and imprinted for this only purpose that amongst them that have to do in the Parliament some godly-minded men may thereat take occasion to speak more in the matter than the author was able to write'. The pamphlet offers a programme of reform by legislation. The second claimed that it 'taught a most present remedy for sedition' and outlined ways for restoring harmony. Both, however have no doubt that the condition of the people of England left a great deal to be desired and that the cause of all the misery are certain greedy exploiters.

Crowley's advice to Parliament started by taking it for granted that the oppression of the poor 'by the possessioners as well of the clergy as of the laity' was the main issue to be discussed, even more than the settlement of religion which nevertheless also called for debate. He sets out grievances on both scores. The poor suffer because the rich act on the principle, 'it is mine own: who shall warn me to do with mine as myself listeth?'. This attitude might serve if there were no God, but 'we have a God' who has told us that he will hold all those who possess wealth to account for their stewardship. Crowley certainly operated on a very different assumption: all men have an equal right to wealth, that is to say what they can earn by their sweat, and 'the whole earth therefore, by right of birth, belongeth to the children of men. They are all inheritors thereof indifferently by nature.'[50] One sees why he felt it necessary to defend himself against any suspicion of communist views,[51] though in the light of such principles his defence does not sound terribly convincing. The main trouble, according to him, is that landlords squeeze every penny out of their lands and the poorer sort can get no property of their own. In consequence, the children of the poor perish: boys quite capable of following the liberal arts ('whereof the realm hath

great need') instead must resign themselves to menial work in support of
their impoverished parents, good girls are forced to stay unmarried or to
marry for money against their inclination, and 'immodest and wanton girls
have hereby been made sisters of the Bank'. It is quite an original line (though
one that echoes Latimer) which finds the worst consequences of the gentlemen's greed in forgone scholarly careers, enforced virginities and the filling
of the brothels. More particularly Crowley lists two abuses: leasemongering
which piles rent upon rent on each piece of property, and inflationary valuations by land surveyors. Both these drive men of modest means out of the
land market. The former is particularly prevalent in London where nine-
tenths of all houses are sub-let down a chain of tenants, so that rents rise
sky-high. Since, however, neither touches 'the wealth of the nobility' – 'yea,
it is rather hindrance to many of them to have these things redressed than
any increase of their wealth' – these evils will not be mentioned in Parliament
unless the pamphleteer draws attention to them.[52] The only other secular
grievance listed concerns usury, Crowley wanting to see the statutory
permission (of 1545) repealed. As a programme of social reform it strikes
one as both limited and idiosyncratic, especially in its manifest concentration
upon London. London also looms large in Crowley's notions of what is wrong
with the spiritual realm: the only matter he specifically complains of is the
tithe as levied in London under arrangements settled by statute.[53] Even
the standard charge against the clergy, that they do not discharge their
true function properly, drags in London: when 'our ministers . . . apply themselves to priesting because they like well the idleness of the life', they behave
like craftsmen seeking the freedom of the city for their own ends. There is a
good deal of passion, backed by scriptural citation, in this pamphlet, but the
substantive content remains pretty slight, especially after the expectations
aroused by its title. Crowley is manifestly very angry, but as a promoter
of reform he prefers cutting phrases to comprehensive analysis.

When two years later this champion of the underdog came to offer his
'present remedy for sedition', he turned out to be yet another broken reed,
though his gift of language had not deserted him. Professing to find a way to
root out the causes of rebellion, he addressed himself in turn to three sorts
of men – the poor, the clergy, and the possessioners. The poor, he knows,
will readily identify the source of their distress: 'Cormorants, greedy gulls:
yea, men that would eat up men, women and children are the causes of
sedition!'[54] It is exploitation that men say rouses them to rebellion – which
of course, is true enough. Does Crowley agree? He feels very sorry for a
poor man, oppressed by those who should be his natural protectors, and he
accepts that without such provocation the false prophets that urged rebellion would have found no following. But 'no cause can be so great to make it
lawful for thee to do against God's ordinance', and the poor are urged to
search their hearts: are not their sufferings perhaps caused by their failure

to obey God's commands? 'Submit thyself wholly to the will of God; do thy labour truly; call upon God continuously.'[55] Humble submission and prayer – those are Crowley's advice to men who suffer from the ruthlessness of their betters. As for those betters, they too have no difficulty in identifying the cause of sedition: in their opinion 'the peasant knaves be too wealthy, provender pricketh them'. And so the knaves wish to do away with rank and 'have all men like themselves, they would have all things common'.[56] Crowley, who for some reason calls the rich 'churl's chickens', has an answer for them too: by your unlawful enclosing, rack-renting and so forth you taught the poor disobedience: you failed to obey the king's proclamation, and rebellion came upon you as God's punishment. They too, therefore, are told to practise humility and (presumably) obedience to the laws which limit their power to do with their wealth as they please – wealth which is really 'the public wealth of England'.[57] The clergy receive advice which mingles the commonplace with the baffling. Noting that 'a great number of your unworthy curates have been the stirrers up of the simple people in the late tumults', he enjoins their spiritual duty upon them in unexceptionable but also unmemorable terms; secondly he demands that they make their extravagant wives behave themselves. Crowley was noticeably obsessed with female extravagance, but even so it is odd that he should have singled out ministers' wives for special condemnation. The point has value, however, because it helps us to understand the man: cranky, prejudiced, without vision but readily moved to indignation, Crowley was the archetypal pamphleteer and a poor peg on which to hang notions of a powerful and deeply concerned reform movement. Also, by the way, a poor peg on which to hang a real understanding of the state of the realm: citing Crowley proves nothing about the economic crisis.

That leaves John Hales – John Hales of Coventry, clerk of the hanaper, an enthusiast for causes who under Edward devoted himself to abolishing enclosures and under Elizabeth promoted the claims to the throne of the Seymour family, getting into trouble on both occasions. There is no need to review at length his ideas touching enclosure which have been sufficiently studied before, except to remark that he has now clearly been deprived of the authorship of *The Discourse of the Common Weal* which is in fact the work of Sir Thomas Smith.[58] What matters here is that unlike the other propagandists discussed Hales was without doubt in close touch with the Duke of Somerset and his government: if there was a commonwealth party active in the reform of the realm, he was it. When after the troubles of 1549 Hales heard that he was accused of being the sole begetter of the agrarian policy which took the blame for the uprisings, he defended himself vigorously by alleging that he had but been the agent of a group of likeminded men. This, if true, is the best evidence for the existence of a body of commonwealth-men; is Hales right? He names no names, but those he calls to witness are a strange company of bedfellows. It was not he at all who had sued out the enclosure commission of 1548, but partly certain poor men protesting against landlords' practices 'and partly . . . some of those that now be most against it', the latter apparently including the king, the Protector and 'many of the council'.[59] One may well believe that protests from the commons drew the government's attention to the need to do something, and it is possible – though less likely – that the first commission had the support of a large part of the government, even though its outcome was so null that their sincerity must stand in much doubt. At any rate, Hales's description excludes the likes of Latimer, Lever or Crowley who even after 1549, while deploring rebellion, charged the gentry with agrarian malpractices including enclosure. In September 1549 Hales presented himself simply as a servant whom it ill became 'to reason with his master': he did as instructed.[60] But in the summer of 1548 Hales, as is well enough known, took an energetic initiative on the commission to which he belonged, and which alone of those appointed attempted to carry out the policy; and his report to Somerset also suggests that it was he who had pushed on that policy. On 22 July he wrote urging the continuance of the commission and reminding the Protector of his own words, spoken when they were discussing the state of the realm: 'that maugre the Devil, private profit, self-love, money and such like the Devil's instruments, it shall go forward'.[61] That sounds much more like an enthusiastic convert's response to his mentor than like the speech of a master instructing his servant in the action to be taken. As for Somerset's motives in espousing Hales's programme, Dr Bush has rightly found them in the duke's eagerness to appear a friend to the common weal without stopping the flow of money required by his Scottish war and supplied by the disastrous debasement of the coinage.[62]

Whatever may be true about the enclosure commission – and the chances are that Hales instigated the policy and attracted official support for it – he really proved his personal responsibility for the agrarian measures of this government by the initiatives he took in the Parliament of 1548–9 for which he prepared three bills of his own devising.[63] What he says about their fate cannot fully be reconciled with the evidence of the Journals of either House, but that difficulty probably reflects only the known defects of those records. Two of his bills Hales rather surprisingly channelled through the Lords. The first was yet another bill for the maintenance of tillage which he says was rejected on first reading. It is not mentioned at all in the *Lords Journal*.[64] The second (which attacked regraters of foodstuffs and especially graziers) passed the Lords after being amended by a small committee (Lord Chancellor Rich and James Hales, serjeant-at-law);[65] John Hales says that it was much debated in the Commons where it was committed and killed by delays, but the *Commons Journal* has no mention of it, even though the clerk noted many bills as introduced which failed. Hales's third bill, introduced (he says) in the Lower House and there defeated after much opposition both to its substantive provisions and to its enforcement clauses, is probably the 'bill for the common weal' which received a first reading on 27 February 1549 and was not mentioned again. It aimed to improve the supply of meat, milk, butter and cheese by compelling sheep farmers to maintain two cows and rear one calf for every 100 sheep they had over 120; and it committed enforcement to the parson and 'two honest men' of the parish who were yearly to survey all pastures and present both breakers and observers of the law.[66] We may (with Hales, if he plays fair to his opponents) think little enough of the arguments allegedly advanced against the main sections of the bill – that scarcity of cattle was better remedied by the tried expedient of temporary bans on the slaughtering of calves, and that supplies would in any case be sufficient if the modern habit of eating butter and cheese in Lent were suppressed – but it is hard to share his contempt for the resistance to the introduction of yet another piece of snooping into village life. So far as their tenor can be reconstructed from his brief remarks, Hales's bills were not, as a matter of fact, particularly sensible or likely to produce that improvement in the common weal that he expected from them. And the reason for his inadequacy is, once again, plain enough: driven to defend his proposals, he can only launch forth into the familiar declamations against greed and covetousness. Something, he cries, must be devised 'to quench this insatiable thirst . . . for it is the destruction of all good things.' The one thing that really links Hales to the preachers is this dedication to a reform of man's nature, but Utopia has never yet been constructed by laws which command no consent among the agencies of enforcement.[67]

Besides, the question remains whether the realm really suffered so exclusively from the covetousness of the possessioners. The diagnosis offered by Latimer, Lever, Crowley and Hales – no 'group or 'party' but certainly men exercised over social distress and trying to do something about it – has until recently been accepted without question, and the authority of Tawney in particular established the orthodox opinion on the subject. Jordan's lengthy discourses also simply endorse those contemporary criticisms, uncritically rehearsing what was said at the time.[68] It has been firmly taken for granted that inflation and pauperization arose from the economic ruthlessness of gentlemen landlords and grasping middlemen, exploiting their advantage without regard for the rights and needs of the labouring poor. A 'new' type of landlord ruined yeomen and husbandmen by the manner in which he maximized his profits; capitalist agriculture revolutionized the rural scene by destroying a happily ordered society in which greed was restrained by the recognition of mutual obligations. We are no longer so well convinced of all this. We are better aware that the purchasers of Crown lands were rarely new and more rarely still of a new type among landowners; we recall the very similar complaints raised against their predecessors; we know rather more now about the agrarian improvements of the age, about the benefits accruing to a tenantry in the main well protected by the customary and common laws, and about the effect of changing conditions which, for instance, reduced sheep farming through the collapse of the wool boom more successfully than anti-enclosure laws ever could have done.[69] There will, of course, be those who see in such historical revisions merely an alternative form of bias, and one more disagreeable than the old one because it seems lacking in compassion and indignation. However, apart from the fact that the newer views rest on better, and better understood, evidence, it should not be forgotten that similar opinions were also advanced in the reign of Edward VI itself. In the most notable piece of economic analysis produced in the century, Sir Thomas Smith's *Discourse of the Common Weal*, we find a much more balanced and penetrating discussion than in all the sermons of Latimer and Lever, the singleminded obsessions of Hales, or the other likeminded writings which have not been discussed here. Smith recognized the weight of many contemporary complaints but showed how they often cancelled one another out and how none of the sectional grievances really explained the crisis; his preferred answer, that a restoration of the coinage alone would lead to the sort of improvement in which the other defects would right themselves naturally, was proved correct when government policy finally abandoned unprofitable moralizing and illconsidered unenforceable legislation in favour of recoinage. And Smith gave the classic answer to the worthy men who wished to root covetousness out of men's hearts:

> But can we devise that all covetousness may be taken from men? No, no more than we can make men without ire, without gladness, without fear, and without all affections. What then? We must take away from men the occasion of their covetousness in this part.[70]

The right answer, he maintained, was to make those activities which benefited the common weal more profitable than those which harmed it. He called not for repressive laws or moral exhortations but for a wise manipulation of the means of gain available, so that men's natural desire to better themselves should redound to the good of all.

A sane prescription, no doubt, but also not one easy to follow, as mankind has discovered often enough. Still, there was wisdom in such counsel beyond the worth of the appalled complaints and bitterness of preachers, pamphleteers and enthusiasts. This spirit of constructive encouragement rather than mere repression had guided the activities of Thomas Cromwell's reform administration and was to make itself felt again in the early years of Elizabeth's reign when William Cecil got his hands on the reins of state. Cecil knew Smith intimately – fellow secretaries both first to Somerset and then to the king – and he possessed a copy of the *Discourse*.[71] Both men were products of that Cambridge in which Cromwell had found many recruits for his administration and which he had endeavoured to turn into a nursery for servants of the state. It is this line of thought and action that now merits better attention: the succession of men who thought coolly, secularly and constructively about the problems of the common weal and who faced the practical tasks involved in turning aspiration into action. They, rather than the laudators of a glorious past that had never been and the lamenters over man's fallen nature, were the true reform party of the sixteenth century.

2

THE DOWNFALL OF ARCHBISHOP GRINDAL AND ITS PLACE IN ELIZABETHAN POLITICAL AND ECCLESIASTICAL HISTORY

Patrick Collinson

If Queen Elizabeth had not been thwarted, her second archbishop of Canterbury would have been the first and indeed the only primate of all England to have been deprived of his great office by judicial process, little more than a year after she had placed him in it.[1] The year was 1577. Saved from annihilation by powerful friends and by the forbidding prospect of unexplored legal terrain, Archbishop Edmund Grindal remained sequestered and suspended from many of his functions for the remainder of his days. Writing about this episode on a previous occasion, I reached for a somewhat strained analogy. In France, in 1572, events had forced another queen into the desperate steps which precipitated the Massacre of St Bartholomew. 'With her surer grasp, Elizabeth merely kept an archbishop in limbo.'[2] The hyperbole was intended to suggest that Grindal's downfall deserves more than the incidental mention it has received in the historical literature, even that it had a certain centrality among the critical choices confronting the Elizabethan régime in the late 1570s.

Grindal has no place in the three volumes and the thousand pages of Conyers Read's *Sir Francis Walsingham and the Policy of Queen Elizabeth*.[3] And if his troubles were given a couple of pages in the same author's *Lord Burghley and Queen Elizabeth*,[4] no connection was made with more salient political questions. Not that Read was insensitive to the interrelation of mid-Elizabethan public issues. 'A half-hundred threads of policy were so knotted and joined that the pulling of any one meant the displacement of all the rest . . . Everything reacted upon everything else.'[5] But whereas Read was disposed to trust that the threads of policy were in good hands, capable of disentangling them, this essay will tend towards Professor Charles Wilson's more recent impression of strange and tortuous dealings, 'a subject of oriental deviousness'[6]: a story not so much of policy as of its absence, or of the neutralization of policy through deep antitheses. By these same antipathies Archbishop Grindal too was neutralized.

We begin with Grindal's two reputations: on the one hand his standing among his contemporaries and immediate posterity; on the other, and in striking conflict, the verdict of history. The annalists' obituary notices were of 'a right famous and worthy prelate.'[7] But if historians for long found little significance in Grindal's disgrace it was because they believed Grindal himself to have been insignificant, rather infamous than famous. His predecessor, Parker, and his successor, Whitgift, while never beyond criticism, have always commanded respect. But Creighton's assessment of Grindal in the *Dictionary of National Biography* was of a weak man, 'infirm of purpose'. Sir Sidney Lee supposed that he 'feebly temporised with dissent',[8] Bishop Frere complained of his 'natural incapacity for government',[9] Gwatkin attributed the elevation of such an unsuitable primate to 'some passing turn of policy',[10] and a modern author has called it 'a mistake'.[11] The misreading of character implied in all these judgments can be traced to the ecclesiastical and political bitterness of the seventeenth century and its aftermath. Thomas Fuller, albeit in a charitable rather than bitter spirit, began the tradition of misrepresentation by casting Grindal as 'our English Eli', blind and broken-hearted at his death. Like Eli who indulged his wicked sons he was accused as a father of the Church for 'too much conniving at the factious disturbers thereof.'[12] For mid-seventeenth century puritans, the heirs of the 'factious disturbers', Grindal provided a stick with which to strike the unacceptable face of prelacy. Milton called him 'the best' of the Elizabethan bishops[13] and William Prynne praised him, and only him, as 'a grave and pious man', while censuring Parker and Whitgift as 'over pontifical and princely'.[14] After two revolutions, and in the unparalleled rancour of public life in the reign of Anne, this archbishop who was revered by puritan nonconformity became a whipping-boy for the high-flying churchman Dr Sacheverell in his notorious political sermon, *The perils of false brethren*. Intending his attack for the archbishop of the day, Thomas Tenison, Sacheverell selected Grindal for denunciation as 'that false son of the Church', 'a perfidious prelate' who was to blame for what he called 'the first plantation of dissenters'.[15]

To the present generation of historians (including more than one contributor to this volume), Grindal's advanced protestantism and moderate churchmanship no longer appear scandalous. The 'Grindalian' tradition is even acknowledged to have been nearly central to the post-Reformation Church of England, long after Grindal's own disgrace. This may constitute the third of his reputations. But the measure has yet to be taken of Grindal's stature, not only as a symbol of moderation and of pastoral excellence but as an effective governor, remembered by the annalist Sir John Hayward as 'a man famous, whilst he lived, for his deep judgment, both in learning and affairs of the world', and as a man of 'magnanimous courage'.[16] When Parker was known to be dying, Alexander Nowell, the Dean of St Paul's, advised William Cecil, Lord Burghley, that the archbishop's place should be 'furnished with a man of great government' and that Grindal, then Archbishop of York, was the man 'of the greatest wisdom and ability to govern, and unto whom the other bishops with best contentation would submit themself [sic].'[17] Burghley needed no prompting[18] and Grindal would later acknowledge him as the 'principal procurer' of all his preferments.[19] Ninety-eight letters are still extant which Grindal addressed to this great patron, most of them in the 1560s when he was Bishop of London and Cecil Secretary of State.[20] They are what the age knew as 'familiar letters', tossed off in the writer's own hand, without deference or artifice, and mostly concerning urgent matters of public policy. Since not even Archbishop Parker was as businesslike in his dealings with Mr Secretary they imply that Grindal rather than his metropolitan was the ecclesiastical counterpart of Cecil in the early Elizabethan régime. This is no more than a hunch, since we have lost all but a few of the records of the Ecclesiastical Commission which was Grindal's principal sphere of activity, and which might have clinched the matter.

Insofar as the translation of such a man to Canterbury aroused partisan expectations among 'forward' protestants it may have been a difficult matter to expedite with the queen. It was not until late November 1575 that Burghley was able to confirm the choice which he himself had made six months earlier: 'I think assuredly her Majesty will have your grace come to this province of Canterbury to take care thereof, and that now, at this Parliament.'[21] Another month was then lost in what may have been more than procedural delays before the *congé d'élire* was at last signed, on Christmas Eve. But Grindal's appointment was also welcomed as bringing an effective hand to the Church's helm after a period of uncertain and uncreative government. Parker in his declining years was an aged man, and his treatment by the Court would have discouraged the most resolute of prelates. But it implied a kind of abdication and an alarming lack of restraint for Parker to draft a letter to Burghley which ran: 'If I had not been so much bound to the mother [Queen Anne Boleyn] I would not so soon have granted to serve the daughter in this place. And if I had not well trusted to have died ere this time, your honours should have sent thrice for me before I would have returned from Cambridge.'[22] It is not recorded that in his even greater extremity Grindal openly regretted having consented to his promotion, although in 1575, as he paused over his reply to Burghley, he confessed to 'many conflicts with myself about that matter.'[23]

The hopefulness but also the delicacy of the circumstances surrounding the transition from Parker to Grindal are conveyed in a letter which, although without signature in the fugitive copy which survives, seems to emanate from a high source and conveyed to Grindal the news of the signing of his *congé d'élire*:

It is greatly hoped for by the godly and well-affected of this realm that your lordship will prove a profitable instrument in that calling; especially in removing the corruptions in the Court of Faculties, which is one of the greatest abuses that remain in this Church of England. For that it is determined that Parliament should hold at the day prefixed, I could wish your lordship to repair hither with as convenient speed as ye may, to the end that there may be some consultation had with some of your brethren how some parts of those Romish dregs remaining in [the Church?],[24] offensive to the godly, may be removed. I know it will be hard for you to do that good that you and your brethren desire. Herein I had rather declare unto your lordship at your repair hither frankly by mouth what I think than to commit the same to letters.[25]

The implication is that matters which historians have associated with 'puritanism' were of interest to the writer, who seems to have been a councillor, and were assumed to have the support of Grindal and other bishops as well.

Illness delayed Grindal's arrival in London until a matter of days before the 1576 Parliament met, and this must have restricted the process of discreet consultation which had been proposed.[26] Nevertheless, the intense interest in the reform of the ministry and discipline of the Church evidenced in this Parliament suggests a broader and more influential constituency than the radical puritan network which Sir John Neale thought he could discern at work. After all, the committee which presented the queen with Parliament's petition for 'supply and reformation of these great wants and grievous abuses' consisted of six privy councillors. But Elizabeth deflected this powerful initiative in the direction of the clergy in Convocation, where she seems to have ensured that the measures for the improvement of the clergy contained in the Canons of 1576 would be of such a limited and conservative character as to earn even from Sir Walter Mildmay (Grindal's anonymous correspondent?) the comment that they were 'little or nothing to the purpose.'[27] Meanwhile the efforts of Grindal and his episcopal colleagues in the House of Lords to stiffen the laws against popish recusancy were nullified, almost certainly by royal intervention.[28]

Grindal's correspondent had drawn particular attention to the archbishop's Court of Faculties, an institution which supplied a variety of dispensations from the constraints of the canon law and which embarrassed many protestants by its evident continuity with pre-Reformation procedures.[29] After the prorogation of Parliament the Privy Council took order, either on its own initiative or that of the archbishop, for the curtailment of the activities of the Faculty Office. Some classes of licence were to be abolished altogether 'as not agreeable to Christian religion in the opinion of the Lords of the Council'. These included dispensations for holding three or more benefices in plurality and for ordination at less than the canonical age, and licences to marry without the calling of banns. Others, considered more tolerable, were to continue, but with the fees differently distributed.[30] In a memorandum justifying the full restitution of the temporalities of the see it was said that Parker had had occasions of wealth 'the possibilities whereof are now taken away',[31] and a predictive statement of income anticipated that with the projected reform the proceeds of the Faculty Office would drop from £60 to £30 a year:[32] a token reduction in a total revenue of more than £3,000 a year[33] but significant as a symbol of intent. There is no evidence that the queen had any part in these transactions or would have approved of them.

In the same late spring of 1576 Grindal called for reports on the state of his remaining courts: the Court of Arches, the Court of Audience, and the Prerogative Court of Canterbury. He received from one of the learned civilians and judges the advice that 'in your grace's Court of Audience, as in all other your courts, so things be out of order that few things be as they should be.'[34]

Enough has been said to suggest that Grindal was expected to effect reforms which would be radical but which it would be inappropriate to label, still less to dismiss, as 'puritan', since they enjoyed solid governmental support. But it was in the nature of things that little had been accomplished when Grindal found himself administratively paralyzed. This happened, after all, only 16 months after his appointment. And Dr Aubrey had found diagnosis of the ills of the courts spiritual an easier matter than the prescription of a cure: 'I am not so able to advertise your grace how to remedy the disease of these delays as to make them known to you.'[35] Recent work on the Prerogative Court of Canterbury, the seat of the archbishop's testamentary jurisdiction, confirms that 'Grindal's projected reforms did not materialize.'[36]

Grindal's troubles began when a cloud the size of a man's hand appeared in the summer sky of 1576: disquieting reports from Northamptonshire and Warwickshire concerning the meetings for preaching and instruction known as prophesyings, to which the archbishop was alerted from the Court, and which he at once referred to the diocesan bishops concerned.[37] There had been trouble over the prophesyings before which had blown over. This time Grindal's awkward conscience would ensure that the matter would come to a head. Macaulay's schoolboy, if he still exists, knows that the prophesyings were the cause of Grindal's disgrace. But the prophesyings themselves are often misunderstood, thanks to the ambiguities surrounding the terms 'prophet', 'prophecy', 'prophesying'.[38] They had nothing to do with ecstatic utterance, nor were they necessarily disorderly or anti-hierarchical. They were meetings in large and centrally located churches under strict moderation, where, in place of the usual sermon, two or three ministers took their turns to expound the text, in the presence of their brethren, and before a lay audience drawn from the surrounding country. They embodied an element of what is nowadays called 'continuing education' and compensated for the deficiencies of the clergy. Institutions like these, taking their name from certain matters discussed by St Paul with the Corinthians, were part of the common resources of the Reformed churches at a primitive stage of their consolidation. They were all but domesticated in many parts of England, including the diocese of Canterbury, in Parker's time. But they were never above controversy and sometimes they were the scene of open disputes or worse scandals. When the queen heard of their existence, which was perhaps not often, they aroused her displeasure. In 1576 unfavourable reports were said to have reached the Court from 'sundry of the bishops and sundry also of her justices of circuit.' Leicester, Walsingham and Burghley all wrote urgently to Grindal about the disorders in the Midlands and on 12 June he was summoned to Court.[39]

What transpired on that occasion we do not know, but Grindal was soon trying to protect the prophesyings both from puritan abuse and from the unfriendly attentions of the Court. He gathered reports from most of the bishops of the province, many of them favourable to the practice.[40] Materials were collected for a scholarly treatise on the subject, 'Tractatus de exercitiis', which survive and have recently been restored to the Library of Lambeth Palace.[41] And finally Grindal composed his 'Orders for the reformation of abuses about the learned exercises and conferences among ministers of the Church.'[42]

There followed a famous set piece of Tudor history: another summons to Court and a painful interview with the queen in which Grindal was instructed to transmit an order to the bishops putting down the prophesyings and 'abridging' the number of preachers; the archbishop, denied the right of verbal expostulation, shaken but resolute, returning home to write his 'book' to the queen, just over four hundred years ago, on 8 December 1576.[43] In this manifesto of more than 6,000 words Grindal defended preaching as the mainstay not only of faith but of civil order as well ('where preaching wanteth, obedience faileth') and, after offering the fruits of his investigations into prophesying ('only backward men in religion do fret against it'), came to that measured but defiant statement in which he withheld the assent of his conscience from the queen's policy and refused to transmit her command:

> I am forced, with all humility, and yet plainly, to profess that I cannot with safe conscience, and without the offence of the majesty of God, give my assent to the suppressing of the said exercises: much less can I send out any injunctions for the utter and universal subversion of the same. . . If it be your Majesty's pleasure, for this or any other cause, to remove me out of this place, I will with all humility yield thereunto, and render again to your Majesty that I received of the same. . . Bear with me, I beseech you Madam, if I choose rather to offend against your earthly Majesty than to offend the heavenly majestey of God.

One historian of the Elizabethan Church called this famous letter 'a particular piece of characteristically puritan crankiness'.[44] But Strype was moved by the passage just quoted to exclaim: 'O episcopus vere apostolicus!'[45] Fuller in the seventeenth century was no less appreciative: 'What could be written with more spirit and less animosity? more humility and less dejection? I see a lamb in his own can be a lion in God and the Church's cause.'[46] But it was gratuitous to end the letter with a peroration composed from the rhetoric of St Ambrose in his celebrated epistles to the emperors Theodosius and Valentinian.[47] For the admonitions of Ambrose echoed a polity foreign to Tudor England, when a bishop could confidently refuse entry to his church to the agents of a still partly alien imperial power.[48] And perhaps there was no need to write at all. As the Dutch divine and man of affairs Loiseleur de Villiers wrote in another connection, three years later: 'I cannot refrain from saying that the way to pacify kings is not to oppose them, or announce by writings, signatures or remarks that one does not approve their doings. It is necessary to be humble, or at least to hold one's tongue. You know why I say this and there is no need of longer discourse.'[49]

But it is by no means clear that the offending letter was the sole or immediate cause of calamity. More than a week after the Earl of Leicester had taken it to Court (and was that a friendly office or not?) there was no royal response. Perhaps the queen had not yet seen the letter. But Leicester and Burghley knew the contents and proposed a compromise. Would Grindal consent to the exclusion from the prophesyings of the lay audience? Grindal could see no reason why the people should not benefit and so closed off this way of escape.[50] As spring approached he was transacting business as usual.[51] In late February Burghley sought to prevent a second confrontation with Elizabeth: 'I could be content your coming to speech with her Majesty were delayed a little longer, and to that end I wish my lord of Leicester were your intercessor, to excuse your absence by reason of your sickness. This I wish for your respects. And yet I refer the order to yourself.'[52] Grindal may never have gone to Court again, as a free agent. By May political efforts to avert disaster had failed. Royal letters went out to the bishops, directly ordering the suppression of the prophesyings, a command obeyed in Grindal's own diocese and peculiars.[53] Soon afterwards the archbishop was sequestered and confined to Lambeth House. The order was apparently made by the Council, after Grindal had made a personal appearance and, in spite of persuasion, had refused to make a perceptible retraction, 'a second offence of disobedience, greater than the first.'[54] The text of the order of sequestration has not survived and its terms are uncertain.

Worse was intended. The queen now called in question the validity of the patents of appointment held by the archbishop's principal officers 'in this time of sequestration' and instructed two ecclesiastical lawyers, Dr Lewyn and Dr Dale, to prepare the ground with the principal law officers of the Crown for the archbishop's deprivation.[55] In mid-July, after seven weeks of confinement, Grindal told a correspondent, probably Leicester: 'I never in all my life numbered days so precisely as I do now, being afore this time never called to answer in any place of judgment.'[56]

If Camden is to be trusted, it is not surprising that Leicester's mediation had failed to save the archbishop since the true author of his misfortune was none other than the earl himself. The root of the matter concerned the marital affairs of Leicester's Italian physician, Giulio Borgarucci, a man with a grudge against Grindal for denying him the means to make an irregular marriage.[57] This story appeared in print as early as 1584, in the notorious libel known to history as *Leicester's Commonwealth*, and variants of it occur in early historical memoirs of the reign and in Fuller's *Church History*, where we find the added suggestion that Leicester had covetous designs on Lambeth House, as Ahab had for Naboth's vineyard. In Peter Heylyn's *Aerius Redivivus* this became Leicester's prime motive.[58] One might discount these rumours from a tainted source but for a letter which 'Dr Julio' sent to Leicester, four days before Grindal addressed himself to the queen in December 1576. This is full of complaints at the frustration of his marriage, directed against the archbishop in person, Grindal having sworn, as Julio's lawyers had reported, that 'I should never obtain this gentlewoman I have married, nor enjoy her.'[59] And when Burghley and Walsingham later discussed the queen's intention to deprive the archbishop Burghley revealed that it was Julio who had instructed an eminent lawyer on what should be done. 'So as I see that he was more of her Majesty's Council than two or three that are of present council.'[60] We cannot remove all traces of ambiguity from Leicester's role in the affair. The rumour was already current that he had furthered the archbishop's troubles.[61] The puritan jungle telegraph was humming with damaging reports about his responsibility for the betrayal of the Midland prophesyings, as well as about his 'ungodly life', which the earl was bound to treat seriously.[62] But Leicester easily aroused mistrust and unpopularity. Camden's hostility is known to have flawed an otherwise impeccable judgment.[63] Ostensibly, Leicester, the chief hope of the forward protestant cause, went out of his way to help Grindal.

So what of Dr Julio? If Julio was Leicester's physician and intimate[64] he was also the queen's physician, and of her chamber.[65] Elizabeth herself became the archbishop's relentless adversary, and we may have no need of the hypothesis that she was influenced against him by some other party or parties: which is not to deny that Grindal's disgrace was welcome to all those at Court who were hostile to his progressive protestantism. There remains the possibility that the affair in its innerness was an episode in the upward progress of the particular favourite of the hour, Christopher Hatton. Hatton too was part of the Italian connection. In 1573 Julio had attended him on a journey to the Spa, just as he later accompanied Leicester to the waters at Buxton.[66] As the patron of Aylmer and Bancroft and the supporter of Whitgift there can be no doubt of

Hatton's political involvement with the rise of a conservative, even reactionary churchmanship which Grindal's fall facilitated.[67] And it is possible that this ecclesiastical strategy was adopted with the intention of outflanking Leicester. Yet there is no positive evidence to link Hatton with Grindal's disgrace, apart from a comment attached to a copy of the archbishop's 'book to the queen' to the effect that in ordering the prophesyings to be put down the queen had been 'moved by Hatton and some other'.[68] This endorsement may not date from 1577 and Hatton, as the enemy of radical puritans, was a natural object of suspicions which may or may not have been well founded. What is documented is that Hatton intervened with the queen on Grindal's behalf in the spring of 1578. It remains possible that it was Hatton's earlier responsibility for the archbishop's discomfiture which invested this initiative with the peculiar importance evidently attached to it.[69]

Clearly Grindal's fall was not the simple consequence of his formal refusal to transmit the queen's order against the prophesyings. So far we have introduced evidence which may seem to trivialize the affair by dissolving it into personal and courtly intrigues. But the struggle of factions and interests in the mid-Elizabethan Court was not at all trivial, connected as it was to events which made these years 'a political and military watershed in European history'.[70] Edmund Spenser had some poetic intuition of Grindal's place in the critical political decisions of the time, which he expressed among the cryptic allegories of *The Shepheardes Calender*:

> He is a shepheard great in gree
> but hath bene long ypent . . .
>
> Ah good *Algrin*, his hap was ill,
> but shall be better in time.[71]

Modern Spenser scholarship claims to have cracked the ciphers and to have made explicit the integration of politics, religion and art in Spenser's poetic rhetoric, especially in its bearing on the Alençon courtship of 1579.[72] But the ecclesiastical crisis of 1577 has yet to be plausibly located in the matrix of contemporary political events.

Let us briefly recall the state of the world, as it appeared to some English eyes, in 1577 and 1578. What Dr Simon Adams has called 'the protestant cause',[73] the cause of 'political puritanism', was espoused by many near to the centre of affairs, including most of those royal servants conducting diplomacy in the sensitive spheres of France, Scotland and, above all, the Netherlands. Their ideology expressed itself in passionate, but by no means irrational, responses to every new turn in international affairs. The queen and the realm were in danger. Their only firm friends were those 'of the religion': in the Netherlands the Prince of Orange above all, who was to be sustained at all costs. Papists were dangerous and deceitful. Policy towards native catholics and in the Netherlands must take account of the ultimate ambition of the Spaniards to overcome England. The reluctance of their mistress to read these signs of the times, her readiness to listen to bad advice, her endless procrastinations, were sources of frustration frequently vented in semi-private diplomatic correspondence.

Here is a selection of the commonplaces contained in memoranda and letters from the period of the Pacification of Ghent and its aftermath: 'The present quiet her Majesty now enjoyeth cannot long continue.' (From 'a brief discourse laying forth the uncertainty of her Majesty's present peace and quietness'.[74]) 'And never will I think that ever any perfect or assured amity will be amongst any that are divided in religion. The queen's Majesty may perhaps mislike my plain writing in these matters after so bold a manner.' (Dr Thomas Wilson to Sir Francis Walsingham, April 1577, in the weeks after the conclusion of the 'perpetual edict' between the Estates and Don John of Austria.[75]) And as Wilson wrote to the queen herself, in June of the same year: 'This is my belief, not to believe' – that is, not to believe papists.[76] In September, with Elizabeth's resolution to support Orange fading and with the Archduke Matthias appearing on the Belgian horizon, Sir Nicholas Bacon, a relatively conservative observer, plucked up the courage to memorialize his mistress to the same effect: 'I see no way so sure for your Majesty as to keep the Prince of Orange in heart and life.' 'Most gracious sovereign, I have been so unquieted with these things.'[77]

In January 1578 the army of the Estates was defeated at Gembloux and according to Charles Wilson the English government scuttled back to perform another set of strange diplomatic quadrilles.[78] Yet what Walsingham reported to Randolph on 20 February was that 'we are now here in daily and earnest consultation what is best to be done, in which generally I see all my lords inclined to one course for her Majesty's safety, if it please God to incline herself to embrace and follow the same.'[79] This course was not to do nothing. Two days later Henry Killigrew wrote to William Davison: 'The Lord give us grace to do that may be to his glory, our own surety and the help of our friends and good neighbours in time.'[80] But in April he wrote: 'Her Majesty hath some that do mar more in a day than all her godly councillors and servants can persuade in a week.'[81] We may spare ourselves the longueurs and distresses of the spring and summer of 1578, culminating in the counter-productive Walsingham–Cobham mission of August: a story which pains Professor Wilson in the telling and which had the principal protagonist, Walsingham, writing by September: 'God send me well to return and I will hereafter take my leave of foreign service.'[82]

This sketch adds nothing to the dense narratives contained in Conyers Read's *Walsingham* and his *Burghley*. But nowadays the strength and broadness of base of the protestant cause appears more impressive than it did to Read, who was over-attracted to the symmetrical model of a Privy Council split between conservative and radical wings, and who attributed too conservative a consistency to Burghley.[83] And from the standpoint of modern scholarship Read made too little of Leicester.

We return to Archbishop Grindal, whose fate was not a wholly separate issue but an aspect, by no means peripheral, of the contention between conservative and progressive forces at Court. It would be too much to claim that the oscillations in Grindal's fortunes corresponded exactly to every barometric variation in the protestant cause. But they can be read as a rough index of the way things were going, a windsock as it were.

This is the significance with which the matter was invested in a letter written to Secretary Wilson by Sir Francis Knollys in January 1578. After general reflections on the familiar theme of vigilance and on the difficulty of conscientiously performing the office of a councillor to a mistress so careless of her safety and so open to false counsel, Knollys comes to particulars:

> The avoiding of her Majesty's danger doth consist in the preventing of the conquest of the Low Countries betimes; secondly, in the preventing of the revolt of Scotland from her Majesty's devotion unto the French and the Queen of Scots; and thirdly, in the timely preventing of the contemptuous growing of the disobedient papists here in England.

'And also', he added, 'if her Majesty will be safe, she must comfort the hearts of those that be her most faithful subjects, even for conscience sake.' And then, in what serves as the rhetorical climax of the discourse: 'But if the bishop of Canterbury shall be deprived, then up starts the pride and practice of the papists. And then King Richard the Second's men will flock into Court apace and will show themselves in their colours.'[84] 'King Richard the Second's men' we must take for the antitypes of Knollys himself, with his robust, protestant plain speaking:[85] smooth-tongued flatterers and 'parasites' who would conceal the truth and bring all to confusion.

In the previous summer of 1577, when the queen had first revealed her radical intention against Grindal, Walsingham conveyed the news to Burghley in a letter which accompanied a discouraging despatch from overseas: 'Her Majesty seemeth to be greatly perplexed with this news. But yet it worketh not that effect, to make her stay her proceedings against the archbishop (which at this time, howsoever he hath offended, were in true policy most requisite), a matter that doth greatly grieve as many as truly love her Majesty.' Details were added of the preliminary steps towards deprivation already taken. 'Thus my good lord you see how we proceed still in making war against God: whose ire we should rather seek to appease that he may keep the wars that most apparently approach towards us from us. God open her Majesty's eyes that she may both see her peril and acknowledge from whence the true remedy is to be sought.' Burghley's response was an echo ('these proceedings cannot but irritate our merciful God') and contained the news of Dr Julio's machinations.

'I think the persons appointed to consult for the deprivation of the archbishop shall be much troubled to find a precedent.'[86]

This was as much as to admit that Burghley, and presumably other councillors, would do all in their power to shelter Grindal from deprivation. It seems significant that the rare glimpses of their efforts which are revealed from time to time occur for the most part in State Papers Foreign, in correspondence with William Davison, the dedicated puritan who had replaced Wilson as ambassador in the Netherlands in July 1577.

On 8 August Davison's cousin and Grindal's secretary, Edward Cheke, reported that he was in daily attendance at Court 'about my lord's business', where he was assured by Leicester and Hatton that it would 'take end very shortly.' 'The queen hath been so troubled with matters of the Low Countries and for the relieving of the protestants in France as it hath [been] the only let of my lord's cause.'[87] A fortnight later Killigrew assured Davison that Grindal had been released from strict confinement,[88] and in mid-September Cheke confirmed that his master had enjoyed 'some enlargement' and that the queen was 'well pacified'.[89] From now onwards the archbishop was free to commute between Lambeth and his manor at Croydon. (There seems to have been no question of a retreat into his diocese, as with other disgraced bishops in earlier times. Indeed one may search in vain for any positive local evidence that Grindal so much as visited Canterbury during his archiepiscopate.[90]) At this point Cheke was optimistic: 'I am now almost despatched from my long travail, for before I go home from the Court I am surely promised to have my lord's liberty.'[91] This was at a time when it appeared likely that Elizabeth would strike the hot iron and intervene in the Netherlands. The same letter from Cheke reported that Leicester was to lead an expedition. 'This is his full determination, but yet unknown unto her Highness, neither shall she be acquainted with it until she be fully resolved to send, which will not be until the Prince of Orange send back again . . . My lord of Leicester is the most desirous to go the chief of this journey that ever you heard of, and doth labour it both by his own policy and by favour of all his friends.'

In October Grindal formally requested the Council to 'be means for me to her Majesty to receive me again into her gracious favour', and acknowledged his particular debt to Leicester, 'who hath from the beginning most carefully and painfully travailed for me to her Majesty.'[92] In November he was 'put in assured hope of liberty.' But then 'a sudden contrary tempest' arose, and at the end of that month he was summoned to appear before the Council, meeting in Star Chamber.[93]

From a remarkable account of what followed, almost certainly composed by Sir Walter Mildmay and surviving among his papers,[94] it appears that the queen had informed the Privy Council that her pleasure was that on his appearance Grindal should either confess his fault or 'receive his deprivation'. When the Council gathered in the Star Chamber on the last two days of

November the judges were also present and the court was in some sense empowered to 'hear and determine' the cause. But before the appointed day the
lords of the Council were said to have met 'all together' at the house of the lord
keeper, Sir Nicholas Bacon, to consider the implications of the queen's instructions. Mildmay suggested to his colleagues that they indicated a 'very strange
course' for which the Council had received no formal commission and which
would involve it in actions beyond its jurisdiction. He asked what would
follow if the archbishop were to appear 'and stiffly maintain his doings', 'the
people addicted to the matter as they were.' It was decided to send Mildmay
himself and Sir Ralph Sadler to sound the archbishop out, while Burghley
wrote to advise him on how to conduct himself at the expected hearing in Star
Chamber, and on the terms of his submission.[95] But Grindal told the two
councillors in uncharacteristically spirited language that before he would yield
'he would be torn in pieces with horses', and he entrusted to Mildmay his own
form of submission which avoided any acknowledgment of guilt.[96]

It was fortunate that illness prevented Grindal from making his appearance
in the Star Chamber on either of the two days appointed, whereupon Lord
Keeper Bacon announced in a short speech that it was thought inexpedient and
by the queen inadmissible to proceed against the archbishop in his absence.[97]
In December Cheke resigned himself to waiting until the following term for a
decision.[98] In at least three collections of Bacon's speeches there survives an
oration intended for use in the Star Chamber, a stern sermon of public rebuke
to be addressed to the archbishop.[99] It is not clear whether this was prepared
for the hearing of late November and never delivered, or whether it belongs
to a subsequent occasion. But since Mildmay conflates elements of both of
Bacon's speeches in his account of what transpired on 30 November and
suggests that this was the end of the matter ('from that time forward he remained in his house as prisoner, continuing in his opinion') it seems most
likely that Grindal never did confront a tribunal charged, however dubiously,
with power to deprive him.[100]

The queen was not pleased. In Burghley's absence from Court it seems to
have fallen to Mildmay to draft a memorandum 'touching the archbishop of
Canterbury in the matter of the exercises', containing arguments which may
have been intended to justify his deprivation.[101] This was dated 22 January.
On the following day Wilson reported to Burghley: 'Her Majesty is much
offended with the archbishop and disliketh our darings for dealing with him so
at large, whom her Highness would have deprived for his contempt committed.' Wilson had advised the queen that the deprivation of an archbishop
could not be so easily arranged, especially since Grindal was likely to contest
the matter. He hoped that on his return Burghley would succeed in persuading
her of the advantages of an arranged resignation, a course 'more safe, more
easy, and as honourable as the other.'[102] A week later Killigrew reported: 'The
bishop of Canterbury is now more likely to be deprived than *at the first*.'[103] But

then, a month later: 'There is hope that the bishop of Canterbury shall do better and better daily', coupled with the news that it was resolved to send Leicester over the North Sea with ten thousand men. 'I would this were a true prognostication.'[104]

At this point Sir Christopher Hatton, newly knighted and preferred to Knollys's old office of vice-chamberlain, became the man upon whose good offices Grindal's reinstatement appeared to depend. On 7 March 1578 Bishop Cox of Ely wrote to a correspondent who could only have been Bishop Aylmer of London, and among other matters asked whether 'by any means we may possibly help our brother', meaning Grindal. 'Ye know the man to be wise, zealous and godly.' His own efforts in this regard had failed. But if Mr Vice-Chamberlain 'could by any prudent means mitigate and assuage her Majesty's displeasure I am persuaded that he should do God high honour and her Majesty good service, and deserve at the hands of those that be zealous and godly infinite thanks and win their hearts for ever.'[105] This was to suggest that Hatton should look for new friends in preserves which were traditionally Leicester's. Two months later, on 2 May, Grindal, in a letter which had no other purpose, thanked Hatton profusely for his 'continual, honourable, and most friendly cares and travails for me, by the which, as also by your sundry comfortable messages at divers times sent unto me, I am brought into an assured hope by your good means to recover her Majesty's grace and favour in time convenient.' Although Hatton's efforts had not yet taken effect, 'yet do I think myself especially bounden to give you most hearty thanks, and that in as ample manner as if I presently enjoyed the fruition of the end of my suit.' The letter suggests that Hatton's intervention was particularly significant. For one thing he was able to exploit a very special relationship with the queen. For another (and this is to speculate) if it was the case that he had initially shared the queen's hostile reaction to the archbishop's letter, or had even provoked her into it, his preparedness to help at this juncture would be all the more likely to succeed. Grindal was more deferential and submissive in this letter than in any other statement he made during this crisis in his affairs.[106] All to no avail. Later in the month the Earl of Huntingdon reported to the Dean of York that the archbishop had been on the point of delivery 'by the good means of Mr Vice-Chamberlain' when reports of a factious puritan sermon conveyed to the queen by Archbishop Sandys of York and Bishop Barnes of Durham were so inflated as 'to make a stay of his deliverance.'[107]

After this the archbishop's cause dragged inconclusively on. Twice in the early months of 1580 he renewed his petition to the Privy Council 'to be means' to the queen for his liberty and restitution.'[108] His health was now broken beyond repair and he was losing his sight.[109] By the New Year of 1583 even the queen's displeasure must have mellowed, for she gave him a 'standing cup', apparently her first gift since the original year of his archiepiscopate.[110] In the following July he forestalled the arrangements at last concluded for his resignation[111] by dying, still in office. He was honourably buried.[112] We need not pursue the details of the story beyond the summer of 1578, for by then the archbishop's cause had reached a kind of plateau. In 1579 the storm over the proposed French marriage shifted attention to another quarter and to a different kind of martyr to the protestant cause, John Stubbs, author of *The gaping gulf*.[113]

An instructive aspect of Grindal's sequestration was the support which he never ceased to enjoy in high places. In public utterance, as in the speeches which Bacon prepared for his appearances before the Council, the archbishop might be reprimanded for his extreme insubordination. Yet surely Bacon gave the game away when he told the company in Star Chamber: 'Some no doubt are apt enough to marvel why her Majesty should so proceed against him. But if it were as well known to you as to my lords here present what reasons her Highness hath to lead her hereunto, I should not need so many words in this matter.'[114] This reflection of public concern is reminiscent of Camden's description of the crowd at John Stubbs's immolation: 'The multitude standing about was altogether silent, either out of horror at this new and unwonted punishment, or else out of pity towards the man, being of the most honest and unblameable report, or else out of hatred of the marriage, which most people perceived would be the overthrow of religion.'[115]

Among the bishops Grindal had but one enemy: Richard Barnes of Durham, a churchman whom he held in contempt as a venal careerist.[116] In February 1578, with the archbishop poised on the brink of deprivation, Barnes found it necessary to defend himself to Burghley against reports that he did not have 'a good mind' to Grindal, and to explain why on a visit to London he had avoided a call at Lambeth.[117] Even conservative bishops such as Cox, Aylmer and Whitgift did nothing to worsen the archbishop's predicament. Cox indeed made use of what he presumed to be a still privileged position to intercede with the queen and Burghley,[118] and, as we have seen, indirectly with Hatton. But it is perhaps significant that in 1580 Whitgift and his ally, Piers of Salisbury, took the initiative in commending to Grindal a form of total retraction and submission,[119] and that three years later Piers was involved in the arrangements for his resignation.[120] In 1581 Convocation and 12 of the bishops presented the queen with formal addresses in favour of their primate's restitution.[121] Admittedly the suspension of the metropolitan was sufficiently prejudicial to the hierarchy as a whole to elicit a united response, almost regardless of the merits of the case. But the absence, or concealment, of any desire to profit from the archbishop's eclipse is nevertheless impressive.

Clearly the sympathetic concern of the protestant nation was firmly engaged on Grindal's behalf. On the other side stood the queen herself and, one must suppose, 'King Richard the Second's men', whose identity one may guess at. They may have included, among privy councillors, Sir James Croft and the Earl of Sussex; and, beyond the Council, the connection of catholics and crypto-catholics of the Court who would later show their hand in the struggle over the French marriage: Lord Henry Howard, Lord Paget, Charles Arundel, Sir Edward Stafford, and the Earl of Oxford, until he was detached from his unsuitable friends by his father-in-law, Burghley.[122] Whether Hatton should be included in their company, at least in the inception of the archbishop's troubles, must remain an open question. Like any account of courtly intrigue, the picture retains its areas of shade and its indefinite outlines.

Finally, what was the state of the Church of England while its senior pastor was under a cloud? This essay has hitherto avoided definition of the legal and administrative intricacies of a suspension from office which was never total, was not set out in any document which survives, and which was not consistently enforced. The relevant facts are in the archiepiscopal Register.[123] As soon as Grindal had been sequestered, in late May 1577, such formal documents as licences for schoolmasters, letters dimissory (vouching for candidates for ordination in another diocese) or commissions to institute to benefices in vacant sees were not only issued by Dr Thomas Yale, as official principal and vicar general, but in his name, rather than that of the archbishop.[124] In November, when Yale took to his deathbed, the Privy Council authorized Grindal to appoint 'two sufficient persons' to take his place. Grindal accordingly issued his own commission to Dr William Drury and Dr Lawrence Hussey.[125] But on 20 January he was informed by Thomas Wilson, as Secretary, that their places as vicars general were to be taken by Dr William Aubrey and Dr William Clark. Aubrey had been nominated by the queen, Clark by the Council, and they were to occupy jointly during royal pleasure the office described at one point in the Register as 'the vicarageship of the archiepiscopal see of Canterbury'. From September 1581 Aubrey appears to have acted alone in the execution of this office.[126]

Among the mandates issued as a matter of course by Aubrey and Clark were commissions to conduct the metropolitan visitation of the various sees. But on 20 January 1583 Grindal inexplicably issued in his own name the commission to visit Lichfield Cathedral.[127] (It was at this time that the queen had favoured him with a New Year's gift.) As for the exercise of his more properly spiritual, episcopal functions, these never seem to have been inhibited by his sequestration. He took part in the consecration of bishops in March 1578, August 1579, September 1580 and September 1581, and mandates to confirm the elections of bishops and for their installation continued to be issued in the archbishop's own name.[128] Moreover, whenever directly instructed to do so by the Council Grindal continued to take a variety of administrative actions, such as the forwarding to the other bishops of royal briefs for charitable collections in aid of distressed individuals or communities, the ordering of enquiries into popish recusancy, and the transmitting of an order of the Council requiring unbeneficed preachers to celebrate communion.[129] On one such occasion he was required to act 'notwithstanding your present sequestration.'[130] In 1579 Grindal was active and authoritative in arbitrating in a major dispute between the cathedral chapter of Canterbury and Queen's College, Cambridge, and in 1581 in efforts to pacify the warring factions in Merton College, Oxford.[131] But such traditional primatial responsibilities as the presidency of Convocation and the appointing of court preachers were assumed by the bishop of London, who also seems to have presided over the Ecclesiastical Commission.[132] In the Parliament of 1581 Archbishop Sandys of York took precedence, although Whitgift of Worcester made an impression which implies that his eventual promotion to Canterbury was already anticipated.[133]

It would require a better sense of the relations between the person of the archbishop and the administrative machinery operated in his name than ecclesiastical historians can yet command to judge how damaging was the absence of personal direction over a period of six years, from the diocese of Canterbury, from the vacant sees, and from the province at large. A memorandum listing 'inconveniences by the sequestration of the archbishop of Canterbury'[134] noted that the processes which normally went out over his name and title would be 'less esteemed' and their validity even doubted when these were lacking. The absence of the archbishop from Convocation was 'a new precedent of dangerous and doubtful sequel.' In vacant sees the archbishop was accustomed to arbitrate personally in major disputes, 'which now he cannot do.' The metropolitan visitation was likely to be ineffective and to leave many dioceses unreformed. The credit and authority of the archbishop were lost to the Ecclesiastical Commission. And

> where as well the bishops and other of the clergy as also of the laity throughout the whole province were wont to resort to the archbishop to consult with him and have his direction in matters of great weight, whereby many controversies and occasions of strife and slander within their dioceses were cut off, although there do arise many like occasions daily, yet there lacketh the authority of the same archbishop for the appeasing thereof.

It was at this personal and political level that the effective headlessness of the Church proved most damaging. Almost half the sees in England seem to have been shaken by storms or scandals of one kind or another between 1575 and 1583. In Sussex and in Norfolk and Suffolk there were major political contests between the bishops and the ruling gentry, and although Bishop Curteys of Chichester was at odds with a conservative, even catholic gentry and Bishop Freke of Norwich with puritans, the two 'country causes' were otherwise of the same order: in both cases the bishop over-reached his political strength in taking on the leaders of local government. The case of Bishop Curteys was a minor reflection of Grindal's greater tragedy: suspension from office, precipitating his death in 1582.[135] Bishop Cox of Ely was being hounded by Lord North and Sir Christopher Hatton and was in serious danger of enforced resignation.[136] Scory of Hereford, who called his diocese a 'purgatory', was under suspicion for 'certain matters of very foul disorder'.[137] Robinson of Bangor had to defend himself against the charge of being a papist[138] and his brother Middleton of St Davids was already linked with the colourful list of crimes which would eventually lead to his degradation.[139] Lichfield witnessed a battle royal for the chancellorship between Dr Becon and Dr Babington, with the ring held by the venal Bishop Overton in a diocese described by Whitgift of Worcester as 'in sundry parts . . . out of frame'.[140] In the north, Archbishop Sandys was in conflict with the lord president, Huntingdon, and with the deans of both York and Durham, Hutton and Whittingham. Then in 1582 came the scandal, juicy if contrived, of the archbishop and the landlord's wife, in an inn at Doncaster.[141] 1580 saw a general enquiry into the wastage of timber in episcopal parks and woods, which exposed many of the bishops as opportunists in estate management.[142]

Above all there was the major scandal of a tripartite delapidations suit involving the senior members of the hierarchy, the two archbishops and the bishop of London, which arose in the first instance from a bitter dispute about the financial affairs of the diocese of London between Sandys and his successor, Aylmer.[143] This quarrel was invested with more than ordinary venom, Sandys writing of Aylmer: 'Coloured covetousness, an envious heart covered with the cloak of dissimulation will, when opportunity serveth, show forth itself.' 'So soon as the bishop of York had holpen him on with his rochet, he was transformed and showed himself in his own nature.'[144]

In retrospect the state of the Church and of religion in the time of Grindal's addled archiepiscopate was both applauded and deplored. The Kentish puritan, Josias Nicholls, recalling that this was a season when preaching ministers were not molested, thought it 'a golden time, full of godly fruit'.[145] But Whitgift's secretary and biographer, Sir George Paule, wrote of 'that crazy state of the Church (for so it was at this archbishop's [Whitgift's] first coming and a long time after'.[146]) Readers who have come thus far will concede that Paule discovered the *mot juste* in 'crazy'.

The contention of this essay has been that Archbishop Grindal's troubles were coherent with the struggle over Elizabethan policy, especially foreign policy. But an almost contradictory argument is equally valid. Once Grindal had written the offending letter and for this and any other contributory causes had incurred the queen's displeasure he became a liability for protestant politicians and it was an important objective of their policy to save him from the worst consequences of his action. But it was no part of policy that Grindal should have written such an undiplomatic letter in the first place and we may be sure that it was without political advice that he put impolitic pen to paper. Policy, even protestant policy, would say: 'It is necessary to be humble, or at least to hold one's tongue.' Grindal represents not political puritanism but that sturdy strain in reformed protestantism which rediscovered the difference between religion and politics and for which 'policy' was almost a term of abuse.[147] In another century and another polity Grindal's 'puritanism' might have been compatible with 'deep judgment' and 'the greatest wisdom and ability to govern'. In Elizabethan England these things were plainly incompatible, and there was a certain inevitability about the archbishop's political extinction.

3

THE ANJOU MATCH AND THE MAKING OF ELIZABETHAN FOREIGN POLICY

Wallace T. MacCaffrey

In December 1576 Secretary Wilson wrote that the whole fate of Christendom depended on three men – Don John of Austria, the Prince of Orange, and the Duke of Anjou.[1] The first of these was in fact to die two years later – young, disappointed and frustrated; the second was to win a prominent niche in the pantheon of European national heroes. The third was to die unlamented, having failed at everything he set his hand to, and having won an unenviable reputation for faithless double-dealing and for almost unrivalled political fecklessness. Nevertheless Anjou played for a few years a prominent role in English politics and for a fleeting moment seemed likely to share sovereign power with Elizabeth. He is in himself a negligible figure but the English phase of his career, examined with care, serves to throw a good deal of light on more important topics.

The flirtation with Anjou – marital and diplomatic – was part of a major episode in English foreign policy, a crucial turning-point in England's unsettled relations with the Hapsburg power. The decisions made in these years were of long-term importance, but the way in which they were shaped is hardly less important than what was decided.

What were the circumstances of English foreign relations at the end of the 1570s? The great preoccupation of the English government since April 1572 had been the rebellion in the Low Countries. The initial explosion had gone off like a series of defective fire-crackers, some exploding cleanly, others mere damp squibs. The result had been that the revolt just barely remained alive but until 1576 its continued survival seemed very doubtful. The English leaders made no bones among themselves as to their hopes for some kind of rebel success[2] – preferably a restoration of the *status quo ante* of Charles V's days when the Netherlands enjoyed a loose autonomy and a high degree of home-rule. England could live comfortably with a régime which guaranteed domestic order in a market so important to English prosperity but which itself did not play a great role in international politics.

But English hopes that the Dutch could achieve this by their own efforts were disappointed. Unluckily the rebels neither succeeded nor quite failed. They could not be abandoned entirely but on the other hand the English dared not risk any substantial stake on a horse so unlikely to stay the course. Consequently England pursued a policy of officially correct neutrality, bent just sufficiently to allow the rebels to acquire supplies (if they paid for them) and to enjoy the assistance of English volunteers.

Then in 1576 there was a dramatic reversal when the inner weaknesses of the Hapsburg monarchy transformed the scene. Spanish power in the Low Countries collapsed as their unpaid troops broke loose from all control. In a few months the 17 provinces were united under the leadership of their own magnates and magistrates in the States-General and England's best hopes seemed in a fair way to be realized. The left-wing protestant internationalists, led by Leicester and Walsingham, pressed the queen hard for active support of the Brussels régime. The option they had always backed – overt support for reasons of both religion and national security – seemed about to be implemented.[3] The queen accorded *de facto* recognition to the States, made them loans – on very niggardly terms – and more than half-promised military aid if Don John and his master would not listen to reason and concede them home rule. Leicester began acquiring harness and armour and wrote that he was about to lead the greatest army to leave English shores in 40 years.[4] But then quite suddenly the weathercocks veered round as the queen backed away, step by hurried step. Promises of military aid faded out in a flurry of explanations; money for the loans was held up; and the most the queen would do was to subsidize the German prince-mercenary, Duke Casimir of the Palatine house, who brought a force into the Low Countries.[5]

What led the queen to reverse her policy at this time? Probably a mixture of forces was at work; the States were displaying a dismaying inability to co-operate among themselves. The catholic princely house of Croye feared the ambitions of the protestantizing house of Orange; protestant populism frightened catholic conservatism; paralysis of will afflicted all the States' affairs. Even their most ardent English supporters recognized their weakness and disunity. The queen disliked dealing with an irregular régime, which for all its protestations of loyalty to the person of Philip II, was patently in rebellion against lawful authority.

But if English influence upon the States were to diminish, the resulting vacuum would almost certainly be filled by a French prince – by the Duke of Anjou. He had been prowling around the edges of the scene for several years, but had been repeatedly distracted by temptations nearer home, championing the Huguenots – or the catholics – against his royal brother. But there was, for the moment, peace in France and his reappearance on the Low Countries stage came at a moment when the threat of Don John (who won a victory over the rebels at Gembloux in January 1578) and English hesitations gave him bargaining power with the States. What was particularly worrying to both English and Netherlands leaders was the question of Anjou's backing. Did he sail under his own colours or those of his royal brother? If the latter were the case, his emergence was as worrying a contingency to English policy as a restored Spanish hegemony.

Hence the first stage of reorienting English policy was to make somewhat diffident approaches to the French prince; it was diplomatically convenient to garb them in the worn but still usable costume of a marriage negotiation between the queen and the duke. This was done in the spring of 1578, but until the new year of 1579 no one did more than mark time. Neither side took seriously the other's intentions. It was the arrival of Simier, the duke's master of the wardrobe, in England in January 1579 which signalled the beginning of another round of wooing – one in which the lady rather than the gentleman took the initiative.

Sometime in the first half of 1579 what had begun as a conventional diplomatic exercise in which – as often before – discussion of a royal marriage was simply a handy vehicle for arriving at some kind of entente, turned into an intense, almost breathless, wooing of François d'Anjou by Elizabeth Tudor. Statesmen from all the interested courts stood in unbelieving astonishment – not least that shop-worn pair of royalties, Henri III and his mother, who stared in cold-eyed disbelief at the behaviour of their island sister. But there was no mistaking the genuine mating note in the calls which she loudly emitted.

The game of match-making opened with the arrival of Simier in January after some delays which had annoyed the queen. Immediately upon his arrival every stop was pulled out in an effort to persuade him of Elizabeth's desire for marriage to his master. Entertainments of the most extravagant kind – feasting, dancing, jousting, masques – were lavished on the Frenchman. While the lords of the court vied in their attentions the queen herself was constantly passing over little gifts – handkerchiefs, gloves, or miniatures of herself – to be sent to Monseigneur. She talked incessantly about marriage and about the duke to anyone who would listen and the ambassador wrote – perhaps somewhat hyperbolically – that she seemed 15 years younger in the excitements of the wooing.[6]

About a month after Simier arrived, Leicester sought out the resident French ambassador, Mauvissière, almost certainly at the queen's direction, and in a long interview did everything he could to persuade the Frenchman of the queen's sincere desire for marriage. He emphasized his own commitment to the match, declaring that he had already bought clothing, horses and equipment for the nuptial celebrations. He retailed his successful efforts to win over the strongly protestant earls of Huntingdon and Bedford as well as other magnates such as Shrewsbury, Pembroke, Rutland, and Arundel. Leicester insisted that the duke would have nothing to do once he presented himself at the English court but to make love. The earl's flow of encouraging speech was slightly marred only by his nervous inquiries as to the real sentiments of the French Court.[7] The queen herself followed up her favourite with similarly auspicious references and even suggested the possibility of a marriage immediately after Easter. Every inducement was laid on to persuade the skittish duke to press his suit before the lady herself. The comedy, one of many acts, had a long run.

Serious bargaining on a marriage treaty began in March, based on the terms granted Philip when he married Mary. At first it seemed the obstacles presented by Anjou's putative role in England and by his religion would block all progress, but the queen brushed these aside, particularly the objection of religion which had always been reserved as a final – and insurmountable – objection in previous negotiations. This time the queen easily conceded private practice of his own religion to the duke. The queen's urgencies at last paid off; the royal suitor arrived – incognito – at Greenwich on 17 August for a 10-day visit.

This whole episode stands out in sharp contrast to earlier royal behaviour. The wooing was very much the queen's own doing, sustained in the face of deep French suspicion and, as we shall see, oblique but powerful obstructiveness in her own court. Moreover, it was the queen who was now making her own policy. In place of her earlier role in which she had listened passively to the proposals nudged forward by her councillors, rejecting or accepting them but rarely taking the lead herself, she was now totally in charge, pressing on under full sail and drawing her councillors in her wake.

What was the policy she now embraced? It rested first on the assumption that France would be drawn to a scheme which would aggrandize the younger brother, Anjou, but also withdraw him from the French political arena. The match accomplished, the new link would draw England and France to act in the closest harmony. Elizabeth and Francis would be the protectors of the French protestants, ensuring them against further catholic oppression, but also guaranteeing to Henri III the loyalty of his reformed subjects. The reverse of this coin would be the end of French (*i.e.*, Guisan) intrigue in England and Scotland. Above all, such an Anglo-French combination would be too powerful for Philip II to ignore and he would be constrained by it to some reasonable compromise with his Netherlands subjects. One stone was to kill a whole flock of blackbirds.

The assumption underlying this proposed line of action – repeatedly brought forward in the various deliberations on the marriage – was the underlying hostility of both France and Spain towards England, which, sooner or later, would eventuate in an intervention in her affairs.[8] At this very juncture the arrival in Ireland of the Fitzmaurice expedition, patronized by Spain, was striking evidence of the dangers. D'Aubigny's arrival in Scotland later in the year would be yet another confirmation of it. In short, one of the great Continental powers had to be not only neutralized but drawn to alliance; it could only be France, first because of the unique matrimonial opportunity; second because of the somewhat less rigid attitude towards the reformed religion which circumstances forced on the French Crown. Roughly speaking, this was the rationale put forward to justify the Anjou marriage. A variant, hinted at from time to time, was alliance without marriage, but this would give the queen much less leverage over the wayward French prince than would the bonds of matrimony.

What moved the queen to shift to so activist a policy, one which would require English initiatives, which might well lead to confrontation with Spain, and one so riddled with dangerous contingencies? The earlier alternative, which the queen had favourably entertained for a time – that of backing the States-General – had soured as the internal fissures among the Low Countries magnates became visible. At the same time Anjou, by his eagerness to intrude himself into Netherlands affairs, had become a serious menace. It seemed all too probable that, following on his flirtations with the French catholics, he might enter the provinces as the ally of Don John (or his successor) and in English eyes this would mean he was merely a stalking-horse for French ambitions to dominate the Netherlands. A third, remoter, element which gradually bore on English political calculations, was the probability after the disaster of Alcazar in the late summer of 1578 that Philip would add Portugal to his dominions and thus dangerously overweight the balance of power in western Europe. Under these circumstances it would become imperative to hold Spain in check in the 17 provinces. As early as September 1579 the queen was expressing her concern over the Portuguese problem to the French and Spanish ambassadors.[9]

But the sum total of these policy considerations does not yield an entirely convincing explanation of this far-reaching shift in Elizabethan policy. We have, I think, to turn to the queen herself, who transformed a conventional round of diplomatic sparring into an intensely personal drama. The diplomatic pretence suddenly acquired a startling and vivid reality. There is of course no direct evidence of Elizabeth's emotional life, now or at any other time, but the circumstantial proof is strong. She had reached the very last term of years in which marriage would be a live option for her. Once she passed child-bearing age the diplomatic value of a match vanished. And with it would vanish one of the great pleasures of Elizabeth's life – the excitements of courtship. It was this knowledge of time's panting urgency which presumably overpowered her normal repugnance to marriage and drove her to headlong pursuit of Anjou. She was not, I think, in love with him as she had been 18 years earlier with Robert Dudley. But she was in love with his rank and dignity; her royal snobbery was gratified by a prospective match with the first prince of the blood of the oldest of the great dynasties. It was possible to paint a plausible picture of the match as a necessary – and wise – act of state policy, but in 1579 the driving force behind the negotiations was the overpowering attraction which matrimony now exerted on Elizabeth.

But as in 1561 the queen would not take the final plunge unless she had the strong and urgent backing of her councillors. For them it was a bewildering dilemma; for years they had urged on her the necessity of marrying and begetting an heir. The dreadful uncertainties of the succession were no less frightening now than at any time in the past. Yet an elementary knowledge of physiology told them what were the risks of any marriage for a 46-year-old woman. They whistled in the dark by dredging up stories of successful late pregnancies, but few of them can have doubted that any marriage was a frightful risk for the queen and the kingdom. There was also the question of the particular candidate now proposed, the heir to the French throne and a prince whose antecedents were to many dubious and to some unsavoury. Dared they risk the very existence of the political and religious establishment on the chances of this incongruous mating?

These were the questions the Council was drawn to debate in October 1579 but their official and private deliberations were overtaken by a public and popular outburst of a novel kind. Sermons had been preached against the marriage since March and an angry queen had threatened to have the preachers whipped. Public criticism was being noised abroad during the summer and during the duke's supposedly secret visit. A few weeks later lampoons against the marriage were posted on the Lord Mayor's door; a surviving couple (probably from autumn 1579) give us an idea of their content and style. One in Latin, the other in English, both are outspoken in their abhorrence of a foreign ruler. 'The king of France shall not advance his ships in English sand! Nor shall his brother Francis have the Ruling of the land.'[10]

But the matter exploded into the open in September with the publication of John Stubbs's *The discovery of a gaping gulf wherein England is like to be swallowed by another French marriage, if the Lord forbid not the banns by letting Her Majesty see the sin and punishment thereof.* The queen's fury at Stubbs's book was almost beyond bounds. A proclamation, ordering its public destruction,[11] denounced it as the work of a seditious libeller, whose object was to 'alienate the love and estimation which her people have of her.' The proclamation defended Anjou's reputation and scornfully repudiated the suggestion that the marriage treaty endangered either the Church or the commonwealth and made the point that any conditions agreed to with Anjou would have to have parliamentary confirmation. The Privy Council sought the assistance both of the London corporation and the bench of bishops in suppressing Stubbs's book. The bishops were to summon meetings of their diocesan clergy to whom the proclamation was to be read. They were to be reassured as to the queen's intentions to 'maintain the state of religion without any alteration or change'. They were also to be warned not to intermeddle in their sermons with any matter of state nor, indeed, in any secular matter. Even before this Aylmer had taken measures and arranged to have a sermon preached against Stubbs's book. He was hopeful that opinion in London itself might be brought round but dubious as to what might be done about preachers in the country who were attacking the match. He feared that summoning them to London for rebuke would only reignite interest in the issue in the capital. Bishop Aylmer reported his success in checking London sermons hostile to the match but had little doubt that the weight of opinion was against it.[12]

The queen's anger is understandable since Stubbs's production had to be taken seriously. It was much more than a zealot's shrill polemic; a rhetorically skilful and wholly literate piece of work, it was addressed to an educated audience. Its central arguments were shrewdly considered, comprehensive, and very knowledgeable. Indeed they were so well-informed – and so close in content to the actual Council debates – that the queen came to suspect that someone in the Council was behind Stubbs.[13]

Stubbs himself was a lawyer and country gentleman, a Cambridge graduate and a member of Lincoln's Inn with left-wing protestant associations aplenty. His sister married Thomas Cartwright and he was a friend of both Walter Travers and William Davison and kin by marriage to the great protestant house of Willoughby d'Eresby. He had a connection with Burghley also, through his life-long friendship with Michael Hickes, secretary to William and friend to Robert Cecil.[14]

Stubbs, his bookseller, Page, and his printer, Singleton, were apprehended shortly after the book was suppressed and swiftly brought to trial. Sentence was pronounced on 30 October and the punishment carried out on 3 November. Its nature is a measure of the royal wrath. Stubbs and Page were tried under a statute of Philip and Mary against publishers of seditious writings. Some lawyers thought the statute had expired with the late queen and although the Chief Justice, Wray, defended its validity, one lawyer who protested against it was sent to the Tower and one of the Justices of Common Pleas was 'so sharply reprehended that he resigned his place'. The penalty was an unusual and brutal one; Stubbs and Page both lost their right hands, chopped off with a cleaver. Camden gives us an eye-witness account and soberly records the silence of the multitude 'either out of an horror at this new and unwonted kind of punishment, or else out of commiseration towards the man, as being of an honest and unblamable repute; or else out of hatred of the marriage, which most men presaged would be the overthrow of religion'.[15] The unlucky lawyer was then taken back to prison where he was to remain until the early months of 1581. But in the course of the 1580s Stubbs would be employed by Burghley to answer Allen's *Defense*; later he sat in the Commons for Great Yarmouth and had the Lord Treasurer's (unsuccessful) backing for an Exchequer post. He was to die serving Lord Willoughby in France.[16]

The book which Stubbs had written displays a wide command of the arguments of all kinds adduced for and against the marriage. He set out to show and to prove 'that this is a counsel against the Church of Christ, an endeavour of no well-advised Englishman, as well in regard of the common state, as of Her Majesty's good estate, to every of which it is pernicious and capital'.[17] The argument that the marriage would endanger the Reformed faith was the first to be taken up. Drawing heavily upon Old Testament precedent, Stubbs casts the English in the role of the Chosen People and likens a match with a Popish prince to a Hebrew marriage with a Canaanite. 'Or shall it be much more ugly before God and his angels when an Hebrew shall marry a Canaanite?'[18]

He goes on to demonstrate that the family of France collectively and this prince singly have been and are enemies of the Gospel, 'a principal prop of the tottering house of Antichrist'.[19] Catherine de Medici was identified with Athaliah and the massacre of St Bartholomew evoked in bloody detail. The argument that Anjou would be converted to his wife's faith was mocked by copious references to the duke's religious tergiversations. The conclusion was plain; marriage with the French duke would be ruinous to true religion in England and would call down the wrath of an angry God upon a faithless generation.

Stubbs turned from the religious argument to the nationalist one. 'It is natural to all men to abhor foreign rule as a burden of Egypt, and to us of England if to any other nation under the sun.' It was against nature that an alien could have those 'natural and brotherlike bowels of tender love towards this people which is required in a governor'.[20] Not so much as a petty constableship should be entrusted to one foreign-born. Stubbs pinpointed his argument by a telling reference to the recent past. The first and chief benefit done by the queen to her people was to redeem them – with the Lord's help – from a foreign king. A marriage with a foreign prince – above all one of the ancient enemy house of France – would be to undo this good work, and to re-enact the miseries of Philip's years as Mary's husband, with the added horror of destroying true religion.

More gravely dangerous are the risks which arise from Duke Francis's position as his childless brother's heir. If he were to succeed to the French Crown Elizabeth must either follow him across the Channel to be a mere 'borrowed majesty as the moon to the sun' or stay at home 'without comfort of her husband, seeing herself despised or not wifelike esteemed and as an eclipsed sun diminished in sovereignty'.[21]

Countering yet another argument – the hope that the royal marriage would bring the long-awaited heir – Stubbs quite baldly points out the high probability of the death of both mother and child, for one of Elizabeth's years. But even if there were a living son, his very succession might reduce England to a mere Naples or Sicily ruled by a French proconsul. No ingenuity of the lawyers could devise legal bonds strong enough to constrain the French prince once he became the husband of the English queen.

The strongest argument for the marriage, Stubbs admits, is the alliance with France and the support of the protestant party within that kingdom which Monsieur would bring in his train. Stubbs quite sensibly points out that Anjou has in fact no base in French politics, no body of steady or respectable supporters either protestant or papist – nothing resembling the power which stands behind either Guise or Condé.[22] And as for the argument of a French alliance, he summons up history – the long saga of Anglo-French enmity – as a witness against its utility. Besides, such an alignment will break the old Burgundian link, still economically vital; cut off the new entente with Scotland, 'a brother in Christ', and forfeit the respect of the protestant princes of Germany. And all this for the deceptive mirage of alliance with an ancient enemy, the protagonist of a false and hostile faith.

Stubbs then moves on to more personal considerations: how will Anjou, the man, suit Elizabeth, the woman? Although he eschews direct accusation, his prose is laden with innuendoes, all of them more than hinting at the depraved tastes and habits of the duke. Nor were his motives in seeking the marriage above suspicion; he was, Stubbs argues, likely to be no more than a pawn for the catholic interest in France and at Rome, a confidant of Guise and a favourer of the Queen of Scots. In short the marriage might be no more than a barely disguised scheme to bring in the old religion.

Stubbs then returns to one of the central arguments supporting the marriage: that Anglo-French power would suffice to bring Philip to terms in the Low Countries. If this is so, why has the duke not already joined us instead of intriguing against Orange and flirting with the Malcontents? And indeed if French forces provided by the king were made available, it would be a French, not an Anglo-French, settlement. There was no more point in England fighting France's wars against Spain than there had been in fighting for Spain against France in Queen Mary's time.[23] The assumption of those who support the French alliance is that Henri's jealousy of Monsieur will lead him to support any move which takes the duke out of French politics. But is this realistic? First of all, would the king advance his brother to another kingdom – to two, England and the Low Countries? And at bottom does such jealousy really exist; will not brothers and mother rally together to support the joint interests of their house? Certainly the least of their care is for the welfare of England.

Appealing again to national pride, Stubbs argues that no alliance is really necessary to protect England; had she not won her freedom from popery by her own exertions? 'The best bridle, therefore, that we can have to keep in proud France are [sic] the naturally bridling bands of the sea, wherewith God hath compassed us about and the surest girths which hold us in the saddle are the peace and good order of our land.'[24] Anjou would bring in his train a whole flock of covetous French or French-Italian cormorants, to batten off the people of England.

In his peroration he reiterates that neither would religion be preserved, the strength and gain of the land maintained, nor English honour served by bringing in 'this odd fellow, by birth a Frenchman, by profession a Papist, an atheist by conversation, an instrument in France of uncleanness, a fly worker in England for Rome and France in this present affair, a sorcerer by common voice and fame'.[25]

The *Gaping gulf* was all in all a powerful and persuasive attack on the whole programme of the Anjou marriage. It assailed the basic policy assumptions of the pro-French party, denying the advantages which would accrue to England by such an alliance. It brought out into the open the worrying contingencies involved in a match with the heir of France. It painted an unflattering but altogether plausible picture of the duke himself. And as a propaganda piece, it appealed powerfully to all the ancient English prejudices against the French and to the newer protestant convictions of so many of the queen's most weighty subjects.

The timing of Stubbs's book is important, for it was published at the very height of a long-drawn out duel in the Council. Discussion of the match had begun in the spring and continued up to the duke's arrival.[26] Opinion within the Council was divided and quite certainly opposition to the marriage was now openly led by Leicester, who, for a long time, had posed as a friend of France and of Anjou. He was treading on dangerous ground, for in the previous year he had secretly married Lettice Knollys, the widowed Countess of Essex, daughter of that staunch puritan, Sir Francis Knollys. The favourite suffered a shrewd blow when Simier was able to reveal this event to the queen[27] – thanks to the assistance of two crypto-catholics, Henry Howard and Charles Arundel, both of them protégés of the Earl of Oxford. That lord was now enjoying a considerable ascendancy at Court and had awakened the jealous hostility of the Leicester-Sidney faction. It was sometime in this summer that the young Philip Sidney had his famous tennis-court quarrel with Oxford, an incident which heightened the rivalry between the two noblemen. Sidney had also composed a letter to the queen deploring the proposed match with Anjou. In late August it was reported that Leicester was holding meetings at Pembroke's house with that lord and with Henry Sidney. Pembroke had been a nephew by marriage of Dudley since his marriage with Mary Sidney in 1577. The deep dismay of the Leicester faction is reflected in Spenser's *Shepheardes Calender*, published in December of 1579.[28]

Discussion in the Council had begun as early as March but up until the duke's visit councillors had evaded the main issue by concentrating on such ancillary topics as the consort's authority (he was to have none), his income or his coronation (decisions shuffled onto the shoulders of a future Parliament). But in October they had to bite the bullet. For the first time the objections voiced hitherto in pulpit and pamphlet were heard at the Council board. Their content was hardly novel; indeed it was so like Stubbs's arguments that it is hardly surprising the queen should suspect a collaboration between the pamphleteer and some member of the anti-Anjou faction in her Council. Those favouring the match emphasized the alliance against Spain, joint action in the Low Countries and the protection of the Huguenots. They made much of the grim consequences of rejecting Anjou; he would marry an infanta; Spain and France would ally against England. Conspiracy at home, focussed on that centre of all discontents, Mary Stuart, would blend with schemes for foreign intervention. And, as Burghley warned the queen, this would entail English reactions – to keep alight the fires of dissidence in France and the Netherlands would mean 'conjunction with heads of factions', soldiers and money, probably a guaranteed annual subsidy.[29]

The opponents of the marriage averred that the marriage 'could not be but dangerous to religion, unsure to Her Majesty and unprofitable to the realm'.[30] And if Mendoza's informant was correct, virtually the whole Council, led by Leicester and Hatton, recommended against the marriage; only Burghley and Sussex favoured it. The opponents warned the queen that if she persisted, there would have to be a campaign of persuasion before Parliament met and that that body would certainly demand the nomination of a successor.

Mendoza may have got the drift of discussion in the Council right but he was wrong as to the actual recommendation made to Elizabeth by that body. What they reported to her was not an outright rejection but a stalling motion, *i.e.*, that they could only report the *pro* and *contra* arguments without coming down on either side. The queen was indignant, fell to tears, and declared she should never have put the question to discussion. In a second interview she reproved those who opposed the match, made light of their fears of Anjou's catholicism, and expressed astonishment that there should be any doubt of the advantages of the match; indeed she had thought there would have been a universal request that she proceed. The Council under this pressure sullenly gave way and agreed 'to offer their services in furtherance of the marriage if it should so like her'; they still evaded any forthright statement of approval.[31] So the matter stuck through October. In early November Mendoza reported that Elizabeth had told the Council she would marry;[32] we know certainly that she did order a newly-appointed committee of ranking councillors to draw up a treaty of marriage. The articles were signed by Simier on 24 November and taken to Paris by him and Edward Stafford in December.[33] Significantly they had a proviso tacked on suspending the treaty for two months, to give the queen time to persuade her people to the match; Parliament was prorogued until January.[34] And sometime before the end of the year the queen was writing to Anjou[35] bemoaning the ill will of those who objected to his faith but admitting that public opinion was too strong to allow her to yield to her inclinations.

Elizabeth had been frustrated in her desire to marry Francis of Anjou. The definitive check had come in the Council itself. After months of polite evasion during which they no doubt hoped that the queen would prove no more serious in this wooing than in previous ones, they had to face the fact that she plainly demanded their enthusiastic support for the marriage. What answer were they to give? With two exceptions – Sussex and more doubtfully Burghley – they obstinately opposed the match. The gross defects of the duke, private and public, the risks of a match with the heir of France, the dangers to the queen's own life, and last but not least the peril in which such a marriage would place the protestant faith, made a conclusive negative case. And so the councillors politely offered 'their services in furtherance of the match' if the queen on her own chose to make it. Resolutely withholding their explicit approval, they refused all responsibility for the marriage and threw the weight of decision back on the unwilling shoulders of their mistress.

In these events the customary roles of queen and Council were in a measure reversed. Normally the initiative rested solely with the ruler; it was she who brought the Council to life, in its collective consultative capacity, by asking its advice; without her command it could not function in this way. She could then take or reject its proffered advice, as she chose. But in this instance the queen needed conciliar backing before she could act. The queen never doubted the greatness of her power, but she was also aware of its limits. The Anjou marriage was too grave a matter for the sovereign to move on her own, unsupported by the greater politicians. The Council's refusal to give any positive assent to her proposal revealed its latent blocking power. Without directly opposing the royal will, its wary coldness towards her intended actions was sufficient to change the whole direction of English policy.

The obstinacy of the lords of Council was sufficient to hold back the queen from marriage, but their opposition was backed up by the great strength of an effectively mobilized popular resentment. Stubbs's book was only the tip of the iceberg. Besides the sermons preached against the marriage, there was Philip Sidney's letter, Bishop Cox's treatise and a body of popular ballads, some still extant. All contemporary witnesses agree as to the extent and the intensity of feeling.

The most sophisticated response is to be found in Edmund Spenser's *Shepheardes Calender*, printed in December 1579 but circulating in manuscript before that date. (It was printed by Stubbs's printer, Singleton.) The November and February eclogues are the two most relevant sections.[36] The first of these emphasizes the ruin of religion (and of the protestants' patron, Leicester) which the Anjou match presaged; the second echoes the court quarrel between Leicester and Oxford, a supporter of the match. The role of the Leicester connection suggests that the outburst of public indignation was by no means an entirely spontaneous phenomenon. We need not doubt, although we cannot prove, that the Leicester-Walsingham faction in the Council made the most of their case. What is important is the existence of this latent body of opinion which needed only a little stimulation to spring to life.

The public opposition to the marriage reveals something else about the nature of the Elizabethan régime. Since the very beginning of the reign the myth-makers had been busily at work in the service of what the twentieth century would call the cult of personality. Poets, preachers, and painters all lavished their art on the task. Some of their efforts were devoted to celebrating those royal characteristics on which Elizabeth particularly prided herself: her virginity, with the related implication of her complete devotion to her people's welfare, her prudence, wisdom, and justice.[37]

But besides these celebrants of the queen's 'official' virtues there was another school composed of those who set up an image of her as the protectress of true religion. This 'unofficial' enterprise was first shaped by the conceptions of that prophet-historian, John Foxe, who in his great book built up a framework of historical and biblical interpretation which provided a stage into which Elizabeth's career could be fitted. She was the English Deborah, the princess set by God's special providence upon the English throne to revive and to fulfil the work of reformation and of renewal. Lesser writers in prose and verse had in the 1560s and 1570s continued this tradition, linking religious and nationalist aspirations into a common pattern.[38] (Spenser's climactic work, of course, still lay in the future.) But this unofficial cult was being built up without the approval of the goddess herself. Indeed, the role of protestant champion which it assigned her was one deeply repugnant to the secular-minded queen. Nevertheless, she could not avoid the fact that the loyalties massed around this religio-nationalist conception had become a substantial proportion of the monarchy's moral capital. The immense popular enthusiasm for the queen rested in no small part on the widely-held vision of her as the defender of a faith at once evangelical and distinctively English. To have married Anjou would have sadly marred that image. In one sense Elizabeth was right in seeing Stubbs's book as an attempt to alienate her people from her. He sought to constrain the queen to act within the stereotype and implicitly threatened her with the loss of popular affection if she did not conform.

While one cannot assess the exact proportions of each of the forces which turned Elizabeth away from marrying Anjou, it is possible to understand this episode as revealing new energies at work within the English political order which were to have a permanent place within its structure. A deep anti-catholic prejudice, as much a xenophobic phenomenon as a theological one, had taken root in important segments of the politically articulate political nation. The literate gentry and townsmen to whom Stubbs addressed his book or the congregations who listened to preachers sympathetic to him represented a latent force but one which could be easily stimulated and which was likely to find voice in Parliament.

The firm although gentle pressure of the councillors had brought the royal train to a halt in its headlong progress towards matrimony. It was to remain stalled for nearly a year and when it began to move again it had been switched to a track which led not to marriage but to alliance. The contrast between English policy in 1579 and in 1581 could not stand out more sharply. In the earlier year the needs of the state were muddled confusingly with the emotional drives of a middle-aged spinster princess. In the latter the interests of the state and the goals which could satisfy them were spelled out with hard-headed clarity. It is not too much to say that in this final 'Angevin' phase English statesmen explicitly described and faced the classic dilemma which their successors were to encounter in various future forms, and which is loosely denominated the 'balance of power'. There is no great Cecilian state paper which sets forth the issues but there is plenty of scattered evidence in the diplomatic instructions – and in the later Council debates of 1584–5[39] – which makes clear that the English government came to see the international situation in its largest dimensions, those of the whole community of Europe. The instructions given Walsingham when he went to Paris in the summer of 1581 are unambiguous.[40] He was to urge upon the French rulers 'how necessary it is for the Crown of France as well as for ours, yea, for all Christendom that the King of Spain's greatness be impeached'. This sentiment – the need to 'impeach' the catholic king's greatness – is repeated again and again in the diplomatic documents of these years. The augmentation of Spanish power brought about by her annexation of Portugal tipped the balance in a way which endangered all other European states.

The remedy which England proposed was straightforwardly 'Machiavellian' in its assumptions. Unlike the tentative entente of 1572 which was coloured by the Huguenot predominance at the French Court, this understanding was to be free of any ideological content. That one power was catholic, the other protestant, and their common foe the most catholic of all kings was quite beside the point. It was the growing greatness of Philip which required England and France to sink all lesser differences in a common alliance against a common menace. This tough-minded argument was put with all possible force by Walsingham when he went as special ambassador to Paris in 1581 in an effort to persuade Henri III and Catherine de Medici to enter such an alliance. He failed, in part because he could not convince France that Spain was a real menace to her, and in part because the French Court deeply distrusted Elizabeth's good faith. They put it quite bluntly; once Spain and France were at one another's throats, Elizabeth would slip the collar and retire to a comfortable grandstand seat to watch the ensuing action.[41]

As a result the English, unable to mobilize French support, had to turn once more to Anjou. He came this time – in November 1581 – in the guise of a suitor and even went through the forms of betrothal. 'The force of modest love in the midst of amorous discourse carried the Queen so far that she drew off a ring from her finger and put it upon the Duke of Anjou upon certain conditions betwixt the two.'[42] But in fact the real business of the visit was a treaty between the English government and the duke; the latter was to become the Governor of the Low Countries and to be generously subsidized with English funds. It was a *pis aller*; instead of the full-fledged alliance with France, England would have to make do with an 'Angevin' régime in the Low Countries which would at least hold Spain in check there. Since additional funds were made available to the duke from his own apanage and from the royal French coffers, there was a *de facto* collaboration of a very loose kind, the shadow of the alliance which Elizabeth had sought in vain.

This second-best strategy ended in unmitigated disaster. The cause of its failure was simple: the total incompetence of the Duke of Anjou as ruler and as general. The pointless – almost obsessive – double-dealing which was the hallmark of this prince's career led him to attempt a feckless coup at Antwerp (and in other Flemish towns) in January 1583. Its predictable failure wiped out whatever residue of trust still existed between him and his Low Countries subjects and forced him to ignominious retreat, tail between his legs.

Anjou's failure in the Low Countries points up the contradictory features of English policy in these years. The diagnosis of England's position had been clear-eyed and tough-minded. The queen had at last come to acknowledge that the combination of English assistance to the Netherlands rebels, and Drake's forays into the Indies was likely to provoke Spanish retaliation – indeed, the two expeditions into Ireland in 1579 and 1580 were an earnest of this. And Spain, now the master of Portuguese resources at home and overseas, would, if she chose to act, be too powerful to be withstood. (Indeed, there was a risk that she would soon be too powerful even for a combination of allied powers.) Hence the need for an immediate Anglo-French alliance, actively cooperating in the Low Countries and in the Portuguese empire, which by its very existence would lead King Philip to second thoughts: to compromise and conciliation. In short, the queen had come round to a view of the international scene which her protestant advisors had long pressed, unsuccessfully, on her. They had consistently held up the image of Spain as an implacable enemy, the very nerve centre of a great conspiracy against the protestant faith. But if she had now come to fear Philip, it was not as confessional champion but as a secular prince whose own secular interests intersected those of the English crown. The analysis was cogently persuasive and all elements in the Council, for different reasons, were prepared to give it hearty support. Yet the whole programme failed of fulfilment; what went wrong?

Obviously its success depended on drawing France into effective alliance. The simplest means to accomplish this end would have been a royal marriage. But by 1581 this was precluded, as we have argued above, by domestic pressures of great intensity. Elizabeth was placed at serious disadvantage and the

French had a useful weapon to hand. They agreed readily to an alliance – if the queen would first marry Anjou. Indeed, they offered to pay all the expenses of a Low Countries expedition. But they insisted on the marriage as the one token that the queen's intentions were honourable. Otherwise, they would not believe she meant a real alliance. This left her in an awkward position with few alternatives. Her best line of action – as Walsingham pointed out – would be a generous and specific commitment of men, arms, and money to the common enterprise, but Elizabeth, always reluctant to give even the most modest hostages to fortune, held back and the French were confirmed – if confirmation were still needed – in their total distrust of her intentions. But not only were they altogether sceptical of the English queen's good faith; they were far from convinced that Spain represented – at this time – a menace to their own security. The French Court had not dabbled in Low Countries affairs; they had sent no volunteers nor made any loans; and they were not tainted with heresy. Why then risk war with a Spain which had no overt reasons to assail them? And so for this combination of reasons, the queen's first ploy – the attempt at alliance – failed. This failure stemmed in no small part from Elizabeth's own style of diplomacy. Her favourite techniques of evasion, delay, objections, half-promises, had often served to dazzle opponents and frequently to win time – to the advantage of England. But this style had also widened the 'credibility gap' to such a breadth that only the one-way bridge of matrimony could close it.

The second stage of Elizabeth's policy in 1581–2 – the subsidization of Anjou – has already been characterized as a failure and blame assigned to the duke. Yet the queen must also bear responsibility since she insisted on giving him the fullest backing, even when he betrayed his Low Countries allies and when his usefulness was obviously at an end. She lavished £60,000 of her scanty resources on the duke in 1581 and 1582.[43] She never quite shed her illusions about her royal protegé; somehow she could not quite accept the fact that he did not embody those imperial virtues to which birth entitled him. But without abandoning her whole strategy – and backing the Prince of Orange – she had no alternative open to her. So as long as Anjou remained in Flanders – and even for a time after his return to France – the queen continued to give him her support until even she had to recognize the bankruptcy of her policy. By June 1583 the whole attempt to check Spain in the Low Countries was in ruins and England could only stand by, a helpless looker-on, while Parma pocketed town after town in his relentless reconquest. Only after the deaths of both Anjou and Orange and under imminent threat to Antwerp did the English government stir from its paralysis and revert finally to the policy of direct assistance to the rebel States.

To sum up: I have argued that in 1578 English foreign policy was personally taken in hand by the queen and turned sharply in a new direction. Already after the events of 1576 Elizabeth had allowed herself to be persuaded into more overt and effective support of the rebel cause. But now she cast aside this line of action, so strongly favoured by the protestant left, and took another tack. Her policy was still interventionist, but it was henceforth to be linked not to the Netherlands but to the King of France. In its earlier version, that of the Anjou marriage, England's involvement would have been far-reaching since the queen would have been at once France's sister, his ally, and the protectress of his protestant subjects. The scheme foundered on the objections of powerful segments of Elizabeth's own subjects. Within the Council itself most of the magnates, at odds on other issues, found common ground in opposing the marriage. In wider circles, in London and in the provinces, members of the politically aware classes, gentry, clergy, and townsmen, rallied behind a cause which was at once puritan and nationalist in character. Fears for the new religion and for national independence were equally effective stimuli for a formidable coalition of opposition. Hence Elizabeth was driven back on a more modest goal – an alliance with France, but one designed not only for intervention in the Low Countries but also to contain the 'greatness of the King of Spain,' now by his annexation of Portugal, at the very zenith of his fortunes – and indeed by his overweening might a threat to all the other states of Christendom. This scheme failed too because of French distrust and Elizabeth's timidity; so did the second-best arrangement by which she subsidized Anjou as governor of the rebel provinces. Her initiative of the years 1578–83, which has been the subject of this paper, now faltered to an ignominious halt. In the intervening years the threat to England's security had increased. Her own actions had further aroused Spanish resentment while Philip himself had acquired substantial new resources. All efforts to find an ally had failed and England, with the sole help of the enfeebled provinces, was left alone to deal with the Hapsburg power.

4

POPULAR PURITAN MENTALITY IN LATE ELIZABETHAN ENGLAND[1]

Nicholas Tyacke

'I wish I had been able to penetrate more deeply into the thoughts and feelings of the mass of the nation. Nothing is, however, more difficult than to descend below the surface to the depths of society: nothing more easy than to be led astray into imagining the chance utterance of some poetaster or pamphleteer to be the echo of the popular mind'. So wrote the founding father of English seventeenth-century historical studies, S. R. Gardiner, pausing amidst his labours on the history of the 'Puritan Revolution'. But, with the best of intentions, can an historian of puritanism ever hope to descend Cousteau-like beneath the waves of sermon and similar literature? For puritans constituted neither a church nor a sect and there seems no satisfactory means of collectively identifying them. Instead the subject appears fated to lead a more or less 'surface' existence. Yet one possible and certainly neglected approach lies via the puritan baptismal names – names like Fear-God, which emerged during the late sixteenth century. Assuming that such names are a genuine echo of puritan mentality, lay as well as clerical, then the children may be able to lead us to their parents, who they were, and what they thought and did.[2]

Everyone has heard of Praise-God Barebone after whom is called the nominated parliament of 1653, and students of English literature at least are familiar with the peculiar names that Ben Jonson gives to some of his characters in *The Alchemist* (1610) and *Bartholomew Fair* (1614): Tribulation Wholesome, Zeal-of-the-land Busy and Win-the-fight Littlewit. Jonson's most likely source was William Camden, his former schoolmaster, who had earlier remarked in print on the 'new names', including Tribulation, given 'upon some singular and precise conceit'. More specific as to the religious context was Richard Bancroft, the future archbishop. In his *Dangerous Positions . . . practised . . . for the Presbyterial Discipline,* he asked rhetorically 'whence else do these new names and fancies proceed: The-Lord-is-near, More-trial, Reformation, Discipline, Joy-again, Sufficient, From-above, Free-gift, More-fruit, Dust and many other such like?' According to him they were an out-growth of 'English Scotizing'. While both Camden and Bancroft agree in assigning the origin of these puritan baptismal names to the later years of Queen Elizabeth neither gives any indication of whereabouts in England they occurred.[3]

The first person seriously to investigate puritan nomenclature was the Victorian vicar C. W. Bardsley, who made a very important distinction between what he called the 'Hebraic invasion' of English parish registers by Old Testament names, dating from the 1560s, and a later crop of baptismal names consisting of 'scriptural phrases, pious ejaculations, or godly admonitions'. This second stage Bardsley linked to the English presbyterian movement of the 1580s, and there are good grounds for thinking him correct. Untenable, however, are his further claims that the new baptismal fashion of the 1580s lasted until the Civil War and moreover spread into every English county 'south of Trent'.[4] In fact the giving of such names was much more delimited than Bardsley thought, both in time and space.

Historiographically these 'scriptural phrases, pious ejaculations, or godly admonitions' came to be associated particularly with the county of Sussex. Thus wide publicity was given by David Hume in his *History* to a list of seventeenth-century Sussex jurymen, all endowed with names like Redeemed Compton of Battle.[5] This and a similar published list together yield 23 identifiable Sussex parishes.[6] All of them are in the eastern part of the county and the possible significance of this can be tested against the extant west Sussex protestation returns of 1642. The latter indicate a total absence of puritan baptismal names originating in west Sussex.[7] A similar east-west contrast exists between names recorded in the archdeaconries of Lewes and Chichester, both of testators and applicants for marriage licences. On the basis of the Lewes wills and marriage licences we can add 22 more east Sussex parishes to our original 23.[8] Finally three other parishes, which have come to my notice, need to be included.[9]

Examination of the relevant parish registers, where available, reveals 18 east Sussex parishes in which puritan baptismal names were being given during the last two decades of the sixteenth century; 15 of these parishes are contiguous, running in an arc from Salehurst on the Kent border to Alfriston on the South Downs.[10] The names occur earliest in a triangle formed by the parishes of Heathfield, Warbleton and Burwash, although the highest concentration of names in any of the 18 parishes is at Warbleton. Between 1587 and 1590 more than half of the children baptized each year at Warbleton received puritan names.[11] The charismatic element seems to have been provided by the local curate, Thomas Hely, who in November 1585 christened his son Much-mercy. This was the second child at Warbleton to be given

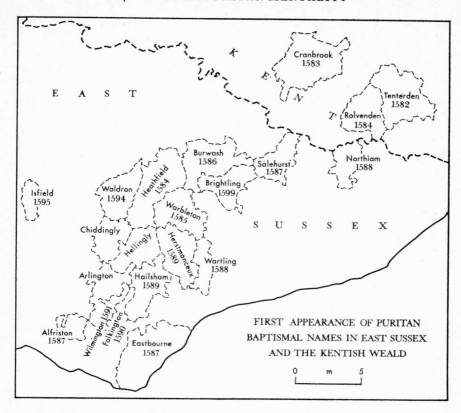

FIRST APPEARANCE OF PURITAN
BAPTISMAL NAMES IN EAST SUSSEX
AND THE KENTISH WEALD

0   m   5

one of the new names, the practice being inaugurated in July 1585 when
Goddard Hepden's son was baptised Return. At neighbouring Heathfield
two children had been given puritan names even earlier: in March 1584
Richard Fuller's son was baptized Obedient and in April 1585 Roger Luff's
son was baptized Zealous.

The vicar of Heathfield, John Miles, was childless but apparently sympathetic to this novel style in names. Certainly he and Hely had close links;
in 1591, for example, Miles witnessed the will of Hely's mother-in-law.[12]
The other witness was Humphrey Sommer, schoolmaster at Heathfield,
who in October 1588 called his daughter Flee-sin. Also associated with Hely
was William Hopkinson, rector of Warbleton and vicar of Salehurst. At
Salehurst, between November 1587 and February 1592, Hopkinson named
his children Endure, Renewed and Safe-on-high. Hely and Miles were both
men of property in their own right by the early 1590s, being assessed for purpose of subsidy on respectively £2 worth of lands and £4 10s. worth of lands.
None of the three clergy had a university degree. Of the earliest Sussex
laity to adopt the new nomenclature, Fuller and Hepden were each substantial

yeomen, while Luff was a husbandman unable as a witness to sign his own name.[13]

Puritan nomenclature did not however originate in Sussex. The chief begetter nationally was almost certainly Dudley Fenner, curate at Cranbrook in Kent by the early 1580s. Fenner previously had been in Antwerp with Thomas Cartwright, one of the 'principal ideologues of the English Presbyterian movement'.[14] At Cranbrook, in December 1583, Fenner named his daughter More-fruit and was most likely involved in the earlier naming, in March 1583, of From-above Hendley, gentleman. From-above was the son of Thomas Hendley, esquire, of Corshorne near Cranbrook, and the nephew of Sir Henry Bowyer of Cuckfield Park in Sussex. Fenner too was of gentry stock and, interestingly, from Sussex. For this may help explain why the giving of puritan names spread from Cranbrook and the nearby parishes of Tenterden and Rolvenden south-west into Sussex rather than north into other parts of Kent.[15]

Fenner states that 'the father's duty is . . . to present the child for the first sacrament, and there to give a name in the mother tongue, which may have some godly signification, . . . so the Greeks in Greek, as Timothy: the fear of God'. Further light is shed by his remarks on the sacrament of baptism and the biblical teaching of *Matthew* xxviii.19, which is usually rendered as 'go ye therefore, and teach all nations, baptizing them *in the name* of the Father, and of the Son, and of the Holy Ghost'. Translating literally from the original Greek, Fenner writes that:

> we are segregated from the world to have fellowship with one God in three persons, as a wife with an husband, which is noted by this '*into the name*', that is to bear the name in being one with these three persons by faith, and by hanging on them for all government, blessing etc. Whereof it cometh that as the wife is called by the name of the husband, and to bear the man's name . . . so to be into the name of God, to bear his name, is to be separated and dedicated to him as his spouse.[16]

The practice seems analogous to the taking of a saint's name by those entering on a monastic vocation, in this case with the new born child being 'separated and dedicated' as the 'spouse' of God.

When Walter Travers, probably advised by Cartwright, drew up the Book of Discipline in the mid-1580s, baptismal names were recommended 'chiefly such whereof there are examples in the Holy Scriptures in the names of those who are reported in them to have been godly and virtuous'. No support was given to the kind of name favoured by Fenner and the reason, I would suggest, was a dislike of their separatist tenor. Yet, as Professor Collinson has pointed out, preachers by distinguishing between 'the godly' and the rest inevitably divided parishes against themselves. 'Hath not Ely set Tenterden, his parish, together by the ears, which before was quiet', asked a hostile contemporary, and 'what broil and contention hath Fenner made in Cranbrook, and all the rest likewise, in their several cures?' George Ely, vicar of Tenterden, did not adopt the new puritan nomenclature for his children although Fenner, in recommending names of 'godly signification', was only taking a few more steps along the same religious road that led, among other things, to congregationalism.[17]

By 1586 Fenner was in exile at Middelburg where he died the next year. At Cranbrook the type of baptismal name that he had popularized continued to be given by a small group of families, all laymen, until the turn of the century. Most remarkable was Thomas Starr who between 1589 and 1600 called his children Comfort, No-strength, More-gift, Mercy, Sure-trust, and Stand-well. Thereafter the family moved to Ashford in the same county, Comfort Starr emigrating as a surgeon to New England in the 1630s. In other parts of Kent the practice seems only to have survived with any vigour at Eastwell, where Josias Nicholls was vicar. Nicholls, in January 1583, named his daughter Above-hope and as late as March 1595 called his son Repent, although few parishioners followed his example. He eventually married Fenner's widow and the two men may have been collaborating closely in the early 1580s.[18]

The heartland of puritan nomenclature was undoubtedly east Sussex and the Kentish border. In other areas, like Essex and Suffolk,[19] the new names never became fashionable. Elsewhere only in Northamptonshire, around Daventry, do puritan names appear to have established a foothold. This was mainly under the influence of John Penry, the future separatist martyr. His wife came from Northampton and in June 1589, at All Saints church, his daughter was christened Deliverance. Earlier at nearby Daventry, in January 1589, the baptism is also recorded of Deliverance Wilton. Thus these Northamptonshire puritans celebrated the defeat of the Spanish Armada and England's deliverance from Antichrist. Penry's other three children, all girls, were named Comfort, Safety and Sure-hope. He was on the move during these last years, because of his clandestine publishing activities, and the Elizabethan authorities finally captured him in March 1593. Executed in May, Penry had formally declared for separatism the previous year, and his defection would seem dramatically to have fulfilled the worst possible fears of the English presbyterian leadership about the new baptismal names. To what extent Penry was influenced by Fenner is unclear although they were both educated, within a few years of each other, at Peterhouse, Cambridge.[20]

In so far as Penry had a Northamptonshire successor this looks to have been John Barebone, rector of Charwelton. The Charwelton parish registers do not survive, but John Barebone was most likely the father of the famous Praise-God. The origins of Praise-God Barebone have never been traced back beyond his appearance in London as a freeman of the Leathersellers'

Company in 1623; from a statement made late in life his birth has been dated to about 1596. The vital clue, however, is the existence of a Fear-God Barebone living at Daventry in the early seventeenth century, for in August 1594 John Barebone had married Mary Roper of Daventry. It is possible to go further and suggest why John Barebone chose these specific names for his sons, because the Elizabethan Prayer Book defines the first cause for which marriage was ordained as 'the procreation of children, to be brought up *in the fear. . . and praise of God*'. If the father was a logical man, this would make Fear-God the elder of the two boys.[21]

John Barebone was deprived for nonconformity in 1605, and Praise-God Barebone became a separatist. Fear-God Barebone, on the other hand, rebelled against his upbringing. We only know of his existence because there survives a collection of verses made by him in the early seventeenth century. The verses are decidedly bawdy and Fear-God writes, in the third person, that he collected them 'for the mending of his hand in writing than worse to bestow his time'. Examples are the lines which begin:

> *I dreamed my love lay in her bed*
> *And twas my chance to take her,*

or the refrain:

> *Tumble, tumble, tumble, tumble,*
> *Up and down the green meadow.*

He also sums up his own philosophy of life in the following quatrain:

> *No foe to fortune,*
> *No friend to faith,*
> *No, no to want,*
> *So Fear-God Barebone saith.*

For him the god Jehovah had apparently been displaced by the goddess Fortuna, faith and fortune proving antipathetic.[22]

2

While puritan names clearly tell us nothing definite about the recipients, how far can we be certain concerning the outlook of those who gave them? At Warbleton, in Sussex, 93 children were given puritan names during the years 1586 to 1596 inclusive.[23] Over the same period at Warbleton 124 children were given non-puritan names.[24] A small group of families, 19 to be exact, gave their children both puritan and non-puritan names. Apart from these, there are 100 Warbleton families who were consistent in the choice of baptismal names between 1586 and 1596. In this 11-year period 42 families consistently chose puritan names, while 58 families consistently chose non-puritan names.

We do not know the relative influence of minister and parents, father and mother, in the giving of these names. Certainly a measure of free choice was exercised by parents because where the local incumbent was unsympathetic, for example at Eastbourne,[25] puritan names none the less occur in the register of baptisms. With regard to the roles of father and mother, Fenner, as already noted, states that it is 'the father's duty' to name his child, and he assumes moreover a family relationship in which the husband is the 'chief or foregovernor . . . over all persons and matters in the house'. From October 1585 to October 1591 Hely, as curate of Warbleton, called his children Much-mercy, Increased, Sin-deny, Fear-not and Constance. Hely was also the leading nonconformist of the parish; in 1583 he crossed swords with Archbishop Whitgift on the subject of clerical subscription and in 1592 he was summoned to appear before the archdeacon's court for failing to use the sign of the cross in baptism and for not observing holy days.[26] Ultimately he was to be deprived. The likelihood is that those of his parishioners who consistently chose puritan names for their children were some of the parents closest to him in matters of religion generally. Conversely those who declined to give names of 'godly signification' in baptism probably included the Warbleton parents least affected by Hely's ministrations.

But if puritan nomenclature is to provide any kind of key to the sociology of puritanism, then both the geographical and chronological limitations of the data need stressing. East Sussex is patently not England. Furthermore there is an important distinction to be drawn between rural and urban environments because puritan names never, so far as I am aware, became popular either in London or in any other major town. As for chronology, puritan baptismal names generally fade out after 1600. Thus we are talking about a late Elizabeth phenomenon, in the context mainly of the Sussex Weald. For there, especially at Warbleton, the highest proportions of puritan names are found.

In agricultural terms Wealden Sussex was a wood-pasture economy of scattered farms and enclosed fields.[27] Warbleton is a parish of nine square miles and as late as the 1930s half the area was pasture and a sixth was woodland; the population in the late sixteenth century numbered some 400 persons.[28] It had no market, unlike the adjoining parishes of Heathfield and Burwash. Iron-working was carried on in the locality and a conveyance of 1617 mentions Rushlake furnace, Warbleton, with its 'water-courses, water-lays, ponds, bays, banks, pens, dams, flood-gates, sluices, ways, workmen's houses, coal places, mine places and other grounds adjoining'. Industrial plant of this kind must have provided some full-time employment and the reference to 'workmen's houses' indicates as much. The local iron industry also meant useful by-employment, digging ore and making charcoal. Most people however seem to have been chiefly engaged in agriculture. Unfortunately very few inventories survive for east Sussex, but a will of 1586 gives some idea of the type of farming practised in the region: William Dungate, of Warbleton, bequeaths to his wife 'all my cattle whatsoever, as kine, steers, twelvemonthings and weaners, and my hogs and all my poultry, and also my corn and hay.'[29]

County gentlemen, defined as potential or actual J. P.s, were thin on the ground and the upper ranks of this society are best described as 'yeomanly gentry', to borrow a later term from Celia Fiennes.[30] Typical representatives of such yeomanly gentry were the brothers Thomas and Goddard Hepden. When their father John Hepden, of Burwash, made his will in 1586 he styled himself yeoman, although one of his two executors was a gentlemen. Both sons, at this stage referred to as yeomen, sired children during the 1580s and 1590s. Between 1586 and 1596 Thomas, the elder brother, named his offspring Martha, Constance, John, Elizabeth, William and Herbert. By contrast Goddard Hepden, between 1585 and 1596, chose the names Return, Good-gift, Hope-still, Fear-not, Thankful and Constant.[31] During this same period Goddard took to signing his name 'Godward', apparently in line with his choice of baptismal names, and in 1591 he was reported by the vicar of Burwash for failing to receive communion there for over a year. By 1609 Thomas Hepden was being called gentleman and Goddard was similarly described the previous year, as a member of the grand jury. The house that Goddard Hepden built at Burwash, Holmshurst, still stands; it is constructed of brick with stone dressings, and has the initials G. H. and the date 1610 carved on the lintel. He describes it in his will of 1632 as 'my house called Holmehurst' and, styling himself gentleman, he had by this stage reverted to signing his name as 'Goddard' Hepden. In the religious preamble to his will he acknow-ledges 'the days of my pilgrimage to be both few and evil' and speaks of 'the small estate and substance which God hath lent me'. He goes on to mention freehold lands in Heathfield and Mayfield, and copyhold land in Brightling, as well as property in Burwash. Two gentlemen of Brightling, 'my loving friends' Thomas Collins and Nehemiah Panton, are appointed overseers. Significant, however, of Goddard Hepden's continuing agricultural horizons is that he arranges for Goddard junior to assist his stepmother in 'her husband-dry'.[32]

Other Wealden families of yeomanly gentry, who also gave their children puritan names, were the Bishops of Northiam and the Collinses of Brightling. Tradition has it that when Queen Elizabeth passed through Northiam in 1573 she was entertained by the Bishop family. George Bishop senior, although his brother John was a catholic recusant, named his son Thankful in 1589. When he came to make a will in 1605 he avoided using any status description and began with an elaborate confession of faith concerning

God's 'testimony . . . to my conscience that I am his elect vessel and chosen child'. He mentions lands in Battle, Bexhill, Northiam and Westfield, and specifies two legacies of £140 each. His eldest son George Bishop styles himself gentleman in his will of 1614 whereas Thankful Bishop, the younger brother, is called yeoman in 1617. Thomas Collins of Brightling, between 1599 and 1606, named his children Changed, Increase and Patience. Like George Bishop senior he avoided a status description in his will of 1612, and like Goddard Hepden referred to the lands and goods which God 'in this life hath lent me'. These included the manor of Socknersh and a blast-furnace. His daughter, Changed, was bequeathed a marriage portion of £500. Thomas Collins junior was, as we have seen, described as a gentleman in Goddard Hepden's will of 1632, and both the Collinses and the Hepdens are included in the heralds' visitation of Sussex in the 1630s.[33]

The term yeomanly gentry implies a blurring of status distinctions which also occured further down the social scale. In his study of east Sussex during the century 1540 to 1640, Dr Colin Brent has written of the Wealden area that 'the distinction between family farmer and smallholder, between smallholder and cottager, and between craftsman and agriculturalist, must often have been difficult to make'. At Warbleton it has proved possible to find status descriptions for 14 laymen who consistently gave their children either puritan or non-puritan names in the period 1586-1596. They consist of six 'yeomen', six 'husbandmen' and two 'tailors'. Of the six yeomen only James Brown and Goddard Hepden, who is called yeoman during the 1590s, gave their children puritan names.[34] This situation is reversed with the husbandmen, four out of the six, William Dorant, Roger Luff, Richard Reve and John Weeks, having given their children puritan names.[35] Of the two tailors one, Roger Elliard, gave his children puritan names, while the other, Timothy Pettet, did not.[36] It would be rash, however, to conclude that puritanism, even at Warbleton, was predominantly the religion of husbandmen. Quite apart from the small numbers involved, the terms yeoman and husbandman are lacking in precision. We need to check them, where possible, against testamentary evidence, and in any case rather more wills survive than do status descriptions.

Seventeen wills exist for laymen who were consistent in the choice of baptismal names at Warbleton during the years 1586–96. Taking the ten non-puritan wills first (see table 1), the earliest dates from 1588 and is that of Henry Stroker. Henry junior receives £11 and three daughters are each bequeathed five marks, two ewes and two lambs. John Hobeme's will, made in 1591, suggests someone economically much more prosperous than Stroker. Hobeme mentions freehold land in Warbleton and copyhold land in Heathfield, and bequeaths a portion of £40 to his daughter Anne; rent from the copyhold is to 'be put out unto the most profit' for the benefit of his son William. He also gives 6s. 8d. to the poor and 3s. 4d. for the church fabric.

Next in time is the will of Richard Browne, dated January 1593. Richard junior receives £50, 'to be put out unto the most profit', and other cash bequests total £40, plus 3s. 4d. for the poor. The second son, Caleb Browne, is described as a carpenter in 1606. William Hobeme, husbandman, made his will in November 1593 and legacies come to £22. John Medherst, in his will of 1596, speaks of a house and lands, bequeaths to his son Richard 'one

TABLE 1 · WILLS OF NON-PURITAN FATHERS AT WARBLETON 1586–96

Name	Date	Status	Land	Money	Interest rate	Poor relief
Henry Stroker	1588			£21		
John Hobeme	1591		Freehold & copyhold	£40	'most profit'	6s. 8d.
Richard Browne	1593			£90	'most profit'	3s. 4d.
William Hobeme	1593	Husband-man		£22		
John Medherst	1596		House and lands			1s.
William Stace alias Shether	1597	Yeoman		£40		3s. 4d.
James Busse	1603		House and tenement	£11 3s. 4d.	'most advantage'	
John Pettet	1606		Lands	£52 + £5 annuity	'best advantage'	£2
William Avery	1607	Yeoman	46 acres	£40		6s.
Ambrose Hunt	1631			4s.		

acre of wheat of the best', and the poor receive one shilling. The following year, 1597, William Stace alias Shether, yeoman, made his will. Portions, all to his daughters, total £40 and the poor receive 3s. 4d. No land is mentioned but Thomas Stolion, gentleman, is named as one of the two overseers. From 1603 comes the will of James Busse. He bequeaths to his wife a house and tenement with 'the stables and shops'. Cash bequests amount to £11 3s. 4d., those to his nieces 'to be put out to the most advantage'.[37]

With John Pettet's will of 1606 we seem to be moving among the yeomanly gentry, albeit of the non-puritan variety, No status is given, but he refers to 'my brother' Thomas Stolion, either the 'gentleman' of ten years earlier or his son, and the Warbleton poor receive £2. Pettet mentions lands in

Heathfield, Hellingly, Herstmonceux, Warbleton and Westham, and other money bequests add up to £52 plus an annuity of £5. The £20 which he wills to his god-daughter is to be 'employed . . . for her best advantage'. William Avery, yeoman, made his will in 1607. Avery is unusual in that he actually gives the acreage of his lands; located in Ashburnham, Warbleton and Wartling, they comprised 46 acres. He bequeaths to his wife all his cattle and 'seven acres of corn on the ground'. Legacies come to £40 plus 6s. to the poor. Lastly, there is the will of Ambrose Hunt, dated 1631. He was by then living at Brightling, but the names of his children indicate that it is the same man who lived at Warbleton in the 1590s. Four children are bequeathed 1s. each and his major wealth seems to consist of 'eleven pounds of linen ready spun'.[38]

TABLE 2 · WILLS OF PURITAN FATHERS AT WARBLETON 1586–96

Name	Date	Status	Land	Money	Interest rate	Poor relief
Edmund Gower	1601			£57		
John Jennings	1603			£64 10s.	'meet'	
Roger Elliard	1603	Tailor		£92	'reasonable increase'	13s. 4d.
Richard Morris	1606					
John Weeks	1610	Husband-man				
Roger Luff	1619	Husband-man		£63 10s.		5s.
Goddard Hepden	1632 (c. 1590)	Gentleman (yeoman)	Freehold & copyhold (£4 subsidyman)	£183 5s. +£23 annuities		£2 10s.

Turning now to the seven puritan wills (see table 2), the earliest is that of Edmund Gower, dated 1601, and cash bequests total £57. In May 1588 he had named a son Be-thankful. Of comparable wealth appears to have been John Jennings, who made his will in April 1603. His legacies come to £64 10s., and his son-in-law receives four bushels of wheat. Between January 1587 and July 1591, his children were christened Faint-not, Increased and Good-gift. Jennings entrusts their portions to John Creasy of Wartling 'and he to give for the use. . that my overseers and executor shall think meet'. From June 1603 dates the will of Roger Elliard, tailor. He gives 13s. 4d. to the poor and further money bequests amount to £92, including sums to his grandchildren which he specifies are 'to be put to some reasonable increase' and 'reasonable profit'. Elliard leaves to his wife 'nine pounds of fleece wool and all the hemp in my house, and seven pounds of linen yarn'. Less expected is the further bequest to her of two kine, one weaner, one heifer, one bullock, 'my best barrow hog and my second sow', 'one goose and six young geese, one crock of six quarts of butter and two cheeses', as well as seams of 'oaten malt' and oats, and two quarters of wheat. Other stock is mentioned, and Elliard's case serves to illustrate the over-simplifications of a status description; if he was a tailor he was also a farmer. In addition to having called his children Unfained and Confidence in April 1586 and January 1588, he speaks in his will of 'my beloved in Christ' Thomas Stolion the younger and Richard Stolion. These presumably were the sons of Thomas Stolion, gentleman.[39]

In apparent contrast to the wealth of Gower, Jennings and Elliard is the situation revealed by Richard Morris's will of 1606; no money or land is mentioned and his son, Thomas, receives two ewes and two lambs. His son Fear-not, baptized in November 1594, was presumably dead. Similarly poor, to judge from his will of 1610, was John Weeks, husbandman. His five children, including Refrain, baptized in May 1595, each receive one ewe and one lamb and nothing else. Seemingly a much more prosperous husbandman was Roger Luff, who made his will in 1619. From March 1588 to November 1594 he had named his children More-fruit, Be-thankful, Sin-deny and Preserved. These four children were all baptized at Warbleton, although an earlier child, Zealous Luff, was baptized at Heathfield and in his will Roger describes himself as of Heathfield. Cash bequests come to £63 10s. and the poor receive 5s. Goddard Hepden did not make his will until 1632, and as evidence for his position in society 30 years earlier it is likely to be misleading. By 1632 he had for many years, as we have seen, been calling himself gentleman and was now possessed of land in three parishes. His money bequests amount to £183 5s. and a further £23 in annuities, plus £2 10s. for the poor. Back in the 1590s, when he was called a yeoman, he had been assessed, for purposes of subsidy, on £4 worth of lands.[40] What then can these wills tell us about lay puritanism?

The wills confirm that yeomen were, in the main, more prosperous than husbandmen and to that extent they underline the preponderance of yeomen over husbandmen among the non-puritans. Taking each group as a whole, in money terms the puritans were twice as wealthy as the rest, although this figure is probably inflated by Goddard Hepden's upward mobility, from yeoman to gentleman. Against this greater puritan liquidity, however, is the imponderable element of land values, for half the non-puritans mention land compared with the solitary puritan instance of Goddard Hepden. There is the additional and insoluble problem of the possible failure by testators to record significant assets. As to individual cases, the puritans Richard Morris and John Weeks have no close counterparts among the non-puritans save Ambrose Hunt, who may have been even poorer; in 1594 Hunt was described as 'labouring' in Dallington, a parish adjacent to Warbleton.[41] Apart from a few sheep, men like Morris and Weeks appear to have owned only household goods. More generally, the donations to poor relief do not seem to indicate any very clear differences – the puritans gave more *in toto*, while more non-puritans gave something.

Wills can also, of course, shed light on literacy. Although the inability to sign one's name, when in good health, does not necessarily mean complete illiteracy – a person can read without being able to write – at the very least it points to semi-literacy. Marks made by testators may simply reflect illness, and in consequence are best ignored, but we commented earlier on the mark made by the puritan husbandman, Roger Luff, as a witness to a will in 1613. Similarly the non-puritan William Avery, yeoman, revealed his inability to write as a deponent in 1607.[42] There are no references to books in any of these Warbleton wills. Nor, with the exception of Goddard Hepden, do any of these testators begin with more than a formal statement of religious belief.

The foregoing evidence seems to indicate that puritan and non-puritan name groups were broadly similar in socio-economic terms, and that the acceptance or rejection of puritanism at Warbleton tended to divide the community along vertical rather than horizontal lines. There are, however, two other differences which run deeper. For the dates at which the wills were made imply that the puritans were in general younger, and this is lent support by the fact that puritan births are more closely spaced than non-puritan ones in the period 1586 to 1596.[43] At the same time there is a marked divergence in attitudes towards the taking of interest. The non-puritans John Hobeme, Richard Browne, James Busse and John Pettet specify, as we have seen, that their money bequests be 'put out unto the most profit' or 'the most advantage', whereas the puritans Roger Elliard and John Jennings speak of 'reasonable increase' and that which is 'meet'. The reality of this distinction is borne out by the will of Humphrey Sommer, the puritan schoolmaster at Heathfield, 'written with my own hand' in 1598. One of his overseers was John Miles, vicar of Heathfield, to whom he willed the 'book between the archbishop and Mr. Cartwright' and 'Mr. Fenner's *Divinity*'. But what matters for immediate purposes is that Sommer bequeathed to his four daughters, Restored, Flee-sin, Constant and Susanna, £10 each 'to be employed by my executors *in such sort as the word of God will warrant*'. Thus the Warbleton puritans stand revealed as young conseratives, unwilling simply to endorse the statutory maximum interest rate of 10 per cent on money lent.[44]

3

Yet something more can be said about the mental and physical universe of those who, in late Elizabethan England, chose either to accept or to reject the gospel according to Fenner and his ilk. For the 1580s saw both an upsurge of invasion panic and the worst harvest since 1562. Rumour flourished even more luxuriantly than usual, and at its most extreme took the form of predictions that the world was due to end in 1588. Prophecies also were current of Queen Elizabeth's violent death. By May 1586 the Privy Council was talking in terms of 'a general dearth of corn and victual' and the previous month rioters at Framilode, in Gloucestershire, had seized a cargo of malt, claiming that they had been driven to feed their children on cats, dogs and nettle roots. At about the same time there was rioting at Romsey, in Hampshire, which by July had escalated into a conspiracy to fire the beacons and during the ensuing chaos to rob the houses of the local gentry. Then in August 1586 broke the news of the Babington plot, and with it came the final act in the long-drawn-out drama of Mary Queen of Scots. Meanwhile, month by month, the prospect of an invasion attempt by Spain became more certain.[45]

Against this background of fear and hardship, the nonconformist preachers and their lay allies were experiencing a crisis of their own. Ever since the appointment of Whitgift to the archbishopric of Canterbury in 1583 they had been under growing pressure to conform and partly as a reaction to this there had sprung up the presbyterian movement. November 1586 saw a renewed, and more extreme, presbyterian campaign in Parliament, which culminated in the imprisonment in March 1587 of Peter Wentworth and his fellow parliamentary agitators. The late 1580s also saw an attempt to secure nationwide approval for the Book of Discipline and one of the stumbling blocks to this was perhaps the subject of baptismal names. For a basic question was after what fashion the new discipline should be erected, with puritan nomenclature arguably constituting one of the 'tokens of an incipient congregationalism'.[46] It may be in this light that we can best understand the baptizing at Daventry, in August 1589, of Discipline Brookbank – as a call for the setting up of communities of visible saints, loosely affiliated, rather than a presbyterian national church.

The giving of puritan names was at its height, in Sussex, Kent and Northamptonshire, during the six-year period 1587-92. Only at Warbleton, however, did a majority of the children baptized in any year receive such names. Elsewhere the proportion was at most a third, as at Northiam in 1592, and a more usual ratio even at the peak was about 1:6, as at Heathfield in 1591. Moreover only at Warbleton can any pattern be detected in the choice of names. There in 1586, out of nine puritan names, three children were called Repent and two Refrain. From January to May of 1587 Be-thankful or

Give-thanks account for three out of seven puritan names, with Repent or Repentance and Obey or Obedience predominating for the rest of the year. Throughout 1588 the names Be-thankful and Good-gift were between them the most popular. The next year, 1589, from January to April three children were baptized Sin-deny, and from May to October three others were baptized Fear-not. January 1590 was characterized by the name Sin-deny or Sorry-for-sin, with Be-thankful the most popular name from February to July. The year 1591 began on the note Repent, which from June turned into Be-thankful, these names together constituting four out of an annual total of six puritan names. This was followed by a final burst of Sin-denys in 1592 – three out of seven puritan names, and thereafter no pattern is discernible.[47]

The most likely explanation of this pattern of puritan names is that it represents a recurring religious cycle of repentance on account of sin followed by thanksgiving for the withdrawal of God's wrath. No examples survive of sermons preached at this time by Hely and like-minded Sussex ministers. Nevertheless there are the strident pamphlets of John Penry who, as we have noted, called his children Deliverance, Comfort, Safety and Sure-hope, and his writings suggest some of the assumptions shared by those who gave their children puritan names. In his pamphlet of 1587, the *Aequity*, Penry is concerned with the evangelization of Wales, as a matter of spiritual life or death for his fellow countrymen. The lack of a Welsh preaching ministry is a crying sin, which must be remedied by the action of queen and Parliament; already God's displeasure at their delay has been made plain.

We feel the Lord's hand many ways against us at this time in regard of the scarcity of all things, and especially of victuals . . . The unseasonable harvest 1585 yielded very little corn. Therefore many were able to sow nothing the last year, because they had not bread corn, much less seed. The winter 1585 destroyed all their cattle well near, so that now the very sinew of their maintenance is gone . . . This famine is for our sins, and the Lord without our repentance saith it shall continue.

After a spell in prison, Penry returned to the theme of Welsh evangelization in his *Exhortation* of 1588. Now with invasion imminent, he prophesies that the Spaniards will 'prevail against this land unless another course be taken for God's glory in Wales . . . than hitherto hath been.' The following year, 1589, appeared the *Supplication* where Penry explicitly associates himself with concurrent attempts to reform the established church in England, and he warns against mininterpreting the meaning of England's recent victory over the Spanish Armada. 'The Lord by that deliverance gave us warning that he passed by us, but so as unless the corruptions of his service be clean done away, with speed . . . [he] meaneth to pass by us no more, but to suffer his whole displeasure to fall upon us.'[48]

But if some parents gave their children names like Deliverance or Preserved,[49] in memory of Spain's defeat, others revealed much more personal concerns. For instance at Isfield in Sussex, in August 1595, Edward Goodman called his daughter Joy-in-sorrow, his son Caleb having died the previous month. We have already suggested that the names Fear-God and Praise-God originated in contemporary marital teaching and the same is probably true of the name Comfort,[50] for the Elizabethan Prayer Book defines the third cause for which marriage was ordained as 'the mutual society, help and *comfort* that the one ought to have for the other'. More difficult to gauge are significant names when bestowed on children born out of wedlock. Of three bastards baptized at Warbleton between 1589–91 only Repent Rowly received a puritan name, which implies that in this case the parents, or one of them, wished to be absolved in the eyes of the godly.

'Sin' for Penry however was pre-eminently a matter of 'wicked ecclesiastical constitutions', and his writings convey a sense of growing desperation at the failure to achieve religious reform. The type of baptismal name that he chose for his children had never found favour with the majority of non-conformist ministers, and the fashion was probably killed more by internal criticism than anything else. Thus John Frewen, rector of Northiam in Sussex, having baptized his two eldest sons Accepted and Thankful, from January 1594 chose the names John and Joseph for his subsequent sons. The gradual abandonment of puritan names during the 1590s perhaps also reflects a collapse of eschatological hopes; the reform programme remained unfulfilled, and God had failed to come in final judgment. From 1597 it became obligatory for parishes to make regular returns to their diocesan registries of all baptisms, marriages and burials and this unaccustomed limelight may further have hastened the demise of puritan nomenclature. Although puritan names did not entirely die out, as part of a religious movement their end is symbolized by the baptism in March 1606, at Isfield, of Deprived Winsbury. For deprivation from their ministries was indeed the fate by this time of Thomas Hely in Sussex, Josias Nicholls in Kent, and John Barebone in Northamptonshire.[51]

At one level puritan baptismal names provide the stuff of endless ribaldry. Yet they also permit us to enter the world of those who were engaged, at this time, in 'rediscovering' the Bible 'as a code of private and public behaviour'. In so far as such names represent an extreme manifestation of popular puritanism they accentuate rather than distort the ethos of a movement which, it has been said, 'constituted a threat . . . to culture as a whole'.[52] Dividing both family and community, puritan counter-culture, in Sussex, was certainly no friend to economic individualism.[53] Indeed, if like Goddard Hepden one conceived of man's life as a spiritual 'pilgrimage', material goods were *ipso facto* of secondary importance. While over against this puritan realm stands Fear-God Barebone, with his firm 'no, no to want' and evident distaste for 'faith'; a poetaster, he may nevertheless be allowed to speak for a very different facet of the popular mind.

5

MILITIA RATES AND MILITIA STATUTES 1558–1663[1]

A. Hassell Smith

The Elizabethan and Stuart militia has recently received considerable attention from historians writing from both the local and the national viewpoint. On the one hand a series of county administrative studies, to which Professor Hurstfield has made a pioneering contribution, have placed militia affairs within the context of county government.[2] Such studies have underlined the diversity which existed within the militia; a diversity which reflected the variety of English county administration and of social and political relationships within those counties. On the other hand the work of Dr Boynton has shown that county magnates and gentry marched, albeit raggedly, to the drum-beat of central administration.[3]

Greater familiarity with the details of Tudor and Stuart militia affairs has, nevertheless, left the historian uneasily aware that some baffling problems remain. Why, for instance, was the 1558 statute 'for having of horse armour and weapon' – the cornerstone of Elizabethan militia administration – repealed in 1604 and not replaced by a more up-to-date measure? Then, within the militia rating system, there is the paradox of ship-money collectors being confronted by spirited opposition when they rated maritime counties in 1596 and 1626, and yet collecting their quotas with little difficulty when they levied the rate throughout England in 1634 and 1635.[4] Most important of all, recent studies have served to underline the disparity between the immense effort to create an efficient militia and the pathetically small achievement. Why, when Englishmen were called upon after 1570 to make modest sacrifices of time and money in order to safeguard their faith, their monarch and their families, did they grumble so much, respond so tardily and default so frequently that, when the moment of truth arrived in 1640, the 'perfect militia' became 'in a matter of days the greatest law enforcement problem in living memory'?[5]

Dr Boynton considers that this breakdown resulted from Charles I's government trying to do too much:

taken by itself the programme for the militia was formidable, but not impossible; but taken in conjunction not only with the tightening-up of all local administration but also with the military expeditions launched between 1624 and 1628, its collapse was predictable. To search deeper for the causes of failure seems hardly necessary.[6]

Necessary or not, it is the purpose of this essay to suggest that down to the 1630s, perhaps not for the last time in history, the government's failure to devise an equitable rating system produced a sense of grievance which, in this instance, undermined militia efficiency. By contrast, as will be shown, after 1630 the government developed rating assessment procedures which reveal both an awareness of the basic problems and an ability to respond creatively.

I

The late-Marian statute 'for having of horse armour and weapon',[7] which will be described hereafter as the 1558 Arms Act, began a new era in the Crown's endeavour to secure a supply of weapons and men for the defence and safety of the realm. Dr Goring has suggested that it established uniform criteria for the provision of weapons and a national system for musters in place of the dual system which had developed during Henry VIII's reign. He has shown how from 1534 onwards Henry not only appointed commissioners in each county to muster all the able men and to inspect their provision of weapons as laid down by the Statute of Winchester, but also revived the practice, which had been superseded by the indenture system, of summoning particular landowners to muster and inspect their tenants, servants and others under their rule and authority. Sometimes, especially when it was necessary to recruit an army, Henry initiated both procedures simultaneously with the result that muster commissioners and landowners summoned the same men: 'the national system came into conflict with the Crown's quasi-feudal arrangements'. The conflict was resolved, Dr Goring suggests, by the 1558 Arms Act which established the county militia system at the expense of the quasi-feudal system: 'the old dualism was ended and the subsequent history of the Tudor army is the history of the Tudor militia.'[8]

The Act repealed the arms clauses of all previous statutes, laid down a graduated scale of arms contributions from all temporal persons, and provided the administration to enforce these provisions. Since those who drafted it could not have foreseen the impending revolution in methods of warfare, they emphasized the provision of traditional weapons rather than the introduction of new ones; they assumed an aptitude for and experience in the use of arms rather than any necessity for special training. Consequently they made no provision for regular musters let alone training (nor were these ensured by the Muster Act which accompanied it). They made no provision for raising funds to cover training expenses such as the purchase of powder and shot or the payment of men's wages whilst absent from work; they did not even specify an assessment procedure by which men could be charged to arms.

If these omissions, only to become significant later, suggest some conservatism in the drafting of this Act, an examination of its provisions reveals that elements of the old dualism were in fact incorporated within its clauses; that as well as creating something new it enshrined much that was old. So much so that there is reason to surmise that it was a composite measure based upon two or three bills,[9] each perhaps harking back to one or other aspect of the Henrician militia arrangements. Clause V placed responsibility for the corporate provision of weapons ('Town arms', or parish arms as they will be termed in order to avoid confusion) upon the inhabitants of a territorial unit – the parish; clause II charged particular persons with arms (private arms) no matter within how many parishes their lands lay. Clauses V and VI gave administrative responsibility to commissioners for musters; clause VIII gave it to J.P.s. Clause II stipulated what each income group should contribute; clause V left this to be negotiated between the muster commissioners and each parish. Clause IV provided for enforcement by informers in any court of record; clause VIII by J.P.s in quarter sessions. These discrepancies may possibly betray elements derived from each of the early Tudor systems of mustering. The clause which makes provision for parish arms supervised by muster commissioners may have been modelled on that part of the Henrician militia system in which commissioners attempted to enforce statutory military obligations upon all subjects. In contrast, the clause which provides for private arms has affinities with the quasi-feudal system. In particular it resembles the Henrician scheme which, according to Sir Robert Cotton, provided 'for an Army Royal to attend Henry 8 into France, in which, on all subjects from £4,000 land or fees to £20 in goods, a proportion is set to find for the King's service proportions of men' – the scheme which Thomas Cromwell may have had in mind in 1539 when he referred to 'A device for defence of the realm in time of invasion, and for every man to contribute according to his behaviour.'[10]

Be that as it may, the 1558 Arms Act embodied sufficient duality to generate tension and grievance once the Elizabethan Council began to organize the trained bands and to demand that they be equipped with modern weapons and regularly instructed in their use. The basis of his organization was territorial. The trained men of each county were divided into companies of foot and bands of horse, each unit drawing upon the manhood of a defined area – usually a hundred or, in the case of the horse, a group of hundreds. The size of these companies varied a little, each area being 'rated' to a given number of men according to its ability as discerned by the justices and muster commissioners.[11]

Unfortunately, while the obligation to provide and equip a company was laid upon a hundred, the 1558 Arms Act operated in such a manner that some hundreds became denuded of arms contributors to the point at which they could not meet their quota, while others were comfortably over-supplied. This inequity arose because the Act did not stipulate procedures for assessing and levying private arms contributions. Militia administrators therefore had to base their assessments upon the subsidy books[12] which valued a man within his parish of residence, albeit his income accrued from estates which straddled other parishes, hundreds or counties. Consequently a landowner who lived in Somerset, but owned extensive estates in Wiltshire, contributed only to the Somerset forces. Likewise the landowner with estates scattered across three hundreds contributed only in one, while the merchant investing heavily in country estates contributed only to the arms of the town in which he resided.

This tendency for rating procedures to deprive particular hundreds of the militia contributions of some of their more substantial landowners was accentuated by the clergy's non-participation in the county militia system. They were exempted by the 1558 Act which limited its obligations to 'every nobleman, gentleman and other temporal person'. In times of emergency the Crown called upon them to muster, train and contribute to its forces, but throughout Elizabeth's reign their organization remained separate from the county forces, bishops assessing their clergy under the direction of the archbishops. Consequently those hundreds with episcopal or capitular estates or the property of parochial clergy lost contributors to their quotas of men and arms.[13]

In many cases, no doubt, some sort of rough justice ensued: the contributions which a hundred lost from the estates of one landowner because he lived outside its bounds might well have been offset by those gained from another who resided there, albeit the bulk of his estates lay elsewhere. But the roughness might well have been more apparent than the justice to captains and constables confronted with a deputy lieutenant's demand for a well-armed company to be mustered at full strength. Nor did rough justice always pertain. In areas in which large estates were common and in which lawyers, government officials and merchants were investing heavily in land, extensive purchases by absentee landowners could suddenly reduce the number of substantial militia contributors in a particular hundred. This situation, with its inequitable consequences, might have caused little complaint had it occurred in a geographically random manner; but there is some basis for surmising that the extensive estates which gave rise to the problem lay chiefly within the champion areas of England. Although at present we know little about the size of estates or the fluidity of the land-market in relation to the 'farming regions' of England, agrarian historians have shown that large farms were a feature of arable areas while smaller holdings characterized the wood-pasture districts.[14] It is interesting that in Norfolk the opposition to late Tudor militia rating occurred almost entirely within the champion areas in the north and west of the county where some of the larger estates were situated.[15] Nor may it be fortuitous that the clearest statement about the difficulties confronting militia captains in hundreds with large estates and absentee landowners came from a captain in the champion area of the county who on more than one occasion failed to muster a full company:[16]

> Every Hundred must supply his proportion all and known part [*sic*]. And if the tax of arms were personal and tied to residence, a captain of an Hundred might justly alledge (in excuse of an unfurnished and imperfect band) that A, B, C, D etc. have £2,000 per annum in his Hundred and they living elsewhere in that or some other county, the personal charge upon them where they reside (for their general estate and value) abates the worth of the Hundred, whereby he cannot raise his full company, being abridged so great a part of the means *without oppression to many*, and therefore justly craves to be abated, which cannot be yielded unto since the charge of the Hundred is and ought to be (in respect of value) fixed and local and not fluctuant or transmissible.[17]

'Without oppression to many'. But no captain who was 'abridged so great a part of the means' could avoid such oppression if he was to muster the quota of men and arms 'layed' upon his hundred. Nor need he try, since the 1558 Arms Act legalized this oppression by laying down a fixed scale of arms contributions from the more wealthy (private arms), while leaving the contributions of the poorer sort subject to negotiation (parish arms). Clause V states that

> the inhabitants of every city, borough, town, parish and hamlet within this realm, other than such as are specially charged before in this Act, shall . . . find . . . and maintain, at their common charges and expenses, such harness and weapon and as much thereof as shall be appointed by the commissioners . . . for the musters.

In short, a captain or his muster commissioners, faced with a shortfall of private arms as a result of absentee landowners who paid elsewhere, could recoup these losses by raising the contributions of parish arms.[18] Hence the frequent complaints from the queen and her councillors that the poorer sort were overburdened while the rich avoided realistic contributions. As Burghley commented: 'if these demands for musters, for powder and new weapons were not demanded of the poor in towns [i.e. townships or parishes], the matter were of less moment, for the rest may well bear the greater. I see a general murmur of people, and malcontented people will increase to the comfort of the enemy.'[19]

As well as the injustice which arose from this drift towards parish arms, inefficiency also ensued. Parochial armour was frequently lost, sub-standard and in a state of disrepair. As one captain put it: 'town [i.e. parish] arms are usually in the custody of the constable for his year, who is usually poor and neglects them in the keeping, and as usually, when he dies or removes, the arms also, or some part of them, die with him or are lost'.[20]

The problems outlined above were aggravated by the necessity, *faute de mieux,* of using the subsidy assessments as the basis for 'laying' private arms. Since subsidy assessments were declining throughout Elizabeth's reign, not only in real but in absolute terms as well,[21] it was inevitable that there should be a concomitant decrease in the supply of private arms. Indeed this relationship between subsidy and arms assessment seems to have worked to the detriment of both, since concern to avoid the burden of military taxes became one of the factors leading to under-assessment in the subsidy – or so one M.P. argued in 1593:

> I could very well agree to the subsidies if they might not be prejudicial to the subject in other services, for the subsidy is in the valuation of every man's land and goods by record called the Queen's books. And according to a man's valuation in subsidy are they at all other charges as to the wars and in time of muster with horse and armour; and this charge maketh man unwilling to be raised in the subsidy . . . the tail and appendage of it being great and higher than the subsidy itself.[22]

Dependence upon subsidy assessments presented further problems for militia administrators because of the relative inflexibility of these assessments in relation to the rapidity with which land changed hands. Even when subsidy assessors were at work it is doubtful, to say the least, if their assessments kept pace with the growth of some estates. But for most of the time they were not at work, since they could only revise assessments when Parliament granted subsidies. Revision was therefore at best intermittent under Elizabeth and non-existent for long periods under the early Stuarts. Consequently estates which were dismembered by death or sale ceased to provide private arms, while long delays could well ensue before the purchasers of these lands could be reassessed. Once again captains tended to be faced with a diminishing pool of private arms contributors.

The sense of grievance generated by the arms rating system, at least among the arms contributors of some hundreds, grew as this system became the model for assessing other onerous military levies, indeed all levies for which there were no statutory assessment procedures. When the Council introduced regular training for selected men (trained bands) in 1573, it called upon the counties to provide funds to compensate militiamen for loss of wages, to equip them with up-to-date weapons, and to provide powder and shot for their training. After 1585 counties had to meet further heavy charges. Maritime shires bore the brunt of repairing or constructing coastal defences, while the expense of the muster-master's salary and the repair and manning of beacons fell on all alike. During the 1590s levies of men and equipment for overseas service, together with the necessary 'coat and conduct' money, were costing each county up to £2,000 annually. Meanwhile, in 1596 maritime counties were called upon to assist their port-towns in providing ships for the Cadiz expedition.[23]

Each county raised money to finance these activities through rates collected by hundred and parish constables. But if the method of collection was clear, the basis of assessment was not. The 1558 Arms Act gave no guidance, while parochial rating systems for the provision of the poor, the repair of highways, and the maintenance of Bridewells were only emerging on an *ad hoc* basis and did not become standardized until the 1597 Act for the relief of the poor.[24] In these circumstances muster commissioners or deputy lieutenants had no alternative but to assess people for these extraordinary rates – general militia rates as they will be called hereafter – on the same basis as they 'layed' people to arms. The results were predictable; by the 1590s constables were meeting with widespread refusal to pay these rates – particularly those for the muster-master's salary and ship-money – while complaints abounded of misappropriation of funds by deputy lieutenants.[25] Undoubtedly the weight and incidence of these rates engendered a reluctance to pay, but many reluctant rate-payers may have been driven to outright refusal by the knowledge, or even the suspicion, that the burden fell inequitably as between hundred and hundred and between rich and poor. As Nathaniel Bacon complained in 1598, when discussing how best to assess for these extraordinary rates: 'the richer sort did occupy lands in sundry parishes and did contribute only in the parish where their dwelling was, and thereby the poorer sort was forced to bear part of their burden.'[26]

Rate-payers' intransigence may have increased as a result of demarcation disputes among militia administrators. These disputes, too, had their origins in the structure of the 1558 Arms Act. Clause V ordained that commissioners for musters should be responsible for parish arms, while clause VIII authorized J.P.s to enforce contributions to private arms. Initially harmony prevailed since membership of the muster commission and the commission of the peace was identical. But the statute empowered the lord keeper to appoint as many J.P.s to the muster commission 'as by his discretion shall be thought meet and convenient'. In 1573 he and his fellow councillors deemed it convenient to entrust militia affairs in each county 'to the care of some *fewer* number being partly for their degrees and calling of more reputation in the county and partly for their knowledge in martial sciences more able to direct the same'.[27] Consequently the majority of J.P.s found themselves in the indeterminate position of having statutory responsibility for the provision of private arms, yet lacking authority to hold musters where such arms could be inspected. They came even closer to redundancy after the regular appointment of lords lieutenant during the 1580s, since the latter usually proceeded to administer each county militia through a small group (normally 3–5) of deputies. Thereafter the majority of justices were in the unenviable position of being asked to grant quarter sessional authority for the collection of rates with which they had little sympathy and over whose expenditure they had no control.[28] In such circumstances it is not surprising that they sometimes refused the necessary warrants. On James's accession their aspirations to regain primacy in militia administration were formulated in a submission to him of 'things grievous and offensive to the commonwealth which may be reformed by your Highness or by a parliament.' They pleaded that the Lieutenancy was

> an office . . . thought unnecessary and inconvenient in time of peace . . . by means whereof the prince's service is abused. . . . This service was and may be done with more ease and expedition by the justices of peace in their precincts, who may see the musters, levies etc. as well performed and keep the soldiers in use of arms at their set times, and being many will not easily all agree in partiality.[29]

2

The 1558 Arms Act was repealed in 1604 in a general Act for the continuation and repeal of divers statutes.[30] There is no record of any debate or discussion about its repeal; most likely there was none, for the simple reason that all parties agreed about the unsatisfactory state of militia administration under this Act. Nobody disputed the need to devise a system whereby militia captains could draw upon the *total* wealth and resources of their hundreds. But there agreement ended. The lieutenancy interest, wishing to tackle the problems in a reasonably professional manner, considered that repeal of the Arms Act would give it a free hand to proceed and would ensure that its policies could no longer be impeded by the justices since they would lose their statutory right to involvement in militia affairs. Moreover, in the absence of statutory norms about the types of weapons and levels of arms assessments, deputy lieutenants would be free to raise or abate assessments arbitrarily without being hampered by assessees' recourse to law. In short, in a period of rapid military and economic change, repeal of the Arms Act would provide the lieutenancy with some much needed flexibility.

Many gentry and most justices, however, wanted precision and definition rather than flexibility.[31] For them militia reform meant a new statute which would, no doubt, have restored primacy in militia administration to justices of the peace; which would have re-stated the nation's militia obligations in terms of up-to-date weapons; and which would have devised a rating system whereby large landowners, merchants and clergy contributed in every hundred where they had land rather than simply in their place of residence.

The latter point provided an intractable issue which frustrated all attempts to replace the 1558 Arms Act. The obvious alternative to assessing arms contributors upon their total income was to use the parochial rating system formalized in the 1597 Act for the Poor.[32] This would have meant treating large estates as if they were a series of small ones, none extending beyond a single parish. While this certainly ensured that within a hundred each landowner contributed proportionately to the area of his land, it provided an absurd solution since there would have been few incomes adequate to provide cavalry or even the more sophisticated fire-arms. A mean had to be struck between the impracticability of a thoroughgoing system of parish arms and the debilitating inequities of basing militia companies upon hundreds while rating arms contributions upon entire estates. Nothing less than a new type of assessment would suffice – a prospect which few landowners relished. Having established a cosy procedure for subsidy assessment, gentry and yeomen disliked any proposal that their incomes should be scrutinized through any other assessment procedures. Such a possibility had contributed to their doubts about compounding for purveyance and wardship,[33] and seems likely to have frustrated all attempts to provide a new statutory basis for militia administration.

Even so, advocacy of a new Arms Act persisted, to judge by the number of appropriately entitled bills in Parliament during the period 1580–1628. In 1581 a 'Bill for furniture of armour and weapons' received a first reading in the Commons. In 1589 the Lords passed a bill 'for having horse armour and weapons', but despite pressure from the Upper House the Commons failed to give it even a first reading. On the initiative of George More in 1597 the Commons appointed a committee to draft a bill concerning 'armour and weapons', but members seem to have been more intent upon dealing with corrupt practices by the Armourers' Company and by captains recruiting soldiers for overseas service.[34] In 1604 a bill had been prepared 'for the better provision of the realm with armour and weapons fit and serviceable', but there is no evidence that it was introduced into either House.[35] In the 1621 Commons Sir William Brereton brought in a bill for 'horse and armour'; meanwhile the Lords passed 'an Act for making the arms of this kingdom more serviceable in times to come' which, to judge from the ensuing debate in the Commons, concentrated upon measures to secure standardization of weapons and shot. In this debate Sir Edward Coke and Sir William Poole emphasized the need for an Act which specified 'what arms every man should find'. The House agreed that the committee on the Lords' bill should 'consider of a Bill for orderly setting every one to his arms and assessing the fees of the muster-master', but in the end all these militia proposals failed.[36] The 1624 House of Commons discussed a measure 'for the authorising of the Lords Lieutenant and deputy lieutenants . . . to appoint what persons shall provide and find horse and armour for the necessary defence of the realm', but rejected it on the first reading.[37] In 1626, in response to a call from Mr Thomas Wentworth, the Commons appointed a committee 'to consider and frame a Bill for the finding of arms and horses and of all things incident thereunto'. Subsequently the House amalgamated this committee with one which had been appointed to consider the inevitable Lords' bill 'to make the arms of this kingdom more serviceable'. All foundered on the nasty issue of rating for arms – or so one would surmise from Mr Wentworth's report to the House that his committee had 'many difficulties about the finding of arms'.[38] The Commons made another attempt to solve this intractable problem in 1628. On 24 March it appointed a committee 'to frame a Bill for the finding of arms and for regulating the power of lieutenants and deputy lieutenants concerning charging men with arms, raising of money, pressing of soldiers, and all other like incidents'. Meanwhile the Lords again concentrated upon a measure to standardize weapons within the militia. In their debate Lord Maynard and the Earl of Northampton realized the primacy of the issues at stake in the Commons and proposed a conference 'for a Bill how to raise the money etc. for their musters and arms'. The Commons appointed a new committee which drafted 'an Act for ordering of musters and assessing of arms' – a stop-gap, compromise measure which recognized the need for more consideration of the vexed rating issues, and which, as one might wearily surmise, suffered the fate of all other militia bills.[39]

'Better to live under severe laws than any man's discretion', had been Sir Edward Coke's characteristic comment in 1621 when he pleaded for a new Act to replace the one repealed in 1604.[40] In the event there was no new Act; instead the 'discretion' of deputy lieutenants was called upon to resolve the problem which successive Parliaments failed to solve: to develop a system of rating for arms whereby the captain of a foot company or horse band could draw upon the resources of everyone who had lands within his hundred or group of hundreds. The repeal of the 1558 Arms Act had removed the principal impediment to a solution, but this ground-clearing operation needed to be followed by some positive measures.

The first anomaly to be tackled was the clergy's exemption from providing arms and mustering within militia bands. The repeal of the 1558 Arms Act, which had exempted clerics from its provisions, weakened the case for their independent musters. Consequently when mustering was renewed in 1608 the Council ordered lords lieutenant to view clerical arms within each militia band and to charge to arms any clergy who were under-assessed or who had escaped any contribution.[41] Bishops resented this challenge to their authority; the clergy resented the muster-master's scrutiny of men and weapons. Gradually a compromise emerged whereby bishops continued to assess their clergy 'according to such directions as hath been or shall be given . . . by the Lord Archbishop of Canterbury', but they conceded that deputy lieutenants could muster and train their assessees 'with the rest of the trained bands'. This undoubtedly enlarged each captain's potential pool of weapons and men, but the gain may have been more apparent than real since episcopal assessments were low and clerical absenteeism high. In 1617 the Norfolk deputy lieutenants confessed: 'there is no certificate at all of the clergy arms, for they default generally'.[42]

Absentee landowners posed the greatest problems for militia administrators. Deputy lieutenants in Norfolk voiced a common complaint when they informed their lord lieutenant 'that divers persons who have great and large possessions in our country are laid with us to no arms because their most abiding is out of the country, and thereby our country is the less able to perform the numbers of horse and foot expected.'[43] Cities and corporate towns posed a similar problem since, under a clause in the Marian statute 'for taking of musters', they claimed exemption from mustering with county forces.[44] Consequently gentry who lived in these towns and merchants who had purchased lands in the county escaped assessment by any deputy lieutenant. In 1618, after widespread complaints from the deputies, the Council ruled on this issue along lines dictated by good sense: the trained bands of each county were to be 'levied and raised out of the owners of lands' lying in that county who were to be assessed 'rateably according to the value and proportion of the lands they hold in the same'. Nobody was to be exempt from contributing 'either in the county where he hath lands and doth not reside, or in the county wherein he dwelleth, for such possessions as he holdeth there'; everyone was to 'bear his rateable part in *each* place where his lands and possessions lay'.[45] Unequivocal though this might be, it did not resolve the entire problem. There is evidence that throughout the 1620s deputy lieutenants had difficulty assessing the parts of an estate lying within their county.[46] Nor did the Council's ruling solve the inequities created by a landowner whose estates lay within a single county but straddled several hundreds. He still, presumably, contributed arms only within his parish of residence to the impoverishment of the arms provision of the other hundreds. Nonetheless the 1620s witnessed a resolute effort to tackle this problem, undoubtedly with some success. Just how much depended, as we shall see, upon the deputy lieutenants' ability to enforce conciliar policy.

Some deputy lieutenants also took steps to prevent the drift towards an increasing provision of parish arms. Such weapons were rarely serviceable, particularly after sophisticated fire-arms had been introduced. Under Elizabeth the practice of 'joint arms' had developed whereby two, three or four parishioners had been made responsible for the provision of a particular weapon.[47] In this way, it was thought, arms would be 'better both kept and served by belonging to the care of a definite . . . number than if it went under the reputation and account of a town arms which seems everyone's care and consequently ends in nobody's care because they all commonly both trust and fail one another.'[48] But by the same argument, weapons produced by individual parishioners would prove most serviceable, and some deputy lieutenants pursued this logic by rating individuals to parish arms – finders of 'particular arms' as they were called.[49]

Even before the 1558 Arms Act had been repealed some county Benches had attempted to assess general militia rates more equitably by using the parish as the unit of assessment rather than the estate. The opportunity for this reform arose when the 1597 Act 'for the relief of the poor' established a clearly defined rating system for common parish payments. Prior to this Act there had been disagreement about whose property should be rated to provide parish funds. Statutes for the relief of the poor had specified that rates should be levied either according to 'agreement of the parishioners' or upon all 'inhabitants'.[50] Problems arose because neither the term 'parishioner' nor 'inhabitant' clarified the position of those landowners who, all too frequently, occupied land in several adjacent parishes. Were they inhabitants and parishioners of them all, or of only the parishes in which they resided? If the latter, then entire parishes could conceivably be left with few, if any, 'parishioners'. The judges of King's Bench ruled on this issue in 1589 in the case of Jeffrey versus the churchwardens of Hailsham. They took the view that 'although the house wherein Jeffrey dwelt be in another parish, yet forasmuch as he had lands in the parish of Hailsham in his proper possession and manurance, he is in law *parochianus de Hailsham*.'[51] This judicial interpretation was embodied in the 1597 statute for the relief of the poor by introducing the word 'occupier'. The Act specified that funds should be provided 'by taxation of every inhabitant and every *occupier* of lands in the said parish'.[52]

Once it had been established that a landowner should be rated within every parish for the land he occupied there, militia administrators began to apply this principle when they levied general militia rates. Within a year, for instance, Norfolk justices had implemented a resolution that in every parish 'levies and taxations for all extraordinary kinds[53] should be guided principally by the value of lands in every man's occupation, and yet regard should be also had to raise or abate every person charged, according to his substance in the said parish besides his lands'. As if to justify this radical departure in assessment procedure they hastened to add that 'the equity of this rule is partly approved by the last statute made for the relief of the poor'.[54]

Despite these efforts to solve some of the principal rating problems arising from the 1558 Arms Act, the repeal of that Act in 1604 created new administrative difficulties which ensured that the Stuart militia would be no more 'perfect' than its Elizabethan counterpart. A militia Act facilitated militia administration in the same way that the Act of Supremacy had underpinned Henry's supreme Headship – it made available the enforcement procedures of the Common Law to implement a policy which the Crown could otherwise pursue only under its prerogative. This, for all its shortcomings, is what the 1558 Act had done. Its repeal left the Stuart lieutenancy with few realistic coercive powers when confronted with an increasing body of sullen ratepayers. It was argued that repeal of the 1558 Act automatically revived the arms clauses of the statute of Winchester which had been repealed by that Act.[55] But the argument was largely theoretical since these clauses were obsolete. Moreover, as if to scotch this argument, they were repealed in 1624.[56]

In any case, most J.P.s, relegated by lieutenancy commissions to the subordinate role of 'aiding, assisting, counselling and helping'[57] lords lieutenant and their deputies, had little enthusiasm for assuming any common-law powers against militia defaulters. In December 1608 the lord lieutenant of Wiltshire and Somerset spoke of 'the doubtfulness of the justices to punish offenders by reason for want of authority in the commission',[58] while in corporate towns the Mayors' courts abandoned the organization of musters and enforcement of arms assessments.[59] Privy Council and militia officials were left to devise their own methods of enforcement. Usually captains of companies returned lists of defaulters to their deputy lieutenants who bound the most obstinate to appear before the lords lieutenant or Privy Council,[60] where all too frequently little appeared to happen. In 1619 one frustrated captain complained to his superiors: 'I every year with a great deal of care and pains return you an exact muster roll, but there being never anything done in it, it may be thought the captains are rather punished than the delinquent soldiers'. Four years later nothing had improved: '[at] this view I was short 80 of my 200, and most of the rest so poor and base as makes me weary of the office, for having only a power to charge and not to punish, what respect can a servile fear bear towards me'.[61] The deputy lieutenants found it all too true and, in turn, beseeched the Council

that for such as either obstinately refuse or undutifully neglect to show or serve with their horses and arms . . . their Lordships will be likewise pleased to prescribe some such certain course to us who be deputy lieu- tenants as may free us from pursuit in law or in parliament by the offenders, if any thing we should do by way of coercion that by law directly is not warranted.[62]

Exemplary punishment by an overworked Council was breaking down and the deputies had no sanctions which they could substitute apart from resort to arbitrary imprisonment with the likely consequence of 'pursuit in law or in parliament'. Militia discipline had collapsed and the deputies started to give notice: 'we . . . do find that without some more especial direction and fortifica- tion of the power given unto us, we shall by no means be able to execute . . . what is by your Lordships required of us . . . [and] we shall be enforced to make a stay of our proceedings in the musters'.[63]

If the deputy lieutenants lacked adequate powers to implement conciliar instructions, the Council, for its part, although attempting some piecemeal reform, showed no ability to diagnose the fundamental causes of militia malaise. Conciliar demands for improved militia efficiency were usually accompanied by bland advice advocating that precedent be followed. The response of the Earl of Northampton in 1611 to his deputy lieutenants' demands for policy direc- tives typifies this attitude:

I do therefore once again will and require you that with all convenient speed possible you take new musters . . . and that all defects may be supplied and so many good and serviceable horses laid upon the county as you shall find to have been borne in the year 1591, or at any time before or since. I doubt not but in the distribution of this charge you will hold that even and just course that shall sort best in true proportion with the worth and ability of every person that is to contribute and that no man shall have just cause to complain . . .[64]

Since councillors and lords lieutenant blundered along, it is not surprising that they created new rating problems – sometimes in the process of correcting old. The development of double rating is a good case in point. The 1558 Arms Act, for all its defects, had been carefully drafted to ensure that a person provided either private arms or parish arms, but not both. After 1604, however, it was not uncommon for deputy lieutenants to order 'that the charge of town armour shall be borne equally with the rest by such as are laid to private armour'.[65] Such double rating made for administrative simplicity since it brought the assessments for parish arms into line with those for maintenance of the poor and other statutory parish rates. It may also have been a device for increasing landowners' militia contributions which, in the absence of any new guide to assessment, continued to be based upon the notoriously low valuations in the subsidy book. Whatever the motives dictating this type of double rating, it did more to engender controversy than to improve militia efficiency or increase the number and quality of arms. As one commentator remarked: 'It hath been a long time and often controverted and as often (almost) diversly resolved and ruled how town [i.e. parish] arms ought to be taxed and assessed, whether upon all inhabitants or those only that find no private arms.'[66]

Even the late-Elizabethan initiatives to lessen rating injustices by assessing general military rates on a parochial basis faltered under the early Stuarts.[67] The resulting chaos is difficult to depict since, in the absence of conciliar direction, deputy lieutenants appear to have raised such money as they could by any means to hand. The muster-master's salary, when it could be collected at all, usually continued to be levied on the basis of arms assessments; so, too, did the rates to provide powder and shot. Similarly the 1626 ship-money levied upon maritime counties, although 'layed' on hundreds, was again assessed on the basis of the subsidy book. There is also some evidence that here and there certain rates continued to be levied parochially. Frequently, to meet the exigencies of the moment, deputy lieutenants and parish officers raided whatever fund was available, be it that for a parish charity, the maimed soldiers, the house of correction or an exchequer reimbursement of 'coat and conduct' money.[68]

This failure to consolidate late-Elizabethan improvements in military rating may have been due, in part at least, to the bifurcation of functions between J.P.s and deputy lieutenants as a result of the repeal of the Arms Act in 1604. Thereafter constables served two masters: sometimes they collected rates on warrants signed by the justices in quarter sessions, sometimes on warrants signed by deputy lieutenants. Nor was this the only difference. In the event of non-payment of these rates, as we have seen, enforcement procedures differed after 1604. Such factors militated against the levying of a common rate for county charges. By 1605 some justices were anxious that constables should be instructed 'to make their taxations several' and to avoid putting

> the assessment for the King's Bench, the lame soldiers, the prisoners, the composition for His Majesty's diet, the poor and all other parish charges whatsoever together, . . . because as the occasions for which those taxations are made are divers and several, so are the means to come by them from those that refuse payment also divers, and cannot by one measure to all be compelled.[69]

The more taxations remained 'several' the less likely became a common and equitable rating system which would have blurred the distinctions between military rates and ordinary parish rates.

3

Ironically, the ship-money levies of the 1630s represent the first government-directed moves towards a system of parochial assessments for general militia rates. On this occasion the Council gave clear instructions as to how this rate should be levied. It empowered the sheriffs to appoint hundred and parish raters who were to assess everyone according to the normal parochial rating system for 'common payments' – an assessment based upon the area of land owned or occupied by each parishioner. For the first time the hybrid procedure which had developed from the 1558 Arms Act, whereby militia taxes were rated upon areas but levied upon individual estates, had been superseded by a thoroughgoing rating system: the total county contribution was proportioned between hundreds; hundred contributions were proportioned between parishes, and parish contributions proportioned between inhabitants and occupiers. Problems still remained. For instance, nobody knew the precise rating potential of each hundred; such information would only be available when each parish had produced proper assessment books. Hence the sheriff's power to adjust arbitrarily the proportions contributed by each hundred – a procedure which was probably no more unjust than had been the dealing of justices or deputy lieutenants when they drew up hundred apportionment tables.

The Council chose to underline its new policy by supplanting its former ship-money collectors – the deputy lieutenants – by the sheriffs. The possibility of maintaining tighter control over a single sheriff than over a group of deputy lieutenants may have been a consideration which influenced the Council's decision. So, too, may have been the desire to differentiate the new rating system from the inequitable one which had become so closely associated with the deputy lieutenants and their oppressive activities. Indeed, ship-money rating marks a resumption of those assessment policies which had been inaugurated on an *ad hoc* basis by county Benches after the enactment of the 1597 poor law.[70] Even the sheriff's power to over-ride parochial assessments (powers which he undoubtedly abused) had been foreshadowed then in instructions to adjust assessments in order to take account of personal as well as real estate, 'to raise or abate every person charged, according to his substance in the . . . parish besides his lands'.[71] Undoubtedly, as Professor Barnes has stressed, sheriffs collected the early ship-money levies so successfully because of the power concentrated in their hands. But the mode of assessment may also have contributed to their success since, despite being widely abused for factional or personal reasons, it eliminated those inconsistencies and injustices which for several decades had soured militia administration, and which, ship-money apart, continued to do so during the 1630s.

Ship-money rating, however, provided a model for the future, for commencing in 1643 parliamentary ordinances for weekly (later monthly) assessments adopted parochial rating as the basis for *all* military taxation. One cannot improve upon Professor Everitt's succinct description of this system:

> The total sum required, to be levied on both real and personal estate, was first apportioned by parliament between the counties. Then the County Committee appointed two, three, or four assessors in each Hundred to ascertain the total county income . . . and fixed the poundage rate necessary to bring in the sum required from Kent. . . . Then they apportioned the county total between the lathal committees and they the lathal total between the Hundreds and parishes. Then collectors were appointed, and collecting began: the parishioners paid their assessments to the parish or hundredal collectors . . .

In short, the parish became the basic unit for assessment and collection of these monthly rates for the maintenance of the army.[72]

The ordinances laid down procedures for appointing assessors and collectors, made provision for appeals against assessment, sanctioned distraint upon defaulters, gave guidance on the vexed problem of assessing the relative income derived from a piece of land by owner and lessee, stipulated that rates should always be paid by lessees who could subsequently recoup such portion as was due from the owner, and ordered parish assessment lists to be compiled and returned to the county committees. Their tenor suggests that they were drafted by men aware of and anxious to remedy the defects within early Stuart militia administration. The clause which dealt with the hitherto intractable problem of assessing a large landowner must suffice to illustrate the point: 'the sum on him rated and set [is] to be levied in every county for the estate he hath . . . in that county only; and if he have an estate . . . in several places in one county', then he is to be rated in each place 'and the sum on him set to be there levied accordingly'.[73]

The ordinances have been criticized for their failure to give precise guidance on all issues; a failure which has been attributed to their authors' 'acute embarrassment at the paternity of the assessment: it was a direct descendant of ship money'.[74] Shortcomings there undoubtedly were, but they were those inherent in the tortuous evolution of a novel taxation system. Seen in perspective, the Civil War assessment ordinances and the sophisticated parochial administration they entailed represent the greatest single achievement in the creation of this system. Nor need their authors have been embarrassed by the paternity of these assessments for it can be attributed to late-Elizabethan justices, albeit the initial success of the ship-money levies underlined the advantages to government of an income derived from a rate rather than a subsidy-type tax.

The monthly assessment records provided militia administrators with the necessary information to rate private persons for arms in a manner which avoided the inequities inherent in assessments based upon the subsidy books. The virtual supersession of subsidies by monthly assessments therefore provided the means to a solution of the problem which had defeated all attempts to place arms provisions on a statutory basis in the early Stuart parliaments. The way had been prepared for the militia Acts of 1662 and 1663.[75]

These Acts resolved the tensions and contradictions within militia administration which had been largely created by the 1558 Arms Act and which had been, if anything, aggravated by its repeal in 1604.[76] They settled rivalry between J.P.s and the lieutenancy about responsibility for militia administration by placing it squarely in the hands of lords lieutenant. But the latter's rule was no longer to be arbitrary; the new statutes empowered them or their deputies to impose fines, distrain, and imprison as occasion demanded; established formally the hundred and parish constables as their subordinate officials; and authorized the appointment of treasurers and clerks. While allowing the lieutenancy discretion over the rating of arms, these statutes provided some clear guidelines within which it had to operate. They ended the duality between private arms and parish arms by abolishing the latter, although making provision for joint horse and foot arms. They allowed the lieutenancy to rate arms upon the basis of estates, but only upon estates within a county. This was similar to the policy adopted by the Council in the 1620s except that the new parochial assessments made it feasible for the lieutenancy to calculate the value of these estates. Finally, they largely severed the tail of general militia rates which had so aggravated the arms rating problem. Ship-money had, of course, been abolished. Meanwhile the lieutenancy was empowered to levy rates, based upon the monthly assessments, to cover the cost of ammunition and 'other necessaries' used in training, to hire carts for the baggage, and to provide officers' pay and 'coat and conduct' money. In case of apparent danger – the type of situation which had caused the counties to be so heavily rated in the 1580s – the lieutenancy was empowered to levy further sums rated according to the 18 months assessment. Other expenses, however –

notably the muster-master's salary and the provision of wages during training – were made the responsibility of those who provided arms. These Acts satisfactorily resolved militia difficulties at the local level, but in so doing they provided a sound militia system which could be misused by the Crown. That, of course, is another story.

4

The militia rating problems discussed above raise some interesting issues. The apparent contradictions within the 1558 Arms Act are reminiscent of those in the Statute of Apprentices which have been so excellently expounded in an essay in honour of one of Professor Hurstfield's predecessors in the Astor Chair of English History.[77] They suggest that Elizabethan statutes, like their Henrician counterparts,[78] could have divers origins; that the processes both in and out of Parliament by which a bill emerged may have been both more subtle and more haphazard than is frequently allowed by a too ready equation between statute and government policy. Indeed the Arms Act's unfortunate consequences for almost a century of militia administration underline the disjunction which could arise between government intent and the administrative reality as embodied in statute or the traditions of local governors. Furthermore, the relative slowness with which the Council perceived the fundamental flaw within the militia rating system, or at least took action to remedy it, gave rise to tensions which percolated far down the social scale and around which faction and private spite luxuriated to the further detriment of militia administration. But fundamentally the 'perfect militia' failed because it was imperfectly constituted.

The unfortunate consequences of these imperfections, however, did not fall equally upon all counties or all areas within a county. They were likely to be most marked in areas of large estates and extreme social differentiation; hardly discernible in areas where estates fell largely within parishes or hundreds. Where present they provided an issue which rumbled on at grass-roots level for decades, stimulating a demand for redress in Parliament.[79] Moreover if, as has been suggested, large estates were a feature of the champion as opposed to the wood-pasture and grazing areas[80] – natural regions which invariably cut across the boundaries of local administration and parliamentary constituencies – then the divergent views likely to arise between each region as to the feasibility of the militia schemes would have tended to stimulate debate *within* counties. In such circumstances the English electorate matured.

6

CROWN, PARLIAMENT AND FINANCE: THE GREAT CONTRACT OF 1610

Alan G. R. Smith

On 14 February 1610, at the beginning of the fourth session of James I's first Parliament, his chief minister and lord treasurer, Robert Cecil, Earl of Salisbury, set before the House of Lords the principal reason for summoning the Parliament; to provide financial assistance 'to relieve his majesty's necessity'. On the following day he repeated his remarks at a conference between Lords and Commons committees, arranged on the initiative of the Lords, indeed at Salisbury's personal suggestion.[1] At these meetings he revealed that the king was substantially in debt and also that there was a large annual deficit. James, therefore, needed both 'supply' – a large grant of money to pay off the debt – and 'support' – a substantial annual sum to meet the deficit and keep him out of debt. This statement must have made the hearts of many members of the Commons sink, as it was they and their constituents who would have to find the money. Salisbury did, however, attempt to sugar the pill by assuring them that the Lords would join with them 'in any reasonable request for the public good, which may serve you for an answer to any that shall object disadvantage to you by conferring with us'.[2] The implication was clear: James was prepared to strike a bargain with his subjects, making concessions to them in return for their money.

It soon became apparent that the Commons were determined to drive a hard bargain. The government's needs were discussed on 19 February in the Commons committee for grievances, which set down ten points of 'retribution', including the abolition of wardship and purveyance.[3] On the 21st Sir Edwin Sandys, for long a denunciator of the evils of wardship, reported the committee's deliberations to the House as a whole. He suggested another conference with the Lords at which particulars could be obtained about the government's proposed concessions; 'to know what we shall have', as he put it. He laid great stress on the need to secure the ending of wardship. The committee he stressed 'could find nothing to pitch upon but tenures and wardships, nothing else valuable'. As far as purveyance was concerned, 'they expected not the grievance only, but the right of purveyance to be released'. The House at once agreed to seek another conference and resolved 'if the Lords did not propound tenures and wardships . . . then to propound them from this House'. The chancellor of the exchequer, Sir Julius Caesar, was then dispatched to the Lords to arrange a conference 'touching the matter of contribution and retribution moving from their lordships'.[4]

The meeting took place on the 25th, when Salisbury told the Commons' representatives that the government wanted £600,000 in supply and £200,000 a year in support. In return he offered ten points by way of retribution. These included the total abolition of purveyance and some reforms in the wardship system, but no suggestion that wardship might be completely extinguished. When the Commons raised that subject Salisbury replied that the Lords committee 'would acquaint the House [of Lords] with our desire, and thereupon make choice of a committee to attend his majesty and know his pleasure'.[5]

The king's answer was given to the Commons at a conference with the Lords on 12 March, when the Earl of Northampton told representatives of the Lower House that James was 'pleased that you have good allowance to treat of tenures'.[6] With that reply serious negotiations began between Crown and Commons for a bargain which would involve a substantial annual support for the Crown in return for the abolition of wardship and purveyance and other less important concessions. Discussions about this 'Great Contract' can however only be fully understood if we appreciate the financial background against which they took place as well as the previous attitudes of both the government and M.P.s towards purveyance and wardship.

When considering the financial situation in Elizabethan and Jacobean England[7] it is useful to distinguish between ordinary and extraordinary revenue and expenditure. At the end of the Middle Ages it was generally assumed that in normal times the Crown would 'live of its own', that is to say it would pay the running expenses of government out of its ordinary revenue – the money coming to it year in year out from such sources as the royal lands, customs duties and the profits of justice. In times of emergency, which effectively meant wartime, the king could ask the help of his subjects in parliament to meet extraordinary expenditure. In the years from 1534 onwards conventions changed. Tudor monarchs asked for and received from Parliament extraordinary revenue for expenses not incurred in war. Elizabeth, however, took justifiable pride in asking as sparingly as possible for parliamentary help, not only in peacetime but in wartime as well. Indeed it is a historical commonplace that one of the principal reasons for her successes was her careful stewardship in financial matters. After 1585 her naval and military commitments necessitated a vast increase in extraordinary expenditure financed partly by a combination of Crown land sales, parliamentary grants and impositions on local communities but also by savings in ordinary expenditure. Her policy in this last field was rigid economy. Between 1590 and 1602 she not only balanced her ordinary budgets but carried to the extraordinary account an annual surplus of about £100,000 which she used to help finance the English war effort against Spain. Thus at the end of the Elizabethan period the queen was saving substantial sums out of her ordinary revenue to help to pay for extraordinary expenditure.

When James came to the throne there was a vast increase in ordinary expenditure. This may have averaged as little as £225,000 a year during the last five years of Elizabeth's reign and it was certainly no more than £300,000 *per annum*. By 1609, however, ordinary expenditure was running at about £500,000 a year, a colossal increase in six years. Ordinary revenue had also increased, but to nothing like the same extent. As a result the Elizabethan surplus on the ordinary account had been wiped out and there was a substantial annual deficit. The Crown's insolvency was particularly glaring in view of the fact that the war with Spain had been concluded in 1604.

The basic reason for James's insolvency is plain: extravagance. The level of ordinary expenditure, as we have seen, soared in five or six years by at least 70 per cent. Inflation cannot have accounted for more than a tiny fraction of this (two price indexes suggest rises of only 3 per cent or 7 per cent in the first decade of the reign) and ordinary expenditure on defence and the diplomatic service in 1609 was only 4 per cent above the average for these items in the period 1598–1603. The increase in the same period in the expenditure on the Household, the Wardrobe, the Chamber, the Privy Purse, the Office of Works and in fees and annuities was on a quite different scale; it more than doubled. The increase in these items reflected, of course, James's lavish expenditure on his own pleasures and his open-handed generosity to his servants. It is clear that a substantial increase in royal grants to courtiers and ministers was in order after the lean last years of Elizabeth, but this could hardly justify the way James spent money like water on needless festivities and greedy Scottish favourites.

Despite the parlous state of the Crown's finances in 1610 attempts had been made to improve the situation in the previous four years when Salisbury and his predecessor, Thomas Sackville, Earl of Dorset, substantially reduced the royal debt. In 1603 this stood at perhaps £350,000.[8] By 1606 it had risen to £735,000. In 1610 it was down to £280,000. This seems at first sight an impressive achievement, but it must be remembered that in 1606 the Crown received parliamentary grants which brought in £453,000 over the next four years. Crown land sales brought in another £445,000 and minor measures £287,000 – a grand total of £1,185,000. This should have been ample to clear off the whole of the 1606 debt and leave a substantial surplus. But in 1610, as we have seen, there was still £280,000 owing. The reason was that large deficits on the ordinary account continued between 1606 and 1610: the deficit in 1610 was about £130,000.[9]

It seems, then, that Salisbury's request for £600,000 supply and an annual support of £200,000 would, if it had been met in full, have solved the Crown's immediate financial problems. The remaining debt could have been paid off and a surplus of about £300,000 left to pay for present and future defence needs. The £200,000 support would certainly have paid off the deficit with a substantial surplus, but here a difficulty arose. The rights which the Crown would have to surrender, especially purveyance and wardship, were worth substantial sums. The £200,000 would only be ample if it was over and above the value of these revenues, later set at £80,000.[10]

James's and Salisbury's appeal to the Commons in 1610 was made, therefore, against a background of royal extravagance which meant a substantial deficit on the ordinary account in peace time, a situation which traditionally represented the epitome of financial mismangement. The efforts of Salisbury in the years before 1610 to improve the situation had been seriously hampered by James's lack of co-operation. Members were being asked to vote unprecedented sums of money on a permanent basis to a spendthrift king. It was not an invitation which any of them could have viewed with enthusiasm.

The most important concessions which the Crown was prepared to make in its proposed bargain with Parliament were the abolition of wardship and purveyance. Purveyance,[11] the traditional method of providing the Court with supplies, was based on the claim of the Crown to compel subjects to sell at a discount to satisfy the needs of the royal household. The practice had been recognized since the early Middle Ages and had always, for obvious reasons, been highly unpopular. To procure goods the Crown sent out purveyors who often behaved badly and aroused resentment. Consequently, throughout the centuries the Crown had been compelled to accept statutes regulating the conduct of purveyors. Between the thirteenth century and 1558 more than 40 Acts of Parliament had been passed dealing with purveyance, some limiting the privileges of purveyors, others prescribing punishments for their misdeeds. Despite these statutes abuses continued and in Elizabeth's reign, between 1563 and 1589, there was a series of parliamentary outbursts against purveyance. The queen and Burghley consistently refused to agree to any new laws on the subject; they rightly argued that existing Acts were sufficient if only they were fully enforced. Burghley, however, did not ignore the outcry. He signed 'composition' agreements with every county in England which could be persuaded to pay a tax towards the upkeep of the royal household in return for the withdrawal of purveyors. By 1597 most shires in the realm had agreed to the new system which Burghley himself regarded as one of the greatest achievements of his career.

Most of the counties, however, only accepted composition after the most serious purveyance crisis of the reign, which broke out in the parliament of 1589.[12] The background to this was the presence in 1588 in south-eastern England of large bands of armed men, assembled to meet the expected invasion from the Spanish Armada. This was a heavy burden on food supplies and in these circumstances the task of provisioning the royal household was doubly felt. Accordingly, when Parliament met during the following year there was an immediate demand for legislation to curb purveyors. The sponsor of the bill was John Hare, a London lawyer and client of Burghley's who later became clerk of the Court of Wards. Among those who were prominent in the debates and committee meetings which followed were George More, son of Sir William More of Loseley and a member of a substantial county family; Robert Wroth, another wealthy gentleman who had been a Marian exile and had sat in the Commons since 1563; and that Elizabethan immortal Francis Bacon, then sitting in his third parliament. These names are very significant. All four appear again in James's reign as leading agitators in the purveyance debates of 1604. Here is important evidence of continuity in both expertise and opposition between the Elizabethan and Jacobean periods. The queen weathered the storm. She resolutely refused to consider legislation and secured a flood of composition agreements in the 1590s. This did not, however, mean that purveyance was no longer an issue by 1603; in some counties, such as Norfolk, there was considerable opposition to compounding.

Existing composition contracts remained valid on James's accession, but new problems about purveyance soon arose. The most serious cause was the greatly increased demand for supplies. During the Elizabethan period there had only been one royal household. Under James there were three, the king's, Queen Anne's, and that of Prince Henry. Contracts made to take care of the needs of Elizabeth's court were no longer adequate and when purveyors were sent out for additional supplies complaints arose on all sides. This, together with the continuing discontents carried over from the Elizabethan period, was the background to the purveyance debates of 1604.

The lead was taken on 23 March, the first business day of the 1604 session, by Robert (now Sir Robert) Wroth, one of the stalwarts of the 1589 campaign. He offered seven issues for consideration by the House, including the 'general abuse and grievance of purveyors and cart-takers'.[13] It has usually been assumed that Wroth's motion represented an unprecedented seizure of the initiative by a private member at the very beginning of James's first Parliament,[14] but recently it has been plausibly argued that Wroth may have been acting as Cecil's spokesman.[15] In any event purveyance was vigorously taken up by the Commons and in the debates that followed Wroth himself, Hare, More and Bacon all played prominent roles.[16] The Commons proceeded first of all by a bill designed to remedy the abuses of purveyance and then by petition to the king showing the necessity of their bill.[17] The petition was presented at the end of April and on 8 May, at a conference with representatives of the Commons, Cecil proposed on behalf of the Lords (and clearly of the government as well) that purveyance should be completely abolished in return for an annual composition of £50,000.[18] During the period from 8 May until 2 June, when they agreed to defer further consideration of purveyance until the next session of Parliament, the Commons discussed the possibility of composition, but although some members were willing to consider it none seems to have been prepared to meet the demand for £50,000 a year.[19]

When Parliament met again in 1606 the subject of purveyance was raised by John Hare, who reminded the Commons of the debates during the last session. The House decided, as in 1604, to proceed by a bill designed to remedy the abuses of the system and, under Hare's leadership, maintained that decision though it soon became apparent that the government again wanted abolition in return for composition. The outcome was that the Commons bill was killed in the Lords, but long before that it had become apparent that there was no chance of the Commons agreeing to composition.[20]

In the 1604 and 1606 sessions of Parliament, therefore, there were consistent government and Commons lines on purveyance. The former wanted the system abolished in return for a fixed annual payment, whereas the majority of M.P.s – led by men whose interest in the subject went back at least as far as the 1589 Parliament – preferred legislation to remedy the abuses of the system. The result was stalemate.

Wardship, the other great concession which the Crown was prepared to consider in its negotiations with the Commons in 1610, had by the sixteenth century lost all the military *raison d'être* which had been its justification in the Middle Ages. It had become a fiscal device exploited to bring profit to the Crown and its servants.[21] All tenants in chief of the king who held their land by knight service were subject to the system. If they succeeded to their property as minors (under 21 if they were men, under 14 if they were women) their lands and the right to arrange their marriages were taken into the Crown's hands. The lands were then leased out in return for annual rents paid by the lessees to the Crown and the wardships of the bodies of the heirs with the right to determine their marriages were sold, often to people who had no obvious interest in the welfare of the ward.

The Crown benefited from the system not only from the direct revenue which it received from wardship – an average of about £15,000 a year during Elizabeth's reign – but also indirectly from the £44,000 or so which was paid out each year by suitors for wardships to middlemen who helped to arrange the sale of wardships and the leasing of wards' lands.[22] Many of these intermediaries were miserably underpaid royal officials and gratuities which they received from hopeful or grateful clients can be regarded as part of their unofficial salaries. The Crown, too poor to pay them adequately itself, accepted the system. The losers were the landed classes, especially the country gentry. Peers and courtiers, though they were themselves subject to wardship, were well placed to obtain custody of wards for themselves and were probably net gainers from the system. Country gentlemen, on the other hand, without the same influence in court circles, had much less chance of getting a ward. They saw all the disadvantages of the system and few of the profits.[23]

In these circumstances it is not surprising that debates in the Commons revealed the widespread unpopularity of wardship. This was evident in the Lower House in 1585[24] and in October 1598, after the end of Burghley's long mastership, rumours were current that the Court of Wards was to be abolished altogether and 'a yearly contribution raised instead . . . which would be more profit to the queen and less grievance to the subject'.[25] The rumours were false – Robert Cecil was appointed to the vacant mastership in 1599 – but they do point the way to the discussions of James's reign.

These began at the very start of his first Parliament. One of the issues raised by Wroth on 23 March was 'the wardship of men's children as a burden and servitude to the subjects of this kingdom'.[26] If Wroth was acting as Cecil's mouthpiece on this occasion – and we have seen that this was at least a possibility – then it may be that the latter was already considering in 1604 a scheme not altogether dissimilar to the Great Contract of 1610. He certainly wanted to compound for purveyance – although the Lower House did not – and when the Commons showed themselves eager to compound for wardship the Lords, led by Cecil, gave their proposals an initially favourable reception.[27] Eventually a conference was arranged between the two Houses for 26 May. At this Sir Edwin Sandys, son of the archbishop of York and to be a notable thorn in the government's flesh for much of the 1604–10 Parliament, put to the Upper House proposals for the abolition of wardship and its replacement by 'a perpetual and certain revenue out of our lands', although the Commons were uncertain whether the tax should be upon all land or just upon that held in chief by knight service. As far as the officers of the Court of Wards were concerned, they were to be compensated by 'an honourable yearly pension', which was to last for life and be 'at the charge of the whole state'.[28] The Lords, however, quashed the Commons ideas. This was a complete *volte face*. As recently as 21 May they had told the Commons that they themselves intended to come to the conference 'furnished with . . . grounds and reasons to induce the king' to agree to the abolition of wardship.[29] Now they advised the Lower House to drop the subject altogether, saying that it was wrong to proceed in such a matter in the king's first Parliament.[30] It seems overwhelmingly likely that the Lords' change of heart was prompted by instructions from members of the government – the Upper House at this time was notoriously subservient to the Crown – and it must be concluded that sometime between 21 and 26 May Salisbury changed his mind. He may have realized that he was not going to get his way on purveyance and decided that a deal with the Commons was only worthwhile if he could obtain composition for that as well as for wardship, or he may have been told by the king to drop the matter; James, as the events of 1610 were to show, was reluctant to surrender his wardship rights. Certainly the Lords' refusal of further co-operation marked the end of the Commons attempt in 1604 to get wardship abolished in return for an annual payment to the Crown.

It was against the above background of discussions and disputes about wardship and purveyance in earlier sessions of Parliament that Salisbury produced his financial plans on 24 February 1610. Members of the Commons, as we have seen, had decided views on the elements of retribution which they wanted if they were seriously to consider the Crown's demands and on 12 March they heard that the king had agreed to their main condition; that wardship should be abolished as part of the deal. Their stress on the absolute necessity of including wardship in any contract is very understandable in light of their views on the subject in 1604, especially when it is remembered that the government's other chief 'concession' in 1610, the abolition of purveyance in return for a fixed annual payment, had not been accepted by the Commons in either 1604 or 1606. In 1610 they were prepared to reconsider their position, but only if composition for purveyance could be included as part of a larger, more attractive bargain. The government's attitude on purveyance was wholly consistent with the line it had taken in both 1604 and 1606 but its policy on wardship requires some further comment. In his original ten points of retribution Salisbury, as already noted, offered only reforms in the wardship system rather than its total abolition. It seems inconceivable that he could have expected the Commons to accept these very limited concessions. He knew very well the strength of feeling in the Lower House on the subject and he had long been personally prepared to consider the total abolition of the Court. As early as August 1603 he 'said he was to have wards turned to a certain annual rent to be propounded in parliament'[31] and we know that his initial response in 1604 to the Commons demands for abolition was a favourable one. The likely explanation is that his original offer in 1610 was a tactical one; he had to have something in reserve to give away to the Commons and he may also have been worried about James's attitude if he had seemed too eager to encourage the abolition of a tenurial system in which James believed that much of his kingly honour was involved. By delaying the offer of a complete abolition of wardship until he was pressed hard by the Commons he could represent to the king that the state's urgent financial needs could only conceivably be met if James agreed to the Commons' demands. This, of course, is speculation,[32] but it seems a plausible interpretation of the events leading up to James's agreement in principle, on 12 March, to consider the abolition of wardship.

On 26 March the Commons offered £100,000 for wardship alone,[33] thus emphasizing their over-riding concern with that aspect of the Contract, but this proposal was quite unacceptable to the government and a month later, on 26 April, Salisbury spelled out the Crown's conditions if the Contract was to include wardship. In the words of Sir Edwin Sandys, who reported the speech which Salisbury made at a Lords-Commons conference,

> He saith not £100,000 is too much or too little for the wards, but the wards is too much for any thing that should come short of the king's first demand.

... The conclusion therefore was that unless we offered that which might give the king a complete satisfaction . . ., *£200,000 a year above whatever we defalked from him by our Contract* the wards will not be had. And if that may be made up then take . . . wards, purveyance and those other incidents with what else the parliament shall think fit.[34]

As the king's concessions were later valued at £80,000[35] the total demand was, in effect, for £280,000. On 2 May the Commons replied with a flat no. They would not proceed further on the basis of the Crown's demands.[36] This blunt rejection of the government's terms probably came as both a shock and a considerable disappointment to James, who had been led by Salisbury to expect a more favourable response[37] – a serious misjudgment by the latter of the mood of the Commons, especially as the Lower House was content to let the matter rest. The issue had to be revived by the Lords on 26 May when they sent a message to the Commons suggesting a conference on wardship that afternoon.[38] By that time the government had clearly had second thoughts. Salisbury made it plain that the king was prepared to reduce his demands but assumed in return that the Commons would advance their offer from £100,000.[39] On 26 June the king asked for £220,000;[40] on 13 July the Commons offered £180,000;[41] and on the 17th of the same month a compromise of £200,000 was agreed, the Commons accepting that figure by a majority of about 60.[42]

So a bargain was struck. It should be noted, however, in view of the limited Commons majority, that many members of the Lower House clearly had grave doubts, even at that time, about the Contract. They could all take some satisfaction, however, from the reflection that they had probably got the better of the detailed bargaining which had taken place with the government. It is true that they had raised their original offer of £100,000 to £200,000 but the £100,000 had been for the abolition of wardship alone, while for the £200,000 they were getting purveyance and other benefits as well. The king on the other hand had reduced his demand from £280,000 for the abolition of wardship and purveyance and other benefits to one of £200,000 for the same concessions. He seems to have made the bigger *relative* sacrifice during the negotiations. The £200,000 it should be remembered was not quite enough to meet the deficit of £130,000 plus the estimated annual loss of £80,000 from the surrender of wardship and purveyance.

The agreement was embodied in Lords and Commons memorials which were entered in the journal of the Upper House.[43] Each memorial cautiously reserved the right of the respective house of parliament, 'addendo, minuendo, interpretando' – that is to say the bargain was not to be regarded by any of the parties as completely firm – but the main outlines of the Contract were clear enough, and it was planned that the whole matter should be finalized at a further session of Parliament, which was to meet again after a summer recess. The chief point, of course, was the abolition of wardship and purveyance in return for an annual payment of £200,000. It was envisaged that the officers of the Court of Wards would be compensated by the king, a change from the 1604 suggestion that such payments should be by state pensions chargeable on the community as a whole.

On 23 July Parliament was prorogued until 16 October. The session ended on a hopeful note. It is true that there had been bitter disputes between king and Commons on the subject of impositions and that the negotiations for the Contract itself had by no means been plain sailing, but the provisional agreement which had finally been achieved on the ending of wardship and purveyance seemed to many to augur a better relationship between the Crown and the Lower House. James himself expressed his satisfaction. At the end of the session, in one of his rare moods of euphoria with Parliament, he told Sir Roger Aston, the master of the wardrobe, that he was 'well pleased with . . . [the Commons] proceedings and chiefly that now he and his people shall part in his favour, with their love and obedience'. Aston had lavish praise for Salisbury 'who, by his wisdom hath so governed all things as they are drawn to a final end. The little beagle hath run a true and perfect scent, which brought the rest of the hounds to a perfect tune, which was before by their voice much divided.' He wrote these words to a close friend of Salisbury's and his remarks cannot be taken entirely at their face value – Salisbury, as we have seen, had not dominated proceedings to the extent which Aston implies. On the other hand Aston's comments do reveal a clear truth; Salisbury had become so closely identified with the Great Contract that his reputation by the summer of 1610 was inseparably linked to its success or failure. Aston concluded his letter by stating that the main issue remaining in the Contract was how to levy the £200,000 which had to be paid to the Crown. That, he went on optimistically, would be decided 'when the commissioners of the Lower House shall return to their countries'.[44]

It was not as simple as that, however, and there can be little doubt that problems raised by the 'levy' are important in explaining the ultimate failure of the Contract. In their memorial the Commons stated: 'not having resolved yet whereupon to raise this revenue, nor in what manner to levy it, this much we are resolved of, that it shall be stable and certain to his majesty and convenient for his majesty's officers to receive and gather it'.[45] That was ominously vague. The Commons in 1604 had envisaged a land tax to replace wardship, though they were unable to decide whether it should be levied on all lands or only on those subject to feudal incidents. In 1610, when purveyance was included in the bargain, they were not even agreed that the whole tax should be on land. The problem was certainly immensely complex. Different classes in the community would clearly have benefited to different extents from the abolition of wardship and purveyance, so that the difficulties in the way of devising an equitable system of raising the money were virtually insuperable. Salisbury himself seems to have envisaged a land tax but many of the country gentlemen in the Commons were – understandably – against the idea of the entire burden being on land. They believed that such people as merchants, office holders and annuitants should contribute.[46] Another problem arose over the Commons demand for security that the Crown would never reimpose any of the burdens which had been abolished. It was provided in their memorial that such security should be 'by act of parliament in as strong sort as can be devised'.[47] The last words reflected fears in the Commons about the ability of statute to bind the prerogative, and the problem of security, like that of the levy, remained to bedevil discussions during the autumn session.

The Commons memorial also contained provisions about how the country was to be informed about the bargain during the recess from July to October. A clear distinction was drawn between the 'better sort' and the 'meaner sort'. The former were to be given a 'view of those things which, in lieu of that sum, we shall receive from his majesty, wherof copies to be taken down by such as please', while the latter were merely to be assured that 'nothing shall be levied upon their ordinary victual, *viz.* bread, beer and corn, nor upon their handy labours.'[48] This stress upon M.P.s informing their constituents is of great interest and importance, especially in view of the recent work of Dr Derek Hirst on the electoral history of early Stuart England.[49]

Constituents would clearly be intensely interested in the details of the bargain. All might expect to benefit from the abolition of wardship and purveyance – the landed classes chiefly from the former and the 'lower orders' mainly from the latter – and equally clearly all would be interested in the taxation system which was to replace them. Moreover, Dr Hirst's researches have revealed that a substantial and growing number of men, both in the counties and in the boroughs, had the right to elect M.P.s in the early seventeenth century, even though not all of these potential electors may have been aware of their rights. The picture which he has painted is very different from the strictly limited electorate which previous historians have depicted and his work lends emphasis to the point that it was sensible for M.P.s to inform their constituents of the details of the bargain and sound out opinion about its merits. This was not simply because these constituents had a direct interest in it but also because a large and growing number of them had a potential voice in electing the M.P.s who had agreed to the scheme.

In May 1610, in a message to the Lords about the Contract, the Commons laid stress on their role as representatives, speaking of 'the trust which so many millions of people have reposed in us',[50] and in July, shortly before the recess, such notable members as Sir Henry Poole, Sir Edwin Sandys and Sir George More stressed the need to carry information about the bargain to the localities during the summer and take soundings among the people.[51] Sir John Holles, another prominent M.P. and a Nottinghamshire man, wrote later on that a decision about the form of the levy had been postponed so that 'first in this vacation we should feel the disposition of our countries thereunto, to the end with more general warranty we might proceed . . . to a desired consummation'.[52] Sir William Twysden, who had wide connections in the south-east of the country, took a more extreme view of M.P.s representative functions, arguing in May that he and his fellow members should 'go into the country and receive resolution and authority' from the people about the Contract.[53] Many of the Lower House would doubtless have rejected Twysden's implied view of M.P.s as delegates, bound to submit to the instructions of their constituents, but it is clear that there was a general feeling that opinion throughout the country should be consulted.

It seems indeed that M.P.s were either sounding out views in their localities or else being made aware of such views even before the end of the fourth session. In June Salisbury referred to 'bitter and sour reports that some of you speak as if your countries were angry and discontented for that you have already offered.'[54] During the recess itself Sir Thomas Beaumont of Leicestershire told his constituents what had been done and asked their advice.   He got a mixed reply. They were:

> glad that the sunshine of his majesty's favour should come so far as to reach them. But they pressed me particularly to tell them whether the impositions, which were resolved in parliament to be unlawful, were determined by the king to be laid down; and then they said so as the levy might be in a reasonable manner, which they hoped should not be all upon land, and all our grievances drawn together into the Contract, they would be willing to give £200,000 a year.[55]

Sir John Holles found that there were also doubts in Nottinghamshire. 'In the better sort', he wrote to Salisbury, there was:

> a very sharp appetite, but in the plebs . . . a very uncertain temper. Yet methought they bit somewhat eagerly at the taking away all manner of purveyance. . . . In tenures they tasted best the removing of escheators and feodaries who, as they said, troubled them most of all upon supposed tenures and that for small patches of land.[56]

Many people in the localities were clearly uneasy about the details of the bargain and in addition some M.P.s must surely have communicated their own doubts to their constituents. This was certainly the view of an anonymous writer who discussed these events a few years later,[57] and it is given credence when we remember that there were many opponents of the Contract in the Commons, which had accepted the final version by a majority of only 60. Members certainly kept the need to satisfy local opinion in the forefront of their minds during the discussions in the fifth session, during which Salisbury spoke disapprovingly of those M.P.s who were still thinking of how to obtain 'commissions to go down to content the people' before they finally concluded the bargain.[58]

It is clear, therefore, that the Contract had been widely discussed outside Parliament before the beginning of the fifth session on 16 October. Both government and M.P.s were aware of the need to inform and consult the people – both the 'better sort' and the 'meaner sort' – at local level, and it is obvious that members took the opinions of their constituents very seriously. It may indeed have been largely because of doubts expressed in the localities that the fifth session got off to such a bad start. The Commons showed no zest at all for proceeding with the Contract. They did not discuss it during the first week of the session and the initiative had to come from the Lords who, no doubt acting with government approval, arranged a Lords-Commons conference on the subject on the 25th of the month. There Salisbury made a long speech,[59] stressing the need for speed. The king, he said, was uneasy about the whole business. 'The longer you are about it, the more will the king's affections kindle against the Contract.'[60]

By October 1610, therefore, the optimism of the previous July had evaporated. Neither king nor Commons was enthusiastic about the Contract and Salisbury's speech on the 25th implicitly recognized this fact – it reads as if it were gloomy and pessimistic in tone. Some of the reasons for the doubts of the Lower House are plain enough. For a start, few members had turned up at the beginning of the session. On 22 October, almost a week after its opening, there were still less than a hundred present, about a fifth of the House.[61] The king himself had angry words about this situation some time later[62] and it is surely of the utmost significance that the great majority of M.P.s stayed away at the start of the session. It must mean that they had decided, after reflection and consultation with their constituents, that they had no great enthusiasm for the Contract. Their absence, together with knowledge of the probable reasons for it, must have depressed the limited number of members who did turn up and may go far in explaining their reluctance to resume consideration of the Contract. Members were worried about the levy and security. When discussions did get underway again they were unable to reach any decision about the former,[63] a problem to which the king referred on 6 November, when he told the Commons that he required satisfaction about the details of the proposed tax, a satisfaction which the Commons were transparently unable to give.[64] As for security, Sir Maurice Berkeley, M.P. for Minehead, expressed Commons fears on the matter on 27 October. [65] James had insisted as long ago as April that tenures in chief themselves should not be abolished – these were a matter of honour – but only the burdens, principally wardship, which depended upon them.[66] The Commons had reluctantly accepted this, but the proposed continuance of the tenures gave point to their fears that the Crown might at some future date revive wardship. The king was very conscious of these fears and tried to allay them. 'For the point of security,' he told the Commons on 31 October, 'he could offer no more than the law could make, and we have enough in our house cunning in that craft.'[67] There seems no reason to doubt James's good intentions but the Commons were still worried about the ability of an Act of Parliament to bind the prerogative as Thomas Wentworth, M.P. for Oxford and son of Peter Wentworth of Elizabethan fame, stressed a few days later.[68] A more widespread fear among M.P.s was about the continued existence of Parliament if the Contract was accepted. As one M.P. put it in November, 'if you give so much then he shall not need a court of parliament.'[69] As a result of these fears demands were voiced at intervals during the negotiations that Parliament should meet automatically once every four, five or seven years.[70]

The king's doubts, which Salisbury had revealed on 25 October, were stressed by James himself in a speech to the Commons during an audience at Whitehall on the last day of the month. He stated ominously that he had 'a just cause to have a loathing and satiety of this Contract' and peremptorily ordered M.P.s to give him 'an answer affirmative or negative' at their next meeting; did they intend to proceed with the bargain or not.[71] The king's lack of enthusiasm – and it must be remembered that from early on in the discussions in the fourth session he had had grave doubts about the wisdom of giving up wardship[72] – was surely reinforced by the pressure to which he was subjected by men whose incomes and jobs would be affected by the Contract, especially, of course, the officers of the Court of Wards.[73] He may also have been influenced by the indictment of the Contract drawn up during the recess by his own chancellor of the exchequer, Sir Julius Caesar.[74] Caesar was out to argue a case and his statistics cannot be accepted at their face value; he inflated both the deficit in 1610 and the actual cost to the Crown of surrendering the revenues from wardship and purveyance. On the other hand he made some shrewd points, indicating that the Contract would give the king a fixed income in an inflationary age and that, if it was accepted, it would be even more difficult than before to persuade Parliament to grant subsidies. Whatever precise effect Caesar's arguments had on James it was certainly the latter who gave what was, in effect, the final blow to the Contract in a message to the Commons on 6 November.[75] In this, besides asking for satisfaction about the levy, he demanded that the Commons should compensate the officers of the Wards and, above all, stated that he must have £500,000 additional supply if he was to proceed with the bargain. The king protested that these were not new terms, they had been implicit in the Contract from the beginning. He had certainly asked for £600,000 in February (and had already received about £100,000 by way of a subsidy plus one-fifteenth and one-tenth in July[76]) but it seems inconceivable that he can have expected the Commons, already doubtful about the bargain, to agree to what *they* clearly regarded as new terms.[77] It looks, in fact, as if this was, from James's point of view, a way of ending the Contract. He effectively raised his terms while protesting that he was not doing so; the refusal could then come from the Commons. If this was his intention, he succeeded admirably. On 7 November, 'the whole House . . ., not five voices excepted'[78] rejected these demands. The Contract was at an end and the king accepted the decision calmly, almost with alacrity.[79]

Salisbury's feelings must have been very different. On 7 November, before the Commons vote took place, in what may have been a last, despairing attempt to keep negotiations going, he sent a message to them saying that he, who had most of all to lose, would not accept any compensation for giving up the mastership of the Wards,[80] and it is clear that he was anxious to keep Parliament in being long after the king himself had given up any hope of bringing it to a satisfactory conclusion. On 6 December, the day Parliament did end, James wrote a cruel letter of reproof to his chief minister in which he told him: 'your greatest error hath been that you ever expected to draw honey out of gall, being a little blinded with the self love of your own counsel in holding together of this parliament, wherof all men were despaired, as I have oft told you, but yourself alone.'[81] In 1610, in fact, Salisbury lost the confidence of both king and Parliament. The collapse of the Great Contract, in which so much of his credit was bound up, was a blow from which his prestige never recovered.[82]

The failure of the Contract was due partly to specific problems arising from the proposed levy and the question of security but perhaps even more to distrust between the Crown and M.P.s. Some of the latter feared for the continuing existence of Parliament and at the same time, and not altogether logically, were worried about the use which the extravagant James, surrounded by greedy courtiers, might make of any money which they voted. Thomas Wentworth put the matter expressively when he asked the Commons, 'what purpose is it for us to draw a silver stream out of the country into the royal cistern if it shall daily run out thence by private cocks?'[83] Members' anxieties were reinforced by the doubts expressed by many of their constituents.

James's fears are less easy to pinpoint, but he must have been swayed by the obvious discontent of the large number of officials who would have lost their jobs and courtiers who would have lost their profits if the Contract had gone through. He may have reflected too that, even if Caesar's memorandum exaggerated the purely financial disadvantage of the Contract to the Crown, the bargain, at best, was only a moderate one for him. The £200,000 would have wiped out the annual deficit and almost compensated him for the loss of wardship and purveyance as well, but it left him no surplus at all to play with at a time of continuing if moderating inflation and put him in a much weaker position in any future appeals to Parliament for assistance. It has been forcibly argued that the fears of M.P.s were the more fundamental and that the basic reason for the failure of the Contract was 'the suspicion with which the Commons regarded the Court.'[84] This may be so, but it must still be insisted that it was the king who finally killed the Contract. His demands on 6 November were just not practical politics.[85]

James may have followed Caesar's advice in rejecting the Contract, but he made little attempt to accept the other, quite vital point in the latter's memorandum; that he should make ends meet by curbing expenditure and reducing corruption. As a result, his debts rose once more, standing at £500,000 in 1612, £700,000 in 1615, and £1,000,000 in 1624.[86] Purveyance and wardship continued and the revenue from the latter source rose sharply during the rest of the early Stuart period, especially in the years of Charles I's 'personal rule', when it reached over £80,000 *per annum* and was one of the major grievances which country gentlemen remembered only too well in the Long Parliament, which abolished the Court by ordinance in 1646.[87] Purveyance had already been suspended by an order of 1642 which seems to have held good until about 1654, and the system was abolished by the second protectorate Parliament in 1657.[88] These abolitions were, of course, regarded as illegal by the government of Charles II and the whole problem had to be tackled again at the Restoration in an Act of 1660,[89] which finally ended purveyance and wardship. In compensation for the latter the Crown was granted an income, expected to be worth at least £100,000 a year, from duties on beer, cider and tea, excises which fell on the whole community. The net effect was to reduce the tax burden on the landed class.[90]

In December 1610 the representatives of that landed class in the Lower House parted from their sovereign amidst mutual distrust. James was scathing in his condemnation of a House of Commons which, after the failure of the Contract, had resolutely refused to consider any alternative means of granting him money and had, into the bargain, launched violent attacks on his Scottish entourage.[91] He described the Lower House to Salisbury as 'this rotten seed of Egypt', and told the Privy Council the next day, 7 December, that 'in all the Lower Houses these seven years past, especially these last two sessions . . . our fame and actions have been daily tossed like tennis balls amongst them, and all that spite and malice might do to disgrace and infame us hath been used.'[92] This release of long-pent-up feelings represented not only James's verdict on the collapse of the Contract and the trouble over impositions, the two issues which had dominated the fourth and fifth sessions, but also his frustration at the failure of his pet project for a 'perfect union' between England and Scotland, which had been the main business of the third session.[93] It was the sessions of 1610, however, as James himself admitted to the Council, which were of crucial importance in his disenchantment with parliaments and it can be argued that he never really recovered a spirit of goodwill towards them. The experience of the 'Addled' Parliament of 1614 merely reinforced a determination not to recall them unless it was absolutely essential and when necessity came again in the 1620s it initiated a period in which Crown and Commons were frequently at loggerheads over both domestic and foreign policy.

The Great Contract was an important element in this 1610 watershed in relations between Crown and Commons. Historians have speculated – and come to very different conclusions – about possible consequences if the Contract had been agreed.[94] Its failure was a turning point in the financial and constitutional history of the early seventeenth century. It demonstrated the inability of Crown and Commons to reach agreement on a fundamental overhaul of an outmoded and unpopular financial system. The consequences were very apparent in the rest of early Stuart history right up to the outbreak of the Civil War.

7

STAGING A PARLIAMENT IN EARLY STUART ENGLAND

Elizabeth Read Foster

In the early seventeenth century, as today, the royal procession at the opening of Parliament was a great show. People thronged the streets, which had been hung with tapestries. Ambassadors rented rooms along the way to watch the pageant as it moved slowly from Whitehall to the Abbey, then from the Abbey to the Old Palace of Westminster where Parliament normally met. First came messengers and trumpeters, then royal judges and privy councillors, bishops in ecclesiastical robes, peers in their Parliament robes of velvet trimmed with ermine. There followed the prince in his Parliament robes, with cap and coronet, and at last the king, preceded by his cap of estate and sword, wearing his Parliament robes and crown, flanked by gentlemen pensioners and followed by his guard. Heralds, splendid in ceremonial attire, marshalled each group.[1] The pageantry of the opening day, the building in which Parliament met, the furnishings, the supplies, the personnel, had all to be paid for. The purpose of this essay – and it is an essay in the original sense of the word – is to retrieve from the royal accounts and other sources details about the physical surroundings of Parliament, about parliamentary personnel, about supplies and provisions which were bought and to attempt to estimate how much it cost the Crown to set the stage for Parliament. No satisfactory totals will emerge. The state of the records and the nature of the accounts make this impossible. But we can perhaps suggest the broad dimensions of the problem.

The responsibility for the Palace and the immediate area around it rested, under the direction of the lord chamberlain, with the Office of Works. Only certain rooms in the Palace were used for Parliament: the Lords' chamber; St Stephen's Chapel where the Commons sat; the Painted Chamber; adjoining rooms for committee meetings or set aside for the king, the lord chancellor, the lord treasurer and the speaker, and those claimed by the clerks. It is not always possible to separate the charges for these rooms from other charges or (in some accounts) to differentiate the charges for Whitehall from those for Westminster. The following totals are therefore offered with diffidence. They serve to indicate the variation from parliamentary year to parliamentary year and of the costs for maintaining the building and the area around it, preparing them for Parliament, and providing some of the necessary furniture. In 1610, when Henry was created Prince of Wales in Parliament, overall costs chargeable to Parliament to be paid by the Crown through the Office of Works came to £395 0s. 6d. This sum included the expense of changes in the chamber of the Court of Requests (within the Palace of Westminster) where the ceremony was held. In 1621, charges for the Palace which can be related to Parliament came to £283 6s. 2d.; in 1625-6, £242 10s.; in 1627-9, £323 9s. 3d. and in 1640, £640 6s.[2] By examining the accounts on which such totals as these are based, we may come to understand them better, and to visualize the preparations for Parliament which the Office of Works undertook.

The procession from Whitehall to the Abbey, the service in the Abbey and the procession from the Abbey to the Parliament House were a significant part of the ceremony of opening Parliament. Thus the charges for a Parliament involved railing streets of access, care of Old Palace Yard, the approach to Parliament and arrangements in the Abbey itself. In preparation for the crowds, streets were railed on both sides from Whitehall to the Abbey.[3] The cost of rails was computed by the rod at 6d. the rod with an additional rate of 4d. for digging post-holes. The number of rods varied from 225 (1613–14) to 243 (1640) and the number of post-holes from 376 (1623–4) to 558 (1640). On each occasion the beadle of Westminster earned a small sum (3s. to 5s.) for proclaiming that posts and rails should not be broken down and taken away after the ceremony. In 1640, the justices of Westminster were ordered to set watches to preserve them.[4] Sometimes the weather caused additional expense. In 1623–4, labourers were paid £5 3s. 4d. 'for digging and breaking the ice in the streets, sweeping and scooping of water out of the ways, spreading of gravel and shovelling up the same again being made all dirt' on the first day when the king was thought to be going to Parliament, and for 'breaking up the ice and sweeping out the water' the second day when he actually did go.[5]

It was the responsibility of the justices of Westminster to see to the paving of the streets to the Abbey;[6] but paving within Old Palace Yard and on the approaches to the two Houses fell to the Office of Works and was included in the charges for a Parliament. The 'confluence of people and coaches' necessitated frequent repaving at considerable expense.[7] In the last years of Elizabeth, paving was laid at the queen's entry to the upper House. In 1614, £400 was to be paid for paving and repairs to the Old Palace. In 1624-5, John Taylor paved the way entering into Old Palace Yard; and in 1626-7, paving was done 'under the gate leading to the Parliament House.' The following year a number of holes between the gates were paved; and in 1639–40, 414 square yards before the Parliament House were laid with ragstones.[8] The traffic in Old Palace Yard became so noisy and troublesome that in 1642 a chain was hung across the entrance to prevent carts from going through. The gentleman usher entrusted the key to Charles Best, who was also to sweep. By 1644 he was still unpaid and had to be relieved from the poor box.[9]

Sometimes the monarch proceeded by water to Parliament, as did many of the members. When the Thames froze over twice in 1621, John Chamberlain reported that 'the watermen are quite undone to lose the benefit . . . of parliament.'[10] Some of the charges for the care of the Palace of Westminster submitted by the Office of Works involved access to the river. There was whitewash for the passage to the waterside in Elizabeth's reign, and in 1603, carpenters made a new door to the water gate. Later a brick wall was built to keep up the wharf of the garden before the Parliament House. In 1645, watermen petitioned for repair of the causeway down from the Parliament stairs. They could not, they said, land a fare at low water. The Lords ordered an inquiry, but whether the work went forward or was paid for is not recorded.[11]

The service in the Abbey which was part of the ceremonial of the opening of Parliament also entailed special arrangements and special expense, all included in the charges of the Office of Works. In 1603, provision was made for hangings around the communion table in order that the king might hear the sermon in an enclosed or private place. In 1627–8, 'ledges' for hangings were again provided on either side of the altar and two rooms were enclosed beyond the altar, 'th'one for the reposing, and th'other for the attiring of his Majesty there.'[12]

The Palace of Westminster was an old building, which constantly required repair and alteration. The roof was a perennial problem, tiles and leads continually in need of replacement – some worn out, others stolen.[13] Over the years, chimneys and hearths were rebuilt, walls and ceilings repaired and whitewashed.[14] Masons in Elizabeth's time had reset steps to the Lords' chamber and provided 'a great step' for the entrance to the gallery or passageway of the upper House.[15] The ceiling of 'old wainscot' in the 'great outer room' of the upper House was made fast in 1606–7. In 1621, a joiner made and set up 13 yards of deal (or board) ceiling in the lower House. Later, plasterers refinished and whitewashed the ceiling in the king's presence chamber of the upper House, 'with the great cornish beneath it.' The ceiling of the prince's chamber (used by the king as a robing room) was hung with blue linen in 1640, and a painter redrew and mended 'with black and white the fret work of the ceiling in the four windows of the upper House . . . and part of the end walls of the said House.'[16]

The two great windows in the upper House were repaired at the end of Elizabeth's reign and again in 1606–7. 'Paper' windows for the upper and lower lights of the great windows of the House of Commons were made in 1645–6. An awning (or 'umbrage') kept the sun out of the large east window.

In 1625–6, John White twice erected this great canvas for the sum of 5s., which included the use of a scaffold;[17] and in 1644–5, a pole 24 feet long strengthened the frame 'of the umbrage . . . being blown down.'[18]

At James's accession, a place was made for the queen near the king's chair of state.[19] More seats were needed in the House of Commons, for the total membership had increased during the Elizabethan period and would continue to do so in the reigns of the first two Stuarts. Carpenters built a large frame with a boarded floor in 1604 to accommodate members and new steps 'to the seats there.'[20] In 1621, they erected a new gallery at the lower end of the Commons' chamber, with 38 'ballesters' and 3 long columns, all painted with two coats of 'rance', a mottled red.[21] Certain changes were made in the lord chancellor's and lord treasurer's rooms in 1606–7.[22] In 1625–6, a 'half-pace' under the chair of state was provided in the upper House and a traverse (or small boarded area) behind the state 'for our ambassador to stand upon' in 1627–8.[23] In 1644–5, various repairs were made to the House of Commons, the passages to the House of Lords, the steps to the Hall from the lower House and the paving of New Palace Yard to an amount exceeding £300.[24]

There were several alterations to accommodate the growing number of records kept in the Old Palace – some of them records of Parliament. In 1603, a new door gave access to the 'House of Records' over the Parliament House.[25] In 1621, renovations to the old Jewel Tower of the Palace transformed it into a repository of the Lords' records and an office for the clerks. In 1623–4 the stone work and timber roof of this building were repaired; and in 1626–7 the expenditure on the office came to £10 13s. 1d. In 1645–6, some rooms were altered for keeping the records of Parliament near the Lords' House. This involved moving two presses and two pairs of stairs, cross-jointing and new boarding the 'Great Room,' the closet and room beneath, making four new doors, two windows and a lantern in the roof to give light to the stairs.[26]

In addition to doing repairs and making renovations, the Office of Works also provided, regularly laid, mended and replaced matting on the floors of the meeting chambers of both Houses, as well as in adjacent rooms – the king's privy chamber, the Commons' committee room, the lobbies, the prince's room and the Lords' 'stool-house'. Matting was also laid on the seats in the Commons' chamber and in the space between the seats.[27]

The charges for making furniture, included in the total charge presented by the Office of Works of which some examples were given above, amounted to £15 18s. 4d. in 1601–2; a similar sum in 1603; £3 14s. in 1609–10; £30 11s. 6d. in 1623–4; £37 16s. 6d. in 1625–6; and £43 3s. 8d. in 1639–40.[28] The furniture comprised a variety of items. For the House of Commons in 1603, joiners made three new deal tables, three trestles, six deal forms (or benches) and six joined stools, in addition to the new benches already mentioned. For the upper House, they mended old forms for the lords to sit upon, and constructed five new forms (16ft long) with square feet. For the privy chamber, a wainscot (or oak) table with two wainscot forms was provided, a court cupboard 4ft high, a dozen high joined stools, and one drawing table of wainscot (4ft long, 3ft broad) with two cupboards in it; for the lord chancellor's room, one wainscot table (10ft long, 3ft broad), and a similar table for the lord treasurer's room; for the clerk of the parliaments, 'a wainscot table with a cupboard to it, and boarded about the sides, being 5 feet long and 3 feet broad.' Richard Dongan received 3s. for the use of a horse block to stand at the higher House in Parliament time. The total sum for furniture of £15 11s. 4d. does not seem to include the new scaffold for the House of Commons. But it does cover payment to Black Rod, the gentleman usher, 'in allowance for certain old tables and old forms, cupboards and trestles which he leaveth in the House at the end of the parliament besides the new stuff which he taketh for his fees.'[29] Since the gentleman usher regularly claimed as his fee all the furniture of the upper House save the 'joined table with drawing boxes [or drawers]' which went to the clerk of the parliaments and since 'one joined table with drawing boxes' was the perquisite of the serjeant-at-arms of the lower House, it was necessary before each Parliament to replace or make payment for much of what had been supplied and paid for before.[30]

Thus in 1609–10 further 'joined work' was provided, including a 'wainscot table with a cupboard in it for the clerk of the council [Parliament] in the upper parliament House, 30s.,' a 'wainscot table with a frame for the king's privy chamber there, 20s.' and '12 wainscot stools' at 24s. each.[31] In 1623–4, there is a long list of joined work for both Houses 'and the rooms and chambers belonging to the same': deal tables of different sizes, forms, trestles, wainscot cupboards, joined stools, a screen, and a case of wainscot for the clock.[32] In 1625–6, 'sundry large forms of deal' with square legs of oak were made 'and boarded together to be lined for the upper House.' The joiner again made a table of wainscot for the clerk of the parliaments and one for the clerk of the crown, a clock case for the upper House 'and other joined works there.'[33] In 1639–40, for the Short Parliament, 39 forms were constructed, two tables, trestles, five court cupboards, a screen and 30 joined stools.[34] In 1644–5, during the Long Parliament, much work was done at St Stephen's, the Commons' chamber. Carpenters made a bench and new frame for a table in a committee room and rebuilt the forms for the House with deal (possibly pine) and oaken backs. During this period of civil war, the Office of Works seems to have taken over some of the customary responsibilities of the Wardrobe. It lined the forms with Yorkshire kersey, covered chairs and a stool for the clerk with the same, supplied 146 yards of canvas 'to make rolls for the seats', which were stuffed with curled hair, provided canvas for the 'umbrage', and 30 yards of serge for making curtains for the 'great windows'.[35] In 1645–6, when further work was done in the Commons' chamber, the speaker's chair was refurbished. In 1640, the king's arms above it had been repainted.[36] Now the chair itself was richly ornamented with 'arkets,' 'round beads,' 'lace in the architrave,' four cornices and capitals, the royal arms and supporters carved in such a way as 'to be seen on both sides' and two scrolls 'in the front piece.' The cost for carving came to £9 13s. 9d. A joiner made the screen behind the chair, the frame for the chair and a step up to it for £17 10s., including materials.[37]

Furnishing the rooms used by Parliament and its officers in the Palace of Westminster was a responsibility shared with the Office of the Great Wardrobe, which normally provided materials for upholstery and curtains, workmanship, an assortment of fire-tools and other small objects. Therefore in picturing the stage on which the drama of Parliament was played out and in estimating the cost of providing and setting that stage, one must add to the charges of the Office of Works, discussed above, those of the Wardrobe.

In 1603, the lord chamberlain, on behalf of the king, ordered the master of the Great Wardrobe to deliver to James Maxwell, gentleman usher and Black Rod, '22 pieces of say of the best and largest size, one hundred and three score ells of good and well made canvas to make sacks to cover the stools and forms withall, twelve todds of very good wool for the stuffing of all the forms and stools within the [Lords'] chamber,' hay to fill the sacks, thread, lyor (or tape), and nails. He was to pay also for workmanship. He was to provide two pairs of brass andirons, two pairs of 'handsome and serviceable' fire shovels and tongs, two pairs of great andirons with large fire shovels, tongs and forks, and three pairs of iron creepers with three fire shovels and tongs,[38] for the '7 rooms with chimneys in the House of Peers.'[39] He was to supply one screen for the royal use, one large down pillow for the lord keeper and ten pounds of lyor to hang the state (the cloth embroidered with royal arms behind the throne and the canopy above it).[40] The same order was repeated with little variation for each Parliament and sometimes for sessions within the same Parliament.[41] Clearly all that had been purchased was regularly disposed of, possibly as the perquisites of the usher. All had to be purchased again. The total charge came to £207 12s. in 1609-10; £211 9s. 8d. in 1614; £138 17s. in 1623-4; £132 10s. 8d. in 1625-6; £150 17s. in 1627-8 and £144 13s. 4d. in 1639-40.[42] £200 was warranted in 1640. In 1657/8, when the Council of State made provision 'for the other House of parliament' and the rooms adjacent, Clement Kynnersley, then in charge of the Wardrobe, was ordered to furnish them 'at the cheapest rates he can, and to hang the said six rooms with baize, or striped stuff,' the total sum to be £200, which did not vary greatly from previous or subsequent expenditures. In 1660, Kynnersley expended £211 4s. 4d. and for the next Parliament £286 6s. 5d. [43]

A closer examination of the accounts provides details which make it possible to visualize the setting of Parliament more clearly. In 1624, the brass andirons were specifically allocated to the king's privy chamber, and another pair was added 'for the use of our dearest son, the Prince' in his chamber.[44]

In this year also bellows appeared (4s. the pair), and three pillows, two for the lord chancellor's seats [sic] and one for the gentleman usher. Oliver Browne, the upholsterer, at a cost of £131 6s. 8d., made four large packs of canvas, filled them with hay and covered them with red say. He also covered all the seats, bars, forms, benches and stools with canvas and stuffed them with wool. Fine crimson tape and copper nails garnished seats, forms, and rails. Two screens made of red say and lined with canvas kept out the wind. A standard (or chest) of seasoned elm boards with hide leather, bound in iron with a lock, was for the Parliament House. In 1625–6 fire-makers (ignatibul) appeared. The pillows were now allocated to the lord keeper, lord treasurer and the gentleman usher; and a frame was set up for filling the 'wool' sacks. In 1627–8, a standard, a cabinet, a large pot or tankard and a leathern cup were provided. An umbella (or sunshade) was made for the use of the king (10s.), and two other umbellas of red say, lined with canvas, and a traverse and seat for the queen. The Wardrobe in 1627–8 supplied 40 ells of canvas to shade the House of Commons. They were fitted and nailed 'over the shed without the great window at the upper end of the lower House.'[45] It was this arrangement or 'umbrage' which blew down and for which the Office of Works made a pole in 1644–5. There was a regular supply of pewter chamber pots and 'necessary' or 'close' stools with pans.[46]

In addition to furnishing the rooms for Parliament, the Wardrobe also provided such items as were needed in the Abbey for the opening ceremonies: in 1627–8 and 1640, two cushions of purple velvet with buttons and tassels of gold and silk, one demi-carpet and one turkey carpet. These were the perquisites of the master of the horse and were doubtless replaced regularly.[47]

With these major charges against the Wardrobe and the Office of Works, there were a number of other figures which must be cast into the account. The labour costs of disposing furniture in the Parliament chambers fell chiefly to the Wardrobe, but cannot always be located. They included also a charge for transferring tapestries, hangings and other items from the king's great store at his other palaces or in the Tower. The upper chamber, Sir Thomas Smith had said, 'is richly tapessed and hanged, a princely and royal throne . . . set in the middest of the higher place thereof.' Other observers also commented on the tapestries. The Painted Chamber and other rooms were similarly hung.[48] In 1628, Kynnersley had been ordered to furnish a dining room for 'Mr Speaker' with five tapestry pieces which told the story of Actaeon and Diana and with ten small carpets of 'turkey making' from the materials in his charge, all to be redelivered at the end of the session.[49] A purple 'state', cushions and stools were to be sent from the Tower. In 1640–1, hangings and 'other stuff' for Parliament were sent from the Tower, from Windsor, and from Oatlands. A new 'state with the furniture thereto' was borrowed from Whitehall.[50] The keeper of the wardrobe at Hampton Court was to deliver seven pieces of hangings 'of the story of Hercules' and seven pieces with the tale of Ahasuerus and Esther to Kynnersley to furnish two rooms at Durham House for Sir John Finch, presiding officer of the House of Lords. 'Rich stuff' came from the Tower for the Abbey.[51] In 1644, hangings hired by the king's upholsterers and still unpaid for were replaced by some of the king's 'shallow' hangings from Oatlands to save expense.[52]

Robert Inkersoll of the Removing Wardrobe in February 1627–8 presented bills for eight labourers in fetching stuff from the Tower to furnish the Parliament House and for ten labourers for ten days in August for returning the stuff to the Tower and Whitehall. John Hamley brought materials from Windsor (nine labourers, eight days). George Clark of the Removing Wardrobe employed eight labourers, eight days, to return 'the stuff' to Oatlands. John Griffith, underkeeper of Oatlands, was in turn paid for airing the stuff in November, January and March 1628–9 and for delivering it out to furnish Parliament in January 1628–9. In 1648, hangings were brought at a charge of £1 for the room in which the Committee for the Advancement of Money worked.[53] Kynnersley's bill for carriage by land and water and for hire of porters and labourers for furnishing Parliament came to £3 10s. 8d. in May 1660 with an additional 14s. 'for coach hire and going by water upon the occasion the House was furnishing.' In December he submitted a comprehensive bill (April–December) for £11 10s. 'for carriage by land and by water of goods towards the furnishing of the House and hire of men.'[54] These sums have already been included in his bills for furnishing Parliament in 1660, cited above. The housekeeper of the House of Lords, John Whynnard, was responsible for placing furniture in the upper House and for removing it. Thus in 1629, he submitted bills for six labourers for 16 days in November 1628 and for six labourers, himself and man 'before and after the last parliament.' The total sum, which included cleaning, is not stated.[55] Many of these charges were relatively small but must be considered in a study of the Crown's expenditures.

Another regular but small cost to the Crown was for cleaning and sweeping. Most of this expense was met by payments authorized by the lord chamberlain's Office in addition to those charges in the Wardrobe and Household already mentioned. The yeoman usher of the House of Lords, Richard Crane, in 1625 and 1626, presented bills to the lord chamberlain for £6 10s. for brooms, 'sweepers' and chimney sweepers for keeping the House clean from 1 February to 16 June 1625, and £5 10s. for brooms, baskets and 'sweepers' at Oxford when Parliament was held there (15 July–25 August 1625).[56] For Parliament in 1628, Crane's bills were £6 11s. for brooms, 'sweepers' and chimney sweepers, fire-making and keeping the House and chimneys clean, and £5 in lieu of his disbursements for boughs, strewing herbs, roses and the like 'for sweetening of the rooms of the said House. . . '. Later his charges included £4 10s. for brooms and the like, at a rate of 12d. *per diem* for 90 days (1 Jan. – end March 1628/9), £3 for 20 days at the same rate in

October and £2 10s. for chimney sweepers.[57] John Whynnard's bill, already mentioned, included 'sweeping, brushing and carrying forth the dust and rubbish and making clean of ye Parliament House' in 1628. These men were also engaged, as we have seen, in placing and removing furniture.[58] Four labourers cleaned the stuff used in the king's barge at his going to Parliament.[59] Charles Best in 1644 complained that he had never been repaid for brooms purchased to sweep Old Palace Yard nor for his services there.[60] In 1644–5, a woman was paid 9d. for cleaning the seats in the House of Commons.[61] In 1660, a woman scoured andirons for 10s. This charge together with payment to porters and labourers who made 'all clean and carried out the soil' came to a total of £1 10s., already included in the Wardrobe accounts. A further sum, also included, was for 12s. for charcoal to air the rooms and for candles.[62]

Charges for cleaning the stool rooms and vaults fell to the Office of Works and seem to be usually in addition to those already cited. In 1628–9, divers labourers were paid for 'shovelling a great quantity of soil in the Old Palace and making the same clean.'[63] In 1645–6, the charge for emptying the vault of the House of Commons was £3. In 1660–1, water was pumped morning and evening into the stool room of the House of Commons at a cost of 15s. per month.[64]

The cost of maintaining fires in rooms adjoining the Lords' chamber and the chamber itself ran high, increasing in cold weather. With each succeeding day of a Parliament, the total mounted. The accounts we have are for four years of the Long Parliament (1642–5) when the House sat more regularly than it had done earlier in the century: £767 3s. 8d. for 1642, £787 5s. for 1643, £783 3s. for 1644, and £781 5s. for 1645 (43s. per diem, 'as well when the House sits as when it is adjourned'). Part of this sum was due to Wilkes Fitchett for wood: '2 load of talwood and 2 loads of billets [that is wood cut to size for fuel] by the day for seven months and half that proportion for 2 months.' Part was due to Joane Shellaker for 84 loads of charcoal yearly: 10 loads for 4 months, 8 loads for 3 months, and 4 loads for 5 months.[65] It would be difficult to attempt to extrapolate from these figures estimates for the cost of fuel for the House of Commons with fewer hearths or for the cost for other Parliaments.[66] But in thinking of the overall expense of a Parliament to the Crown, fuel is a significant item.

The cost of books, stationery and similar supplies for the clerks and other officers of both Houses increased as the life of a Parliament continued and was paid by the Crown to the king's printer, Robert Barker, or his assigns. Itemized bills have survived among the Lords' papers, among the Wardrobe accounts (where they are impossible to differentiate as clearly related to Parliament) and in miscellaneous papers now classified under the Office of Works. In 1604, supplies delivered to the clerk of the parliaments cost £20 12s. 10d.[67] In 1610, those delivered to the clerk and to the gentleman usher came to £127 10s. and £20 was authorized for the clerk of the lower

House for 'books and necessaries'.[68] In 1614, the clerk received items in the amount of £94 18s. These chance survivals probably do not constitute the total sums for James's first and second Parliaments. An undated memorandum, in the clerk's hand, indicates that more paper and parchment should be delivered 'as occasion shall serve.'[69] In the years 1640–2, when we have the next detailed parliamentary accounts, supplies were delivered periodically throughout the session to the upper and lower Houses, in the amount of £763 15s. 2d.; in 1642–5, in the amount of £752 12s.; and in 1645–8, in the amount of £443 11s. 5d., a total of £1959 18s. 7d. for the Long Parliament up to and including 1648.[70]

Just what was provided? First of all, in 1604 the king's printer brought a small library of books for the upper House: statutes, abridgments, books of computation, several Bibles and a *Book of Common Prayer*. In 1614, he again brought statutes, abridgments, Bibles and a *Book of Common Prayer* together with copies of Holinshed, Speed, and Foxe's *Book of Martyrs*.[71] Most of these books could be justified as necessary to the functions of the House, but Speed, Holinshed and Foxe seem questionable. The duplication makes it clear that they were sold or appropriated at the end of a Parliament, probably as the perquisite of the clerk. When we come to the wonderfully detailed accounts of the Long Parliament, it is apparent that books were delivered to and probably retained or sold by several officers of each House. In 1640–2, the clerk of the parliaments required a Bible, eight books of *Common Prayer* or service books, 15 almanacs and various sets of statutes. The gentleman usher required a Bible, two service books and an almanac. The speaker of the House of Commons began to buy in a library at the expense of the Crown: three almanacs, statutes, abridgments, several Bibles, a service book, registers of writs, Fulbecke's *Law*, Coke on Littleton, Pliny's *History*, Plutarch's *Lives*, the works of Seneca, an English translation of Tacitus, a *French Academy*, *Flores Doctorum*, *Office of Executors*, Kitchen's *Courts Leet*, Matthew Paris, the *Adages* of Erasmus, Du Bartas, *The souls solace*, and Gerard's *Herbal*. The clerk of the House of Commons received a Latin Bible.[72]

In the period 1642–5, book buying continued. The clerk of the parliaments acquired Coke's *Reports*, and the newly issued volumes of his *Institutes*.[73] The gentleman usher was furnished with additional almanacs. The clerk of the lower House now also received Coke's *Fourth Institute*, another Latin Bible and two volumes of Seneca. Lenthall, speaker of the House of Commons, added a wide range of books to his collection, over 60 titles: further works of Tacitus, Livy, Coke's *First* and *Second Institutes*, Caesar's *Commentaries*, Aristotle, Erasmus' *Dialogues*, Ovid, Cicero, several dictionaries, Virgil, the works of William Perkins, Browne's *Religio Medici*, Balzac's *Epistles* in three volumes, Comines, Foxe, the works of Bede and of Camden, all of Baker's works, Calvin's *Institutes*, Milles's *Catalogue of Honor*, a French Bible and two 'Scottish' Bibles, Du Bartas (for the second time), various almanacs,

Brightman on *Revelation*, Boccaccio's *Decameron*, Burton's *Melancholy*, Hakewill's *Apology*, and the works of Hall.[74] He was more restrained in the next period (1645–7), limiting himself to a Bible and almanacs. Manchester, presiding officer of the House of Lords, acquired Foxe, several almanacs, statutes and abridgments. The clerk of the parliaments also obtained Foxe, Coke's *Institutes* and a book of notes on the Bible. The clerk of the House of Commons had Bibles, almanacs, statutes, Cotton's *Concordance*, the Thirty-Nine Articles, 'Mr Roger's notes' and a *Harmony of the Confession of Faith*.[75]

The needs of the two Houses were more appropriately served by deliveries from week to week of writing materials, all set down in detail: paper of different kinds in loose sheets and in books, parchment of different qualities, pens and pen knives, cedar pencils, ink, standishes, 'hanging ink horns' with silken strings and inkhorns to fasten to clerks' desks, sand (black and white), bags of leather and of canvas, trunks of different sizes and materials, glue, cotton, wax, thread, needles, bodkins and 'carnation tape'.[76] The printer also delivered large quantities of printed Acts, declarations, votes, orders, ordinances and other public documents to both Houses, as well as to other offices. Since all had been paid for by the Crown, it would be interesting to know whether there was a further charge to the ultimate recipients of these printed materials.[77]

The king's printer did binding for both Houses, bringing his presses and tools by water to Westminster in order to do it on the premises.[78] There was a charge of £2 in 1641 'for 3 volume covers fully gilt with large King's Arms upon them wherein were bound the Remonstrance of both Houses, with silk strings;' and in 1643 and 1647 there were charges for binding journals in the House of Lords 'together with an alphabet and claspt.'[79] Besides supplying stationery and doing binding, the king's printer did all the printing connected with Parliament and provided forms used by both Houses and the king.[80] A printer followed the king to Berwick in 1639 and later to York, Shrewsbury and Oxford.[81] Leonard Lichfield, printer to the University, worked for the king at Oxford, submitting a bill of £676 8d. for the period 29 October, 1642–3 February 1643/4.[82] At Westminster, after 1642, each House had its own printer, usually John Wright for the upper House and Edward Husbands for the lower.[83] Husbands's bill (July 1642) for printing for the House of Commons came to £211 5s. Later, in April 1648, Lords and Commons ordered that he should be paid £617 15s. 6d. 'upon accompt.'[84] Other accounts do not seem to have survived.

Next, there is the panoply of royalty to consider, robes and the royal barge. The initial expense of making parliament robes for the king and for the princes, for maintaining robes, beating, airing, brushing and 'sweetening' them was a further item in the cost of Parliament to the Crown, paid through the Wardrobe. Two robes, made in 1603, for King James and Prince Henry, came to £617 7s. 8d.[85] In 1614, after the death of Henry, a charge occurred of 100s. for making a Parliament robe, kirtle and cap for Prince Charles of crimson velvet, bordered with fustian and strengthened with canvas and buckram, with some minor charges for materials. Perhaps Charles' robe was simpler (he was only 14 years old) or the ermine (always very expensive) was borrowed from the robe made for Henry. In 1623–4, the king's robe, kirtle, hood, cap of maintenance and 'the cap the crown is worn upon' were retrimmed with fresh ermine and repaired for £8 15s.[86] In 1627–8, a chest was made for the sword of state at a cost of 20s. A scabbard of crimson velvet was provided, and the pommel, guard and blade refurbished for 26s. 8d.[87] The annual cost of airing, brushing, beating and perfuming the king's robe varied. Often the coronation robes (stored at the Tower with the Parliament robes) and sometimes the robes at Whitehall (1627–8) were included as well as the cost of wood, charcoal, sweet powder and brushes. A sure figure is therefore difficult to obtain; but it was an expense to be reckoned with, running from 100s. in 1614 to over £100 in 1627–8.[88]

Sometimes the king proceeded to Parliament by barge, seeking to avoid the crowds and the danger of plague. Sometimes, as Queen Elizabeth had done, he left Parliament by the east door and went down the Parliament steps where his barge lay ready.[89] In 1620–1, he allocated £400 'for a privy barge to be forthwith made for our service this next parliament', painted and gilded with two other barges 'belonging thereto', probably for attendants. A barge cloth was also ordered, embroidered with the king's arms, crests, crowns and supporters, for the sum of £150. In preparation for Parliament in 1640, the king ordered a new barge, and advanced £620 'to enable and encourage the workmen.'[90]

There are a number of problems in estimating the cost of staffing Parliament. The personnel – presiding officers, clerks and their assistants, serjeants, gentleman usher, yeoman usher and doorkeepers – were paid in a variety of ways. Their chief support came not from the small salaries they received from the Crown, but from fees they collected from members and from those who did business with Parliament. Certain officers and servants were paid annually by the Crown, and temporarily assigned to Parliament when it was sitting – for example, the lord chancellor (or keeper), the judges and other assistants in the upper House, who sometimes also received 'rewards' at the end of Parliament.[91] The serjeants, gentleman usher and His Majesty's groom porter's servant were also paid annually by the crown, as well as the clerk of parliaments, his assistant in the lower House, and the clerk of the Crown. The speaker of the House of Commons, on the other hand, was paid only in Parliament time and usually by the session. Some officers received lodging and diet at court, robes and regular 'gifts'. It is questionable whether, in a strict accounting, the charge for officers of Parliament on the annual pay roll should be included as one of the expenses of Parliament, and there is a good argument for omitting altogether personnel items of this nature. Certain figures may, however, prove interesting and worth recording if they are used with caution. The salaries of judges (including the lord chancellor or lord keeper) have not been considered here.

In the upper House, the clerk received £40 *per annum*. In 1605, he was paid an additional £40 'for his charges and pains in writing and transferring the general parliament roll for the last Parliament' into the court of Chancery.[92] He also claimed his desk as fee, [93] and possibly stationery supplies and books. The gentleman usher, or Black Rod, received 5s. *per diem* for himself and men. His additional expenses for travel were probably usually paid by those to whom he delivered parliamentary orders and the like, but possibly some were met by the Crown.[94] He claimed as his fee all the joined work in the upper House, with the exception of the desks and table allocated to the clerks. He either took the furniture which was his due or compounded for it.[95] Perhaps he also had some claim on the upholstery materials and on stationery delivered to him – points which are not clear. He received a New Year's gift of £6 in 1628–9 and 15 yards of crimson satin for a robe in 1640, with '5 ells of white taffeta to line the same.' He was also entitled to lodging at Whitehall.[96] The serjeant, assigned to the lord chancellor, was paid 12d. *per diem*. The yeoman usher received 3s. *per diem* for himself and his servant. The groom porter's servant, assigned to the upper House, received 20d. *per diem*.[97] In the lower House, the speaker could normally expect £100 for a session, though in 1621 Richardson complained that he 'had no penny recompense for any my pains, charge and loss.'[98] The clerk was paid £10 annually and may have claimed certain furniture and stationery as his perquisites.[99] The serjeant-at-arms, assigned to the speaker, received 12d. *per diem* and his livery. He claimed 'one joined table with drawing boxes.'[100] Staffing Parliament did not cost the Crown a great deal. The total sum for any one Parliament (with the exception of the Long Parliament) came to less than £500.

Certain royal officers and servants received special remuneration for services connected with Parliament. The clerk of the Crown (whose annual salary of £40 has not been included here) was paid 53s. 4d. in 1571 'for exemplifying of the general pardon and writing the same in the form of a mittimus, into the Exchequer.' In 1605, Sir George Coppin, then clerk of the Crown, received 13s. 4d. for his charges in writing and expediting each of three commissions for the prorogation of Parliament.[101] £20 was to be divided among several messengers for delivering writs of Parliament in Elizabeth's reign. In 1605, they were to be paid £24 for riding 'into all the counties, cities, and principal towns' with proclamations for the prorogation, and in 1610 the same amount for carrying proclamations concerning the king's determination to dissolve Parliament.[102] Charges for the delivery of a writ for a by-election came to £5 in 1675. There were also charges for the delivery of writs to new lords during a session.[103]

The treasurer of the Household was empowered to provide diets and other necessaries incident to the attendance of the lords in Parliament, and also to provide the same for judges, serjeants-at-law, the attorney general and the solicitor for their attendance and service in Parliaments.[104] It is not clear from any of the records whether all the lords were entitled to diets during Parliament time or whether this provision applied only to lords and others of the Council. Sometimes the cofferer's account speaks specifically of 'Lords of the Council in time of parliament'[105] or 'Lords and others of our privy council . . . during the continuance of this our present parliament.' Sometimes the phrase is shortened to 'Lords during the time of this present parliament', 'Lords of parliament', or 'Lords in parliament'.[106]

The amount expended on diets varied greatly. For the first session of 1621 it came to £559 5s. 4d., which would average out to £8 4s. 5d. per diem. For 22 days in 1624, the cost was £536 7s. 1d., or £24 7s. 7d. per diem. For 1626, the average per diem was £51 17s. For the lords of the Short Parliament, diet in April came to £589 1s. 10d. or £42 1s. 6d. per diem.[107] From 3 November 1640 to 20 March 1640/1, the grand total was said to be £1500, an overall average of about £12 12s. 1d. per diem, whereas the rate from March 1640/1 to 31 December 1641 was £4 13s. 3d. per diem.[108] The cost of diets thus ranged from about £4 to £51 per diem,[109] doubtless reflecting the shift in the number attending. When a Parliament dragged on, diet could become one of the most significant costs.

At the end of this journey among the ledgers, rolls, account books and other records – this 'wilderness of accompt', to borrow Lord Salisbury's phrase in 1610[110] – though much research remains to be done, we can see more clearly the setting of Parliament and its personnel. We can also roughly estimate the cost of Parliament to the Crown. In arriving at such an estimate, there are a number of difficulties. The allocation of some charges must be arbitrary. Certain officers were paid annually and only temporarily assigned to parliamentary duties. The Office of Works made repairs over a number of years and carried them forward whether Parliament met or not. The king used the barge on other occasions. When the figures which have been given are arranged in tabular form, additional deficiencies became obvious. Items to be included are available for some Parliaments and not for others. However, if to the figures which are known we add charges which may be safely estimated, the outline of the cost of individual Parliaments begins to emerge. It is best to look at each Parliament by itself. Comparisons are not very satisfactory and must, of course, take account of the number of days of sitting. The Long Parliament presents particular problems. The figures are not comparable to those of other Parliaments. The Long Parliament was exceptional both in duration and in the scope of its business. We are looking here at an institution which had taken over the functions, and hence the expenses, of a number of government departments. There has, therefore, been no attempt to extrapolate from the figures we have the total cost of diets or the payments to officials. Yet the Long Parliament provides some of the most interesting accounts, particularly for fuel and stationery, and has been included for this reason.

The total cost of staging a Parliament, or indeed a session, is probably irretrievable and the investigation of it would run far beyond the scope of this essay. The major part of the cost was paid in the same way as the cost of other branches of the government.[111] It was spread widely among those who used Parliament, who paid the numerous fees to clerks and others, who carried the various charges for elections and who sent members to Parliament. Even the privilege of Parliament was said to be a charge on the subject – heavier than the subsidy, a member asserted in 1625 with pardonable exaggeration – particularly in and about London. Members did not pay their debts and many suits at law were stopped. If Parliament (and privilege) continued over a long period, as in 1640, the burden might well be insupportable. Lords in the upper House also paid for Parliament and so did members below, who in addition to meeting some of the charges and fees enumerated above must support themselves in Westminster or London. Such wages as were issued to commoners were wholly inadequate for this purpose.[112]

The Crown also paid for Parliament, both directly and indirectly.[113] Among indirect costs were bills of grace (to sweeten a Parliament for supply)[114] and the general pardon which also cut into royal revenue. Though all the profits of justice did not come to the king's coffers, they enriched many of his subjects and thus made it unnecessary for him to remunerate them in other ways. The pardon, Solicitor-General Heath urged in 1621, would be worth three subsidies. In 1623/4, the pardon was said to have diminished royal revenue by £10,132, a more sober estimate, probably closer to the mark.[115]

The direct cost of Parliament to the Crown, investigated here, was rather modest. In normal times, it did not come to very much – less than the amount of a nobleman's funeral, for example.[116] Certain charges mounted as the days went by, *per diem* wages for cleaning, fuel, stationery, lords' diets. Other charges (repairs, maintenance, robes, the barge) fell more heavily in some years than in others. Overall, a few thousand pounds at most set the stage for king, Lords and Commons for a single Parliament. In determining the life or death of a Parliament, the question of its direct cost could not have greatly influenced the king. The total for all James's Parliaments together (making allowance for the first three sessions of the first Parliament) might have been £10,000 or so. For Charles' reign, without taking account of the Long Parliament, the amount would have been about £8,000.

While pursuing these matters, we have met many of the people involved in a Parliament: the messengers who rode off to all parts of the realm with the king's writ, with word of prorogation or dissolution, the officers, the housekeeper, the yeoman usher, those who swept, cleaned and polished, who supplied fuel and kept the chain in Old Palace Yard, the printers and stationers.

TABLE 3 · THE COST OF PARLIAMENT: 1610–40

	1610 4th session: 165 days 5th session: 52 days inclusive	1614 64 days inclusive	1621 1st session: 126 days 2nd session: 29 days inclusive	1624 108 days inclusive
	£ s. d.	£ s. d.	£ s. d.	£ s. d.
Repairs and furnishings[1] (Works)	395 0 6	400 0 0	283 6 2	
Stationery[2]	147 10 0	94 18 0		
Furnishings[3] (Wardrobe)	207 12 0	211 9 8		138 17 0
Robes[4]		5 0 0		8 15 0
Care of robes[5]		100 0 0	59 8 0	50 6 0
Fuel[6]				
Officers[7]	[378 11 8]	[187 0 0]	[145 10 0]	[215 0 0]
Diets[8]			[748 1 3] (91 days)	[1852 16 4] (76 days)
Cleaning[9]	[10 17 0]	[3 4 0]	[7 15 0]	[5 8 0]
Barge[10]			550 0 0	
Printing[11]				
Messengers[12]	[24 0 0]	[24 0 0]	[144 0 0]	[48 0 0]
Total	[1163 11 2]	[1025 11 8]	[1938 0 5]	[2319 2 4]

Estimated figures are indicated by square brackets.

1. For these figures, see p. 130, n. 2. See also PRO, E 403/1718 (1614); AO 1/2424 (55) (1625); E 351/3262 (1629).
2. See p. 138, nn. 68–70.
3. See p. 134, n. 42.
4. See p. 140, nn. 86, 87.
5. See p. 140, n. 88.
6. See p. 137, n. 65.

1625 1st session: 24 days 2nd session: 12 days inclusive	1626 130 days inclusive	1628–9 1st session: 102 days 2nd session: 54 days inclusive	1640 Short Parliament 23 days inclusive	1640 Long Parliament
£ s. d.	£ s. d.	£ s. d.	£ s. d.	£ s. d.
147 12 11	242 10 0	323 9 3	640 6 0	
				1959 18 7 (1640–8)
	132 10 8	150 17 0	144 13 4	200 0 0
	2 6 8			
	168 1 4			
				3118 16 8 (1642–5)
[175 0 0]	[226 10 0]	[392 6 8]	[163 8 4]	
607 0 1 (27 days)	1244 8 5 (24 days)	1605 11 10 (104 days)	[757 7 10] (18 days)	1553 2 0 (1640–1)
12 0 0	[6 10 0]	21 11 0	[1 3]	
				620 0 0
				(for King) 676 0 8
				(for House of Commons) 657 15 6
[72 0 0]	[48 0 0]	[72 0 0]	[24 0 0]	[24 0 0]
[1013 13 0]	[2070 17 1]	[2565 15 9]	[1729 16 9]	[8809 13 5]

7. See p. 141, nn.92–103. The estimated figures have been compiled by adding the annual salary of the two clerks, the sessional salary for the speaker (except for the Parliament of 1621 when he was apparently not paid) and the total *per diem* costs for other officers (obtained by multiplying the total number of days of the life of the sessions of a Parliament by the appropriate *per diem* rate). Payments to the clerk of the Crown for commissions (at 13s. 4d. each) have been projected from the record in the Lords Journal.

8. See p. 142, nn. 107–9. The estimated figures have been obtained by multiplying

the average *per diem* (when obtainable) for a given Parliament, session or part of a session, by the total number of days the lords actually sat.

9. See pp. 136–7, nn. 56–64. The wages of the yeoman usher of the upper House, responsible for cleaning, and of His Majesty's groom porter's servant, are included with parliamentary personnel. Estimates for cleaning were obtained by multiplying 12*d. per diem* by the total number of days in each session, although as indicated in nn. 56 and 57, the charges do not always correspond with days Parliament was in session.

10. See p. 140, n. 90.

11. See p. 139, nn. 80–4. For £40 claimed by Hunscot from the House of Commons which has been included in the total, see 'The humble Petition and Information of John Hunscot Stationer, . . . to both Houses of Parliament' [1646] (BL Thomason Tract, E.340.15).

12. See p. 141. The charge for carrying writs has been estimated at £24, which seems to be the accepted rate in the Stuart period for general delivery throughout the realm. The charges listed are for writs and for proclamations concerning adjournment, prorogation, or dissolution.

The setting within which parliament met has become clearer. As preparations for the opening day go forward, we know that traffic on the river becomes heavier. Men carry additional provisions to Whitehall. Porters unload tapestries and furniture at the 'back door' of the Old Palace, near the Parliament steps. We hear workmen hammering on the roof of the Old Palace, and others, directed by John White, nailing up an awning by the great east window of the Commons' chamber. Down below there is the clatter of paving-stones replaced and the sound of post-holes driven into the street for railings to hold back the crowds. As darkness comes, strange noises betray those who come out to steal supplies.

Inside the Old Palace, in the Lords' chamber, upholsterers are busy with a frame to fill the woolsacks (alas!) with hay. Their small hammers pound copper nails to fasten crimson tape on the forms. In the Commons' chamber, new matting goes down, new benches for an enlarging House. Men are setting in place the clerks' desks, the tables and benches in committee rooms, the tankards, the chests for records, screens against draughts, and a royal chair of estate. Fire-tools are by the fire-places, bellows, shovels, and lighters. Down cushions are ready for chancellor, treasurer, and Black Rod. The rooms are fresh with the smell of herbs. The king's printer arrives with parchment, paper, pens, tape, ink and a small library of books.

The opening day of Parliament has arrived. In the frosty morning, we hear shovels scraping ice from the street, the flutter of tapestries in the chill wind, the snuffle and stamping of horses. Crowds strain against the railings. Trumpets blare. Peers and bishops in their scarlet robes ride by. The heralds march in brilliant coats. The railings crack as the crowds press forward. The king is coming to seek God's blessing in the Abbey before addressing his Parliament. The setting is complete. The drama can begin.

8

THE PARLIAMENTARY CAREER
OF JOHN PYM, 1621–9

Conrad Russell

On the morning of 27 November 1621, two members of the House of Commons caught Mr Speaker's eye together, and the man who sat down was John Pym.[1] This incident is symbolic of the early career of Pym, who, both in the House of Commons and outside it, was a surprisingly inconspicuous member. In the amply reported Parliament of 1621, he is known to have delivered 37 speeches and one report. The figure should be compared with 62 speeches by William Mallory, 336 speeches by Sir Robert Phelips, and 447 speeches by Sir Edward Coke. Even among these 37 speeches, the majority were brief procedural interventions, only noticed by a minority of the diarists. Even his later friend Sir Thomas Barrington appears not to have known who he was, and reported him under the most inappropriate name of 'Mr Pope'.[2] In a Parliament which proliferated committees on such a scale that leading members were literally unable to fulfil their commitments, Pym was only named to 13 committees. It only took one man, not the whole House, to name a member to a committee. For that reason, one may wonder whether a man who was named to so few was a rather friendless man. When he was named to his first committee, after four weeks, he took home one of its papers and kept it, apparently as a souvenir.[3]

In this, as in many other ways, Pym was a very untypical member of the Commons. To a purist, of course, any individual member is by definition untypical, yet Pym is much more untypical than most. It is therefore the more unfortunate that, because of his importance 20 years later, he is more often used as a 'typical member' than most. This is misleading because the subjects on which he is most often quoted as typical of his fellow-members – his attitudes to recusants, Spain and the Duke of Buckingham – are in fact among the subjects on which the consistency of his views is most nearly unique. All remarks in this essay are meant to apply to Pym alone, unless otherwise stated.

One of the most unusual things about Pym is his lack of a county community. Professor Barnes, Professor Everitt, Dr Hirst, Dr Morrill and others have rightly taught us that to study a seventeenth-century M. P., we need to see him in his local context. It is perhaps Pym's greatest peculiarity that he is an exception to this rule: when he spoke of his country, he did *not* mean his county. Indeed, it is an open question which his county was. What used to be thought to be his single appearance as a J.P. has now vanished before the scrutiny of Mr Richard Cust.[4] In his approach to the work of a Westminster legislator, he was immune from the restraining influence of local office. He belonged to no local community, enjoyed no local power base, and appears to have been uninfluenced in the House of Commons by any ties of localist sentiment.

He was born in Somerset, where his rather scanty hereditary estates were, but before he reached the age of four, his mother's second marriage took him out of the county. He was brought up in Cornwall, in the home of his step-father, Sir Anthony Rous. Kinship counted for as much in Pym's loyalties as neighbourhood counted for little, and his friendships with members of the Rous family lasted till his death, when his step-brother Francis Rous was one of his executors.[5] His wife, Anne Hooke of Bramshott in Hampshire, was a collateral of the Rous family,[6] and gave him tenuous contacts in yet a third county. In 1607, this Hampshire contact was reinforced by his appointment to the only office which exercised a significant influence on his outlook: that of Receiver of Crown Lands for Wiltshire, Hampshire and Gloucestershire. Yet even as a receiver, he appears to have felt that his real loyalties were to the Exchequer, rather than to the counties in which he worked. The Pym who claimed in 1626 that 'the custom of the Exchequer is the law of the kingdom, for so much as concerneth the revenue', was showing the real centre of his loyalties. Chamberlain, with his usual thumbnail accuracy, characterized him as 'one Pym, a receiver'.[7]

The implied social sneer is an important part of this characterization, for in local society, Pym was definitely not 'county'. When he came of age, he appears to have tried to establish himself in Somerset, and failed. He was still trying in 1621, when he gave enthusiastic support to attempts to restore the parliamentary representation of Ilchester and Minehead,[8] but he never even secured appointment as a Somerset commissioner of sewers. One minor Somerset gentleman was bound for him when he became a receiver, and another was one of his feoffees to uses in 1614.[9] With these two exceptions, Somerset gentlemen are conspicuous by their absence from lists of his non-parliamentary contacts. During the 1620s, he made a second attempt to establish himself as a country gentlemen, this time in Hampshire, which seems to have been his base for most of the decade. This attempt was equally unsuccessful. By 1630, he seems to have abandoned it, and was living in the parish of St Andrew's, Holborn. By 1638, he had taken refuge in ideologically congenial company, and was living in what Clarendon called 'a kind of classis' in the house of his friend Richard Knightley of Fawsley in Northamptonshire.[10] This, then, was a man who offended against the most sacred canon of Tudor and Stuart respectability: he had no fixed address.[11] He was, then, able to be uniquely his own man in his contributions to debate in the House of Commons.

Why did Pym fail to establish himself in county society? Part of the answer must be the smallness of his estate, and perhaps also his recklessly long leasing of it. His estate only gave him a marginal claim to be a J.P., yet both his father Alexander and his younger son Charles supported the dignity of a J.P. on the same estate. Perhaps, then, Pym's county failure was in part social. He was a good and expeditious man of business, yet somewhat lacked the light touch. His surviving letters appear to be more single-minded in their concentration on the business in hand than those of any other contemporary except Robert Cecil. In all his adult life, he is only known to have made one joke, and even that was perhaps not meant to be funny. In his diary for 1621, reporting the debate on whether Oxford or Cambridge should be mentioned first in the bill of subsidy, he wrote: 'all those that had been of either University inclined to that place of which they were. But such as had been of neither remained indifferent and were only swayed by reason. So that, upon question, the precedence was appointed to Oxford'. Even here, being a careful man, Pym felt compelled to add: 'confirmed by order'.[12] Except for his loyalty to Oxford, he appears to have been almost devoid of non-functional interests. It is no ground for surprise that a letter about racing should turn out not to be written by John Pym, but by someone else of the same name.[13] Even in the Pym papers, the letter from a Somerset neighbour saying: 'I long to vent my passion for my horses on you which you may furiously expect',[14] could only have been written to its actual recipient, his younger son Charles. When Pym's daughter Dorothy set her heart on a pair of second-hand virginals, which she hoped might be cheap because they were going out of fashion, her request did not go to her father. It went, as such requests do, to the real seat of power, to 'my solicitor general, a pretty preferment I tell you for a young lawyer': it went to her brother Charles.[15]

It was likely to be difficult for a man with so few local roots to secure election to the House of Commons. His first two elections, for the Wiltshire boroughs of Calne in 1621 and Chippenham in 1624, appear to be due to his position as receiver. He sat for Chippenham as the candidate of the corporation franchise, and his chances of future election to the Commons seemed to be severely threatened when the committee of privileges quashed his election in favour of that of Sir Francis Popham, the candidate of the wider freeman franchise. Pym contested this case with passion, and continued to contest the principle of it after he had waived his own election and decided to sit elsewhere. Dr Hirst has shown that he believed in the corporation franchise, but this is not enough to explain why this was one of the rare occasions in his parliamentary career when he made a fool of himself. In the words of Hawarde's diary, having made his election, and now being no party 'he was permitted not only to sit at the committee (of privileges) but heard at large with much favour to say what he could. He was very large, but to very little purpose, in so much as Mr Brooke said he had delivered a great deal of false doctrine'.[16]

It appears to be the lesson of the Chippenham case that Pym could not count on election to the Commons without the assistance of a patron. It was fortunate for him that it coincided with the appearance of a patron able to offer him a regular seat. He was Francis, second Lord Russell of Thornhaugh, who bought up the estates of the bankrupt Earl of Bedford in 1617, and succeeded to his title in 1627.[17] Bedford supplied him with a regular seat, and he never looked elsewhere. Even in 1640, it is doubtful whether he could have secured a seat without the help of a patron. In Bedford (as he will be called for convenience throughout this essay) Pym was fortunate to have acquired a patron who was almost as literal-minded as he was, and one who did very little to limit Pym's freedom of action. Bedford appears to have had an even more insatiable appetite for exact information than Pym, and Pym's chief service to him seems to have been supplying copies of his Commons' diaries, which Bedford read and annotated with scrupulous care.[18] The acquisition of a patron in the Lords doubtless strengthened one of Pym's deepest reflexes, which was to encourage the House of Commons, in moments of crisis, to turn for good correspondency, and indeed for rescue, to the Upper House. However, since this tendency was already apparent in Pym in 1621, before there is any evidence that he enjoyed Bedford's patronage, Bedford cannot be credited with creating it, but only with reinforcing it.[19]

There are a number of occasions on which the two men can be shown to have worked together, such as the impeachment of Manwaring. On one occasion, their collaboration appears to have averted a potentially serious dispute between the Houses. On 3 March 1626, the House of Lords set up a committee, including Bedford, to complain of a breach of their privileges by the House of Commons in sending for the Duke of Buckingham without asking leave of the Lords. The next morning Pym, apparently briefed on what was happening in the Lords, drew attention to what appears to have been a genuine error in the Commons' Journal, and said that they should take the chance to correct a further error by the clerk in claiming that they had 'sent for' Buckingham before they received any message from the Lords. Pym's fiction was duly accepted by all parties to the dispute (including the clerk).[20] One of the most successful examples of Pym's tendency to turn for rescue to the House of Lords concerned the arrest of Digges and Eliot, later in the Parliament of 1626, for words spoken at a committee of both Houses. Pym proposed that all members of both Houses who were present should make a protestation that Digges and Eliot had not spoken the words with which they were charged. Bedford's readiness to make the protestation as soon as it was put before the Lords suggests that he may have been involved in the planning of it, and it was successful: Digges and Eliot were released.[21]

Yet, though it is possible to show many instances of common action between two like-minded people, it is surprisingly hard to show any case of Pym accepting a 'line' either from Bedford, or from his other noble patron, the Earl of Warwick. Pym's persistent, if vain, support for bills to legalize the militia supported a cause strongly backed by Bedford as lord lieutenant of Devon, but there is no reason to doubt that they also represented his own conviction.[22] Perhaps the clearest case of Pym following a patron's line is in his strong support of the private bill to settle the estate of the Earl of Devon, to whom Bedford was a feoffee to uses.[23] On the impeachment of Buckingham, an issue on which people were particularly keen to seek the protection of patrons, Pym followed Bedford's line of speaking against the duke from the beginning, rather than the more cautious waiting game played by Warwick, yet there is no evidence that he needed Bedford's prompting to do so.[24] There is, indeed, one example of Pym's freedom of action being unhampered by his patron's evident disapproval. In his first draft for the 1625 petition on religion, Pym proposed the reform of impropriations, to allow impropriators to be charged to pay higher maintenance to their vicars. Bedford, in his copy of Pym's parliamentary diary, wrote in enormous capitals, 'NO'. Yet Pym's activity in trying to reform impropriations appears to have been undiminished.[25] On the whole, seventeenth-century patrons appear to have operated a political 'whip' only on issues which personally concerned themselves, or on issues where it was necessary for like-minded men to seek safety in numbers and in combined tactics. The Earl of Devon's private bill and the impeachment of Buckingham may serve for examples of the two types of issue.

There were two obsessive themes which ran through the majority of Pym's speeches in the 1620s, and Bedford was largely in agreement with one of them, and wholly in agreement with the other. The two themes, which, appropriately, were the subjects of Pym's first two speeches in the Commons, were the purity of the true religion, and the sanctity of the king's revenue. Pym was, from the beginning of his parliamentary career, one of those who believed the world was a perpetual struggle between the forces of good and evil, of Christ and Antichrist, a battle in which there was no resolution short of final victory. Evil, in the form of popery covert and overt, was constantly present, and 'the remedies of this contagious and dangerous disease we conceive to be of two kinds, the first to consist in strengthening our own religion, the second to the weaking [sic] and abating of theirs'.[26] Pym, partly because he was so nearly immune from the countervailing pressure of good neighbourhood, was able to approach the task of hunting out corrupt and popish religion with a single-mindedness which was shared only by Richard Knightley in Northamptonshire and Sir Thomas Posthumus Hoby in Yorkshire. In this hunt for the forces of evil, he seems to have been particularly on the watch for those who would 'divide us among ourselves, exasperating one party by the odious and factious name of Puritans'. This was the occasion of his maiden speech, an attack on a church papist member of the Commons called Shepherd, who had opposed the Sabbath bill on the ground that it was a 'Puritan' bill. Shepherd annoyed the Commons, but enraged Pym. He held Shepherd guilty of an offence 'against the state, which is the highest object that civil offences can reach unto'. Only Pym thought his offence was '*generale generalissimum*, against the flourishing estate of the kingdom', or that 'such small seeds of tumult and sedition grow up into great dangers, even to the overthrow of states'. He showed very clearly one of the distinguishing marks of his creed, the belief in the universality of evil: 'nothing', he said 'is so apt to multiply as evil'. 'Sins against God are infinite in respect of the object, because they offend an infinite Majesty'. This attempt to divide protestants, he thought, could threaten the overthrow of the state by breeding boldness in the 'common adversary'. He wanted Shepherd expelled, imprisoned during pleasure, fined £100, and exempted out of the general pardon. In 1621, this speech did not catch the mood of the House, and no less a pair of recusant-hunters than Sir Edward Seymour and Sir James Perrott condemned it as 'too violent'. To Pym's obvious disappointment 'the sentence consisted only of his expulsion'.[27] Thus, in his maiden speech, Pym set out what was to become one of his lifelong themes. In 1624, he tried unsuccessfully to have the town of Liverpool punished for contempt for electing a non-communicant, but unconvicted, papist as a member of Parliament. He wanted attacks on papists to be directed at church papists as much as at formal recusants, and stressed that they should consider 'those who by their practice show what they are, as well as those that are convicted'. He wanted to root out popish office-holders, especially deputy lieutenants.[28] The extent to which this determination overrode considerations of immediate political advantage is nowhere more clearly shown than on 3 May 1626, the day after the Commons had decided to transmit their charges against Buckingham to the Lords. On that day, he tried to ensure that the list of recusant office holders presented by the Commons should include the Earl of Arundel, one of the chief supporters of the impeachment, on the ground that he had three recusant servants.[29] There is no need to multiply examples of this kind.

If the gravest crime in Pym's political calendar was that of destroying the purity and the unity of true religion, the second gravest crime was that of defrauding the king of his lawful revenue. This was the offence for which he attacked Sir Giles Mompesson. His attack was almost confined to Mompesson's patent for concealed Crown lands. Others attacked Mompesson for oppressing the subjects: Pym's attack on him was almost entirely confined to the charge of defrauding the king. The wording of Mompesson's patent on conceal-ments allowed him to find as concealed all lands which were not in charge before the auditor of the Exchequer: 'by pretence whereof, he hath gone about to pass some parts of forests, which are not in charge; no more are houses of access, divers ancient castles, other houses, grounds, and woods reserved for his Majesty's own use'.[30] This theme is even clearer in the Parliament Roll text of the declaration in which the concealments charge was ultimately presented to the Lords. In this Pym, to put it no higher, had a very big hand. This declaration draws heavily on Pym's knowledge of Exchequer procedure. For example, the declaration expresses outrage at Mompesson's power to pass land which had been encroached upon; 'herein he may gain things of great and unknown value from his Majesty and thereby dismember most of his Majesty's manors'. Inquisitions to find the value of concealed land could be taken at unsuitable places (for example, inquisitions of land held of the manor of East Greenwich were taken *at* East Greenwich). The values of the inquisitions were accepted even if they showed a lesser value than the lands had formerly yielded to the Crown, and since Mompesson's particulars were made out by the king's remembrancer, the auditor was unable to exercise any control on the finding of lands at under values. The wording of his grant had enabled him to find lands as being concealed which were legitimately in charge in the Pipe Office, and even to acquire some parts of the entailed lands.[31]

This speech shows detailed knowledge of royal revenue, and a serious concern with reforming it: it shows the Pym of whom it has been well said that the Excise is his most enduring memorial. It is, moreover, a concern which is constant throughout Pym's career. This accountant's mind enabled him, alone among the Commons, to see material for a proper legal charge against Buckingham in the case of the prize ship *St Peter*. When Pym heard that the duke's men had removed a number of bags of gold and silver from the ship, he wanted to know 'by what warrant they delivered the money of the King or the Frenchmen to the Duke'. It is the same administrative Pym who complained, in the impeachment of Buckingham, of the reprising of bailiffs' fees in lands granted to the duke. He complained of exchanges between the duke and the Crown, whereby the duke, he said, was enabled to cut down woods, enfranchise copyholders and make new leases, and then surrender the land back to the Crown at an unchanged rent. Pym referred approvingly to the fact that under the civil law 'public treasure was held in the same reputation with that which was dedicated to God and religion' – perhaps the strongest image a man of Pym's outlook could employ.[32]

This is a man who carries more credibility than the rest of the Commons when he claims that 'the Commoners aim not at judgement only, but at reformation'. In this speech, he proposed an Act of Resumption of Crown lands, and also that lands should be entailed upon particular titles, so that the Crown should again benefit from land coming in by escheat. In revenue and supply debates, Pym showed that he was as good as his word. He was prepared to delay supply for the impeachment of Buckingham and for the Petition of Right, but with these two exceptions, every speech he made on subsidies was in favour of giving the largest possible number of subsidies in the shortest possible time, in order, as he put it on 3 May 1626, 'that the bounty of the subsidy may give the King occasion'. On 19 April 1628, he collaborated with Digges and Rich in throwing out a bill for the royal manors of Bromefield and Yale, because the bill was drafted with insufficient care for the royal revenue. In 1626, he prefaced his first attack on the duke with a proposal for 'a select committee to consider of the king's estate and revenues . . . that we may with the Lords . . . take a course for the enabling of the King and preventing danger.' It was the same financial realist who intervened in the 1626 project for a West India Company, to fight the king of Spain on £200,000 a year, with a calculation that the rigging alone for the required ships would cost £120,000.[33]

He was, then, a man for whom the state's service took priority over everything except God's service. Where a man has two such obsessive themes, it is natural to ask whether they were in any way connected with each other. In such matters as the valuation of recusants' estates, there is a direct, but ultimately superficial, connection. Is there a deeper connection between the two obsessions? In the reign of James, it seems that perhaps there was. Pym's views of foreign policy were those of Sir Francis Walsingham and John Foxe: 'your Majesty is the chief head and defender of those who profess the reformed religion, and . . . another prince is the head of the popish religion'.[34] The monarchy, had a divine purpose, which was incompatible with popery. For this divine purpose, the monarchy enjoyed divine right:

> As God, together with the being of things, had infused into them certain
> special qualities and instincts, aptest for the preservation of that being, so,
> by a kind of proportion and resemblance, it might be said, that the state of
> monarchy, which is the perfectest state of government, doth breed in the
> hearts of all princes certain inclinations and affections, apt to preserve
> monarchies . . . every prince desireth (touching human dependency) to be
> within his own dominions, as God is in the world; that all power and favour
> should be derived from him, all services dedicated to him. This indepen-
> dancy upon others is broken in all that party adhering to the church of
> Rome, by their subjection to foreign ecclesiastical jurisdiction.

In the true tradition of Foxe's cult of the Christian Emperor and of the Act of Supremacy, he thought that popery was incompatible with monarchy, and incompatible in part because of 'the popularity of them, against which in itself all kings have a kind of repugnancy'.[35]

The king, then, ruled by divine right: 'the image of God's power is expressed in your regal dignity'.[36] But the English monarchy enjoyed divine right for a purpose: the purpose of warring against God's enemies. For this purpose, the monarchy was too weak. Pym the financial realist was well aware that the monarchy lacked the resources for the task allotted to it by Pym the religious enthusiast. On 27 November 1621, he commented on possible plans for a Continental land war: 'that this war must be supplied by money, wherein we are too weak for the King of Spain'.[37] Seeing so fundamental a defect, Pym was of course committed to rectifying it. The bounty received by the Duke of Buckingham he thought the more dangerous because it was had in time of war, 'when there appears great wants and hazards of the kingdom, for the provision of the navy, and guard of the seas in his own charge, the kingdoms threatened with invasions, and potent enemies'.[38] The security of the monarchy, then, was essential to the security of religion.

So long as Pym was certain he lived under a protestant prince, his themes could be reconciled. In 1624, when war against Spain was being prepared, reconciling them was a simple work of piety and patriotism. In the subsidy debate, he said that 'we have made one step from the greatest danger that ever threatened us God grant we relapse not again' and moved to grant the full sum of six subsidies and twelve fifteenths which the king was requesting and to agree on the particulars at a committee of both houses.[39] On 2 March he seconded a motion by Digges 'to give thanks to the Lords for the correspondency between the Houses, to the prince for his favour and constancy to religion, to the King for accepting our advice in so great a work, and that he will declare himself to the world, and that there may be through the kingdom a general thanks to God for his gracious favour herein' – a speech recorded in the more secular glass of Hawarde's diary as 'Mr. Pym *al* no purpose'.[40]

For the whole of James's reign, Pym retained his confidence that he was living under a protestant prince. He might often think that James was asleep at his post, and that 'his Majesty's . . . royal disposition is not yet bent to that which we desire'. It might be necessary to explain to James that, in believing he could avoid popish plots by lenity in executing the recusancy laws, he had, literally, failed to understand the nature of the beast: 'for having gotten favour they will expect a toleration, after toleration they will look for equality, after equality for superiority, and after superiority they will seek the subversion of that religion which is contrary to theirs'. Pym seems to have been pleased with this sentence, since he got it copied into the Commons' petitions on religion in both 1621 and 1625.[41] Yet he always thought James was a protestant. It was, after all, hard to regard the man who had been on the throne on the fifth of November 1605 as an agent of the international popish conspiracy. Moreover, as Pym often remembered, James had spent 'upwards of sixty pages' proving the pope to be Antichrist. It might be advisable to protect James, as it had been advisable to protect the equally misguided Queen Elizabeth, by reviving the Bond of Association, to ensure that offices were held by those who were loyal both to religion and the king's person. Yet even if Pym did not believe James was well cast in the role of godly prince, he did not believe he was beyond the reach of a prompter. Thus he was enabled to work with the grain of the political system in which he lived, and to regard a Parliament as an agent, not for the fruitless task of trying to coerce a king, but for the more congenial and practicable one of persuading him: 'herein lies the principal part of our labour, to win the King, for he is the first mover, from whence all the prosperity of this and other affairs of Parliament must be derived'.[42]

This belief was crucial to the views of the Jacobean Pym about the nature and function of a Parliament. His was the administrative view of Pym the receiver, the view of a man of business almost untouched by Cokeian legalism. On 7 December 1621, he said that 'the liberties and privileges of the House are but accessory, and bills are the end of a Parliament. And therefore he would not that the end of preserving our liberties should hinder the end for which we came hither'. On 18 December he repeated the same point: 'moved to settle the good bills and articles now in agitation, and then if we have any more time to spend it about our privileges, for that thother are *magis principale*'.[43] His diary also gives the impression that in 1621 he did not want, either to start a privilege dispute, or to enter into any detailed foreign policy debate. He noted that the first attempt to make an issue of the restraint of Sir Edwin Sandys was 'well passed over' by the House, and the speech of Sir George Hastings, the only attempt at a really detailed discussion of foreign affairs, is dismissed in the words 'here were interposed some unseasonable motions'.[44] By contrast, he recorded the contents of bills in unusual and valuable detail, and showed himself much concerned about such practical points as whether it should be possible to convict a drunkard on the unsupported oath of his drinking companion.[45] Yet he showed a readiness to leave things to administrative action which his colleagues sometimes found surprising. For example, he seems to have offended Coke and Alford by maintaining that James's proclamation condemning the patent for alehouse recognizances was a sufficient condemnation of the patent, without the support of an Act of Parliament.[46] A week later, he persuaded the House to throw out a bill to move a court leet on one of Sir William Brereton's manors, on the ground that the king could, if it pleased him, perfectly well do this without an Act of Parliament, and therefore it was not worth passing one.[47]

His attitude to parliamentary privilege appears to have been strictly functional, immune from the element of self-importance which was so essential a part of the subject in the minds of Coke and Phelips. He objected to the banning of discussion, and to the imprisonment of members, yet when he saw a privilege dispute beginning, he wished 'to cast balm to heal the wound, not to make it wider'. In 1626, Coke, who was claiming to be a member in spite of being a sheriff, claimed parliamentary privilege in a lawsuit. Pym commented: 'our privileges given us [sic] as in respect of our attendance: if we have forbore his attendance we may forbear his privilege'. In 1628, when Phelips objected to the king's message asking them to have no Easter recess, Pym asked 'cannot we accept a motion from his Majesty as willingly as we do from a member of this House?'[48] As late as the end of May 1628, Pym was still arguing in a way which convinced Sir Edward Coke he did not have the root of the matter in him. The Commons were debating Monson's revival of Lepton's patent for a monopoly of engrossing bills and processes in the Council of the North. Pym agreed to the condemnation of the patent because he thought the monopoly of engrossing bills a grievance because Monson was unskilful in it, yet he insisted on dividing the House to prevent a condemnation of the monopoly of making processes. He said: 'as for the process it is in the king to erect a court, shall not he that erects the court appoint who shall make the process'? Coke claimed that this speech showed that Pym did not understand the statute of Monopolies.[49]

All these views on the nature and function of a Parliament were inoffensive to the monarchy, even if offensive to Coke or Alford. Under James, there is no evidence, except on the single subject of impeachment, that Pym had any wish to change the place or function of Parliament in the state. Parliament, like other things, was to be made, as far as possible, an efficient instrument of business. This committed Pym to a concern with efficient procedure, to a dislike of time-wasting debate,[50] to the voting of sufficient supply, and to the dispatch and efficient drafting of bills. In the words of Hawarde's law French: 'Mr. Pym will no bill sans order. Private bills in le morning'.[51] Under James, there is nothing which justifies classifying him as in any sense a member of a parliamentary opposition.

If this is the case, it is necessary to explain why he was imprisoned after the 1621 session. The real reasons for the 1621 imprisonments may not have been the same as their ostensible grounds.[52] The ostensible grounds for Pym's imprisonment appear to have concerned his speeches of 27 and 28 November. It is possible to look through these speeches, and find passages which might have given offence. The proposal to revive the Bond of Association, the proposal for the king to employ a commission drawn from both Houses to execute the recusancy laws and a reference to the king's 'wariness of his own person' might all have given offence.[53]

Yet it is worth looking at the comment of a sensitive contemporary writing without hindsight, even from a week later. On 1 December Chamberlain commented: 'I have heard extraordinary commendation of a neat speech made by one Pimme, a receiver, wherein he laboured to show that the King's clemency, justice, bounty, facility, peaceable disposition and other his natural virtues were by the adverse party perverted and turned to a quite contrary course; and though he were somewhat long in the explanation of these particulars, yet he had great attention, and was exceedingly commended both for matter and manner'.[54] It is hard to believe that Chamberlain or his informants had so little capacity to recognize an offensive speech. It is therefore worth wondering whether Pym had done anything which might have encouraged the duke or any other councillor to give exaggerated reports of his speech to the king. He had: there is one thing that all those punished after the 1621 Parliament had in common: they were all on the short list of members who had impeded Buckingham's plans and endangered his security by taking up the case of Lepton and Goldsmith. In this case, Pym's contribution had been one of the most effective. It was his immediate motion to seal their studies and search their papers which had made the whole case possible.[55] If this is the cause, the duke and not the king was largely responsible for Pym's imprisonment. The imprisonment does not appear to have soured his attitude to the king, nor to have alienated him from the Court as a whole. He was released on the intercession of Bedford's friend Lord Treasurer Cranfield, who required his services on official business.[56] In 1624, he made no attempt to support the making of a privilege issue out of his imprisonment, and even opposed the very limited motion of Mallory, that in future the clerk, who appears to have been the Council's informant, should not set down a man's name to a motion. Unlike many of his leading parliamentary colleagues, he seems to have never made any attempt to come to terms with the duke, but until the death of James, there was apparently nothing else to disqualify him from using his administrative talents as a holder of high office.

Pym's eagerness to develop the process of impeachment cannot be held to have disqualified him as a candidate for office. If it were a disqualification, it would have ruled out many of the Council, led by Pembroke, Arundel, the duke and the Prince of Wales. It was Pym, well before any other member, who formed a clear picture of what later became the recognized procedure of impeachment, with the Commons as prosecutors and the Lords as judges, and it was in the impeachment of Manwaring, in 1628, that he first turned this picture into fact.[57] The Commons, he thought, should be responsible for what he called 'the inquisition of the fact', the Lords for judgment, and the king for its execution. As he put it, 'the high court of Parliament is the great eye of the kingdom to find out offences and punish them'. It was a task which was to be undertaken in collaboration with the king, not in opposition to him: 'for execution, left to the king wholly, who hath the sword'.[58] For this reason, impeachment in the 1620s was not a suitable weapon to secure ministerial responsibility. It is, as we have recent cause to remember, possible to use the power of pardon to frustrate the purpose of an impeachment. Pym was well aware of this fact, and had no idea of making any use of impeachments without the king's consent. Indeed, many of the numerous delinquents he pursued were much too small to be put through the cumbrous process of an impeachment. Instead, the king was to be petitioned to take the necessary action against them.

That Pym's aim was not ministerial responsibility is perhaps best shown by listing the delinquents he attacked, most of whom could not by any stretch of imagination be called ministers. They are Shepherd, Mompesson, Sir John Bennet (a corrupt probate judge), Floyd, Lambe and Cradock (two corrupt officials of ecclesiastical courts), Lepton and Goldsmith, Dr Anian, president of Corpus Christi College, Oxford, who was charged with bribery, buggery and disparagement of preaching, Simon Dormer, a Popish schoolmaster, the town of Liverpool, Richard Montagu the Arminian, Bishop Harsnett of Norwich, Buckingham's client Edward Clerke (for rude words about Sir Edward Coke), Cleydon and Lewis (two more popish schoolmasters), the Duke of Buckingham, More and Dyott (for ill-advised speech in the House of Commons), Boyd, a projector, and John Cosin the Arminian. In 1628, Pym had a new list: Baber, recorder of Wells, Walter Brooke, who had carried a young woman beyond seas, where she suffered a fate worse than death (by becoming a nun), Burgess, vicar of Witney, who had made rude remarks about puritans, the deputy lieutenants of Cornwall, Roger Manwaring, William Welby, deputy lieutenant, Edmund Sawyer auditor of the Exchequer, and the Countess of Buckingham. In 1629, he added Aleyn, who had made rude remarks about puritans, Lord Lambert, who had illegally levied militia rates, and Bishop Neile.[59] Of these, only the cases of Buckingham and Neile really raise issues of ministerial responsibility. On the cases of Cranfield and Bacon, Pym remained silent. Pym's attacks on these delinquents, like the attacks of earlier parliaments on Mary Queen of Scots, were not meant to hinder the monarchy: they were meant to help it. Yet they do show the extraordinary force of Pym's zeal for rooting out delinquents: if the members of the 1620s were to be nicknamed along the lines of Sir John Neale's famous 'choir', Pym would indubitably be classed as 'Pym the prosecutor'.

Under James, Pym's rather excessive loyalty was in a tradition which had been well established in the days of Sir Francis Walsingham and Sir Walter Mildmay. If he had more concern for the king's safety than the king himself, they had had more concern for the queen's safety than she had herself. If he thought the king allowed some men to hold office in the Church who were less godly than they should be, Walsingham and Mildmay had thought Queen Elizabeth did the same. James's attitude to Abbot could even be compared favourably to Queen Elizabeth's attitude to Grindal.

For Pym, the confidence that he lived under a protestant prince was rapidly destroyed during the first three years of the reign of Charles I. The cause of the destruction was the rise of Arminianism. It is perhaps a significant coincidence that the rise of Arminianism happened at exactly the same time as Pym began to acquire some knowledge of the inner workings of the Court. Before he was taken up by Warwick, Pym had enjoyed an exceptional ignorance of Court affairs. Most leading members had their Court contact: Pym, except for what appears to have been a purely business contact with Cranfield, did not. The Pym who, in 1621, had believed that a royal proclamation was a sufficient security for the abolition of a monopoly was showing a naïveté which only ignorance could explain. For such a man, the discovery that the Court was not always what it seemed was likely to be a shock at any time. When this shock merged with the shock of the rise of Arminianism, the reverberations lasted the rest of Pym's life.

Dr Tyacke has identified Pym as the leader of anti-Arminian feeling in the

Commons,[60] and similarly, the rise of Arminianism should be identified as a watershed in Pym's career. For Pym, who had been a friend of John Preston before his election to Parliament,[61] the belief in predestination and election was one of the central and defining points, not of puritanism, but of international protestantism.[62] This belief runs through the whole of his circle of friends: every surviving will we have from a friend of Pym or from a member of the Rous family asserts, with dogmatic clarity, its certainty of its author's own election.[63] For Pym, predestination was the doctrine of the Church of England because it was so laid down by law. It was laid down in the Thirty-Nine Articles and the Book of Homilies, both of which were confirmed by Act of Parliament. For Pym, then, an assault on predestination was an assault on protestantism, an assault on law, and an assault on the position of Parliament within the state. Above all, it was an attempt to subvert the state, both by depriving it of that religious unity without which it could not function, and by destroying that unity between king and people without which no government could be other than arbitrary.

Dr Tyacke emphasizes the far-reaching re-definition of 'puritanism' attempted by the Arminians, and this appears to have been one of the points which offended Pym most. The Committee of Religion reported, possibly in Pym's words, in 1625: 'if Puritans be so bad, it were good we knew them. But Mr Montague leaves this uncertain, for by his opinion we may all be Puritans. Mr Ward and Mr Yates are Puritans, and yet these are men that subscribe and conform'. In Pym's words in 1628:

> He seems to make a difference between the church in foreign parts and the church of England. As for his charge of sedition, it is clear by dividing the kingdom under the name of Puritans, labouring to bring his Majesty in jealousy with his subjects and to stir up others in hatred against such. First he lays the name Puritans upon the King's subjects that are dutiful and honest subjects in truth. At the first this word was given to them that severed themselves from the church, but he says there are Puritans in heart and Puritans in doctrine, as of predestination and reprobation. Also this division and aspersion is new, and under this name he comprehends some of our bishops. Also he labours to bring these persons into dislike with his Majesty as dangerous persons.[64]

Pym was the first member of the Commons to take up the issue of Arminianism, in 1624, yet it appears that his initial reflex was to look for help to authority. He believed that James's warrant for the printing of Montagu's first book had been procured 'without his privity, as it should seem', and after James's death, he showed an entire, and justified confidence in the readiness of Archbishop Abbot to put down the new doctrine if he could. Alarmed though he was, Pym seems to have continued to believe for some time that he was dealing with 'boldness of private men', which, with the aid of the House of Lords, could be duly put down by authority.[65] The idea that the centre of popery was actually at the English Court was one so dreadful that it seems to have taken Pym a long time to absorb it. He took part in the attack on the duke, yet he did not attack the duke's religion. It was Sherland, not Pym, who accused the duke of being the patron of a semi-Pelagian semi-popish faction.[66] Pym thought the duke had brought the state into danger of 'final destruction' by exhausting its revenues, but in May 1626, he does not yet appear to have thought that the duke was an agent of international popery. The realization that Arminianism was being securely, openly and knowingly supported from within the Court appears to have come to him during the campaign to elect the duke chancellor of Cambridge University. On 3 June 1626, he said 'that a member of the Lords' house went to Cambridge to solicit this business for the Duke, with the consent of some others who have been agents to utter Montague's book, as Dr Cosins and Mr Mason have explained themselves about this that it may be to perfect a conspiracy to bring in Arminianism'.[67] For Pym, this speech appears to have been the crossing of the Rubicon, the moment at which the notion that the Court harboured a 'popish and malignant party' was born.

When Parliament reassembled in 1628, the Pym who came back to Westminster had changed as fundamentally as the Church of England. He had also suddenly become a frequent speaker. Over a third of all Pym's speeches during the 1620s were made in the Parliament of 1628. He had also suddenly acquired an intense concern with questions of law and liberties, on which his previous silence had been so complete as to be deafening. As Hexter said, 'Pym's love of the law had about it a certain quality of intermittency'.[68] His support for the Petition of Right was enthusiastic, vocal and unyielding, and in stating it, he began the enunciation of a rapidly developing body of political ideas. He used the concept of the birthright: 'a man as soon as he is born is born into the world, not into a prison'. He became one of the surprisingly few vocal adherents of Coke's doctrine of the ancient constitution: 'we are upon the point of imprisonment. Sir Edward Coke can say much and tell you what a plain right the subject enjoys. Nay the conqueror himself though he conquered the kingdom he conquered not the law.'[69] He later claimed that William the Conqueror had obtained the Crown by composition with the people.[70] He was so eager to reject notions of arbitrary power and reason of state that he came perilously close to denying the Scriptural text 'render unto Caesar the things that are Caesar's':

And though he would not presume to expound a place of Scripture, yet as an historical observation he desired their Lordships to remember that the Jews were at that time a conquered nation, and so for their laws persons and estates subject to the absolute power of the Romans who were the conquerors, whereby this case is far different from the case of this kingdom, which hath been always free and hereditary.[71]

Pym's new cult of the law and the ancient constitution was not meant to diminish the monarchy: king and law were, for him, coeval and interdependent. As he put it, 'we are subject to a kingly power with an established law'. Both, in their turn, rested on the law of God, the ultimate source of all authority: 'no king, no council, no judge, either by God's law or man's, can lay imprisonment without cause, which not at his pleasure, but originally in the party himself'.[72]

Yet, even in the middle of his new cult of law, Pym had too much appreciation of the facts of political power to believe that it was possible to use the law as a coercive force to bind the king. On one offer to confirm liberties in general words, he commented: 'we have it already and it has been broken already', and significantly went straight on to express his deepening concern about martial law.[73] Pym was well aware that the king possessed soldiers, and that *inter arma silent leges*: 'these heads are most considerable, the unlawfulness of these men, the forced contributions, the exemption of them from law, the superinducing of an unlegal authority, the uselessness of them, and the jealousness and religion of them'.[74]

Pym was well aware that the king could not be forcibly controlled by law: the law was an instrument for proceeding against lesser mortals, and, if the king so chose, one of the greatest guarantees of the love and loyalty of his subjects. In the debate of 6 May about whether to take the king's word for a confirmation of their liberties, Pym's objection was not to taking the king's word: in the last resort, he knew there was no other security. His objection was that the king had not said the right word:

> the King's word were enough if we knew how far he meant to express that word. A comfort to us to hear the King. If he understood the laws, he would not err. We have a greater tie on him, at his coronation, in his conscience. If the King should say that he is better satisfied in the law than he was the last year, and apply it to our business, I should rely upon it. But I hear not the King say that we shall have no more imprisonments for loans, nor that his name shall not be used in such like; that it shall not be pretended to be matter of state when it is not so.[75]

It would seem clear on chronology alone, even without the aid of logic, that it was the rise of Arminianism which first persuaded Pym that the rule of law was in danger. Yet, believing it was in danger, he did not become less eager to supply the king with money. He moved that 'the King may not lose Tonnage and Poundage, nor yet take it against law', and offered to 'settle it in as ample ways as ever any of his predecessors enjoyed it'. He said the same in 1629, claiming that voting Tonnage and Poundage was the only way to 'sweeten the business with the King', and that by comparison with the liberties of the kingdom, 'the privilege of this House is but a mean matter'.[76]

In trying to 'sweeten the King', Pym was trying to preserve something which was, for him, bigger than the law, though it was interdependent with it. He was trying to prevent something akin to what Locke was later to call 'the dissolution of society'. A threat to the principle of government was more than simply a threat to the rule of law: 'there are some laws which are co-essential and con-natural with government, which being broken, all things run into confusion'.[77] For Pym, the greatest threat came from what he saw as the making of a division between the king and the people. Without unity all the circumstances which made a rule of law possible would be lacking. The destruction of unity was a task Pym believed had been begun by the Arminians, and he saw it carried on most dangerously by Roger Manwaring, a clergyman who had preached that the Forced Loan was due by the law of God, and that those who refused it were, as he put it 'temporal recusants'.[78] Pym was well aware of the danger which arose if such arguments were put to the king while parliaments were not adequately supplying him, and took the occasion to remind his hearers once again of the need for a greater permanent endowment for the Crown. Yet, if the king would have practical excuse for listening to Manwaring, this merely appeared to make his insinuations more dangerous. Pym accused him of 'a wicked intention to avert his Majesty's mind from calling of Parliaments', and when he thought of what would happen if there were no Parliaments, it was, significantly, their function in rooting out offences of which he thought first: 'If Parliaments be taken away, mischiefs and disorders must needs abound without any possibility of good laws to reform them; grievances will daily increase without opportunity or means to redress them, and what readier way can there be to distractions betwixt the king and people, to tumults and distempers in the state than this?'.

This threatened the grounds of political obligation: 'he hath acted the part of the Romish Jesuits, they labour our destruction by dissolving the Oath of Allegiance taken by the people, he doth the same work by dissolving the oath of protection, and justice, taken by the King'. It was an attempt to corrupt 'his Majesty's conscience, which is the sovereign principle of all moral actions'. In one of his most revealing phrases, Pym said that if taxation should cease to be by consent, the subjects would lose the means 'by any act of bounty or benevolence to ingratiate themselves to their sovereign'. It was, as he put it, an attempt to alienate the king's affections from his subjects. He claimed, as he was to claim again in the trial of Strafford, that the like offence had never before been committed. He thought that Manwaring was doing no less than dissolving the ancient constitution, a dissolution which he thought threatened the king as much as it threatened the subjects.[79] There is an ominous warning in the description of Manwaring's doctrine as 'spiritual poison offered to the ear of the king, appropriating omnipotency to princes. Where we note the grace of the king, not to be taken up by these immodest terms: Herod, consenting to the blasphemy etc, was eaten up of worms'.[80]

Pym's speech to the Lords on Manwaring came early in the miserable week between the king's first and second answers to the Petition of Right. In the next two days Pym first began the remonstrance debate by moving, through his tears, for the doors to be locked, and 'then added the state of Ireland for matter of religion. Many companies soldiers there commanded by popish recusants'.[81] In this picture of an army in Ireland which may be employed here to reduce this kingdom, we are suddenly within measureable distance of the Pym of 1640. It is, then, no surprise to read, in Oliver St John's obituary tribute to Pym that, about 1630, 'fearing that popery might overgrow this kingdom', he intended to make 'some plantation in foreign parts, where the profession of the Gospel might have a free course'.[82] St John was undoubtedly right in the priority he gave to religious over constitutional issues in Pym's intellectual make-up. Pym was not much interested in the privileges of Parliament, and even the rule of law perhaps mattered to him more because it guaranteed the true religion in England than for any other reason. When Pym accused Montagu of laying the charge of puritanism upon 'conformable persons', it was law which gave him the measure of the degree of conformity he regarded as acceptable.[83] For him, the rule of law without the security of true religion could never be more than the most tenuous form of security. Law, for him, was a measure of the mutual obligation of king and people to each other, and without unity in religion, such a sense of mutual obligation would be quickly replaced by something approaching Hobbes's state of war. Without a common body of belief, he believed there could be no consent, no law, and no liberty. It was this common body of belief which he believed to have been destroyed by the Arminians. Was it a self-fulfilling prophecy in which he said, in April 1626, that 'the raising of a division or distemper in religion doth often meet in this *tertio*, to ruin the body of the church and state'?

If Pym was making self-fulfilling prophecies, it was not an activity in which he and his friends could claim a monopoly. It is equally arguable that Laud was making a self-fulfilling prophecy when he said, also in 1626:

> 'they, whoever they be, would overthrow *sedes ecclesiae*, the seats of ecclesiastical government, will not spare (if ever they get power), to have a pluck at the throne of David. And there is not a man that is for parity, all fellows in the church, but he is not for monarchy in the state. And certainly either he is but half-headed to his own principles, or he can be but half-hearted to the throne of David.

In 1626, Pym was no more genuinely in favour of 'parity' than Laud was in favour of 'popery'. These two growing fears present a mirror image to each other, and came to enjoy a curious interdependence, each being necessary to validate the other. Francis Rous's fear of popish frogs out of the bottomless pit is curiously similar to Richard Montagu's fear of puritan 'allobrogical dormice'. Throughout the reign of James, this mutual commerce of fear had been soothed by the near-certainty that nothing very dramatic was going to happen. In 1625, the accession of a young and energetic king brought these mutual fears to a point where they became uncontrollable. As Laud remarked, 'break unity once, and farewell strength'.[84]

Dr Tyacke is indubitably right that in starting the chain of events it was Charles and Laud who were the innovators.[85] The gulf between the Pym of 1624 and the Pym of 1628 shows how quickly a shrewd observer reacted to them. It is worth remembering that both Clarendon and the Grand Remonstrance, from their very different points of view, firmly claimed that the origins of the crisis of 1640–2 should not be sought any further back than the accession of Charles I.[86] When we find that, as early as 1628–9, John Pym was already looking back to the days of King James, the man who had proved the pope to be Antichrist and upheld the decrees of the Synod of Dort, the man who had censured Vorstius and condemned Cowell,[87] it is time for us to wonder whether what they tell us three times is true.

9

'THE RAMOTH-GILEAD OF THE GOOD': URBAN CHANGE AND POLITICAL RADICALISM AT GLOUCESTER 1540–1640

Peter Clark

Few provincial towns more amply justified Edward Hyde's attack on 'that factious humour which possessed most corporations' during the Civil War than the county town of Gloucester. From the late 1620s the city was increasingly at odds with the Crown over political and religious issues and in 1640 returned as a burgess to the Long Parliament, Thomas Pury, one of the leading supporters of the Root and Branch bill.[2] In 1643 Gloucester held out valiantly against a lengthy royalist siege and the defenders' success was, to quote Bishop Goodman, 'indeed the turning of the wheel, for ever after the parliament-forces prevailed . . .' Despite the vicissitudes of war and political settlement, the city remained loyal to successive parliamentary régimes. After the Restoration it was duly and harshly punished by the Crown.[3]

To understand Gloucester's development as a leading radical stronghold we shall need to examine not only the short-term influences of the decade or so before 1640, but also the major secular problems and pressures affecting all aspects of the community from the mid-sixteenth century. Many of these problems – demographic, economic, social, political, and cultural – were not unique to Gloucester but exemplified the general dislocation which has recently been seen as widespread among English county towns during the Tudor and early Stuart periods.[4] On the other hand, it will be argued here that the very intensity of Gloucester's problems helped forge a particularist strategy of civic survival – a vision of an embattled godly commonwealth, of a city on the hill. It was this perception of the community which in the rapidly changing religious and political climate of the late 1620s and 1630s played a vital part in the progressively bitter conflict between the city and the Crown.

I

Gloucester was fairly typical of the hundred or so second-rank towns in Tudor England. A Roman settlement, it owed much of its early importance to its location at the first easy crossing place above the mouth of the Severn and at the centre of a communication network stretching north–south along the Severn valley and east–west towards London and Wales. By 1483 it had acquired an impressive array of corporate privileges including an extensive jurisdiction over two hundreds of the county, the so-called inshire. John Leland noted in the 1530s: 'the town of Gloucester is ancient, well builded of timber and large and strongly defended with walls'.[5] At this time it had a population approaching 4,000 and held second place (after Bristol) in a county hierarchy of nearly 30 urban centres, most of them small market towns.[6]

In the century before 1640 Gloucester's population grew substantially to just over 5,000. Part of the increase resulted from natural growth, but the major share came from immigration. While parish register evidence indicates there may have been a surplus of baptisms over burials in better-off inner parishes like Holy Trinity, this was almost certainly cancelled out by deficits in poorer outer parishes such as St Aldate's. With plague increasingly an urban phenomenon, there were serious outbreaks at Gloucester in 1573, 1578, 1593–4, 1603–4, 1625–6 and 1637–8.[7] In critical decades like the 1590s even respectable parishes incurred net losses of population and had to recruit new inhabitants from outside the community. Gloucester witnesses appearing before the diocesan courts between 1595 and 1640 provide substantial biographical data to confirm that migration was a dominant feature in the city's demographic growth (see table 4).[8]

Less than a quarter of the witnesses had failed to move at some time in their lives, nearly a half had previously resided outside the city limits, while about

TABLE 4 · PHYSICAL MOBILITY AMONG GLOUCESTER
WITNESSES 1595–1640

	male %	female %
Stationary	27.2	19.0
Unspecified move	16.2	23.0
Move within city	7.6	10.0
Move from county	23.8	22.0
Extra county move	25.2	26.0
Sample	210	100

25 per cent had come to Gloucester from outside the county – from adjoining areas like Herefordshire and Worcestershire as well as from further afield. Though our sample is too small to make any positive correlation between migrational patterns and occupational groupings, a significant number of the incomers were what we might call *betterment* migrants, respectable men and women travelling fairly short distances in the hope of economic improvement. Many of them became urban apprentices. Thus of 1,643 apprentices whose indentures were enrolled at Gloucester between 1595 and 1640 31 per cent were city-born, 44 per cent had come from the county, whereas only 16 per cent had travelled from outside Gloucestershire. Again over 40 per cent were the offspring of gentlemen, yeomen, or substantial distributive traders.[9]

A very different and, in magisterial eyes, far less acceptable kind of physical mobility before 1640 involved *subsistence* migrants – poor servants, labourers, and petty craftsmen who had been driven on to the road by dire necessity and who poured into Gloucester, particularly during periods of major difficulty like the 1620s. Of the many vagrant poor arrested in the city in the early seventeenth century, a substantial number had tramped over 100 miles, mostly travelling across western England.[10] Others, however, came from nearer home. Rural over-population was a severe problem in Elizabethan Gloucestershire, especially in the poorer pastoral areas of the Vale of Tewkesbury and the Cotswold slopes where the situation was aggravated by enclosure.[11] Some poor labourers migrated into local market towns or squatted in the Forest of Dean; others flocked to Gloucester hoping for work, relief, or a few scraps from the bustling markets. Swelling the ranks of the city's many indigenous poor they posed a serious threat to social order and civic government.[12] In this way demographic pressure was a key variable affecting city fortunes and the mentality of the ruling classes before the Civil War.

2

The crucial difficulty with Gloucester's population growth, both native and immigrant, was that it coincided almost exactly with a period of profound and in certain respects brutal change for the city's economic structure. During the late Middle Ages Gloucester had a strongly pluralistic economy, its markets servicing the neighbouring countryside, its port trafficking in coastal and foreign commerce, its religious houses attracting pilgrims and other visitors, its industries employing many citizens. In the fifteenth century Gloucester's leading industry was still the manufacture of woollen cloth, though the making of metalware ran it close, with capping not far behind. The overall picture both before and after 1500 seems to have been one of moderate prosperity.[13] In 1487–8 it is true the city fathers complained to the king of 'the great ruin and decay of the habitations, mansions and tenements of the said town . . .', but such complaints were part of the conventional rhetoric of petitioning the Crown. When, in 1536, the city secured its inclusion in a general statute for the repair of towns one suspects that Gloucester was jumping on a bandwagon set in motion by other centres. Certainly there is little hard evidence that the city was undergoing that deep-seated economic crisis which we are told was affecting many established towns, particularly in eastern England, during the first half of the sixteenth century. Judging from the freemen's lists clothing and capping were still prospering,[14] while Gloucester merchants built ships to trade with France and the Mediterranean and expanded ties with Bristol, which was also enjoying fairly buoyant trading conditions until mid-century. Even the economic loss of the old religious houses in Gloucester was more than offset by the accession of a large episcopal household and church courts as a result of the creation of the new diocese in 1541.[15]

Severe difficulty in Gloucester's economy mainly occurred after 1550. At root was the contraction of the city's textile industries. In the early 1580s the magistrates asked: 'whether the trades of cappers and clothiers be not much decayed in Gloucester within twenty or thirty years past?' To some extent the answer can be discerned from the changing occupational structure outlined in table 5.[16]

Even making allowance for the difficulties in comparing the sets of data, there seems to be little doubt that the textile and allied clothing trades registered a major fall in importance. From their leading position in the occupational

TABLE 5 · OCCUPATIONAL STRUCTURE OF TUDOR AND
STUART GLOUCESTER
(EXPRESSED AS % OF PERIOD SAMPLE)

		1535–54	1608	1653–72
1	Gentlemen	1.7	9.4	7.5
2	Professional	0.2	0.3	0.5
3	Distributive	8.3	16.9	7.7
4	Service workers	2.9	2.6	3.9
5	Agricultural	10.5	5.4	1.4
6	Food processors	15.2	14.9	18.1
7	Metal processors	5.2	8.2	12.3
8	Wood workers	3.8	3.4	6.3
9	Textile workers	15.4	12.2	5.8
10	Leather crafts	12.9	12.2	18.8
11	Clothing workers	17.1	8.2	11.3
12	Building workers	2.8	3.8	1.3
13	Misc. skilled	1.2	2.5	4.9
14	Marine	2.8	0.0	0.2
	Sample	421	390	586

order in the early Tudor period, they had fallen by the seventeenth century to secondary status, out-paced by a number of other trades. As one weaver declared about 1635: 'whereas there were heretofore above a hundred looms going, now there are not above six or seven looms constantly wrought in all the city'. Those clothiers and weavers who remained employed only a few workers. The collapse of capping was no less striking. In 1583 it was said that 'before Sir Thomas Bell and one Mr Falkoner kept great numbers of people at work spinning and knitting of caps . . . [but] now there are very few set to work in that trade'.[17] Clothing suffered from stiff rural competition encouraged by the exemption of the city's main rivals, the Stroudwater clothiers, from the 1557 Act which sought to confine clothing to towns.[18] But Gloucester's plight was further exacerbated by the growing dominance of London merchants in the marketing of cloth which destroyed the city's chances of serving as an outlet for rural textiles. In the case of capping, the principal culprit seems to have been a growing fashion for more fanciful headgear, probably imported from London.[19]

We know less about metal-working in the city. If the data tabulated in table 5 is any guide, the period before 1640 was one of modest growth, but from a lower base than in the fifteenth century – perhaps due to the decline of the important specialist craft of bell-founding after the Reformation. Pin-making, introduced in the 1620s, was mainly a late Stuart success story. One of the few industries which obviously continued to flourish in our period was leather-working, notably tanning. As in other towns, this undoubtedly reflected strong demand for leather products, especially from better-off rural consumers. On the other hand, most of Gloucester's tanners were small men (few bore civic office) and there was little growth of secondary industries. Tanning was unable to lead the city economy out of its industrial decline.[20]

With its industrial sector in disarray Gloucester came to depend heavily on its marketing role. By 1608 distributive traders formed the largest specific occupational grouping in the city (see table 5), while mercers held nearly a quarter of the common council seats between 1580 and 1600. Gloucester, like other towns, did increasingly well catering for the new prosperity of rural society.[21] From their large shops near the High Cross mercers and haberdashers sold luxury or semi-luxury wares to visiting gentry and yeomen farmers as well as supplying the small part-time stores which started to appear in the countryside. By the 1610s we find nearly a dozen country carriers coming from up to 15 miles away to collect goods.[22] Some of the wares in Gloucester shops had been imported via Bristol like the large quantities of oranges, wines, oils, and raisins listed in 1583; others, particularly the latest fashions in dress, came overland from London. 'Returning' money to pay for purchases from the metropolis was a well-established practice by 1600, and at least two carriers operated weekly between Gloucester and London in the 1630s. At the same time, the city did not have everything its own way in the marketing field.

There was strenuous competition from the multitude of smaller market towns in the county, particularly in the provision of more basic commodities, while Bristol to the south took some of the cream of gentle custom with its more sophisticated range of high quality goods.[23]

Gloucester's main strength in inland trade derived from its role as a marketing centre for cereals. As Bristol's magistrates remarked jealously about 1583: 'Gloucester stands not upon any trade of merchandise but of corn and grain'. In the Elizabethan period the Vales of Berkeley, Gloucester and Tewkesbury were fertile corn-growing areas selling their grain principally through Gloucester. Leading city merchants like Thomas Rich, John Taylor and Thomas Machin shipped vast amounts of wheat and malt down-river to Bristol, the West Country, Wales and southern Ireland. They benefited especially from the recovery of Bristol's long-distance commerce in the 1580s and 1590s, supplying much of the grain which Bristol ships carried into the Mediterranean and further afield.[24]

Another growth point in the city economy was its service sector. 'Gloucester', we hear in the 1580s, 'is a great thoroughfare . . . and a great market situated in the heart of the country where great concourse of people is'. Justices, jurors, witnesses, and litigants flocked to the city: to the church courts in the cathedral; to county quarter sessions, the main political and administrative forum of the nascent county community, held at the castle or a city inn; to the assizes sitting twice a year in the Boothall; occasionally to the Council of the Marches meeting (as in 1592) in the cathedral close.[25] Prosperous visitors lodged in the 12 great inns along the main streets (often packed to capacity at peak times); other lesser folk made do with the city taverns or numerous alehouses. Despite civic ordinances the larger victualling establishments not only lodged merchants and traders but increasingly provided the venue for business deals and negotiations, away from the inclement hurlyburly of the open market.[26]

Professional men also exploited the town's growing importance as a social centre. None did better than the lawyers who served the great tide of litigation encouraged by landed prosperity: by the turn of the century there were about 20 Gloucester-based practitioners – counsellors, attorneys and proctors. But well-heeled country clients also lined the pockets of physicians, surgeons, scriveners, and schoolmasters. The cathedral school in particular taught the children of gentry families from a wide area of western England. Some country gentry began to reside in the city for part of the year, renting perhaps a house in the cathedral close. Lesser landowners moved there permanently like Richard Pope of the Leigh, concerned 'for the education of [his] divers small children', or Henry Gilbert of Whaddon living there 'for his better service of God and for recovery of his wife's health by physic'.[27]

The expansion of the tertiary sector undoubtedly took up some of the slack in urban economic activity, but it worked no miracles for local prosperity.

Indeed in some ways this expansion aggravated the instability of the economy. With its greater reliance on rural demand the city's economic performance was now highly vulnerable to those sharp oscillations of the agrarian economy which recurred in the late sixteenth and early seventeenth centuries. Too often problems caused by harvest difficulty were compounded by plague epidemics which caused the isolation of the city from its hinterland. Naturally in times of dearth Gloucester's grain trade still yielded lucrative returns for leading merchants shipping corn, but this merely underlined the falling level of general demand among ordinary citizens faced with soaring food prices. Increased coastal traffic had other drawbacks for the urban economy, encouraging a desertion of the old longer-distance trades and leaving city commerce at the mercy of the erratic fortunes of Bristol and other West Country ports. Last but not least, Gloucester's economy was vulnerable in one further way. The growth of the city as a social centre depended to a large extent on the fickle patronage of county gentry. This custom might easily transfer itself to a rival town if the city fathers failed to play up to the gentry's political sensitivities.

In the mid-1620s all the problem birds came home to roost and there was a full-scale crisis. Foreign war dealt a mortal blow at the fading cloth industry; harvest failure created food shortage and widespread poverty; plague brought inland trade to a standstill (for a while); coastal shipping was disrupted by a commercial crisis at Bristol and difficulties in the North Atlantic fishery; county patronage was seriously alienated by the city's bitter opposition to gentry demands for concessions over the inshire (discussed below). Gloucester's economy remained badly depressed into the 1640s. As we shall see, these years of crisis, the culmination of a prolonged period of economic instability, had a considerable influence on the growing radical outlook of city leaders prior to the summoning of the Long Parliament.[28]

3

Another vital factor helping to engender a radical mentality in the years before 1640 was the growth of social polarization and tension. Already by the 1520s the subsidy rolls suggest that over 40 per cent of those taxed were assessed at the lowest rate, while only 6 per cent were rated at more than £40. By the mid-seventeenth century the wealth pyramid may have been more steeply tapered. Though the Hearth Tax returns are not directly comparable with the earlier subsidy rolls they do shed some crude light on the pattern of wealth: thus of those taxed in 1664, only 5 per cent paid at the highest rates of nine hearths or above, whereas 54 per cent were assessed at the minimum rate of one or two hearths. If there was a trend towards increased economic inequality, it probably reflected the industrial malaise from the mid-sixteenth century with the resultant decline in the number of substantial clothiers, as well as the way that medium-rank traders were discouraged from staying in Gloucester by the heavy burdens of civic office-holding. No less important, it also mirrored the high prosperity of leading Stuart merchants, their fortunes based on the large profits of inland and coastal trade.[29]

Not only were the Gloucester *potentiores* increasingly wealthy compared to ordinary freemen and poorer inhabitants, but they displayed their wealth in more conspicuous forms – in new and better buildings in the centre of town, in household furnishings, books, plate, and dress. Though statistical data is lacking for Gloucester, we do have evidence for Canterbury, a similar county centre. There a sample of probate inventories 1560–1640 demonstrates that distributive traders spent three times as much on their apparel as building craftsmen. In the late sixteenth century they invested about twice as much in luxury furnishings as building craftsmen; in the next 40 years it was nearly four times as much. At Gloucester city magnates aped the manners and fashions of the landed gentry, styling themselves gentlemen and procuring coats of arms. They even began to acquire rural residences: in 1624 we know that at least half the aldermanic bench had houses in the adjoining country-side.[30]

While the urban elite began to develop its own class consciousness and identity, at the bottom end of the social spectrum there was massive, escalating poverty as the urban economy proved unable to adjust to rising demographic pressure. In St Aldate's parish, for instance, the number of poor receiving relief trebled between the late 1570s and the 1630s and in the crisis years of the 1620s nearly 40 per cent of the parish was probably destitute. As in other provincial centres the hard core of traditional impotent poor was now steadily overshadowed by a looming mass of labouring poor, unable to secure work or afford rising food prices; many had been forced into tramping and vagrancy as a last resort. In addition, years of prolonged depression forced even marginal poor, the semi-skilled or small craftsmen, on to the poverty line.[31]

Along with the growth of poverty went increased social segregation. Just as the city magnates tended to live in great houses near the main market at the Tolsey, or by the wharves in St Nicholas's parish, the poor were crowded into squalid housing in outer parishes like St Aldate's and St Mary de Lode, the latter in unhealthy marshland. Though never ghettoes in the modern sense, such areas developed their own fairly distinctive social physiognomy. They were afflicted by a high incidence of morbidity and mortality: plague made its first appearance at Gloucester in 1638 in St Mary de Lode, while St Aldate's had the heaviest known mortality of city parishes during the 1630s.[32] Such areas were also prone to high levels of crime and disorder. Taking offenders indicted before city quarter sessions 1639–43 we find the largest contingents came from St Mary de Lode and Barton Street, both impoverished districts. Among the offenders from these areas were numerous alehouse keepers, often running unlicensed establishments in back alleys. Such houses not only victualled and lodged the countless incoming poor, but also offered a meeting-place for local paupers; there they might forget their misery with cheap alcohol and illicit sex. In addition, poor tippling houses often had a communal or neighbourhood role, serving as the centre for more traditional folk rituals and attracting the lower orders away from church services. Poor alehouses, in fact, seemed to many wealthier tradesmen the mainspring of an underground world of immoral, irreligious poor which threatened the mores, power and institutions of established society.[33]

Increased social polarization spawned tension and sometimes conflict. There was recurrent criticism of the ruling elite and during 1586 clothworkers rioted in and about the city over shipments of grain and malt out of Gloucester at a time of acute local shortage. Again in 1604 at the height of the plague epidemic 'disorder and unruliness of the people' was widespread, with a particularly serious disturbance over magisterial directives for the burial of the dead. Fresh disorder broke out in St Mary de Lode parish during the epidemic of 1638.[34]

The poverty problem and the associated order issue dominated the debates and decisions of the ruling elite in the decades before 1640. In response the city established, mostly piecemeal, an intricate system of poor relief. By comparison with eastern towns Gloucester introduced only a handful of limited measures during the early sixteenth century. Concerted action came from the 1560s as the city economy deteriorated. Parishes levied statutory poor rates, a house of correction was opened, and the city experimented with various schemes to set the poor on work.[35] The critical decade of the 1590s provoked the usual flurry of expedients: beadles to whip vagrants out of town; the isolation and relief of plague victims; and the establishment of coal and grain stocks for the poor. In the years of worst difficulty city officials imported grain from Bristol, Shrewsbury, London, and the Continent to provision the destitute.[36] As well as instituting these general measures the city fathers sought to alleviate the special plight of the local poor through revamping hospitals and almshouses. St Bartholomew's, a major almshouse, was reorganized and extended in 1569; during the 1590s the city secured control of St Mary Magdalen Hospital which was refounded in 1617 with an annual pension from the Crown; finally all the main hospitals were brought under centralized aldermanic control in the 1630s. In addition there was a high level of magisterial charity, mostly directed at founding work stocks and encouraging small or young tradesmen with interest-free loans. Overall, Gloucester's relief measures lacked the grand complexity of the schemes found in certain other puritan cities like Salisbury or Norwich, but they seem to have been implemented with drive and relative efficiency, particularly after the turn of the century.[37]

On top of these relief measures Gloucester magistrates endeavoured to combat the dual menace of poverty and disorder through a progressive tightening up of the administrative machinery. Exploiting to the full their power as justices of the peace, small groups of aldermen met several times a week to deal summarily with vagrants and other suspected persons, and to keep a close eye on parish officials. From the mid-Tudor period the city council had issued a series of ordinances against disorderly alehouses and these were strictly enforced from the 1620s. As well as clamping down on unlicensed alehouses the magistrates sought to compel all victuallers to buy supplies from a small group of common brewers under magisterial control.[38] In 1635 the new orders for the city hospitals excluded those poor who had previously kept alehouses. The same regulations also appointed an 'overseer of the manners of the poor'. Concerned with the large numbers of poor who never went to church, the magistracy inaugurated (in September 1632) a special lectureship to preach godly obedience to the poor in St Mary de Lode church and St Bartholomew's, while their puritan betters heard their own sermons at St Nicholas. Godly preaching was as important an instrument of social control as statutory relief and endowed charity.[39]

Thus the city fathers mobilized a battery of measures to overcome the massive social problems and pressures which menaced the city before 1640. Up to a point their tactics were successful. There was no breakdown of public order. Yet the measures themselves did little to resolve the underlying problems; at best they were palliatives. In the 1620s and for much of the 1630s, when the city faced severe economic recession, the situation was tense and difficult.

4

Civic attempts to preserve social order and stability had powerful repercussions so far as the political structure was concerned. Rising expenditure on various forms of poor relief contributed to the growing insolvency of city government. In the early 1550s there was still a regular surplus on the stewards' accounts, but from the 1560s the deficits mounted inexorably – by the 1580s the average was £45 a year and still rising. The problem was that while expenditure increased (boosted by price inflation) traditional sources of revenue (rents, tolls) stagnated. In consequence, members of the corporation had to dip into their own pockets in order to keep the city afloat. By the 1570s the convention was established that the four incoming stewards would lend the chamber cash to clear the current deficit; they in turn would be reimbursed by their successors the following year. In 1579 the new stewards refused to pay up and precipitated a financial crisis, though they eventually submitted. Six years later steward John Brooke held out obdurately and financial collapse was only averted by the outgoing steward accepting payment a year late. Likewise, the sheriffs and mayor frequently incurred expenditure on the city's behalf which proved difficult to recover. In 1604 townspeople witnessed the unseemly spectacle of the sheriffs distraining and carting away the shop goods of the mayor, Thomas Rich, because they claimed they had received insufficient revenue to pay the city fee-farm at the Exchequer.[40]

The financial burdens imposed by office-holding had wide-ranging consequences for civic politics, accelerating the trend towards oligarchy. The political situation at Gloucester was similar to that in most corporate towns with basic political privileges confined to a minority of inhabitants – the freemen. By the early seventeenth century there were about 500 freemen, between 30 and 40 per cent of the adult male population. From their ranks were recruited the members of the main civic assembly, the 40-strong common council, which in turn supplied the mayor and aldermen. The growing cost of office-holding made this step-ladder to power, always awkward to climb, appear downright dangerous. Once elected, councillors had to run the costly official gauntlet of serving two years as steward and then twice as sheriff. Predictably a rising number of freemen refused to accept election to the council and those who did tended to be well-established merchants and traders. Even so, a significant proportion found the financial strain too much and dropped out of the council after one or more spells of official service.[41]

Almost by definition members of the aldermanic bench were wealthy citizens able to survive the gruelling exigencies of office. After serving an extended period as ordinary councillors most entered the inner circle when they were at the peak of their business careers, usually aged about 50. From the subsidy records for the 1590s we can see that the bench comprised many of the wealthiest inhabitants. A few were mini-tycoons with over £3,000 in real and personal possessions, but the average estate was probably somewhat under £1,000. A large part of aldermanic wealth was invested in property, a growing amount outside the city walls.[42] Group identity was fostered by joint business enterprises and credit connections as well as by the ubiquitous ties of kinship. Aldermanic power was also buttressed in two other ways. Firstly there was the authority of age and long service. Many aldermen served for 20 years or more: the average age of members of the bench in the 1580s and 1590s was nearly 60. Secondly, the decades before 1640 saw the bench monopolize almost all the principal non-conciliar offices in the city. They were masters of the main craft gilds, governors of the numerous city hospitals, and justices of the peace *ex officio*, while two-thirds of the city's burgesses in Parliament 1601–40 were likewise aldermen.[43]

The growth of oligarchic government was the most obvious political development in Gloucester in the decades before 1640. At the heart of civic politics there was a steady shift of power away from the ordinary councillors towards an inner cabinet of mayor and aldermen. The royal charter of 1483 placed the election of the mayor in the hands not of the council as a whole but of the aldermen and twelve 'more lawful and discreet' members of the council; in 1605 James I's charter limited the electoral college to the aldermanic bench alone, though the rights of senior councillors were restored in 1627. Aldermen themselves were co-opted on to the bench in our period and while other elections to civic office were made by the council as a whole, there was a large measure of aldermanic influence. By the seventeenth century this influence was brought to bear through a pre-election day meeting of the mayor and aldermen which nominated candidates for the various offices. Even more crucial, given the many pressing problems of the city, was the way that members of the bench took charge of day-to-day administration through the Friday court of aldermen at the Tolsey and through more informal meetings during the week. Again as justices the same men presided over city quarter sessions which by 1600 wielded many new administrative powers, particularly in the field of social order. Controlling sessions the aldermen also had at their beck and call a bevy of new officials – overseers of the poor, highway surveyors and the like. Finally, the increasingly powerful office of town clerk was largely filled by clients of the bench.[44]

Meantime, the common council as a whole suffered a marked diminution in its political importance. Despite the major expansion of local administrative business, the number of council meetings remained static with an average of only ten a year, while meetings were often rigged to the oligarchy's advantage. In 1603–4, for instance, it was said that mayor Rich summoned meetings at short notice when he 'well knew divers of the council to be forth of the city'. Even when a crisis compelled action by the whole council – as over conflict with the inshire gentry in 1624 – the bench ensured that authority was delegated to a committee dominated by aldermen. Oligarchic power made itself felt outside the council chamber too. At parliamentary elections, one of the few occasions when ordinary freemen could make their views heard, aldermanic gerrymandering was the order of the day. In the 1597 election the veteran populist candidate Thomas Atkins claimed that members of the bench had rushed proceedings and ignored the voices of nearly 100 freemen. In 1604 there was another magisterial campaign to railroad their candidate through the election meeting though this time they were foiled by a dissident alderman. But thereafter at elections the bench seems to have had its own way.[45]

Civic ritual in the medieval city had brought together in formal unity all the members of the body politic in quasi-religious drinkings and processions, as at Midsummer and St Peter's eve. But by the late sixteenth century ceremonies served primarily to demonstrate oligarchic power and control. Most civic ritual was focussed on the bench and chief officials with formal progresses to sermon or court in scarlet or puce ritual dress and with ever more elaborate civic regalia. By the mid-seventeenth century the high point in the civic calendar was an elaborate dinner on Nomination Day when, as we have seen, the city leaders effectively fixed the names of incoming officers.[46]

As we shall discover this growing concentration of civic power and initiative in the hands of a small group of magnates was to have major political implications for the city, particularly in the years before 1640. At the same time it is important to see this development in the context of the critical problems and difficulties which Gloucester faced from the mid-sixteenth century: the decay of its staple industries; the problems of civic finance; the high cost of office-holding and the reluctance of many citizens to serve. All these factors undoubtedly contributed to the oligarchic trend, as did the expansion of civic administration due to rising poverty and other internal problems, which dictated the need for a semi-permanent committee of leading townsmen. Of course external pressures were also significant. Not only did the mounting demands of central government increase the work-load of town governors but the Crown showed a clear preference for local cliques of reliable men. As well as wanting active local agents to implement royal policies, the government was increasingly concerned at the severe social pressures in towns and the danger that non-oligarchic rule might open the door to social and political anarchy. Such concern was also shared by leading townspeople. As the Gloucester magistrates declared in 1584, 'experience has taught us what a difficult thing it has always been to deal in any matter where the multitude of burgesses have voice'.[47]

Oligarchic rule led to constant complaints of corruption and abuse. Some were clearly justified. In the 1590s there was a series of frauds involving the corn stock for the poor: Alderman Garnons was said to have profited by up to £160. But most abuse was less glaring, at least after the turn of the century when the ruling elite with its increasingly puritan complexion dealt harshly with serious offenders. On the other hand, low-key abuse was undoubtedly widespread before 1640. Leases of city lands at beneficial rates were hurried, huggermugger, through council for aldermanic clients; town offices were sold; aldermen under-assessed each other for the subsidy; city contracts had a habit of going to members of the bench (in 1604 plague victims were buried in civic shrouds bought from the mayor's shop). Structural abuse of this kind was probably inevitable given the need to compensate town governors for the oppressive burdens of office-holding. But it was also a mechanism by which the ruling elite managed to secure friends and clients and consolidate their control over the common council and burgesses generally.[48]

Resentment over increased oligarchic power and abuse sometimes chimed in with wider social discontent to produce serious agitation – as in 1604. But communal conflict never became as threatening and large-scale as in other provincial towns: the ruling elite never lost command. One reason for this may have been the growing effectiveness of the magisterial apparatus of social and political control. Another may have been the responsibility and cohesiveness of the ruling group particularly after 1600, with its progressively puritan identity. In addition most respectable members of the body politic probably recognized the need to avoid rocking the boat at a time when the city was faced by massive internal problems as well as by mounting opposition to its corporate privileges from outside.[49]

Prior to the Reformation the city had clashed repeatedly with the abbey of St Peter's over their respective common land rights. Some of this rivalry continued after the abbey's refoundation as a cathedral, but the last major dispute occurred in 1583–4 and ended firmly in the city's favour. Thereafter relations with the close were good, much better than in most cathedral cities.[50] More worrying for the oligarchy was growing friction with the inshire, the county hundreds controlled by the city. Crucial here was the magisterial policy of weighting taxes and other royal levies against the country areas, thereby lessening the burden on the economically depressed city, while at the same time consistently refusing inshire inhabitants any say in civic government or the election of M.P.s. A number of clashes occurred in the late Elizabethan period, but the real crisis came in the 1620s. Then a group of inshire gentry organized petitions to Parliament calling for the right to representation and secured from the Crown a commission of association which enabled them to sit as justices at city quarter sessions. The magistracy protested vehemently against this innovation, 'whereby an ill example will be given for knights and gentlemen to infringe and invade the liberties of all cities of England'. The next two years were spent in the frantic re-assertion of corporate rights, ending in the costly acquisition of a new charter in 1627. Resistance continued, however, and eventually triumphed at the Restoration when the inshire was returned to county jurisdiction.[51]

City control over the inshire provoked further trouble with the county authorities. In the last part of the sixteenth century the lords lieutenant tried to force the city to pay more than its customary share of royal levies because of the prosperity of the inshire. Relations between the corporation and the county justices became equally strained. In 1595, for example, the justices kept the mayor and aldermen kicking their heels waiting for a meeting to discuss grain exports only to leave town without telling them. Mutual suspicion continued to overshadow dealings between the county and city right up to 1640.[52]

The Council in the Marches of Wales was another source of anxiety for city rulers. There were several nasty collisions and in 1597 the mayor was fined and imprisoned. But in general the Council was too far away to pose a real threat, while conciliar process could sometimes be used to overawe outsiders.[53]

Ambivalence also coloured relations with the Crown. On the one hand the central government could be an invaluable patron, granting new economic privileges such as the customs house in 1580, supporting the magistracy against popular agitation, helping to ward off gentry attacks. On the other hand, the expansion of Tudor government led to mounting interference in the urban community, most notably during the crisis of the 1590s. In addition, Court magnates, eager to extend their party patronage networks, sought to nominate their clients as recorders, town clerks and M.P.s. The Earl of Leicester, for instance, managed to secure the reversion of the Gloucester recordership for Richard Davies in 1587. Three years before, however, he had been sharply rebuffed when he had demanded the right to appoint one of the burgesses in Parliament.[54] In fact for most of the period Gloucester managed to retain royal favour without making too many concessions. Here it was helped by the fragmented nature of Court politics in the Elizabethan and Jacobean periods. From the 1570s the city enjoyed the patronage of William Cecil, Lord Burghley and later his son the Earl of Salisbury. Their support was invaluable in winning royal grants and in frightening off predatory courtiers and their country clients. In grateful return the city granted annuities and promised its political loyalty.[55]

From the 1620s relations with the Crown began to deteriorate. One obvious reason was the high level of royal demands during a period of acute economic and social difficulty for the city. Thus the Forced Loan met growing resistance from local lawyers, members of the elite, and ordinary burgesses, while there was widespread opposition to billeting in 1627 and 1628. The city was incensed at the high and uncustomary level of military burdens imposed upon it and frightened at the disorders which the troops caused. Despite protests to the government the magistrates could obtain no redress.[56] Fundamental was the growing limitation on provincial access to the Court evident by Charles I's accession. Already in 1624 Gloucester had experienced great difficulty in getting its views on the inshire dispute heard at Court; by the late 1620s the communication problem had become almost insuperable. It was not just that the Court was less open than in the past, but it was increasingly antipathetic to provincial opinions with a puritan intonation. Unable to secure any satisfaction at Court the city demonstrated its resentment in increasingly forthright and principled terms. Not only was Parliament's Remonstrance against Tunnage and Poundage entered in the city records, but in February 1629 John Browne junior, a leading alderman and one of the city's burgesses, declared in the Commons: 'The strength of the king is in the hearts of his subjects. They do the king the greatest disservice that persuade' him to levy customs 'against the good will of the subjects . . . A curse upon all such as shall infringe the liberty of the subject'. Though Browne was probably a moderate puritan, it seems likely that there was by now a core of leading citizens committed to more radical religious beliefs.[57]

5

At this juncture we need to look in detail at urban ideology, one of the most vital and combustible elements in the interaction of urban change and political radicalism. Religion undoubtedly continued to be the dominant force in the city's cultural matrix after the Reformation. Gloucester had an early reputation as a centre of religious reform. During the 1530s there was an active protestant following in the city and within a decade or so most of the traditional religious superstructure had been demolished.[58] From the 1580s we have clear signs of a growing puritan bias: godly preachers, civic lectureships, attacks on catholics, private annotation of sermons, bans on players, conventicles in inns. In 1617 when Laud as dean of Gloucester sought to reform cathedral services it was said of the city opposition: 'Assuredly these zealous people are our precisians, the number whereof is great in this place'.[59]

How do we explain the growing tide of puritan activity? A major factor was the appalling state of the established ministry. In 1603 two-thirds of the city parishes were too impoverished to have resident ministers and for most of our period had to make do with poor, unlearned curates. Nor did the catehdral generally offer much in the form of godly enlightenment. For most of Elizabeth's reign it was beset by internecine feuding, corruption, and episcopal conservatism, while the following period was dominated by chronic non-residence.[60] Disenchantment with the established religious order was compounded by wider changes in the cultural life of substantial citizens. Most important was the expansion of educational facilities. By 1600 there were probably upwards of a dozen petty schools in Gloucester, plus the two endowed grammar schools – the municipal Crypt school and the cathedral school.[61] One result was a high level of male literacy. This can be seen from the subscriptions of witnesses before the church courts (see table 6), though it has to be remembered that the data is possibly biased towards upper social groups.[62]

TABLE 6 · OVERALL LITERACY OF GLOUCESTER
WITNESSES 1595–1640

	per cent literate	n
Male	64.4	205
Female	4.1	100

The incidence of literacy was particularly high in those occupational categories associated with marketing and internal trade (see table 7).

Enhanced literacy was almost certainly accompanied by increased reading and ownership of books. Though the city library proposed by Bishop Goodman in 1629 did not materialize until the late 1640s, citizens had access to small parish libraries and many probably bought books from the two or three stationers operating in early Stuart Gloucester. Such developments permitted and possibly encouraged a greater stress on the reading of the scriptures and other religious works and a more critical attitude towards the established Church. By the 1620s John Deighton, a city surgeon, who owned a number of medical and religious books (including Foxe), was busy supplementing Foxe's account of the Marian martyrdoms in Gloucestershire by talking with parishioners and descendants.[63]

Table 7 · Male literacy at Gloucester

According to occupational groupings 1595–1640
(expressed as % of sample)

	Occupational group	Signatures
1	Gentlemen	91.2
2	Professional	100.0
3	Clothing trades	63.6
4	Leather trades	61.5
5	Food and drink	69.6
6	Textile	74.2
7	Household goods	0.0*
8	Distributive	100.0
9	Building trades	62.5*
10	Yeomen	73.3
11	Husbandmen	8.3
12	Labourers	0.0*
13	Rural miscellaneous	0.0*
14	Service industries	18.2
15	Servants	40.0*
16	Miscellaneous	16.6*
17	Unspecified	55.5*

* = small sample

Puritan activity in Gloucester was also promoted by some of the major social and economic developments affecting the community before 1640. The city's expanding coasting trade brought it into close contact with puritan Bristol and those other godly towns of the South-West, Barnstaple and Bridgewater, while many city mercers and drapers doubtless imbibed the radical truths of metropolitan Puritanism. A growing number of the Gloucestershire gentry who patronized city shops and services also had a staunchly puritan outlook. Even the cathedral, which was plagued by non-residence and abuse, housed a handful of puritan luminaries from the 1580s to the 1620s, men with a following in the city and its vicinity. Among these were Dean Anthony Rudd, Bishop Miles Smith and Thomas Prior, who was both sub-dean and a city lecturer.[64]

Yet there can be little question that the key to the puritan advance in the community lay in the role of the urban elite. As we have already seen, Gloucester's economic and social structure in this period was dominated by a narrow group of merchants and traders who through their position on the magisterial bench also kept a tight rein on city government. It was this group which took the lead in the spread of puritanism in the city. By the 1590s if not before we know that a number of aldermen and senior councillors were actively sympathetic. In 1598 they secured the appointment of William Groves, a local puritan, to a weekly lectureship in the elite parish of St Michael's, with the city chamber making up any shortfall in voluntary donations. From 1611 the magistrates established a twice-weekly lectureship which was served in succession by two committed Calvinists, Thomas Prior and John Workman. In 1617 the agitation against Laud's erection of an altar in the cathedral was largely orchestrated by puritan aldermen.[65] During the first part of James' reign the puritan caucus faced opposition from a faction led by Alderman John Jones, the diocesan registrar, with support from the close and lesser freemen. But by the late 1610s the puritan group was dominant. In 1618, despite the king's recent Declaration of Sports, the maypole in St Nicholas parish was pulled down and a country conservative, Christopher Windle, blamed puritan ministers aided and abetted by the magistrates and mayor. During the 1620s and 1630s the city fathers patronized distinguished puritan schoolmasters and apparently tried to remodel the city hospitals on more puritan lines.[66]

Influential in the progressively puritan bias of Gloucester's rulers were some of the general variables noted earlier. Almost all were educated men; quite a number were distributive traders with close ties with London or Bristol; one or two also had family connections with the cathedral godly. The son of Alderman Christopher Caple, Richard, was a distinguished puritan preacher in the county who suffered suspension during the 1630s. Having said this, we also need to take into account other pressures directly or indirectly related to the host of structural problems which assailed the city in the century before 1640. To civic leaders trying to govern a community beset by rising population, economic instability, widespread poverty, and other social and political difficulties, puritanism, with its emphasis on public control and godly discipline, had a powerful appeal. Puritan ideology served to buttress and justify measures concerning the poor and lower classes. It further served to consolidate oligarchic authority and to unite the ruling elite during a period of sustained communal stress.

A further aspect of the ruling elite's growing commitment to puritan ideology also needs to be considered here. In a critical period when the city was menaced not just by internal difficulties but by external threats, from the county and the Crown, the concept of a godly civic commonwealth led by committed puritan magistrates offered a vehicle for resurrecting in a modified form some of the communal cohesion and particularist cultural identity of the older, medieval city. Gloucester was to be a sober, orderly city on the hill, its preachers and almshouses, schools and citizenry a godly beacon to the villages and market towns of the shire. And in part the vision was realized. Thus after a visit in 1642 Richard Baxter declared (with some understandable exaggeration), that he had found 'a civil, courteous and religious people as different from those at Worcester as if they had lived under another government'.[67]

6

We have argued then that the long-term changes and stresses in the urban community from the mid-sixteenth century created acute fears of social breakdown and, equally important, accelerated the trend towards oligarchic government. We have also analysed how the new all-powerful ruling elite increasingly patronized puritan tenets and values. Yet if all this helps us to understand why Gloucester became an important puritan centre in the early Stuart period, it does not by itself provide a sufficient explanation of the city's growing commitment to radical politics before and after 1640. How did the puritan county town of the first part of the century, with its concern for social order and communal survival, turn into the embattled radical citadel of the 1640s ready to risk almost everything for the parliamentary cause?

A vital factor in the growing political and religious radicalism of the city was the sharp deterioration in Gloucester's economic fortunes during the 1620s and 1630s. We noted earlier how a conjunction of long- and short-term economic problems caused a major recession in the mid-1620s. This depression persisted through the next decade: industry continued to decay and trade on the Severn stagnated.[68] In consequence poverty was endemic, reaching crisis proportions with the dearth of 1630 and the massive outbreak of plague in 1638. On the political front civic finance tottered on the verge of bankruptcy (the cumulative deficit had reached nearly £700 by 1640), and there was open conflict with the county gentry (thus in 1638 the county refused to come to the aid of the plague-stricken city).[69]

In this grave situation, with magistrates almost overwhelmed by difficulty, the policies and actions of the Caroline regime seemed to pose a direct threat to civic survival. As we know, the Crown's repeated financial and military exactions during the late 1620s provoked considerable opposition in Gloucester; after 1634 there was growing discontent over ship money. Not only did the successive levies weigh heavily on a badly depressed community, but they opened the door to further acrimonious conflict with the gentry of the inshire and the county.[70]

Equally disturbing was the Crown's new religious strategy with its emphasis on more ritualistic services, its devaluation of puritan concern with the godly discipline of the lower orders, and its rejection of the long-standing Calvinist consensus over Church theology. Though Arminian tenets were never apparently ennunciated from city pulpits at this time, puritan worthies had only to look at the new-found confidence of city recusants (including the new diocesan registrar Henry Jones) to suspect that the Caroline hierarchy was already well on the way to Rome. On the other hand, it would be wrong to exaggerate the city's alarm at this theological turnaround. At the local level, the magistrates remained on good terms with their maverick conservative bishop, Godfrey Goodman. Even the Laudian innovations in church worship (including the railing of altars) caused no serious trouble: many city parishes apparently ignored the diocesan directives with impunity.[71]

Where serious conflict with the hierarchy did occur was in regard to those central pillars of the godly commonwealth – the city's preachers, hospitals and schools. In the mid-1620s there may have been a dispute with cathedral conservatives over a projected lectureship there. In 1633 major trouble erupted when John Workman, the city's leading puritan divine and principal lecturer for more than a decade, used the occasion of an assize sermon to condemn continuing abuses in the Church, superstitious images and, that bane of public order, popular dancing. The attack on dancing was interpreted (rightly) as a counter-blast to the recently re-issued Declaration of Sports which encouraged popular activities of that sort, and Workman was summoned before High Commission. Strongly supporting their preacher, the city magistracy voted Workman his stipend indefinitely. At this point Archbishop Laud, who doubtless recalled how city puritans had crossed him in 1617, determined to humiliate Gloucester's governors: a number were hauled up to London and eventually fined (the total cost in fines and expenses was later estimated at £200). Workman himself was hounded out of the diocese.[72]

Nor was this the end of Laud's onslaught. In 1635 he authorized a rigorous inquest into the recent magisterial reorganization of the city hospitals and the supposed appointment of a nonconformist to a hospital living. Once again the city fathers had to appear before High Commission and produce the city council books in their defence: the proceedings lasted until 1638. Within two years the archbishop was intervening again, this time to prevent the corporation dismissing the Laudian John Bird as master of the Crypt school. According to the magistrates, Bird had so neglected the school 'that very few able scholars have been sent thence to the university'. In place of Bird they wanted to appoint the eminent puritan John Langley who had recently been removed by Laud's visitors from successful charge of the cathedral school. With Laud's support Bird managed to stave off removal until 1641. Overall, in this attack on the city's schools, hospitals and preachers, in the determined attempt to disgrace the city's magistrates, the hierarchy, with royal support, appeared hell bent on demolishing the bulwarks of the godly commonwealth, on opening the doors wide to social anarchy.[73]

By the mid-1630s if not before the city's attitude towards the Crown was one of sullen hostility. Under concerted royal attack the former preoccupation with puritan stability and order was transmuted into a new strategy of radical resistance. Early in 1640 the city fathers may have had some hand in the planned voyage from Gloucester of 100 colonists to the puritan safety of New England. But salvation was near at hand. During 1639 one of the city's radical curates went to Scotland, quite probably with magisterial connivance, and made contact with presbyterian opponents of the régime. Once the Long

Parliament met, the city lobbied hard for radical religious reform and when war broke out Gloucester determined, in the words of John Corbet, 'not to stand neutral in action but to adhere unto one party with which they resolved to stand or fall'.[74]

7

To sum up, we need to see the growth of radical politics at Gloucester in a wider urban perspective, to ask how far Gloucester's experience was shared by other English towns in the run-up to Civil War. Though we know less about political developments in towns than about changes at the county level, all the signs are that Gloucester's route march to militancy was fairly atypical. Several towns, like Winchester or Chester, became supporters of the king during the early 1640s,[75] while of those centres which eventually adhered to the parliamentary cause, many were clearly unenthusiastic and intermittently expressed a strong preference for neutralism. Quite often urban rulers had been pushed into opposing the king – both before and after 1640 – by communal agitation. In such towns, like Canterbury, Chichester, Norwich, Hull, Leicester, and Newcastle, there was frequently a long record of civic division and factionalism, with town oligarchies unable to maintain effective control; as often as not these divisions were exacerbated by gentry interference and religious sectarianism. This was in striking contrast to the situation at Gloucester where, as we know, the puritan magistracy exercised firm control before 1640. The socio-economic background also differed. While many provincial towns undoubtedly suffered some economic and social dislocation in the century before 1640, most appear to have escaped those intense pressures which Gloucester suffered, particularly in the 1620s and 1630s, pressures which helped forge the powerful political cohesion and radical mentality of that city and its leaders.[76]

At the same time, Gloucester's radical experience was probably not unique. A number of corporate towns like Northampton, Salisbury, Barnstaple, Taunton, Colchester and possibly Coventry,[77] as well as unincorporated centres like Birmingham and Manchester, distinguished themselves by a similar staunch opposition to the king and his armies.[78] Like Gloucester they were bastions of the parliamentary cause, rallying points for the provincial godly. Though we lack detailed information on some of these communities, all or most of them seem to have had two features in common with radical Gloucester: firstly, they were dominated, on a formal or informal basis, by thoroughgoing puritan *potentiores*; secondly, they may well have suffered acute economic and social instability in the years before 1640. If the declining gentry have now been exorcised from the putative ranks of the parliamentary party, we must not ignore the major contribution to the Revolution of declining or economically unstable towns.

PALATINE PERFORMANCE IN THE SEVENTEENTH CENTURY

W. J. Jones

Were it possible to draw an administrative chart of early Stuart England, it would show an almost genealogical network, 'a complex pattern of interlocking, overlapping, and conflicting jurisdictions'.[1] Administration *in* the localities and *of* the localities was the essential element in governing. Local officials and personalities were an expression of authority more real than that provided by occasionally glimpsed Privy Councillors or pronouncements from Westminster. People were most aware of institutions in their immediate vicinity. This was appreciated by Sir John Neale: 'To describe the England of those days as a federation of counties would be legally ridiculous, yet such a misnomer conveys a valuable truth. The central government was for its time an effective and efficient machine, but it had relatively little contact with the individual.'[2]

The palatines and provincial Councils were to some extent mirrors of Westminster although none, of course, embraced the seat of a parliament. Each had its seals and a range of courts, jurisdictions and procedures – civil and criminal, common law and equitable. The palatines – Chester and Flint, Durham, Lancaster – were of medieval origin but had decayed by the end of the fifteenth century. However, their administrative and judicial capacity was to be transformed. By Elizabeth's death they were operating as effective agencies and as integral parts of a national system. From being a devolution of royal authority to private persons, they were now a local expression of that authority. Symbolic of this development was a statute of 1563 which confirmed that bargains and sales, if entered within six months before the appropriate assize justices or palatine Chancery courts, were as good as if enrolled at Westminster.[3] Chester and Lancaster were encouraged because their activity suited both central government and important men holding palatine office. The same trends aided Durham, but it was not easy to shake off the Council of the North. Owing much to an internal drive during the last years of Elizabeth and the advocacy of Bishop Matthew, Durham established its new position after the other two. Its privileges, however, were rather more distinctive and it came nearest to being a petty principality.

Between the palatines there were many differences. The diverse agriculture of Cheshire, renowned for bacon and cheese, was vastly different from that of Durham. Lancashire combined a prosperous zone in its south-east, and growing economic expectations in its western regions, with some of the poorest sections of England. Durham was entangled with the wider estate concerns of the bishopric. Lancaster was a poor relation of the Duchy and dominated by its officials. Chester, an ancient buffer between England and Wales, had its complicated association with Flint and with the Great Sessions. Crown and common pleas were handled by the North Wales circuit, headed by the Chief Justice of Chester who was also *de facto* deputy head of the Council at Ludlow and the only permanent legal member of that body. At Durham and Lancaster this jurisdiction was handled by justices of the northern circuit, acting under warrant on behalf of the respective palatine authorities. Error at Durham lay first to the bishop, whereas in the other two palatines it lay direct to King's Bench. Contrasts there may have been, but there is sufficient similarity to justify treatment of these three palatines on the same level.

Embracing compact county societies, the palatines had a distinct local flavour which even the Councils could not match. Furthermore, resident judges combined long tenure and personal association with the locality, whereas justices on circuit throughout most of England had only a brief acquaintance with the counties they visited. Both conciliar and palatine arrangements fitted contemporary ideas as to how more distant areas should be managed. One idea mooted in 1604, were there indeed to be a union with Scotland, was that a Council modelled on that of Wales should be established at Berwick or Carlisle with powers in both countries.[4] The short-lived palatine of Avalon in Newfoundland, designed in partial imitation of Durham, inspired the proprietary charter of Maryland.

Renewed life for the three palatines, discernible in most areas of administration and jurisdiction, was most notable with respect to their Chancery courts.[5] These, as was the case with other English bill courts in England and Wales, experienced an evident growth in business and were healthy, thriving institutions during the reigns of the first two Stuarts. They lapsed with the onset of civil war, resumed operations at the Restoration, and survived into the nineteenth century. However the former impetus was gone, and in the late seventeenth century they were of only minor significance with respect to both the quality and quantity of litigation. While the impact of wars and Interregnum is inescapable, the disruption of 1642–60 is inadequate as the sole explanation for their subsequent and reduced circumstances. Instead it seems that these courts were damaged by developments and restrictions apparent before the great upheaval. Many other arenas of civil litigation suffered the same fate. Professor Hurstfield has posed the question, would the Restoration see a restoration of local government?[6] From this standpoint, the answer must be in the negative.

There was a clear geographical relationship between major provincial authorities and national institutions. Indeed if Westminster is taken as the centre, a fairly even arc can be drawn running south-west from the Humber to the southern tip of Cheshire; this line, turning south and leaving the Severn to the west, dissects the headwaters of the Avon and the Thames. To the north and west were the two provincial Councils and the three palatines. Close to the border with Scotland were the Marches, each under a warden. In south-west England were the Stannary courts, linked to the heartland of the Duchy of Cornwall. The picture would be even clearer if Henry VIII's Council of the West had survived. The great courts of Westminster – Chancery and Exchequer with their ability in both common law and English bill procedures, Common Pleas, King's Bench, and Star Chamber – had a regional function insofar as they exerted a natural pull on those living in central, east, south, and west England. However, on various grounds they also received suits from the whole country. They claimed and established – Star Chamber perhaps being the exception – a responsibility to supervise other courts, not least to ensure that such jurisdictions observed their own jurisdictions and rules. Few things are more evocative than the sub-title to Thomas Powell's *The Attornies Almanacke*: 'For the general ease and daily use of all such as shall have occasion to remove any person, cause or record from an inferior court to any the higher courts at Westminster.'[7]

Contemporary debates over the jurisdiction of courts had much to do with constitutional and legal theory. This was natural because royal government had such extensive means to indicate its will. Nonetheless most difficulties stemmed from practical problems. The proximity of jurisdictions invited dispute, and the ability of individual litigants to foster disagreements between institutions was inevitable. One Exchequer plaintiff commenced suit for the same matter in Common Pleas and King's Bench. Another noted that bills in different courts might concern the same dispute and yet vary in material matters.[8] Duplication of litigation was a natural consequence of the jurisdictional mosaic. Lord Chancellor Ellesmere said that verdict was put against verdict, judgment against judgment.[9] Coke described the system, 'the bounds of all and every several courts being most necessary to be known'. He urged that usurping and encroaching, not least because of the 'confusion' caused, should be eliminated and only 'proper' jurisdiction exercised.[10] Francis Bacon was of like mind. 'There are many courts, some superior, some provincial, and of a lower orb. It were to be wished, and it is fit to be so ordered, that every of them keep themselves within their proper spheres.'[11] Ordinary people and leading authorities said the same thing about the need to achieve definition, erase unnecessary suits, and reduce the number of conflicts. James I and Coke, far from always being antagonists, shared a conventional analysis of the problem. Difficulties arose on narrower issues. What were the powers of particular jurisdictions or the responsibilities of superior judges? How should such matters be approached?

Although disputes attract deserved notice, more attention has been paid to some spectacular arguments than to the many agreements and definitions which were attained. Furthermore, examples of courts assisting each other and supporting lesser brethren are prolific. Often, however, stands were taken for fear that otherwise there would be a general erosion of powers and privileges. That was why the Manchester court leet, claiming that no burgess or towns-man should sue a fellow 'in any court saving in the lord's of this manor' and seeking to control townships in the barony, struggled against the hundred court of Salford for almost two centuries.[12] We should not exaggerate conflicts, but equally we should not concentrate solely upon those which surfaced at Westminster.

Judicial authority and procedures were normal components of governing, and courts blended 'what we today would separate as administration and justice'.[13] Hence, as Dr Williams has observed, the Tudors 'developed a hierarchy of courts to supervise and control national life'.[14] Even at the private level much litigation supplied a need which later might be handled through other means. Availability, convenience and survival are not the only reasons why so many historians turn to judicial records in order to describe the circumstances of ordinary people. An extension and sophistication of medieval methods governed most activities: conveyances, credit, marriage settlements, or securing entry. Normal arrangements, particularly the extensive use of recorded bonds and resulting objections to execution, do much to explain the phenomenal development – 'this intense activity' – of English bill proceedings. 'It is already clear', wrote Plucknett about the late sixteenth century, 'that one royal court of equity is not enough.'[15] In fact there were a number of such courts in active existence long before Elizabeth died.

Only if we appreciate the dispersion, mass and nature of English bill litigation can the history of early Stuart administration, law and equity be grasped. Major provincial courts – those at Chester, Durham, Lancaster, Ludlow, and York – were inundated with business, and there were many other jurisdictions of this type: for example, the lord mayor's court at London and the lord warden's Chancery at Dover. It is not possible to provide satisfactory figures for the number of bills, but an impression can be obtained from evidence of hearings. In the decade before 1640, the Welsh Council was hearing between 1,200 and 1,500 cases a year. A figure of 2,000 cases pending, probably exaggerated, conveys a similar story about the Council of the North. The Durham Chancery, the records of which are severely fragmented, made between 100 and 150 major orders and decrees each year during the early Stuart period, and its impressive entry book for 1633–42 has 699 pages. Chester averaged about 300 major orders and decrees *per annum*. One entry book there for 1593–1600 has over 1,100 pages, and that for 1639–42 over 1,200 pages. Duchy Chamber, which despite its location was really cognizant of a dispersed local jurisdiction, certainly received more bills than did the Exchequer at Westminster. Appreciation of the overall picture contains a basic truth stressed by Coke. The national Chancery received thousands of bills, and Francis Bacon claimed to make 2,000 orders and decrees in a year, but Westminster must be seen in context. Against the total mass of business elsewhere in the country, the developing jurisdiction in the Exchequer – according to Dr Bryson between 300 and 400 bills were filed annually between 1600 and 1650 – appears miniscule as does that of Star Chamber. It is true that in provincial courts many cases were for small amounts and involved poor sections of the community, but this litigation cannot be written off as negligible or as avoiding tricky points of equity. Many suits involved valuable properties, large sums, and persons of consequence.[16]

Chester presents the most coherent story.[17] Henry VIII created the bishopric and M.P.s were introduced for the city and shire. Palatine jurisdiction was confirmed in 1568–9 when the claims of the Council at Ludlow were rejected. Chamberlains great in the area, in the state or in the law – two earls of Derby, Leicester and Egerton – had a decisive impact. As the palatine Exchequer's most enthusiastic supporter said with reference to the defeat of the Welsh Council, 'now the court of Chester became very absolute, both in state and authority'.[18]

The Lancaster Chancery had its home in Lancaster Castle, but further up the Ribble estuary there were also offices at Preston, where sittings were sometimes held. Pleadings were exhibited in both places, counsel and clients might be separated, and delays ensued. Causes centred on Duchy property were easily transmitted to Duchy Chamber, which also accepted a number of bills concerning palatine jurisdiction and officials. However, although the chancellor was also that of the Duchy, and there can be no doubt as to which was his more important function, the palatine seal – unlike that of the Duchy it was a great seal – remained in the county.[19]

The Durham Chancery was meshed with the bishop's Exchequer which handled his revenues and tenants. The bishop's jurisdiction was complicated since the diocese covered Northumberland, and his estates included Bedlington and Norham in that county and Allertonshire and Howdenshire in Yorkshire. The Court of Pleas at Durham, eventually comprising circuit judges authorized under the bishop's great seal, heard civil matters and pleas of the Crown. Halmote courts were held under the bishop's commission before the escheator of the palatine.[20]

Legislation of 1536, and that concerning the Council of the North in 1537, almost extinguished medieval implications. Durham city was designated as one of the Council's seats. 'The living organism with which we were concerned has become a heap of dry bones', wrote Lapsley. However, unlike Chester and Lancaster, M.P.s had not been introduced. From 1556, the Lord President of the Council was no longer required to hold general sessions at Durham, but Elizabeth included the palatine in his commission. Tunstall's dual position as both bishop and president may have enhanced difficulties. In 1560 the chancellor, Serjeant Robert Meynell, who was also a member of the Council, asked Lord Treasurer Winchester for help. For years there were disputes over jurisdiction, entangled with conflicts involving the lay and ecclesiastical authorities at Durham and York. It was said in 1580 that interference from York made justice impossible in the Durham Chancery, but Lord President Huntingdon demanded recognition of his authority over the reluctant bishopric. It was not a straightforward matter. As had happened previously between Chester and the Council in the Marches, provincial jurisdictions were already engaged in a struggle to determine ability which would later shift in emphasis to the national courts.[21]

The Council was in difficulties after Huntingdon's death in 1595. It was rent by faction, the national Chancery was active with restraining process, Berwick and other places sought recognition of their supposed privileges, and Yorkshire J.P.s complained to the Privy Council about cases being removed from their jurisdiction. The Durham Chancery apparently directed injunctions to plaintiffs at York. By the instructions of 1599 the lord president, when seeking to apprehend persons within the palatine, was henceforth required to write to the bishop. The latter's jurisdiction was thus acknowledged, and about this time it became the regular practice for justices on the northern circuit to operate within the palatine by commission under the bishop's seal.[22]

The quality of the three Chancery benches was generally good and sometimes exceptional. At Lancaster and Preston the practical work was done by a vice-chancellor, this position being jointly filled by two persons for much of James's reign. In late 1604 these were Sir Thomas Hesketh, Attorney of the Wards, and William Bromley. Thomas Tyldesley, later knighted, replaced Hesketh and continued until the end of the reign with various partners, notably Christopher Bannister who sat until the Civil War. At Chester, there was an outstanding team during Elizabeth's last decade when Egerton, the chamberlain, was also lord keeper and master of the rolls. His deputy, Peter Warburton, was a Common Pleas justice from 1600. Between 1603 and 1621, the vice-chamberlain and second justice at Chester was Sir Henry Townshend, a solid common lawyer. The Earl of Derby, the chamberlain, sat on occasion but, as when he reviewed an order made by Townshend, expert assistants joined him on the bench. In the particular case noted these were justices Walmesley and Williams from Westminster. The chief justice of Chester was occasionally called upon, but because of his other duties he was rarely involved.[23]

In 1600 the temporal chancellor at Durham, Thomas Calverley, was joined by a circuit justice, Serjeant Edward Drewe, in hearing a case. Some years later, Richard Hutton became chancellor. Experienced as a circuit judge and recorder of York, he had also been from 1599 a member of the Council of the North. From 1617 until his death in 1639 he was a celebrated justice of the

Common Pleas. Having this responsibility, he could not always be present at Durham and sometimes held sittings in London. He nonetheless emerges across three decades as the outstanding palatine Chancery judge of the early Stuart period, not least because of his orders governing practice and procedure, notably those of 1610 which expanded guidelines promulgated in 1596. As a chancellor, he was to the community of Durham what an Ellesmere or a Coventrye were to England.[24]

One clue to the development of equity and English bill proceedings, national and provincial, is to be found in the efforts of Westminster justices and other common lawyers. If the palatine Chancery courts owed much to those who sat on the bench, this was typical of greater courts. At Westminster, the Exchequer had its own barons. The Chancery was run by the lord chancellor and the master of the rolls – only Lord Keeper Williams was not a common lawyer – and assistance was frequently provided by justices of the Common Pleas and King's Bench. Hearings in Duchy Chamber were dominated by its 'judges assistant': in the 1630s these were Berkeley, Crawley and Vernon, all Westminster justices.

The necessity of keeping in touch with decisions and orders was a practical matter which went beyond the burgeoning reliance on precedent. Reports made by individuals, however selective and ambiguous, were increasingly a support for lawyers. Francis Bacon praised those of Coke, without which 'the law by this time had been almost like a ship without ballast',[25] but he had reason to advise the appointment of court reporters for the major common law jurisdictions at Westminster. Although English bill courts were also the subject of various compilations, they were in a much better situation because of their entry books, those of the Exchequer being outstanding. In the palatines, although so much has been lost or damaged, there seems to have been a steady improvement. Despite gaps, notably 1609–25, the major books for Chester are rather good. Durham has suffered most, and before 1633 we have to rely on draft orders, some of which seem to have been the working papers of Hutton. The Lancaster books slowly improve. It was, nevertheless, difficult for the clerks to keep up with the mass of litigation and orders. None of these courts could match record developments of the national Chancery and Exchequer.

Local convenience and speed were supposed to be advantages, although in fact some suits seemed interminable. On the other hand, in comparison with developments at Westminster, many practices in the palatine Chancery courts could appear almost summary, and in addition such things as the questionable procedure of common bill and confession, as utilized at Chester, cannot be ignored. Some of this may be reflected in a contemporary guide which tells us that these courts 'in the formality of their proceedings do all imitate the practice of the Chancery . . . and in some things they are led by their proper customs and prescription respectively'.[26]

The substance of litigation was also similar to that in the Westminster

Chancery. Title or freehold could not be determined, but orders for preserva-
tion or restitution of possession might be decisive. Trial of title at law through
eictione firmae, making use of depositions taken, was frequently ordered. Many
bills secured the deposit in court of documents or the examination of witnesses.
Much of this related to law suits in other tribunals. Bills were couched in terms
of equity and conscience, claims of violence or prejudice. Disputed debts and
property were at the heart of most litigation. Small values were the norm, but
sums over £100 were common. A suit at Durham was for lands worth £7,000,
the sale of which was covered by a recognizance for a penalty twice that figure.
Tiny tracts or many acres were involved, single beasts or flocks, contracts,
leases, small debts, performance of bargains, grants, and promises. There was
litigation about mortgages, trusts and uses. In 1599, on a point of equity, the
opinion of Attorney General Coke that verbal consent could not take away
title was entered as an order by the Chester Exchequer. Suits to preserve or
challenge right of way were prolific. These were often a means whereby the
sheriff could be authorized to arrange an inquest determining ways and
passages.[27]

A striking theme is provided by the incessant grant of injunctions, requiring
parties and their lawyers to stay proceedings at law in other courts, and by the
issue of *certiorari* to remove the record from another court. Quite often these
writs were soon dissolved, and hence complaints about vexatious litigants and
corrupt clerks abounded. Major orders governing procedure, notably at
Durham and Lancaster, tried to regulate the situation even to the point of
giving borough and other inferior authorities some discretion. In September
1638, Hutton empowered the clerk of the county court not to receive *certiorari*
unless the defendant in that court had entered bail. At Lancaster, plaintiffs
seeking stay of proceedings were required to attend the inferior court in
person.[28]

The majority of common injunctions were issued on grounds of conscience
and equity for stay of execution upon recorded bonds – recognizances, statutes
merchant, and statutes staple. These were judgments and the normal penalty,
now the sum in dispute, was double value. There were thousands of disputed
executions. The consequent demand for injunctions is so consistent at Westminster and in the provinces that it can almost seem a standard procedure.
Perhaps it was. At any rate, the situation is central to our understanding of the
growth of English bill courts.

Criminal jurisdiction was represented by informations, mostly brought by
the palatine attorneys general. Those prosecuted at Chester were mainly
defaulting local officials, particularly with respect to the upkeep of bridges,
ditches and roads. Ordinary people were accused of affrays, misdemeanours,
assaults on process servers, and failure to pay taxes to a local constable. There
does not seem to have been any exceptional activity in the 20 years before
1640.[29] The Lancaster Chancery provides even less evidence, but informations

exhibited in Duchy Chamber may have largely supplanted the palatine court in this respect. At Durham most informations concerned the bishop's estates and revenues. In 1623, an information claiming money from a clerk implies peculation, and in the 1630s a number of such informations concerned beasts, intrusions and wrecks.[30] As Dr Williams has found for the Council at Ludlow, this procedure appears to have had few if any political overtones.[31] The number of prosecutions was not remarkable, and in any case it seems probable that the Crown's interests were increasingly protected through informations brought by the king's attorney general in the Westminster Exchequer.

Responsibility for local government took various forms. In 1608, acting on petitions from J.P.s and others, the chamberlain of Chester issued orders from the bench, *pro rege at republica*, instituting commissions of enquiry into the responsibility of head constables for the repair of bridges with power to advise, after taking examinations, whether immediate inhabitants or the whole county should bear the cost of reparation. Other matters, such as the affairs of industries and guilds, combined private and public interest. Orders controlling salt mining and coal mining were common at Chester and Durham respectively.[32]

The element of supervision was most notable with respect to lesser courts. Strictly speaking the latter were only to entertain cases in which every detail permitted jurisdiction, impartiality was ensured, and proper procedures followed. A fight for judicial independence, centred on problems of definition, was under way before Elizabeth died. The difficulties are illustrated by the experience of the Council of the North which was denounced in 1596 for staying suits in a myriad of lesser jurisdictions. It argued that too many lesser courts were marred by improper proceedings, unfair penalties, and partial judges. The city of York fought hardest, but despite appeals to Privy Council and Parliament – M.P.s of Beverley, Hull and York combined in 1621 – the lord president had more or less established his authority over all boroughs in the area by the 1620s.[33]

The palatines, being small and compact, had less trouble. Their internal claims, perhaps with the exception of Durham, were less ambitious than those of the Councils. They reminded cities, boroughs and manors that jurisdiction was limited to resident litigants and matters arising within boundaries. Considerations of equity, influence and partiality might justify stay or transference of proceedings, but assistance was also given to lesser courts in many ways, including commissions, provision of examinations, and supporting orders. Many cases were referred to borough and manor courts, either totally or with the equity reserved. Decisions of lesser courts were approved, and sometimes entered as orders in palatine Chanceries. The course and conduct of common law proceedings were often directed. Assistance and restraint, however, still meant that supervision was being applied from above and definition imposed. Every lesser court was subjected to the same treatment, from the most minute to the larger ones, such as those in Chester city, Liverpool, Macclesfield, Nantwich, and Preston.

Each borough had its own structure, but a common feature was the late Elizabethan trend towards oligarchy, encouraged by the Crown, which paralleled confirmation of some internal powers claimed by borough officials. Approval of authority suited the central government so long as its exercise was not influenced unduly by the community. At the same time greater courts were insisting upon a strict observance of the rules. The problem was that charters and letters patent tended to be rather specific about jurisdiction and less so about the definition of freemen.[34]

Freemen in Liverpool, whose number almost doubled between 1620 and 1640, were sworn not to sue an inhabitant outside the town 'unless it be for want of justice and right there to be ministered'. In 1642, Preston had nearly 800 in-burgesses and nearly 1,000 out-burgesses. Such figures were absurd in relation to population. Honorary freemen posed a problem, but in fairness to the boroughs it must be said that there was a trend towards treating them as no more than such. The trouble was that palatine courts used residence as their yardstick whereas boroughs, of necessity supporting individuals for fear that general privileges might be undermined, stressed the rights of freemen. The city of Chester tried to prevent freemen from resorting to the palatine Exchequer in disputes against their fellows: process to remove suits from the Portmote was to be brought in person, licence to sue in the Exchequer had to be obtained from the mayor, and fines were imposed on offenders. In 1636, the burgesses of Liverpool agreed to sustain the costs of those summoned, unlawfully in their eyes, before the Lancaster admiralty. Boroughs were able to organize some defence of their liberties.[35]

Liverpool, where plaintiffs were so often restrained by injunctions from Lancaster Castle, had several tussles with the palatine Chancery as to which should have custody of prisoners. The borough made effective use of its charter of 1626 and its position as part of the Duchy, the authority which dominated its adversary. Similar arguments were used to combat any assumption that it was part of the 'port' of Chester, which ran from Barmouth to north Lancashire. Indeed Liverpool's claim to customs independence on the north shore of the Mersey had received some acceptance in 1578 after enquiries and litigation in Duchy Chamber and the Westminster Exchequer. After decades of dispute this was confirmed in 1658 and again at the Restoration.[36]

Chester city had once claimed to be outside the palatine, but in 1574 – a few years after the latter's victory over Ludlow – the Privy Council and the Westminster Exchequer confirmed the chamberlain's authority. Thereafter relations were normal but marked by the odd angry clash. In 1608, after a suit had been removed from the Portmote, the national Exchequer apparently upheld the palatine authorities. In 1611, the city begged the chamberlain not to issue writs of *corpus cum causa* in respect of persons properly imprisoned by its courts. The cathedral precincts and the castle, headquarters of the palatine, were outside the city. So too was Gloverstone, an area within the walls, which was a haven for fugitives and a commercial centre for non-freemen. Disputes over its boundaries and independence went on for years, involving not only the city and palatine authorities but also the Court of Wards and Privy Council.[37]

Municipal feuds prompted recourse to greater courts. Between 1599 and 1611, sporadic disputes concerning the clerk of the Pentice in Chester went to the palatine Exchequer. The monopoly of the Chester Brewers, when challenged, was carried to Star Chamber, the Privy Council was consulted, and the affair was subsequently referred to the chamberlain. Other dissensions had their impact. The Westminster Exchequer issued an attachment after a palatine officer, trying to impound plate belonging to the city, was restrained by the mayor of Chester. In 1636–7, Robert Dobson, dismissed as town clerk of Liverpool after much contention, turned to the assizes. Restraining process and arbitration followed, but the damage had been done. Liverpool like other places would find in future that claims of privilege before the assizes might require production of the town's charter.[38]

Borough disputes might be entertained by a palatine court, but the frustrated could turn to Westminster in the hope of outranking that authority if the matter concerned jurisdiction and privilege. A palatine Chancery had no more right to determine its own position, once the question was raised, than did a lesser court. Whether or not palatine authority was subsequently upheld is not the point. In 1610, it was the Westminster Exchequer which, after years of dispute and a charter which seemed to point in another direction, confirmed the bishop's exceptional sway over the city of Durham. In 1626, the attorney general questioned the bishop's temporalities in an Exchequer information. In 1637, that same national court stayed proceedings at Durham and imposed its own conditions, including valuation, in a tithes dispute. Durham, because of the bishop's diverse interests, is exceptional but the same thing can be found elsewhere. Jurisdiction and privileges were being determined from above, and the national courts applied the same principles to palatines as the latter did to lesser courts within their area.[39]

Certainly the palatine courts had their own internal problems. If many judges belonged simultaneously to greater courts, combination of position was most apparent at lower levels and in conjunction with lesser jurisdictions. Many officials, notably attorneys, were borough officials or related to such. The communication provided was an advantage, but it also spawned allegations of partiality and neglect of duty.

Most institutions experienced an increase in the number of officials. 'Once a new office had established itself, it tended to be continued indefinitely, long after the reason for its creation had been forgotten.'[40] Plurality of office contributed as much to the proliferation of deputies as did the self-seeking petitions of suitors. Administration increased: the office created at Lancaster in

1615 to keep depositions taken by commission is only one example.[41] Resistance to administration increased accordingly. Despite the mass of litigation, it was as astonishing to some people at Chester as it was to outsiders that the number of attorneys in the local Exchequer grew to nine by the early Stuart period whereas the national Chancery had six. The four 'ancient' attorneys failed to convince the chamberlain about this, but they did secure rules to prevent the poaching of staff.[42] It was widely assumed that the number of officials was a factor in increasing costs, and that the multitude of bills made it difficult for litigants, particularly defendants, to secure a hearing, proper copies or entries, unless palms were greased. As at Westminster, it was commonly believed that *certiorari*, injunctions and prohibitions were allowed on surmise or made out by clerks without authority, perhaps without a bill having been filed. Whatever happened, the clerks got their fee.

Private profit and office were interlocked, disputes between officials were often related to local faction, and feud might become a matter of jurisdiction. Early in James's reign Edward Dod, baron of the Exchequer at Chester, had to defend his perquisites against both the examiner and Alexander Cotes, a fascinating figure on the local scene. Formerly deputy baron, Cotes still claimed privilege including the right not to pay fees. Dod said that he brought needless suits and instigated 'incessant troubles, wrongs and scandals'. Cotes was imprisoned but he obtained writs of *habeas corpus* from Westminster directed to the sheriff and to the constable of the castle. Since these circumvented the chamberlain and did 'proceed from above', Derby ordered that they were to be ignored. This was not the last litigation fostered by Cotes in his constant assault on the current establishment.[43]

Error and treason apart, Westminster process was properly directed to the palatine authority – bishop, chamberlain, or chancellor – who would issue the like process under his seal directed to the appropriate party or official, for example a sheriff. Prohibitions went to the palatine head. Injunctions applied to parties, not courts, and hence there was no reason why the palatine should assist. On a different level there is ample evidence that the bishop of Durham was required by *mandamus* to issue process for attendance at Westminster, the arrest of persons wanted there, imprisonment of debtors, and the sale of goods.[44]

Palatine courts could not direct process beyond their boundaries, and they were hampered by strict observance of this geographical limitation upon service of writs and the execution of commissions. Some individuals moved back and forth across palatine boundaries. A single witness beyond reach might necessitate recourse to another court in order to secure examination. If a resident, let us assume without reason, began proceedings at Westminster, it had been understood since the end of Elizabeth's reign that provincial courts could not stay the suit. Orders might be issued, but little could be done to enforce them. Action against the individual, imprisonment if the recalcitrant was within jurisdiction, was questionable and likely to produce a reaction from

Westminster. Something could be done, as when the plaintiff in an enclosure dispute at Chester was ordered to cease his later action of trespass in the Westminster Exchequer, but this was conditional upon the defendant filing a proper answer. It was more tricky when the palatine defendant was the plaintiff at Westminster, but there are examples of such persons agreeing to stay their suits, as when the principal debt plus costs was deposited in the local court. Much was possible unless individuals were intransigent, and even then a provincial court might make its point. One plaintiff at Chester, after a palatine decree ordering his discharge in the Common Pleas, was imprisoned in the castle subsequent to a *capias* from Westminster. However, his opponent, being within jurisdiction and deemed contemptuous, was also imprisoned in the same place on an attachment from the Exchequer at Chester.[45]

There seem to have been few problems with major specialized jurisdictions. In 1587, Chester secured an agreement as to jurisdiction over Duchy lands within the palatine, and the Court of Wards was accepted. Lancaster also deferred to the Wards unless the Duchy had a claim. Lapsley's belief that the bishop did not 'maintain' a Court of Wards is misplaced. The bishop's Chancery appointed commissions for idiots and lunatics, traverses of inquisitions were allowed after exhibition of petitions, grants of custody and wardship were made, licences for marriage or entry without proof of age were issued. If, however, the land was held of the Crown in chief, as distinct from the bishop, the Wards had jurisdiction. Then there was the bishop's admiralty jurisdiction, not notable but acknowledged after the Restoration. He defended it through an information in Star Chamber, exhibited by Coke as attorney general, and again in 1640 against a grant of rights on the Wear made by the lord admiral.[46]

The initiative in going to a superior court, or of demurring, lay with the individual. This granted, the essential point to be argued was that of privilege, particularly that of an area or jurisdiction. Litigants with, for example, disputed interests in both Cheshire and Lancashire, a common circumstance, could not be embraced by one palatine jurisdiction. Officials were privileged to sue and be sued in their own court, insofar as it had jurisdiction, but this was not so if one of their associates in the dispute lacked this qualification or was non-resident, or if a single adversary could claim privilege in a higher court. Hence the impact of Westminster was conventional. All parties had to live within designated boundaries, the matter in dispute had to be located there, and claims of institutional privilege had to be watertight. A single straw party could shatter jurisdiction. The bounds of palatine competence were becoming very limited even if the amount of business was impressive.

Furthermore many issues, superficially local in respect of persons and subject, could be grasped by Westminster because they had national and regal implications. A major dispute between the customer of Chester and merchants of that city was entertained by the Westminster Exchequer. Crown lessees, grantees and officials could turn to that court. The attorney general, even if acting on behalf of a relator, was not easily denied. Early in Charles I's reign, litigants in the Chester Exchequer were stayed by injunction on an information in the Westminster Exchequer dealing with residents, lands and tenements within the palatine.[47]

Disputes as to authority and jurisdiction invited adjudication from above. Customary tenants petitioned the House of Commons against a decree of the Durham Chancery; in 1629 another group of tenants approached the Privy Council and were advised to proceed in Star Chamber with their protest against actions of the Dean and Chapter. After the national Chancery in 1617 accepted a claim of Chester privilege, there was a long imbroglio in which one party, repeatedly applying to Parliament, in 1628 secured an order that the matter was in fact to be heard at Westminster. In 1607–9, the great dispute over the Dee causeway, which involved Denbighshire as well as those living within the palatine of Chester and Flint, was referred by the Privy Council to the two chief justices and the chief baron.[48]

The situation was weighted against palatine authority, not least because in any dispute it would be courts such as the Chancery and Exchequer at Westminster which had the edge in decision. Even if all circumstances justified palatine jurisdiction, a defendant in the Westminster Chancery might find that the onus was on him to appear and plead. In fact, Chancery often dismissed bills, thus recognizing palatine and other courts, but the required procedures consumed time and thus undermined a supposed convenience of local jurisdiction. Supporters of palatine authority had some reason to demand vigilance: 'that no causes be sued forth of the county palatine [of Chester] in any court at Westminster, but the same to be presently called back, and the parties plaintiffs to be severely punished'. Townshend in 1605 complained about encroachments from Westminster, in particular the number of prohibitions from Common Pleas directed to the chamberlain of Chester. Three years later there were grumbles about suits decreed at Chester being called into other courts. The exposed nature of palatine jurisdiction with respect to residence of litigants is illustrated by a case of 1622. The examiner of the palatine Exchequer, resisting execution of an obligation in Common Pleas which concerned a contract made in Chester, claimed privilege and obtained an injunction from his court. Chief Justice Hobart acknowledged that there was equity in the matter, but a single defendant living in London justified a prohibition to the chamberlain and Hobart's conclusion that the matter properly belonged to the Westminster Chancery.[49]

Durham disintegrated under the Scottish invasion of 1640, but the courts at Chester and Lancaster only lapsed after the summer of 1642. Commonwealth and Protectorate did not heed requests for revival, but a series of orders permitted continuation of actions and pleas left hanging or pending before the assizes when the wars started. One factor behind popular petitions for reinstatement was the business which these courts had brought to parent towns, but equally important were arguments stressing local convenience, speed, and the expense of going to Westminster for trivial matters. A similar mixture of motives produced support for the two provincial Councils. As Dr Brooks has written of the petitioning citizens of York in 1661: 'they knew more about the Council as a working institution than we are ever likely to do, and they wanted it back'.[50]

The Council of the North was not revived at the Restoration. The Welsh Council, no longer claiming border counties, survived until 1689 but it was decrepit, and its organization was as poor as its jurisdiction. In any case, as the abolishing statute observed, matters could be determined elsewhere. The palatines continued into the Victorian era, but their Chancery courts were ghosts of former activity. In the eighteenth century, the Chester Exchequer was dependent upon those wretched common bills without which, it was said, business would have been negligible and no attorney of reputation would have attended. The deputy baron sat once a week, the vice-chamberlain twice a year, and the positions of chamberlain and baron were almost sinecures. The Durham Chancery sat for only a few days in the year and its records were in a terrible state. The palatine principle was still alive, but the circumstances had changed. Judges were no longer of national standing: indeed one, it is said, tried to apprehend John Doe and Richard Roe because of their litigious habits. By 1700, provincial Chanceries received a negligible number of bills, the Westminster Chancery dominated but was almost overwhelmed, and the Exchequer reached its feeble peak of about 750 bills *per annum*. Yet, apart from the deletion in 1641 of jurisdiction 'like' to that of Star Chamber, no statute had limited palatine ability.[51]

The reduced circumstances of palatine chancery courts during the Restoration must be seen in context. Their difficulties were not exceptional although, of course, each institution has its own history. The courts of Great Sessions have been described as anomalous bodies staffed by inferior men and operating according to questionable procedures. Yet, it must be noted, civil business on English assize circuits was declining by the 1690s, although the quality of judges and procedures cannot be questioned. The lord warden's Chancery at Dover had fewer suits, and the joint courts of the head towns of the Cinque Ports only met five times between 1698 and 1857. Manchester and Salford reached an unofficial accommodation of their ancient dispute in the eighteenth century, but by that time neither the hundred nor the leet had an ability to match theoretical competence. Shire and lesser courts lost their grip on local government. Borough courts of orphans died across the Stuart century – the collapse of those at Bristol, Exeter and Worcester was apparent before 1640 – unless, as in London, there was a specific vested interest to maintain them. The communal advantages of manorial courts could not match the attraction of greater courts and the force of common law remedies. They were held for formal matters of copyhold tenure, but there was no longer anything to encourage lords to maintain a court for such things as debt and damages. It is a common story at all levels. One result was that there was a wave of demands for new local courts, and indeed some 'courts of requests' were actually established.[52]

People living within the boundaries of the Councils, the palatines or, for example, the Cinque Ports could still file bills in a court that was reasonably close. However, prior to 1640 a strict observance of boundaries and jurisdiction provided, quite properly, one inescapable wall. Furthermore, proceedings that were relatively cheap and speedy, methods suitable for handling a multitude of local cases in as little time as possible, would lose attraction if their authority was questionable. Many cases had been conducted with a formality comparable to that at Westminster, but much was done by methods which in comparison seemed abbreviated: hearings after initial pleadings, sweeping use of *viva voce* examinations at hearings, and a readiness to decree against defendants who failed to appear and answer. Procedural sophistication and record-keeping, although vastly improved, did not keep pace with Westminster standards and its complicated machinery of pleadings, proofs and hearings. Granted geography and convenience, the palatine chanceries could do nothing that their national counterparts at Westminster could not do. Yet the latter could do so much more. Limited and tied to established jurisdiction and procedures, palatine courts could not adapt and soon they would not cope. New aspects of law were unlikely to be embraced. However the national courts, those that had a capability to supervise lesser tribunals, were not constrained. Recorded bonds would be rivalled by other methods of handling credit and money, agreements and contracts. Palatine courts could match neither new requirements of law and society nor the development of equity as understood in Nottingham's Chancery. As Plucknett pointed out, equity and its procedures developed from the institution.[53] There were many variations because there were many institutions, but by the later seventeenth century this divergence was no longer viable.

Revolution and war, political activity and legislation, during the middle of the seventeenth century had a tremendous impact on local courts. Equally important were developments across the entire Elizabethan and Stuart period. The Restoration, accepting much when legal proceedings of the last 18 years were confirmed, ignored tensions and problems which had been apparent before 1640. The palatine Chancery courts, circumscribed and defined, had lost their former capacity. The Westminster Chancery, despite some support from the Exchequer, was overwhelmed by a mass of litigation which before 1640 might in part have been handled elsewhere. Indeed we are looking at a broader factor, the disintegration of a Tudor state based upon competent local authorities. The nineteenth century would inherit a centralized system, described by Holdsworth as 'almost a denial of justice' to the poor man.[54]

THE HISTORICAL WRITINGS OF JOEL HURSTFIELD

1944 TO 1978

1. BOOKS, ARTICLES AND LECTURES

1944 'The control of British raw material supplies, 1919–1939', *EcHR*, 1st ser. XIV, 1–31.

1946 Section 'The sixteenth century' in the Historical Association's *Annual Bulletin of Historical Literature*, XXXI, 20–2; and in 1948–51 inclusive: XXXII, 20–2; XXXIII, 20–3; XXXIV, 23–5; XXXV, 22–4; XXXVI, 33–5.

1949 'The Greenwich Tenures of the reign of Edward VI', *Law Quarterly Review*, LXV, 72–81.

'Lord Burghley as Master of the Court of Wards, 1561–98', *TRHS*, 4th ser. XXXI, 95–114.

1950 'Constitutional development', *Life under the Tudors*, ed. J. E. Morpurgo (Falcon Educational Books), 29–43.

1952 'The revival of feudalism in early Tudor England'. A paper read to the Stubbs Society of the University of Oxford in November, 1949. *History* n.s. XXXVII, 131–45.

1953 *The Control of Raw Materials* (H. M. Stationery Office and Longmans, Green). A volume in the War Production Series of the Second World War, United Kingdom Civil Series.

'Corruption and reform under Edward VI and Mary: the example of wardship', *EHR*, LXVIII, 22–36. [Reprinted in *Freedom, Corruption and Government in Elizabethan England* (1973) 163–82.]

'That arch-liar Froude', *Listener*, 9 July, L, 62–3.

1954 'Wardship and marriage under Elizabeth I', *History Today*, IV no. 9, 605–12.

1955 'The profits of fiscal feudalism, 1541–1602', *EcHR*, 2nd ser. VIII, 53–61.

1956 'The Tudor age', *The Connoisseur Period Guides: The Sixteenth Century*, 1–15.

'William Cecil, Lord Burghley: minister to Elizabeth I', *History Today*, VI no. 12, 791–9.

1957 'County government, c.1530–c.1660', *The Victoria History of the Counties of England:*

Wiltshire, ed. R. B. Pugh and Elizabeth Crittal, V. 80–110. [Reprinted in *Freedom, Corruption and Government in Elizabethan England* (1973), 236–93.]

'Robert Cecil, Earl of Salisbury: minister of Elizabeth I and James I', *History Today*, VII no. 5, 279–89.

Letters on Raleigh's Treason and the Great Contract, *ibid.*, VII no. 7, 480; no. 8, 552.

1958   *The Queen's Wards: Wardship and Marriage under Elizabeth I* (Longmans, Green). 2nd edn 1973 (Frank Cass).

1959   Section III: Constitutional History, 1485–1603, *Bibliography of British History. Tudor Period, 1485–1603*, ed. Conyers Read (2nd edn Oxford: Clarendon Press), 86–117.

1960   *Elizabeth I and the Unity of England* (The English Universities Press in the 'Teach Yourself History' series). [Also published in Penguin Books (Pelican Books): Harmondsworth, 1971.]

'Conyers Read and historical biography', *Listener*, 28 Apr., LXIII, 747–8.

Liberty and Authority under Elizabeth I. Inaugural lecture delivered at University College, London, 12 May 1960 (H. K. Lewis). A shortened version was printed in *Listener*, 29 Dec., LXIV, 1177–79.

'Elizabeth I', *New Universal Encyclopaedia*, VI, 3027–8.

1961   'The Succession struggle in late Elizabethan England', *Elizabethan Government and Society*, Essays presented to Sir John Neale, ed. S. T. Bindoff, J. Hurstfield and C. H. Williams (Athlone Press), 369–96. [Reprinted in *Freedom, Corruption and Government in Elizabethan England* (1973), 104–34.]

'Professor R. R. Betts: an appreciation', *Slavonic and East European Review*, XL, 2–6.

1962   'Some Elizabethans', *History*, XLVII, 18–31.

1963   'John Stow'. An address delivered on 7 March 1962, at the Annual Stow Commemoration Service. *Trans. London and Middlesex Archaeological Soc.*, XXI pt 1, 62–4.

1964   *The Elizabethan Nation* (B.B.C. Publications).

'The Elizabethan people in the age of Shakespeare'. A lecture delivered at University College London to commemorate the fourth centenary of the birth of Shakespeare, in *Shakespeare's World*, ed. James Sutherland and Joel Hurstfield (Edward Arnold), 27–47.

'Elizabethan England in the year of Shakespeare's birth', *History Today*, XIV no. 2, 79–87.

Tudor Times (English History in Pictures), ed. Joel Hurstfield (The Historical Association: Routledge and Kegan Paul).

Foreword, Alice Clare Carter, *The English Reformed Church in Amsterdam in the Seventeenth Century* (Publications of the Municipal Archives of Amsterdam, no. 3. Amsterdam: Scheltema and Holkema), 5.

1965 'Church and state, 1558–1612: the task of the Cecils', *Studies in Church History*, ed. G. J. Cuming (Nelson), II, 119–40. [Reprinted in *Freedom, Corruption and Government in Elizabethan England* (1973), 79–103.]

'John Norden's view of London, 1600. The London setting', *London Topographical Record*, XXII, 5–13.

'Liberty under the first Elizabeth', *Commonwealth Journal*, VIII, 219–22.

'The crisis of the aristocracy, 1558–1641', *Listener*, 24 June, LXXIII, 934–5.

'The framework of crisis' and 'The search for compromise in England and France', *Reformation Crisis*, ed. Joel Hurstfield (Edward Arnold), 1–7, 95–106. [Also published New York: Barnes and Noble, 1966; New York: Harper and Row, Torchbook, 1966.]

1967 'Was there a Tudor despotism after all?', *TRHS*, 5th ser. XVII, 83–108. [Reprinted in *Freedom, Corruption and Government in Elizabethan England* (1973), 23–49.]

'Political corruption in modern England: the historian's problem', *History*, LII, 16–34. An earlier version was read at the Anglo–American Conference of Historians in London in July 1963. [Reprinted in *Freedom, Corruption and Government in Elizabethan England* (1973), 137–62.]

'Tradition and change: English society under the Tudors', *The Age of the Renaissance*, ed. Denys Hay (Thames and Hudson), 250–78. [Reprinted as 'Tradition and change in the English Renaissance' in *Freedom, Corruption and Government in Elizabethan England* (1973), 199–235.]

'Froude, James Anthony', 'May, Thomas', 'Stow, John', *Encyclopaedia Britannica*, IX, 963–4; XV, 4–5; XXI, 281.

1968 'Social structure, office-holding and politics, chiefly in western Europe', *The New Cambridge Modern History*, III (The Counter-Reformation and Price Revolution 1559–1610), ed. R. B. Wernham (Cambridge University Press), 126–48. [A slightly revised version, 'Office-holding and government mainly in England and France', printed in *Freedom, Corruption and Government in Elizabethan England* (1973), 294–325.]

'The Gospel according to Galbraith – Professor V. H. Galbraith talks to Professor Joel Hurstfield about the work of the historian', *Listener*, 4 Apr., LXXIX, 439–40.

'The historian's commitment', *Times Educational Supplement*, 26 Apr., 1383–4.

'Professor Alfred Cobban, 1901–68', *History Today* XVIII, no. 6, 431.

'The causes and consequences of Mr Guy Fawkes', *Listener*, 14 Nov., LXXX, 635–7.

1970 'Gunpowder Plot and the politics of dissent', *Early Stuart Studies*, Essays in Honour of David Harris Willson, ed. Howard S. Reinmuth (University of Minnesota Press), 95–121. [Reprinted in *Freedom, Corruption and Government in Elizabethan England* (1973), 327–51.]

'Monopolies and corruption' and 'The Essex rebellion', *History of the English-Speaking Peoples*, 1348–50, 1356–8.

'"Sometimes I go about and poison wells" – Marlowe, Shakespeare and the Jews', *Listener*, 24 Sept., LXXXIV, 400, 402.

1971 'The historical and social background', *A New Companion to Shakespeare Studies*, ed. Kenneth Muir and S. Schoenbaum (Cambridge University Press), 168–79. [Reprinted as 'The close of the Tudor age' in *The Historical Association book of The Tudors*, ed. Joel Hurstfield (1973), 204–19.]

'Henry and Elizabeth', *Listener*, 11 Mar., LXXXV, 289–92.

'The political morality of early Stuart statesmen', *History*, LVI, 235–43. [Reprinted in *Freedom, Corruption and Government in Elizabethan England* (1973), 183–96.]

1972 'The paradox of liberty in Shakespeare's England', *Essays and Studies* (in honour of Beatrice White), ed. T. S. Dorsch (John Murray), 57–82. This paper is a revised version of the Shakespeare Birthday Lecture delivered at the Folger Shakespeare Library, Washington, in 1969. [Reprinted in *Freedom, Corruption and Government in Elizabethan England* (1973), 50–76.]

Elizabethan People: state and society (A collection of sources), ed. Joel Hurstfield and Alan G. R. Smith (Edward Arnold; New York: St Martin's Press).

'Personal and political biography: a note on Mary Tudor', *University of Newcastle (Australia) Historical Journal*, 11, 17–23.

1973 *Freedom, Corruption and Government in Elizabethan England* (Jonathan Cape). Introduction and 'The close of the Tudor age', *The Historical Association book of The Tudors*, ed. Joel Hurstfield (Sidgwick and Jackson), 7–12, 204–19. ['The close of the Tudor age' originally published as 'The historical and social background' in *A New Companion to Shakespeare Studies*, ed. Kenneth Muir and S. Schoenbaum (Cambridge University Press, 1971), 168–79.]

'Gunpowder Plot', *Folio*, 3–13.

'A medieval evils lesson', *Washington Post*, Apr. 14.

1975 *The Historian as Moralist: Reflections on the Study of Tudor England.* John Coffin

Memorial Lecture delivered at University College London, 25 Feb. 1974 (Athlone Press).

'The politics of corruption in Shakespeare's England', *Shakespeare Survey*, ed. Kenneth Muir (Cambridge University Press), XXVIII, 15–28.

'Queen and State: the emergence of an Elizabethan myth'. A paper delivered to the fifth Anglo-Dutch Historical Conference. This is a revised version of a paper, 'The Elizabethan myth', read at the Folger Shakespeare Library, Washington, in May 1973, in *Britain and the Netherlands*, ed. J. S. Bromley and E. H. Kossmann (The Hague: Martinus Nijhoff), V, 58–77.

'Shakespeare, historical criticism and the historian', *Shakespeare Newsletter* (University of Illinois), XXV, no. 5, 42.

1976　'Elizabethan England', Joel Hurstfield and A. G. R. Smith, *The Tudors and Stuarts*, ed. William Lamont (Sussex Books) (Sussex Publications), 61–79.

1977　'Two inspiring masters of the historian's craft: V. H. Galbraith and J. E. Neale', *Times Higher Education Supplement*, 11 Nov. no. 314, 17.

1978　'The search for the good society in Shakespeare's day and our own', *Shakespeare: Pattern of Excelling Nature*, ed. D. Bevington and J. L. Halio (University of Delaware Press).

Professor Joel Hurstfield has published articles on historical and other subjects in *The Times*, *The Times Higher Education Supplement*, *The Daily Telegraph*, *The Guardian*, *The Spectator* and other periodicals.

2. REVIEWS

1944　Joseph Borkin and Charles A. Welsh, *Germany's Master Plan* (EcHR, 1st ser. XIV, 206–7).

1945　T. H. Burnham and G. O. Hoskins, *Iron and Steel in Great Britain, 1870–1930* (EcHR, 1st ser. XV, 104–5).

1951　*Prerogativa Regis*. Tertia Lectura Roberti Constable de Lyncolnis Inne Anno 11 H.7, ed. S. E. Thorne (*Law Quarterly Review*, LXVII, 401–3).

H. Maynard Smith, *Henry VIII and the Reformation* (*History*, n.s. XXXVI, 123–4).

Arthur Ogle, *The Tragedy of the Lollards' Tower* (*ibid.*, 266). *Calendar of the Patent Rolls, Elizabeth, Vol. II, 1560–1563* (*ibid.*, 266–7).

1952　W. Schenk, *Reginald Pole, Cardinal of England* (*History*, n.s. XXXVII, 163).

1953　*Materials in the National Archives relating to the historical programs of civilian government agencies during World War II* (*Archives*, II, 111–12).

1954 John Clapham, *Elizabeth of England: Certain observations concerning the life and reign of Queen Elizabeth*, ed. Evelyn Plummer Read and Conyers Read; John Gerard, *The Autobiography of an Elizabethan*, ed. Philip Caraman (*History*, n.s. XXXIX, 110–11).

G. R. Elton, *The Tudor Revolution in Government* (*EcHR*, 2nd ser. VII, 110–11).

1955 J. D. Mackie, *The Earlier Tudors, 1485–1558;* J. A. Williamson, *The Tudor Age* (*History*, n.s. XL, 127–9).

Conyers Read, *Mr. Secretary Cecil and Queen Elizabeth* (*Spectator*, 20 May, CXCIV, 653).

Records of the Court of Augmentations relating to Wales and Monmouthshire, ed. E. A. Lewis and J. Conway Davies (Board of Celtic Studies, History and Law Series, no. 13) (*EHR*, LXX, 450–2).

P. E. Russell, *The English Intervention in Spain and Portugal in the Time of Edward III and Richard II;* Joyceline G. Dickinson, *The Congress of Arras, 1435* (*Spectator*, 30 Sept., CXCV, 428).

Barbara Winchester, *Tudor Family Portrait* (*History Today*, V no. 11, 795).

G. R. Elton, *England under the Tudors* (ibid., V no. 12, 874–5).

1956 *Devon monastic lands: Calendar of particulars for grants 1536–1558*, ed. Joyce Youings (Devon and Cornwall Record Soc., n.s. I) (*Archives*, II, 445–6).

Calendar of State Papers, Spanish, Vol. XIII, 1554–8, ed. Royal Tyler (*EcHR*, 2nd ser. IX, 142).

Lacey Baldwin Smith, *Tudor Prelates and Politics, 1536–1538* (Princeton Studies in History, vol. 8); Harold S. Darby, *Hugh Latimer* (*History*, n.s. XLI, 223–4).

John Izon, *Sir Thomas Stucley, c. 1525–1578: Traitor Extraordinary* (*History Today*, VI no. 11, 781).

1957 *The Third Book of Remembrance of Southampton, Vol. I, 1514–1540, and Vol. II*, ed. A. L. Merson; *Elizabethan Peterborough, Tudor Documents*, Part III, ed. W. T. Mellows and Daphne H. Gifford (Northants. Record Soc., 1956); H. P. R. Finberg, *The Gostwicks of Willington and other Studies* (Beds. Record Soc., vol. 36); *The Chantry Certificates for Cornwall*, ed. L. S. Snell; *The Edwardian Inventories of Church Goods for Cornwall*, ed. L. S. Snell; C. A. Ritchie, *The Ecclesiastical Courts of York* (*History*, XLII, 149–51).

1958 *The Calendar of the Caernarvonshire Quarter Sessions Records, Vol. I, 1541–58*, ed. W. Ogwen Williams (*EHR*, LXXIII, 109–10).

Calendar of Inquisitions Post Mortem, and other analogous documents preserved in the Public Record Office: Henry VII, Vol. III (*EcHR*, 2nd ser. X, 486).

The Thought and Culture of the English Renaissance. An Anthology of Tudor Prose,

1481–1555, ed. Elizabeth M. Nugent; *The Elizabethans,* ed. Allardyce Nicoll (*History,* XLIII, 139–41).

Mary E. Finch, *The Wealth of Five Northamptonshire Families, 1540–1640* (Northants. Record Soc., 1956) (*ibid.,* 142).

Lu Emily Pearson, *Elizabethans at Home* (*ibid.,* 232–3).

Philip Caraman, *Henry Morse, Priest of the Plague* (*ibid.,* 237–8).

Thomas Woodrooffe, *The Enterprise of England* (*History Today,* VIII no. 10, 733–4).

1959   A. Tindal Hart, *The Country Clergy in Elizabethan and Stuart times, 1558–1660* (*EHR,* LXXIV, 527).

A. L. Rowse, *The Elizabethans and America* (*Listener,* 15 Oct., LXII, 642).

1960   Millar Maclure, *The Paul's Cross Sermons 1534–1642* (*EHR,* LXXV, 122–4).

The Other Face. Catholic Life under Elizabeth I, ed. Philip Caraman (*Listener,* 7 Apr., LXIII, 629).

1961   P. M. Handover, *The Second Cecil* (*EHR,* LXXVI, 150).

Penry Williams, *The Council in the Marches of Wales under Elizabeth* (*Welsh History Review,* I, 232–4).

1962   Léon Cahen and Maurice Braure, *L'Evolution politique de L'Angleterre moderne, 1485–1660* in the third section of *L'Evolution de l'humanité* (*EHR,* LXXVII, 149–50).

Thomas Wotton's Letter-Book 1574–1586, ed. G. Eland (*ibid.,* 154).

Waldo Hilary Dunn, *James Anthony Froude. A Biography, 1818–56* (*History,* XLVII, 88–9).

V. J. K. Brook, *A Life of Archbishop Parker* (*Listener,* 8 Mar., LXVII, 445).

G. P. V. Akrigg, *Jacobean Pageant* (*ibid.,* 14 June, LXVII, 1040).

F. Smith Fussner, *The Historical Revolution; Approaches to History,* ed. H. P. R. Finberg (*ibid.,* 9 Aug., LXVIII, 219–20).

A Tudor Book of Rates, ed. T. S. Willan (*History,* XLVII, 304–5).

The Tudor Constitution, ed. G. R. Elton (*EHR,* LXXVII, 727–31).

Ian Dunlop, *Palaces and Progresses of Elizabeth I* (*Listener,* 22 Nov., LXVIII, 872).

Elizabeth Burton, *The Jacobeans at Home* (*ibid.,* 20 Dec., LXVIII, 1057).

1963   Hester Chapman, *Lady Jane Grey* (*Listener,* 14 Mar., LXIX, 472–3).

Sir Charles Petrie, *Philip II of Spain* (*ibid.,* 13 June, LXIX, 1008, 1011).

Historical Essays, 1600–1750, presented to David Ogg, ed. H. E. Bell and R. L. Ollard (*ibid.,* 12 Sept., LXX, 393–4).

W. G. Hoskins, *Provincial England: Essays in Social and Economic History* (*ibid.,* 28 Nov., LXX, 895).

1964 W. K. Jordan, *Social Institutions in Kent, 1480–1660, A Study of the changing pattern of social aspirations* (Kent Archaeological Soc., 1961); W. K. Jordan, *The Charities of Rural England, 1480–1660, The aspirations and the achievements of rural society* (*EHR,* LXXIX, 109–11).

William Lambarde and Local Government, ed. Conyers Read (The Folger Documents of Tudor and Stuart Civilization); *Advice to a Son,* ed. L. B. Wright (The Folger Documents of Tudor and Stuart Civilization) (*ibid.,* 411–13).

Fulton H. Anderson, *Francis Bacon, His career and his thought* (*ibid.,* 603).

Michael Strachan, *The Life and Adventures of Thomas Coryate* (*ibid.,* 845–6).

Clifford Letters in the Sixteenth Century, ed. A. G. Dickens (Surtees Soc., CLXXII) (*Journal of Ecclesiastical History,* XV, 116–7).

G. Dyfnallt Owen, *Elizabethan Wales* (The Social Scene) (*Welsh History Review,* II, 101–2).

1965 Amos C. Miller, *Sir Henry Killigrew, Elizabethan Soldier and Diplomat* (*EHR,* LXXX, 161–2).

C. M. Gray, *Copyhold, Equity, and the Common Law* (*ibid.,* 393–4).

1966 Waldo Hilary Dunn, *James Anthony Froude: Vol. II, 1859–1894* (*History,* LI, 240–1).

William R. Trimble, *The Catholic Laity in Elizabethan England, 1558–1603* (*Journal of Ecclesiastical History,* XVII, 273–4).

Sales of Wards in Somerset, 1603–1641, ed. M. J. Hawkins (Somerset Record Soc., LXVII) (*EcHR,* 2nd ser. XIX, 664–5).

R. B. Wernham, *Before the Armada. The growth of English foreign policy, 1485–1588* (*History Today,* XVI no. 12, 867–8).

1968 D. M. Loades, *Two Tudor Conspiracies* (*Journal of Ecclesiastical History,* XIX, 125–6).

Mary M. Luke, *Catherine the Queen;* G. P. V. Akrigg, *Shakespeare and the Earl of Southampton* (*Spectator,* 20 Sept., CCXXI, 404–5).

The Third Book of Remembrance of Southampton, 1514–1662, Vol. III, ed. A. L. Merson (*History,* LIII, 425).

E. E. Reynolds, *The Field is Won* (*Spectator,* 13 Dec., CCXXI, 842–3).

1969 *Calendar of the Patent Rolls, Elizabeth I, Vol. V, 1569–1572* (*EHR,* LXXXIV, 173–5).

W. K. Jordan, *Edward VI: the Young King, the Protectorship of the Duke of Somerset;* Robert Ashton, *James I by his Contemporaries* (*Spectator,* 31 Jan., CCXXII, 140–1).

Joan Simon, *Education and Society in Tudor England* (*Journal of Ecclesiastical History,* XX, 371–2).

J. H. Plumb, *The Death of the Past* (*Spectator,* 13 Dec., CCXXIII, 826).

1970   Mortimer Levine, *The Early Elizabethan Succession Question, 1558–1568* (*EHR,* LXXXV, 413–4).

Whitney R. D. Jones, *The Tudor Commonwealth, 1529–1559* (*Spectator,* 4 Apr., CCXXIV, 446).

Charles Wilson, *Queen Elizabeth and the Revolt of the Netherlands* (*ibid.,* 25 July, CCXXV, 77–8).

1971   J. A. van Dorsten, *The Radical Arts: first Decade of an Elizabethan Renaissance* (*Journal of Ecclesiastical History,* XXII, 173).

1972   W. J. Jones, *The Elizabethan Court of Chancery* (*EcHR,* 2nd ser. XXV, 162–3).

Claire Cross, *The Royal Supremacy in the Elizabethan Church* (Historical Problems Studies and Documents, 8) (*Journal of Ecclesiastical History,* XXIII, 281–2).

1973   B. L. Joseph, *Shakespeare's Eden: The Commonwealth of England, 1558–1629* (*Modern Language Review,* LXVIII, 148–9).

1974   J. H. Hexter, *The Vision of Politics on the Eve of the Reformation: More, Machiavelli, and Seyssel* (*American Historical Review,* LXXIX, 1172–3).

Arthur Joseph Slavin, *The Precarious Balance: English Government and Society* (*The Borzoi History of England, Volume 3: 1450–1640*) (*ibid.,* 1546–7).

1975   Antonia Fraser, *King James VI of Scotland, I of England* (*Times Literary Supplement,* 18 Apr., 420–1).

Letters discussing King James I (*ibid.,* 23 May, 567; 1 Aug., 874).

Samuel Rhea Gammon, *Statesman and Schemer: William, First Lord Paget, Tudor Minister* (*American Historical Review,* LXXX, 1329).

G. D. Ramsay, *The City of London in International Politics at the Accession of Elizabeth* (*London Journal,* I, 279–80).

1976   *Calendar of the Patent Rolls, Elizabeth I, Vol. VI, 1572–1575* (EHR, XCI, 127–9).

V. Norskov Olsen, *John Foxe and the Elizabethan Church* (*Catholic Historical Review,* LXII, 134–5).

The Report of the Royal Commission of 1552, ed. W. C. Richardson (Archives of British History and Culture, 3) (*EcHR,* 2nd ser. XXIX, 152–3).

Stephen J. Greenblatt, *Sir Walter Ralegh The Renaissance Man and His Roles* (*Modern Language Review*, LXXI, 373–4).

1977   E. D. Pendry, *Elizabethan Prisons and Prison Scenes* (Salzburg Studies in English Literature, Elizabethan and Renaissance Studies, 17) (*Yearbook of English Studies*, VII, 216).

Glamorgan County History, *IV*, *Early Modern Glamorgan*, ed. Glanmor Williams (*EHR*, XCII, 608–12).

Professor Joel Hurstfield has also published many reviews in *The Times*, *The Daily Telegraph*, *The Guardian* and other journals.

ABBREVIATIONS

Add.	Additional
AO	Archives Office
APC	*Acts of the Privy Council*
BIHR	*Bulletin of the Institute of Historical Research*
BL	British Library
Bodl.	Bodleian Library, Oxford
CJ	*Commons Journals*
CSPD	*Calendar of State Papers, Domestic*
DNB	*Dictionary of National Biography*
EcHR	*Economic History Review*
EHR	*English Historical Review*
HMC	*Historical Manuscripts Commission Reports*
LJ	*Lords Journals*
LP	*Letters and Papers of Henry VIII*
PRO	Public Record Office
RO	Record Office
STC	*Short-Title Catalogue of English Books 1475–1640*
TRHS	*Transactions of the Royal Historical Society*
VCH	*Victoria County History*

Note Places of publication are given only for works published outside the United Kingdom.

NOTES

1 REFORM AND THE 'COMMONWEALTH-MEN' OF EDWARD VI'S REIGN

1. *England under the Tudors* (2nd edn, 1974), 206.
2. W. K. Jordan (ed.), *The Chronicle and Political Papers of King Edward VI* (1966), xxv.
3. W. R. D. Jones, *The Tudor Commonwealth 1529–1559* (1970), 24ff., 27, 32.
4. S. T. Bindoff, *Tudor England* (1950), 129f.; D. M. Loades, *Politics and the Nation* (1974), 209; C. S. L. Davies, *Peace, Print and Protestantism* (1976), 272ff. (who denies that they said anything very new but accepts their influence). For the Cromwellian group see G. R. Elton, *Reform and Renewal: Thomas Cromwell and the Common Weal* (1973).
5. M. L. Bush, *The Government Policy of Protector Somerset* (1976), 61ff.
6. R. W. Dixon, *History of the Church of England* (1895), II, 505ff.; J. A. Froude, *History of England* (Standard edn, n. d.), IV, 354ff.
7. A. F. Pollard, *England under the Protector Somerset* (1900), 215f.
8. PRO, SP 10/8, no. 56.
9. Pollard, *Somerset*, 256, 268, 281n.
10. A. F. Pollard, *Political History of England*, VI: 1547–1603 (1910), 31.
11. R. H. Tawney, *Religion and the Rise of Capitalism* (1926), 145.
12. Elton, *op. cit.*, 7.
13. Acts touching the Iceland fishery, the making of malt, the tanning of leather, commons and wastes, and sewers (2 & 3 Edward VI cc. 6, 10, 11; 3 & 4 Edward VI cc. 3, 8).
14. Acts touching vagabonds, tinkers and alehouses (1 Edward VI c. 3; 5 & 6 Edward VI, cc. 21, 25).
15. Unlawful assemblies (3 & 4 Edward VI c. 5).
16. *Tudor Royal Proclamations*, ed. P. L. Hughes and J. F. Larkin, I (1964), nos. 328, 331, 334, 336, 337, 341.
17. *Ibid.*, no. 309.
18. 2 & 3 Edward VI c. 15; 5 & 6 Edward VI cc. 5, 6, 20.
19. *Tudor Royal Proclamations*, I, nos. 366, 367, 371, 377–81.
20. *Political History*, VI, 32. On the same page another of Latimer's sermons is used to support the statement that 'fraud was employed to supplement intimidation'. On the page cited I can find nothing to justify the allegation.
21. All references are to *Sermons of Hugh Latimer*, ed. G. L. Corrie (Parker Soc., 1844).
22. pp. 59ff.
23. p. 67.
24. p. 68.
25. Latimer was quite right: charitable bequests began to decline in the 1530s. See the recalculation of W. K. Jordan's figures by W. G. Bittle and R. Todd Lane in *EcHR*, n.s. XXIX (1976), 203ff.
26. pp. 95, 98–9, 100, 101–2.

27. pp. 127, 211.
28. pp. 134–6.
29. pp. 196–7.
30. p. 249.
31. p. 247.
32. pp. 244–5. Coming back later to the same theme, he asks that lechers be excommunicated (p. 258): why if they had already been hanged?
33. p. 279.
34. H. C. Porter, 'The gloomy dean and the law: John Colet, 1466–1519,' *Essays in Modern English Church History in Memory of Norman Sykes,* ed. G. V. Bennett and J. D. Walsh (1966), 18ff.; see esp. p. 19.
35. Thomas Lever, *Sermons* (1550). Reference to this unpaginated original printing has to be by signatures. I have modernized spelling and punctuation.
36. Witness the splendid outburst against inadequate incumbents (sig. E.viii): 'Yes, forsooth, he ministreth God's sacraments, he saith his service, and he readeth the Homilies, as you fine flattering courtiers . . . term it; but the rude lobs of the country, which be too simple to paint a lie, speak foul and truly as they find it, and say: he minishes God's sacraments, he flubbers up his service, and he cannot read his Humbles.'
37. Sig. A.iii.
38. Sig. I.i.
39. Sig. E.vi^v.
40. Sigs. F.i–G.i.
41. Sig. A.vi^v.
42. Sigs. B.viii^v–C.i.
43. Sig. B.vi.
44. Sig. C.i. We recall Somerset's appeal to the Cornish rebels: 'And dareth any of you with the name of a subject stand against an act of Parliament, a law of the realm? What is our power if laws should be thus neglected, or what is your surety if laws be not kept?' (*Grafton's Chronicle,* repr. 1809, II, 518).
45. Sigs. D.i–ii.
46. Sig. A.vi^v.
47. Sigs. B.v^v–vi. Cf. also sigs. H.iv^v–v: 'The chief cause why the commons do not love, trust or obey the gentlemen and officers is because the gentlemen and officers build many fair houses and keep few good houses . . .'.
48. Tawney, *op. cit.,* 145; followed blindly by Jones, *op. cit.,* 53.
49. *The Select Works of Robert Crowley,* ed. J. M. Cowper (Early English Text Soc., 1872), 153ff. and 132ff.; spelling and punctuation here modernized.
50. pp. 163–4.
51. p. 156.
52. pp. 166–7.
53. p. 171.
54. pp. 132–3 (part of the passage cited above, p. 32).
55. pp. 133–4, 141.
56. pp. 142–3.
57. p. 149.
58. For Hales's activities see the introduction to the *Discourse of the Common Weal,*

ed. E. Lamond (1893), hereafter cited as Lamond; Smith's paternity of that impressive treatise has been convincingly proved by Mary Dewar, e.g. in her new edition of the work (1969). One economic measure – the sheep tax of 1549 – needs further study; for the present there is no convincing evidence that Hales was responsible for it.

59. Lamond, LIV.
60. *Ibid.*
61. P. F. Tytler, *England under the Reigns of Edward VI and Mary* (1839), I, 115–16.
62. Bush, *op. cit.*, 40–3.
63. Lamond, LXII–III.
64. Lamond (XLV–LII) prints a draft which very probably was this bill. Its long and impassioned preamble makes no mention of the commonwealth.
65. *Lords Journals*, I, 318b, 333b, 334b.
66. Lamond, LXIII–V.
67. As Crowley once echoed Latimer (above, p. 33). so a phrase of Hales's – 'it may not be lawful for any man to use his own wealth as him listeth' (Lamond, LXIII) – recalls Crowley (above, p. 34). Those who want to make them into a 'party' on the strength of such possible borrowings are welcome to do so.
68. W. K. Jordan, *Edward VI the Young King* (1968), esp. 416–38.
69. These large issues obviously require more research, freed from traditional preconceptions and able to see that conditions and behaviour were uniform neither through the governing classes nor through the whole age; for the present see in particular the work of E. Kerridge: *The Agricultural Revolution* (1967) and *Agrarian Problems of the Sixteenth Century and After* (1969).
70. *Discourse* (ed. Dewar), 118.
71. *HMC*, Salisbury MSS., I, no. 225.

2 THE DOWNFALL OF ARCHBISHOP GRINDAL AND ITS PLACE IN ELIZABETHAN POLITICAL AND ECCLESIASTICAL HISTORY

1. Archbishop William Sancroft's deprivation in 1690 was by Act of Parliament.
2. *The Elizabethan Puritan Movement* (1967), 200.
3. 1925.
4. 1960.
5. *Sir Francis Walsingham*, II, 1.
6. *Queen Elizabeth and the Revolt of the Netherlands* (1970), 2.
7. Thomas Rogers, *The Catholic Doctrine of the Church of England* (1607), ed. J. J. S. Perowne (Parker Soc., 1854), 9.
8. *Cambridge Modern History*, III (1907), 341.
9. W. H. Frere, *The English Church in the Reigns of Elizabeth and James I* (1904), 19.
10. H. M. Gwatkin, *Church and State in England to the Death of Queen Anne* (1917), 255.
11. P. A. Welsby, *George Abbot the Unwanted Archbishop 1562–1633* (1962), 1.
12. Thomas Fuller, *The Church History of Britain*, V (1845), 58.
13. *Of reformation, touching church-discipline in England* (1641), 15.

14. *The antipathie of the English lordly prelacie both to royall monarchy and civil unity* (1641), 147–9.

15. *The tryal of Dr Henry Sacheverell* (1710). For the context, see Geoffrey Holmes, *The Trial of Doctor Sacheverell* (1973); and for the relevance of the Sacheverell affair for the publication of John Strype's *Life of Grindal* see Cecile Zinberg, 'The usable dissenting past: John Strype and Elizabethan puritanism', in *The Dissenting Tradition*, ed. C. R. Cole and M. E. Moody (Athens, Ohio, 1975), 123–39.

16. *Annals of the First Four Years of the Reign of Queen Elizabeth*, ed. J. Bruce (Camden Soc., O.S. vii, 1840), 89.

17. Nowell to Burghley, 16 May 1575: PRO, SP 12/103/49. See also the Earl of Huntingdon's commendation of Grindal to Burghley, 24 June 1575: BL, Lansdowne MS. 20, no. 50, f.130.

18. Burghley to Sir Francis Walsingham, 15 May 1575: PRO, SP 12/103/48.

19. Grindal to Burghley, 27 February 1583: BL, Lansdowne MS. 37, no. 23, f.50.

20. With two exceptions the letters are in BL, Lansdowne MSS. and PRO, State Papers Domestic (SP 12), in roughly equal proportions. A letter of 3 August 1564 is in BL, Add. MS. 35831, no. 86, f.184 and another of 25 November 1575 in Inner Temple Library, Petyt MS. 538/47, no. 267, f.502. Of the 98 letters, 61 are printed, in whole or part, in *The Remains of Edmund Grindal*, ed. W. Nicholson (Parker Soc., 1843; hereafter cited as *Remains*), and occupy 82 of the 484 pages of *Remains*.

21. Burghley to Grindal (holograph), 25 November 1575: Inner Temple Library, Petyt MS. 538/47, no. 267, f.502.

22. A letter neither signed, nor addressed, nor dated, but in Parker's hand: BL, Lansdowne MS. 15, no. 34, f.66. Parker appears to apologize for this outburst in a letter to Burghley, endorsed 6 October 1572: *ibid.*, no. 43, f.84.

23. Grindal to Burghley, 10 December 1575: BL, Lansdowne MS. 20, no. 69, f.168.

24. Blank in the MS.

25. PRO, SP 59/19, f.248v. The item is numbered '983' from its old location in SP 70/141 (see *Calendar of State Papers, Foreign, 1575–7*, 468–9), from where it was transferred to State Papers, Scotland and the Borders.

26. The minutes of the dean and chapter of Canterbury record the awarding of additional expenses to the dean, who had travelled to London to pay his respects to the archbishop and to present the certificate of his election, 'by reason of attending and waiting for the coming of the said archbishop from York, which happened by reason the said archbishop was stayed by sickness.' (Cathedral Archives and Library, Canterbury, MS. Y.11.3, Chapter Acta, f.93; Misc. Accounts 41, accounts for 1576.)

27. J. E. Neale, *Elizabeth I and her Parliaments, 1559–1581* (1953), 349–53; Collinson, *op. cit.*, 161–3. The canons of 1576 are printed in *Synodalia*, ed. E. Cardwell, I (1842), 132–8.

28. F. X. Walker, 'The implementation of the Elizabethan statutes against recusants, 1581–1603' (unpublished Ph.D. thesis, London University, 1961), 36–118.

29. See *Faculty Office Registers, 1534–1549*, ed. D. S. Chambers (1966).

30. There is one copy of these orders in BL, Lansdowne MS. 23, no. 61, f.127 and two further copies in PRO, SP 12/129/25, 26. Two of these copies bear the names of

nine privy councillors: Bacon, Burghley, Lincoln, Sussex, Arundel, Bedford, Knollys, Croft and Mildmay. The last section of the orders is unaccountably dated in the first SP 12 copy '13 January 1578'.

31. PRO, SP 12/107/41.

32. *Ibid.*, SP 15/24/72.

33. Canterbury was variously valued at about the time of Grindal's translation at £3,093 18s. 8d. (BL, Lansdowne MS. 21, no. 20, f.40) and £3,4531 8s. 8d. (*ibid.*, Lansdowne MS. 23, no. 60, fos. 125–6).

34. A substantial collection of reports in Inner Temple Library, Petyt MS. 538/54, fos. 265–71, 282r, 284: partly printed, J. Strype, *Life of Grindal* (1821 edn), 300–9. One of a group of related papers, concerning a dispute about precedence between the archbishop's leading officials (Petyt MS. 538/54, fos. 7–11, 16–18, 21–2, 23–5, 64–7) is dated 3 May 1576 (not 23 May as in Strype, *op. cit.*, 309). Further copies of many of these documents are in Bodl., Tanner MS. 280.

35. Memorandum of Dr William Aubrey, 30 April 1576: Inner Temple Library, Petyt MS. 538/54, fos. 268–71.

36. C. Kitching, 'The Prerogative Court of Canterbury from Warham to Whitgift', in *Continuity and Change: Personnel and Administration of the Church in England, 1500–1642*, ed. R. O'Day and F. Heal (1976), 191, 207.

37. Grindal to Burghley, 10 June 1576: BL, Lansdowne MS. 23, no. 4, f.7; further references and documentation in my *Letters of Thomas Wood, Puritan, 1566–1577*, *BIHR*, special supplement 5 (1960), XVIII–XIX, 9–24.

38. See my attempts to remove misunderstandings in *Elizabethan Puritan Movement*, 168–76; and in 'Lectures by combination: structures and characteristics of church life in seventeenth-century England', *BIHR*, XLVIII (1975), 198–9.

39. Sir Nicholas Bacon's speech to Grindal in Council: BL, Harleian MS. 5176, f.95; Grindal to Burghley, 10 June 1576: BL, Lansdowne MS. 23, no. 4, f.7.

40. Lambeth Palace Library, MS. 2003, fos. 1–34; eighteenth-century copies of most of these with a letter from the Bishop of Gloucester, not otherwise extant, in BL, Add. MS. 29546, fos. 36–57; extracts from the correspondence in Lambeth Palace Library, MS. 2003, fos. 35–6, and in BL, Add. MS. 21565, f.26, adding information from four letters no longer extant; imperfect transcripts of much of the material from the Lambeth MSS. in S. E. Lehmberg, 'Archbishop Grindal and the prophesyings', *Historical Magazine of the Protestant Episcopal Church*, XXXIV (1965), 87–145.

41. Lambeth Palace Library, MS. 2014, fos. 72–80, MS. 2007, fos. 126–44; further material relating to the *tractatus* recently recovered by Lambeth Palace Library is in MS. 2872, fos. 10–11.

42. BL, Lansdowne MS. 109, no. 2, fos. 3, 5.

43. The contemporary fame of the letter is reflected in the many copies which survive: e.g., in BL, Add. MSS. 22587, 33271, Harleian MS. 1877 (imperfect and dated 12 November 1578), Lambeth Palace Library MS. 595, Bodl., Tanner MS. 79, Queen's College Oxford, MS. 292, Northamptonshire Record Office, Fitzwilliam of Milton Papers, F.(M).P.54. The text in *Remains* is taken from BL, Lansdowne MS. 23, no. 12, fos. 24–9, which is endorsed by Burghley 'December 20th 1576', a dating repeated in other copies. The copy in the Morrice MSS. in Dr Williams's Library (*Seconde Parte of a Register*, ed. A. Peel, 1915, I, 135) is dated

'the 10th of December 1576'. The correct date is inferred from Grindal's letter to Burghley of 16 December (*Remains*, 391).

44. Frere, *op. cit.*, 192.
45. *Remains*, 387.
46. *Op. cit.*, IV, 454.
47. Among the books bequeathed by Grindal at his death to the Queen's College Oxford and still extant is his copy of the Erasmian text of the *Opera* of St Ambrose in the Basle edition of 1538. The passages from the Epistles of Ambrose which are quoted in the letter to the queen are extensively annotated in Grindal's hand.
48. 'The palace belongs to the emperor, the churches to the bishop.' (*Early Latin Theology*, ed. S. L. Greenslade, Library of Christian Classics, V, 1956, 178–81.)
49. *Calendar of State Papers, Foreign*, 1578–80, 99–100.
50. Letters to Burghley, 16, 17 December 1576: *Remains*, 391–2.
51. See, for example, Grindal's letter to the Earl of Sussex, 30 January 1576(/7), enclosing a list of Lenten preachers for the Court: BL, Harleian MS. 6992, no. 34, f.69. Grindal's Register records no abnormalities before late May 1577. The earliest commission issued in the name of the vicar general, Dr Yale, is dated 1 June 1577. (Lambeth Palace Library, Grindal's Register, f.406.)
52. Burghley to Grindal (holograph), 23 February 1576(/7): Lambeth Palace Library, MS. 2003, f.39.
53. BL, Lansdowne MS. 25, no. 44, fos. 92–3 contains two alternative drafts of royal letters to the bishops, one of them addressed to the bishop of Lincoln and endorsed 'Aprill 1577. A minute of a letter to be written from her Majesty to the bishops concerning the exercise of prophetie.' BL, Lansdowne MS. 25, no. 44 (3), fos. 94–5 is a draft of a different letter, the one actually despatched, annotated by Burghley and endorsed in his hand: '7 Maii 1577. The queen's Majesty's letter to the bishops to stay of all rites in the Church not warranted by law.' A fair copy of this version in BL, Cotton MS. Cleopatra F. II, f.289 is printed by Strype (574–6) and in *Remains* (467–9). A copy bearing the queen's signet and received and endorsed by Whitgift as bishop of Worcester is in Lambeth Palace Library, MS. 2003, fos. 40–1. That the royal command was obeyed in Grindal's own diocese and peculiars is asserted in the form of submission prepared for him by bishops Whitgift and Piers (See p. 53 below).
54. This is the most likely reconstruction of events, by inference from Bacon's speech to Grindal in Council on a later occasion (BL, Harleian MS. 5176, f.95).
55. Walsingham to Burghley, 31 May 1577: PRO, SP 12/113/17.
56. Grindal to Leicester (?), 13 July 1577: Lambeth Palace Library, MS. 2004, f.1. The reference to 'mediation' in this letter suggests that it was intended for Leicester rather than Burghley, who did not publicly make himself Grindal's advocate.
57. William Camden, *History of the most renowned and victorious princess Elizabeth* (1688 edn), 287–8.
58. *The copie of a leter wryten by a master of arte of Cambridge* (1584), 26–7; John Harington, *A briefe view of the state of the Church of England* (1608) (1653 edn), 6–7; Fuller, *op. cit.*, IV, 455; Peter Heylyn, *Aerius Redevivus* (1672), 248. The impediment to Julio's marriage seems to have been that the lady was previously married, or contracted, and that the parties were related within the prohibited

degrees of affinity. The case had been before the bishop of London, the Master of the Rolls and the High Commission since 1573 (Strype, *op. cit.*, 333–6). The author of *Leicester's Commonwealth (The copie of a leter)* and Fuller confusingly suggest that it was Julio himself who was already married.

59. Giulio Borgarucci to Leicester, 4 December 1576: BL, Cotton MS. Titus B.VII, f.36. I owe this reference to Mr D. C. Peck, late of Ohio State University.

60. Burghley to Walsingham, 31 May 1577: BL, Add. MS. 5935, f.68. This is a late (eighteenth-century?) copy of a letter not otherwise extant.

61. Bishop Richard Barnes of Durham to Burghley, 11 February 1577(/8): BL, Lansdowne MS. 25, no. 78, fos. 161–2.

62. See my *Letters of Thomas Wood, op. cit.*

63. H. R. Trevor-Roper, *Queen Elizabeth's First Historian: William Camden and the Beginnings of English 'Civil History'* (1971).

64. On 25 June 1578 Leicester wrote to Burghley from Buxton: 'My lord, having so convenient a messenger as Mr Dr Julio . . .' (BL, Harleian MS. 6992, no. 51, f.102.)

65. *Calendar of State Papers, Venetian*, 1558–1580, 545.

66. H. Nicolas, *Memoirs of Life and Times of Christopher Hatton, K.G.* (1847), 24.

67. Collinson, *Elizabethan Puritan Movement*, 193–4, 201, 245, 259, 282, 312–14.

68. *HMC*, Hastings MSS., I, 433. I have not seen the original of this document, which is in the Huntington Library.

69. See p. 52 below.

70. Wilson, *op. cit.*, 43.

71. *The Shepheardes Calender* (1579), f.29v.

72. J. J. Higgenson, *Spenser's 'Shepheardes Calender' in Relation to Contemporary Affairs* (New York, 1912); E. Greenlaw, 'The Shepheards Calender', *Publications of the Modern Language Association of America*, XXVI (1911), 419–51; P. E. McLane, *Spenser's Shepheardes Calender A Study in Elizabethan Allegory* (Notre Dame, 1961), esp. 140–57.

73. I quote from the title of S. L. Adams's Oxford D. Phil. thesis of 1973, 'The protestant cause: religious alliance with the west European Calvinist communities as a political issue in England, 1585–1630'.

74. PRO, SP 12/108/82.

75. PRO, SP 70/144/1164.

76. PRO, SP 70/145/1242.

77. PRO, SP 12/115/24. See Robert Tittler, *Nicholas Bacon: The Making of a Tudor Statesman* (1976), 168–86.

78. *Op. cit.*, 49.

79. BL, Harleian MS. 6992, no. 48, f.95.

80. PRO, SP 15/35/74.

81. PRO, SP 15/25/79.

82. Wilson, *op. cit.*, 70.

83. Conyers Read, 'Walsingham and Burghley in Queen Elizabeth's Privy Council', *EHR*, XXVIII (1913), 34.

84. Knollys to Wilson, 9 January 1577(/8); BL, Harleian MS. 6992, no. 44, f.89.

85. W. D. J. Cargill Thompson, 'Sir Francis Knollys' campaign against the *Jure Divino* theory of episcopacy', in Cole and Moody, *op. cit.*, 39–77.

86. Walsingham to Burghley, 31 May 1577; PRO, SP 12/113/17. Burghley to
    Walsingham, 31 May 1577; BL, Add. MS. 5935, f.68. Since both letters bear the
    same date and both parties seem to have been at Court, it may be that only the
    need to convey the ambassadorial report to Burghley with accompanying
    comments led to the committing to paper of highly confidential matters and
    reflections which might otherwise have been confined to word of mouth.
87. PRO, SP 15/25/30.
88. PRO, SP 83/2/43.
89. PRO, SP 15/25/35.
90. My own investigations have covered the city and dean and chapter archives
    which survive for this period and which are preserved in the Cathedral Archives
    and Library, Canterbury.
91. PRO, SP 15/25/35.
92. Grindal to the Privy Council, 24 October 1577; PRO, SP 12/117/9.
93. Grindal to Matthew Hutton, Dean of York, 2 December 1577; *Remains*, 394–5.
94. Northamptonshire RO, Fitzwilliam of Milton Papers, F. (M).P.70. This MS.
    contains three items, wholly or partly in Mildmay's hand. They are a
    memorandum (item c) headed: 'The occasion whereupon the displeasure grew
    from the queen's Majesty to the Archbishop of Canterbury'; an account (item a)
    of proceedings in the Star Chamber on 30 November 1577; and notes for a
    memorandum (item b) headed 'Touching the Archbishop of Canterbury in the
    matter of the exercises. 22 January 1577(/8)'. These documents are discussed by
    Stanford E. Lehmberg, *Sir Walter Mildmay and Tudor Government* (Austin, Texas,
    1964), 148–53, but without specific reference to the meeting at Bacon's house.
95. Strype, *op. cit.*, 348–50.
96. Copies in BL, Cotton MS. Cleopatra F.2, f.273 (whence printed by Strype, *op. cit.*,
    350–2), endorsed '29 No[vember] 1577. The request of the Archbishop of
    Canterbury to my lords of the Privy Council'; and in BL, Lansdowne MS. 25,
    no. 79, fos. 163–4, endorsed: 'The humble submission of Edmund Archbishop of
    Canterbury to the lords of her Majesty's Privy Council in the Star Chamber.
    Touching the exercise of prophesying. Sent by Sir Walter Mildmay.' A nearly
    illegible date follows which has been (mistakenly) read as 3 March 1577(/8).
    Both copies bear Grindal's signature.
97. Copies of Bacon's speech in BL, Harleian MS. 398, f.12; and in Folger Shakespeare
    Library, MS. V.a.197, f.19. A somewhat fuller version of what Bacon reportedly
    said is in Northamptonshire RO, F.(M).P.70a.
98. PRO, SP 15/25/50.
99. BL, Harleian MS. 5176, f.95 (whence printed, *Remains*, 471–3); Harleian MS. 36,
    no. 55, f.391; Huntington Library, MS. EL 2579, fos. 59–60r. A passage,
    purportedly from the Huntington Library copy of this speech and quoted by
    Tittler in his study of Bacon (*op. cit.*, 172), in fact occurs in Mildmay's account of
    the transactions in the Star Chamber of 30 November 1577. (Northamptonshire
    RO, F.(M).P.70.a.)
100. *Ibid.*
101. Northamptonshire RO, F.(M).P.70.b. From the form of this paper it is clear that
    it cannot be read as Lehmberg reads it (*op. cit.*, 153), as an expression of
    Mildmay's private views.

102. PRO, SP 12/122/15.
103. Henry Killigrew to William Davison, 29 January 1578; PRO, SP 15/25/71. The letter has been damaged by damp and uncertainty persists about the reading of the words italicized after prolonged scrutiny under ultraviolet light.
104. Killigrew to Davison, 22 February 1577(/8); PRO, SP 15/25/74.
105. Gonville and Caius College Cambridge, MS. 30/53, f.53.
106. The letter is printed verbatim by H. Nicolas from BL, Add. MS. 15891, f.30: *op. cit.*, 52–3.
107. Huntingdon to Matthew Hutton, 20 May 1578: *The Correspondence of Dr Matthew Hutton*, ed. J. Raines (Surtees Soc., XVII, 1843), 59–60.
108. BL, Cotton MS. Vespasian F. XII, f.192.
109. The archbishop's physical degeneration may be traced through the following letters: Grindal to Hutton, 2 December 1577 and 18 February 1579: *Remains*, 394–6; Grindal to Leicester, 15 August 1581: PRO, SP 12/150/5; Grindal to Walsingham, 7 July 1582: PRO, SP 12/154/61; Grindal to Burghley, 30 January 1583: BL, Lansdowne MS. 37, no. 17, f.36.
110. The cup is mentioned in Grindal's will: Strype, *op. cit.*, 601.
111. The draft of the formal instrument of resignation is in PRO, SP 12/160/31. The negotiations over its terms are documented in Grindal's letters to Burghley, 30 January, 9 February, 27 February, 12 April 1583, in BL, Lansdowne MSS. 37 and 38; printed, *Remains*, 397–403.
112. See 'Things prepared at the funeral of Edmund Grindal Archbishop of Canterbury, who died on Saturday 6 July 1583', PRO, SP 14/89/6; and 'The proceedings in the church at Croydon at the burial of the Archbishop of Canterbury, 1583, Lammas Day [1 August]', Bodl., Ashmolean MS. 817, f.25.
113. *John Stubbs's Gaping Gulf with Letters and Other Relevant Documents*, ed. L. E. Berry (Charlottesville, Va., 1968).
114. BL, Harleian MS. 398, f.12.
115. Quoted, Berry, *op. cit.*, xi.
116. The deterioration of their relations can be documented from Grindal's time as archbishop of York. On 28 April 1577 he told Dean Hutton of York: 'If I had had any special credit when Durham and Carlisle were bestowed some had not sped so well. But blame yourself and Sir Thomas Gargrave. Ye two commended him to be rid of him and now Simon is as good as Peter.' (*Hutton Correspondence*, 56–7.) Barnes was in turn suffragan bishop of Nottingham, bishop of Carlisle and bishop of Durham.
117. Barnes to Burghley, 11 February 1577(/8): BL, Lansdowne MS. 25, no. 78, fos. 161–2.
118. Cox to Burghley, 12 June 1577: BL, Lansdowne MS. 25, no. 29, f.61; Cox to the queen, 8 June 1577, 8 January 1577(/8): Gonville and Caius College, MS. 30/53, fos. 50, 43.
119. Endorsed 'A form of submission devised and sent by the Bishops of Sarum and Worcester 21 January 1580', BL, Add. MS. 32091, f.22. Strype (*op. cit.*, 403–4) printed another version of this document which lacked the endorsement. His assumption that Grindal actually made such a submission is unsupported.
120. Grindal to Burghley, 30 January 1583: BL, Lansdowne MS. 37, no. 17, f.36. Whitgift's secretary and first biographer Sir George Paule is the source of the

tradition that his master 'utterly refused' to accept the primacy *per resignationem* and 'besought pardon in not accepting thereof upon any condition whatsoever in the lifetime of the other'. (*Life of Whitgift*, 1699 edn, 35.) Piers's involvement in the arrangements for Grindal's resignation must place this matter in some doubt.

121. Convocation engaged for this purpose the celebrated eloquence of Dr Toby Matthew, the future archbishop of York. Bodl., MS. Top Oxon. c. 5 contains Matthew's 'oratio' to the upper house on this occasion (pp. 1–7) and (pp. 45–7) the 'supplicatio' prepared by Matthew and subscribed: 'Serenissimae tuae maiestatis observantissimi episcopi, decani, archidiaconi et reliqui ministri ecclesiae Anglicanae presenti hoc synodo congregati'. Another copy is in BL, Sloane MS. 1710, fos. 106v–7r. The text in Wilkins's *Concilia* (IV, 295) is taken from Fuller, *op. cit.*, I.ix.120. The bishops' letter is in Bodl., MS. e. Museo. 55, no. 1, f.3.

122. Identified with the aid of J. Bossy, 'English catholics and the French marriage, 1577–81', *Recusant History*, V (1959), 2–16; and of an as yet unpublished paper by my colleague Dr P. R. Roberts on the political background to the publication of *Leicester's Commonwealth* which he kindly allowed me to read.

123. In Lambeth Palace Library.

124. The earliest commission issued in Yale's name (to visit the diocese of Salisbury with the archdeaconry of Dorset) is dated 1 June 1577 (Grindal's Register, f.406).

125. Privy Council to Grindal, 7 November 1577: *ibid.*, f.157v. The original patent of appointment of Drury and Hussey is in Lambeth Palace Library, Cartae Misc. XII/52.

126. Grindal's Register, fos. 167, 159v, 239v, 244v.

127. *Ibid.*, f.140. The original commission is in Lambeth Palace Library, Cartae Misc. II/79. All but one of the subsequent documents connected with this visitation were issued in the name of Dr Aubrey (Register, fos. 141–3).

128. *Ibid.*, fos. 48, 49, 53, 54, 58v, 59v, 64v, 66r, 70v, 71v, 77.

129. Examples in Register, fos. 158, 164, 171v, 176, 191, 193–5, 198v–9r, 206, 234, 235, 236v–7. For evidence of Grindal's participation in the enquiry into recusancy of October–November 1577, see *APC*, 1577–8, 87–8; PRO, SP 12/117/9, 14.

130. Register, f.234.

131. BL, Add. MS. 32092, fos. 13–21; Register, fos. 591–8.

132. Strype, *op. cit.*, 382; Wilkins, *Concilia*, IV, 292; Bishop Aylmer to the Earl of Sussex (as lord chamberlain), 27 January 1577(/8): BL, Harleian MS. 6992, no. 46, f.92. For an account of Aylmer's activities at this time, see H. G. Owen, 'The London parish clergy in the reign of Elizabeth I' (unpublished Ph.D. thesis, London University, 1957), 540–52; and John Strype, *Life of Aylmer* (1821 edn), esp. 60–4.

133. Collinson, *Elizabethan Puritan Movement*, 205–7.

134. Copies in Bodl., Tanner MS. 280, f.330v, Inner Temple Library, Petyt MS. 538/54, f.278.

135. For Bishop Curteys and his troubles see R. B. Manning, *Religion and Society in Elizabethan Sussex* (1969), 91–125. The controversy between Bishop Freke of Norwich and a faction of Norfolk gentry is documented in PRO, SP 12/126 and SP 15/25. See A. H. Smith, *County and Court: Government and Politics in Norfolk*,

1558–1603 (1974), 210–25. Bishop Freke's subsequent struggle with the puritan J.P.s of Suffolk is described in detail in my unpublished London University Ph.D. thesis, 'The puritan classical movement in the reign of Elizabeth I' (1957), 881–929, which is followed by J. S. Cockburn, *A History of English Assizes, 1558–1714* (1972), 199–206.

136. Walsingham sent Burghley on 8 December 1575 details of 'the principal matters wherewith the Bishop of Ely is to be charged', agreeing with Burghley's opinion that the penalty should 'light upon him and not upon the see'. (BL, Harleian MS. 6992, no. 16, f.31.) A page of Burghley's rough memoranda (PRO, SP 12/136/10) bears a note: 'Bishop of Ely resignation'. The account of Cox in F. O. White, *Lives of the Elizabethan Bishops* (1898), 78–95, may now be compared with the unpublished Cambridge University Ph.D. theses by G. L. Blackman, 'The career and influence of Bishop Richard Cox, 1547–1581' (1953) and F. Heal, 'The bishops of Ely and their diocese during the Reformation period: *c.* 1515–1600' (1972).

137. Privy Council memorandum to the archbishop of Canterbury 'concerning the Bishop of Hereford', June 1583: BL, Egerton MS. 3048, fos. 207v–8. Cf. White, *op. cit.*, 13–19.

138. Robinson to Walsingham, 28 May 1582: PRO, SP 12/153/66.

139. White, *op. cit.*, 251–9; R. E. Head, *Royal Supremacy and the Trials of Bishops* (1962), 23–8.

140. Documentation in PRO, SP 12/158/1, 22, 22 II, 38, 41. Becon, whose chequered career took him from Freke's Norwich through Curteys's Chichester to Overton's Lichfield had this to say about the bishops: 'Having such experience of bishops as I have . . . I had rather live a poor student in St Johns, where I was brought up, than to enjoy their lordships' palaces.' (SP 12/158/41.)

141. Compare the account in White, *op. cit.*, 97–108 and *DNB*, Sandys, Edwin, with the modern unpublished theses by I. P. Ellis, 'Edwin Sandys and the Settlement of religion in England, 1558–88' (unpublished B. Litt. thesis, Oxford University, 1962) and S. Storer, 'The life and times of Edwin Sandys, archbishop of York' (unpublished M.Phil. thesis, London University, 1973).

142. The bishops' certificates, detailing the felling of timber on their estates, are in PRO, SP 12/136 and 137.

143. Cause papers and summaries in PRO, SP 12/112/45 I, 131/22, 137/39, 54, 55, 149/17–27. Letters from Sandys to Walsingham, 30 April 1577: SP 12/112/45; Sandys to Walsingham and Aylmer to Walsingham, April–June 1579: SP 12/130/39, 131/14, 21.

144. PRO, SP 12/112/45, 45 I.

145. Josias Nicholls, *The plea of the innocent* (1602), 9–10. For Nicholls, see P. Clark, 'Josias Nicholls and religious radicalism, 1553–1639', *Journal of Ecclesiastical History*, XXVIII (1977), 135–50.

146. Paule, *op. cit.*, 82.

147. Dr Peter Lake of Clare College helped me to see this point by his comments when I read a paper at Professor Hurstfield's evening seminar at the Institute of Historical Research. It is pleasant to have occasion to record the latest of very many debts incurred around this table in the England Room, where I first met Joel Hurstfield in October 1952.

3 THE ANJOU MATCH AND THE MAKING OF ELIZABETHAN FOREIGN POLICY

1. J. M. B. C. Kervyn de Lettenhove (ed.), *Relations politiques des Pays-Bas et de l'Angleterre sous le règne de Philippe II* (Brussels, 1882–1900), IX, 68 (hereafter *KL, Rel. Pol.*).
2. For Burghley's views see Dudley Digges, *The Compleat Ambassador* (1655), 189, 203.
3. See *Calendar of State Papers, Foreign, Elizabeth*, XII, 201, 203 (hereafter *CSPF*); *KL, Rel. Pol.*, IX, 540, 550; X, 103.
4. *CSPF*, XII, 204, 260.
5. *CSPF*, XII, 529–30, 530–1, 556.
6. PRO, Baschet Transcripts, 1 January, 8 March, 29 April 1579 (hereafter Baschet).
7. Baschet, 22 February 1579.
8. For full documentation on the development of this argument see below n. 29.
9. *Calendar of State Papers, Spanish, Elizabeth*, II, 696 (hereafter *CSPSp*); *CSPF*, XIV, 205.
10. For references to anti-Anjou sermons see *CSPSp*, II, 659; and Edmund Lodge, *Illustrations of British History* (1838), II, 148–50; for other criticisms see Baschet, 30 July 1579, *CSPSp*, II, 692, 701. Bishop Cox wrote a treatise against the match, BL, Lansdowne MS. 28, no. 70. For the ballads see *Ballads from Manuscripts*, ed. F. J. Furnivall and W. R. Morfill (1873), II, 114.
11. P. L. Hughes and J. F. Larkin (eds.), *Tudor Royal Proclamations*, II (1969), 445–9.
12. For the letter to the London corporation see Folger Library, MS. V.b.142, f.54, quoted in the introduction to *John Stubbs' Gaping Gulf with Letters and Other Relevant Documents*, ed. L. E. Berry (Charlottesville, Va., 1968), xxviii; the Council letter to the bishops is in John Strype, *The History of the Life and Acts of Edmund Grindal* (1821), 584–86; the order for sending it to 11 bishops of the southern province is in *APC*, 1578–80, XI, 276. Aylmer's letter is in H. Nicolas, *Memoirs of Life and Times of Christopher Hatton, K.G.* (1847), 132–34.
13. Baschet, 29 October 1579.
14. A. G. R. Smith, *Servant of the Cecils* (1977), 92–96.
15. William Camden, *Annals of Queen Elizabeth* (1675 edn), 270.
16. *DNB*, Stubbs, John.
17. Stubbs, *Gaping Gulf*, ed. Berry.
18. *Ibid.*, 9.
19. *Ibid.*, 22.
20. *Ibid.*, 34.
21. *Ibid.*, 49.
22. *Ibid.*, 59–60.
23. *Ibid.*, 82.
24. *Ibid.*, 88.
25. *Ibid.*, 92.
26. Baschet, 29 May, 30 July 1579.
27. Camden, *op. cit.*, 232; *HMC*, Salisbury MSS., II, 277.
28. For the Sidney letter see Fulke Greville, *Life of Sir Philip Sidney*, ed. Nowell Smith

(1907), 63–9 and for the meetings see *CSPSp*, II, 693. See also n. 35 below.

29. For these Council debates see *HMC*, Salisbury MSS., II, 238, 239, 249, 253, 267.
30. For the opposition to the match see *HMC*, Salisbury MSS., II, 267, 271; *CSPSp*, II, 702.
31. *HMC*, Salisbury MSS., II, 272–3.
32. *CSPSp*, II, 704.
33. *CSPF*, XIV, 95–97, 108–9; *HMC*, Salisbury MSS., II, 275.
34. *Ibid.*, 293.
35. *Ibid.*, 298.
36. For what follows see P. E. McLane, *Spenser's Shepheardes Calender: A Study in Elizabethan Allegory* (Notre Dame, 1961), *passim*.
37. See F. Yates, *Astraea* (1975), *passim*.
38. See E. C. Wilson, *England's Eliza* (New York, 1966) chapters I and II, *passim*.
39. *CSPF*, XIX, 84–85, 95–98; *HMC*, Salisbury MSS., III, 67–70.
40. Digges, *op. cit.*, 352–54; *CSPF*, XV, 277.
41. *Ibid.*, 363.
42. Camden, *op. cit.*, 268.
43. PRO, SP 78/10/339, fos. 308–35.

4 POPULAR PURITAN MENTALITY IN LATE ELIZABETHAN ENGLAND

1. The research on which this essay is based would have been impossible without membership of the Society of Genealogists and consequent access to their unrivalled collection of parish register copies; the latter are listed in *Parish Register Copies, Pt I: Society of Genealogists Collection* (1975). For making available to me parish registers, either originals or copies, and other records in their keeping, I am grateful to the staffs of the East Sussex, Essex, Kent, Northamptonshire and West Sussex Record Offices, the Sussex Archaeological Society, Messrs Phillimore and Co. Ltd, and also to Rev. D. R. Corfe (Eastwell) and Rev. D. Shacklock (Northiam). Advice and information on various points has been generously given by Mr M. J. Burchall, Dr Claire Cross, Mr R. Cust, Dr J. J. Goring, Dr G. F. Nuttall, Dr W. J. Sheils, Mr D. Thomas and Mr A. G. Watson. I am indebted to the members of Professor F. J. Fisher's Seminar for their stringent criticisms, and to Mr D. A. Coleman, Professor P. Collinson, Dr Goring, Mr N. B. Harte and Mr C. S. R. Russell for reading the essay, or part of it, in draft. Finally I must thank my wife, Sarah Tyacke, for her unfailing encouragement.
2. S. R. Gardiner, *The Personal Government of Charles I* (1877), I, ix. An alternative approach to that adopted here would be to investigate a parish, or parishes, where religious differences brought large numbers of parishioners before the ecclesiastical courts, both as plaintiffs and defendants.
3. W. Camden, *Remains of a Greater Work* (1605), 33; R. Bancroft, *Dangerous Positions* (1593), 104.
4. C. W. Bardsley, *Curiosities of Puritan Nomenclature* (1880). For a memoir of

Bardsley see his posthumously published *Dictionary of English and Welsh Surnames* (1901), v–xi.

5. D. Hume, *The History of Great Britain* (1754–7), II, 51. These names were probably extracted from the quarter sessions rolls. Hume was of course mistaken in regarding them as names assumed in adult life.

6. M. A. Lower, *English Surnames* (1842), 134–7. The 23 parishes are Battle, Brightling, Burwash, Chiddingly, Crowhurst, Cuckfield, Ewhurst, Hailsham, Heathfield, Hellingly, East Hoathly, Lewes, Northiam, Pevensey, Rye, Salehurst, Shoreham, Uckfield, Waldron, Warbleton, Wartling, Westham and Withyam.

7. R. G. Rice (ed.), *West Sussex Protestation Returns* (Sussex Rec. Soc., V, 1906). The only two puritan names recorded are Desire Smith and Free-gift Collins, both of St Peter the Great, Chichester. Neither is to be found among the St Peter the Great baptisms.

8. W. H. Hall (ed.), *Calendar of Wills and Administrations . . . Lewes, 1541–1660* (British Rec. Soc., XXIV, 1901), E. A. Fry (ed.), *Calendar of Wills . . . Chichester, 1482–1800* (British Rec. Soc., XLIX, 1915), E. H. W. Dunkin (ed.), *Calendar of Sussex Marriage Licences . . . Lewes, 1586–1643* (Sussex Rec. Soc., I, 1902) and *Calendar of Sussex Marriage Licences . . . Chichester, 1575–1730* (Sussex Rec. Soc., IX, 1909). The 22 parishes are Arlington, Beddingham, Bexhill, Bishopstone, Brede, Brighton, Eastbourne, West Firle, Folkington, Framfield, Frant, Hastings, Little Horsted, Lullington, Maresfield, Ninfield, Playden, Seaford, Southover, Ticehurst, Wilmington, and Wivelsfield.

9. Alfriston, Herstmonceux and Isfield.

10. See map. Where no date is given this is because, lacking a contemporary register, puritan baptismal names have been inferred from the later clustering of such names among those married *c.* 1620. An invaluable guide to the existence and whereabouts of east Sussex parish registers is M. J. Burchall, *Index of East Sussex Parish Records, 1275–1870* (1975).

11. 1587: 14/20; 1588: 13/22; 1589: 13/23; 1590: 13/23.

12. East Sussex RO (hereafter ESRO), Lewes Wills, Bk A 9, f.10. Miles, in his will of 1601, bequeathed to Hely his 'best gown' and Rheims Testament. PRO, PROB 11/98/51.

13. West Sussex RO (hereafter WSRO), Ep.II/5/5, f.198v.; PRO, E 179/190/332, Hawksborough Hundred; BL, Add. MS. 39326, Biographies of Sussex Clergy; ESRO, Lewes Wills, Bks A8, fos. 341v–2v, A14, f.114, A17, f.39r–v.

14. A. F. Scott Pearson, *Thomas Cartwright and Elizabethan Puritanism, 1535–1603* (1925), 274; P. Collinson, *The Elizabethan Puritan Movement* (1967), 294.

15. J. Comber, *Sussex Genealogies: Ardingly Centre* (1932), 233; F. W. T. Attree (ed.), *Notes of Post Mortem Inquisitions . . . Sussex* (Sussex Rec. Soc., XIV, 1912), 89. I owe this reference to Mr Burchall. As indicated on the map, Puritan names leap-frog from the Cranbrook area to that of Warbleton and a further clue may be Hely's own Kentish origins, for he was ordained in 1574–5 by Richard Rogers, suffragan bishop of Dover, and in his will of 1605 refers to a brother, Stephen Hely, at Maidstone: BL, Add. MS. 39326 (46), f.1394; PRO, PROB 11/106/71.

16. D. Fenner, *The Arts of Logic and Rhetoric* (Middelburg, ? 1588), sigs. F5v–F6, and *The Whole Doctrine of the Sacraments* (Middelburg, 1588), sigs. C2r–v.

17. *A Directory of Church Government* (1644), sig. B2; P. Collinson, 'The godly: aspects

of popular protestantism in Elizabethan England' (papers presented to the *Past and Present* Conference on Popular Religion, 1966), 6 and *passim*. Between December 1581 and March 1591, George Ely called his children Obadiah, Lydia, Daniel and Abigail.

18. B. P. Starr, *A History of the Starr Family of New England* (Hartford, Conn., 1879), i–iv. Faint-not Fenner, in her will of 1604, refers to Josias Nicholls as 'father-in-law' i.e. stepfather: PRO, PROB 11/104/85.

19. F. G. Emmison (ed.), *Wills at Chelmsford, 1620–1720* (British Rec. Soc., LXXIX, 1959–60); C. E. Banks (ed.), *Able Men of Suffolk, 1638* (Boston, Mass., 1931).

20. W. Pierce, *John Penry* (1923), 207, 367–72, 385, 416.

21. *DNB*, Barebone, Praise-God, and H. I. Longden, *Northamptonshire and Rutland Clergy* (1938), I, 179.

22. BL, Harleian MS. 7332, fos. 41, 47v, 48 and 49v.

23. These puritan names, in order of popularity, are Sin-deny (10), Be-thankful (9), Repent (9), Patience (7), Free-gift (5), Good-gift (5), Refrain (5), Fear-not (4), Abuse-not (2), Constance (2), Depend (2), Faint-not (2), Give-thanks (2), Increased (2), Magnify (2), Much-mercy (2), Obedient (2), Preserved (2), Renewed (2), Be-steadfast (1), Confidence (1), Eschew-evil (1), Faithful (1), Fear-God (1), Indued (1), Lament (1), Learn-wisdom (1), More-fruit (1), No-merit (1), Obey (1), Repentance (1), Return (1), Silence (1), Sorry-for-sin (1), Unfeigned (1) and Zealous (1).

24. These non-puritan names, in order of popularity, are Mary (16), Thomas (16), John (10), Richard (9), Elizabeth (8), Edward (5), William (5), Anne (4), Joan (4), Margaret (4), Samuel (4), Sara (3), Susan (3), Dorothy (2), Ellen (2), George (2), Lydia (2), Priscilla (2), Stephen (2), Abel (1), Abraham (1), Agnes (1), Alice (1), Ananias (1), Anthony (1), Benjamin (1), Cornelius (1), Denys (1), Edmond (1), Effagina (1), Henry (1), Judith (1), Michael (1), Obadiah (1), Odiane (1), Rebecca (1), Roger (1), Silas (1), Silvester (1) and Winifred (1). The popularity of the name Mary is especially striking given that a modern authority has written that it 'suffered an eclipse after the Reformation and was seldom used during Elizabeth's reign': E. G. Withycombe, *The Oxford Dictionary of English Christian Names* (1977), 211.

25. Between March 1590 and September 1602, Richard Vernon, vicar of Eastbourne, called his children Mary, George, Caesar, Margaret, Elizabeth and John.

26. D. Fenner, *The Arts of Logic and Rhetoric* (Middelburg, ? 1588), sig. E8; A. Peel, ed. *The Seconde Parte of a Register* (1915), I, 214. William Hopkinson, rector of Warbleton, was also a member of the 1583 Sussex delegation to Whitgift: *ibid.*; WSRO, Ep.II/9/6, f.57.

27. I have found particularly helpful C. Brent, 'Employment, land tenure and population in east Sussex, 1540–1640' (unpublished Ph.D. thesis, Sussex University, 1974) and J. L. M. Gulley, 'The Wealden landscape in the early seventeenth century' (unpublished Ph.D. thesis, London University, 1960).

28. Brent, thesis 65; *VCH*, Sussex, IX, 204, 206. My population figure represents the median annual number of deaths (13) in the period 1570–1600, multiplied by 31.

29. Gulley, thesis, 190, 521–3; BL, Add. charter 30920, and E. Straker, *Wealden Iron* (1931), 359–61, 377–80; ESRO, Lewes Wills, Bk A8, fos. 27v–8.

30. C. Morris (ed.), *The Journeys of Celia Fiennes* (1947), 136. The term is used apropos Goudhurst, in the Kentish Weald and adjacent to Cranbrook.

31. PRO, PROB 11/66/20 and St Ch 5/M16/22; WSRO, Ep.II/5/5, f.342v.

32. ESRO, Lewes Wills, Bks A11, f.19 and A22, fos. 89–96. The originals of these wills are extant; WSRO, Ep.II/9/5 f.305 r–v; Dunkin (Sussex Rec. Soc., I, 1902), 67 and J. S. Cockburn (ed.), *Calendar of Assize Records: Sussex Indictments James I* (1975) 21; *VCH*, Sussex, IX, 195, where the name is given incorrectly as 'Hepburn'.

33. A. L. Frewen, *A History of Brickwall in Sussex and of the Parishes of Northiam and Brede* (1909), 45; J. Bishop, *A Courteous Conference with the English Catholics Roman* (1598), sig. A2v.; PRO, PROB 11/106/55; ESRO, Lewes Wills, Bk A14, f.197. This is calendared incorrectly as the will of 'John' Bishop. Hall (British Rec. Soc., XXIV, 1901), 163; Dunkin, *op. cit.*, 105; PRO, PROB 11/120/75; W. B. Bannerman (ed.), *The Visitations of the County of Sussex . . . 1633–4* (Harleian Soc., LIII, 1905), 133, 169–70.

34. Brent, thesis, 226. The other four Warbleton yeomen are William Avery, John Delve, William Stace alias Shether and George Wattell: ESRO, Lewes Wills, Bks A10, f.103r–v, A12, fos. 248–9; WSRO, Ep.II/5/3, f.38v, Ep.II/5/8, f.21v; Dunkin, *op. cit.*, 20.

35. The other two Warbleton husbandmen are Thomas Breach and William Hobeme: ESRO, Lewes Wills, Bks A9, f.227r–v, A16, f.113, A17, f.39r–v and QR/E/3, f.82. For help with Sussex quarter sessions material I am grateful to Mr C. Whittick; WSRO, Ep.II/5/1, f.144v; Dunkin, *op. cit.*, 40.

36. ESRO, Lewes Wills, Bk A11, fos. 223–4; Dunkin, *op. cit.*, 23.

37. ESRO, Lewes Wills, Bks A8, f.446, A9, fos. 114v–15, 174v–5, 227r–v, A10, fos. 4r–v, 103 r–v, A12, fos. 6v–7, and QR/E/7, f.29.

38. ESRO, Lewes Wills, Bks A12, fos. 148–9, 248–9, A21, fos. 101v–2.

39. ESRO, Lewes Wills, Bk A11, fos. 99r–v, 215v, 223–4.

40. ESRO, Lewes Wills, Bks A12, f.156v, A16, f.113, A17, f.39r–v, A22, fos. 89–96; PRO, E 179/190/332, Hawksborough Hundred.

41. WSRO, Ep.II/9/7, f.119v.

42. M. Spufford, 'The schooling of the peasantry in Cambridgeshire, 1575–1700', in J. Thirsk (ed.), *Land, Church and People* (1970), 121–2, 134–6; WSRO, Ep.II/5/8, f.22v.

43. Out of 11 puritan families the mean baptismal interval is 28.4 months (median: 27.2) whereas out of 20 non-Puritan families the mean baptismal interval is 33.6 months (median: 30).

44. PRO, PROB 11/91/42. The language of these testators has to be understood in the light of contemporary views concerning usury. Many ordinary people regarded the 1571 statute 'as sanctioning interest up to ten per cent' while 'theologians and moralists' *all* glossed it in a more restrictive sense. The Warbleton puritans here followed their religious teachers: R. H. Tawney (ed.), *A Discourse upon Usury . . . by Thomas Wilson* (1925), 118–19, 165, 170. The nature of the Warbleton evidence moreover suggests that, in a rural context, a major solvent of traditional attitudes towards usury was the experience of inflation; it must have become increasingly obvious that cash bequests payable some years hence, to children on reaching their majorities, would by then be worth less in real terms.

45. W. G. Hoskins, Harvest fluctuations and English economic history, 1480–1619',
    Agricultural History Review, XII (1964), 39; W. Perkins, 'A fruitful dialogue
    concerning the end of the world', *Works* (1608–9), III, 467–77; *APC*, 1586–7, 91,
    119; *CSPD*, 1581–90, 323, 326, 340, 343–4, 347, 364 and index references to
    'Armada'. For unrest in 1587 see P. Clark, 'Popular protest and disturbance in
    Kent, 1558–1640', *EcHR*, XXIX (1976), 367.

46. P. Collinson, *The Elizabethan Puritan Movement* (1967), 291–329, 333.

47. Cf. n.11 above.

48. D. Williams (ed.), *Three Treatises Concerning Wales [by John Penry]* (1960), xviii,
    41–2, 162.

49. Preserved Holman was christened at Warbleton on 1 August 1588. To my
    knowledge this is the first use of Preserved as a baptismal name.

50. In addition to Comfort Starr and Comfort Penry, Comfort Tamkin was
    christened at Wartling, Sussex, in April 1600.

51. R. B. Manning, *Religion and Society in Elizabethan Sussex* (1969), 201, 211; P. Clark,
    'Josias Nicholls and religious radicalism, 1553–1639', *Journal of Ecclesiastical
    History*, XXVIII (1977), 145; Longden, *loc. cit.*

52. J. Hurstfield, *Freedom, Corruption and Government in Elizabethan England* (1973), 68–9.

53. R. H. Tawney, *Religion and the Rise of Capitalism* (1926), 175–93.

5 MILITIA RATES AND MILITIA STATUTES 1558–1663

1. The theme of this paper derives from conversations with Miss Claire Gittings and
   manuscript references supplied by Mr Victor Morgan. I am also grateful to
   Professor Robert Ashton, Professor James Jones and Dr Roger Virgoe, who have
   made valuable criticisms, to Mr Conrad Russell who has supplied many
   references to parliamentary sources, and to the editors, all of whom have helped
   me in the final stages.

2. J. Hurstfield, 'County government c.1530–c.1660', in *VCH, Wiltshire*, V, 80–110.

3. L. Boynton, *The Elizabethan Militia 1558–1638* (1967) (hereafter cited as Boynton,
   Militia).

4. T. G. Barnes, *Somerset 1625–1640* (1961) (hereafter cited as Barnes, *Somerset*),
   ch. viii; A. H. Lewis, *A study of Elizabethan Ship-Money 1558–1603* (Philadelphia,
   1928); A. Hassell Smith, *County and Court: Government and politics in Norfolk
   1558–1603* (1974) (hereafter cited as Smith, *Norfolk*), 281–3; M. D. Gordon, 'The
   collection of ship-money in the reign of Charles I', *TRHS*, 3rd ser., IV (1910),
   141–62; J. S. Morrill, *Cheshire 1630–1660* (1974), 28; A. Fletcher, *A County
   Community in Peace and War: Sussex 1600–1660* (1975), 205–7.

5. Barnes, *Somerset*, 277.

6. Boynton, *Militia*, 269–70.

7. 4 and 5 Ph. and Mar. c. 2.

8. J. J. Goring, 'The military obligations of the English people 1511–58' (unpublished
   Ph.D. thesis, London University, 1955), *passim*, esp. 70, 277–80, 287; *idem.*,
   'Social change and military decline in mid-Tudor England', *History*, LX (1975),
   192–7.

9. For further evidence of its composite nature see C. G. Ericson, 'Parliament as a legislative institution in the reigns of Edward VI and Mary' (unpublished Ph.D. thesis, London University, 1974), 261–70.

10. Goring, thesis, 121–2 and 313.

11. In the early seventeenth century Norfolk companies of foot were based upon hundreds and varied between 120 and 200 men. The number apportioned to each hundred seems to have been arrived at by a process of discussion and bargaining among J.P.s or commissioners. Occasionally a hundred's quota was raised or lowered slightly, but there appears to be no direct relationship between size of a company and size or wealth of a hundred.

12. Boynton, *Militia*, 63, 71, 94; Norfolk RO, MSS. BL VIIb (2), letter dated 19 July 1599, Norwich Assembly Books 1585–1613, fos. 92v, 160v, 175, 193, 203, 212v, 215v; Folger Library, MSS. L.d.455, 750; BL, Cotton MS. Titus F. II, f. 32; *CSPD*, Addenda 1625–1649, 86 and 321–2; W. Lambarde, *Archeion* (ed. C. H. McIlwain and P. L. Ward, 1957), 104. (I am indebted to Mr C. Russell for this reference).

13. Boynton, *Militia*, 33–36; J. J. N. McGurk, 'The clergy and the militia 1580–1610, *History*, LX (1975), 198–210. His statement that 'since Mary's reign the clergy were bound under statute to provide a special amount of armour and weapons for inspection and use at the shire musters' is based upon a misreading of a document in J. Strype, *Life and Acts of Matthew Parker* (1821 edn), I, 542.

14. See, for instance, Joan Thirsk, 'Seventeenth-century agriculture and social change, in *Land, Church and People*, ed. J. Thirsk (1970); E. Kerridge, 'Agriculture 1500–1793' in *VCH*, Wiltshire, IV, 58–64.

15. Smith, *Norfolk*, ch. xiii, esp. 282–3. A divergence of view as between the sheep-corn and wood-pasture regions emerges even more clearly over the issue of compounding for purveyance (see esp. 298).

16. BL, Kings MS. 265, fos. 328b, 331. Norfolk RO, MS. Martyn, bundle 9, letter dated 22 Oct. 1616.

17. BL, Harleian MS. 168, f. 61v. My italics.

18. Boynton, *Militia*, 175; *The musters returns for divers Hundreds in the county of Norfolk, 1569, 1572, 1574 and 1577*, ed. H. L. Bradfer-Lawrence (Norfolk Rec. Soc., VI, 1935), 59–113; Norfolk RO, MS. WAL XVII/2, letter dated 13 Oct. 1617; Yorkshire Diocesan Registry, MSS. PR Y/J 17, fos. 4, 14v, Y/MCS 16, pp. 179, 190, 195, Y/MG 19, pp. 60, 70, 76, 78, 82, 102.

19. Boynton, *Militia*, 158.

20. BL, Harleian MS., 168, f.63v.

21. C. Russell, 'Parliamentary history in perspective 1604–1629', *History*, LXI (1976), 12.

22. BL, Cotton MS. Titus F.II, f.32.

23. Smith, *Norfolk*, 277–9; Boynton, *Militia*, 165–206.

24. See below, p. 104.

25. Smith, *Norfolk*, 280–84; Boynton, *Militia*, 167–80; Folger Library, MSS. X.d.502, L.d.951; *The Earl of Hertford's Lieutenancy papers 1603–1612*, ed. W. P. D. Murphy (Wiltshire Rec. Soc., XXIII, 1969), 17–108 (hereafter cited as Murphy, *Lieutenancy Papers*); PRO, SP 14/5/77.

26. Norfolk RO, MS. BL VIIb (2), letter dated 2 Dec. 1598.

27. Cambridge University Library, MS. Mm.v. 7; BL, Cotton MS. Titus B.V, fos. 59–79.

28. Smith, *Norfolk*, 280.

29. PRO, SP 14/1/68, f.1v. Undated, but internal evidence leaves no doubt that it was compiled early in the reign of James I.

30. 1 Jac. I. c. 25.

31. Folger Library, MS. X.d.502, letters dated 22 Oct. 1607 and 14 Jan. 1617/18. Norfolk RO, MSS. Martyn, bundle 18, undated letter from Nath. Bacon to William Dix and remembrances for meeting at Norwich dated 31 Oct. 1615. *CSPD*, 1628–9, 18.

32. See below, p. 104.

33. See, for instance, *The parliamentary diary of Robert Bowyer 1606–7*, ed. D. H. Willson (Minneapolis, 1931), 75.

34. *A compleat journal of the . . . House of Lords and House of Commons throughout the whole reign of Queen Elizabeth*, ed. S. D'Ewes (1708), 552–3.

35. PRO, SP 14/6/99.

36. *CJ*, I, 513a, 522a, 542–3, 569b, 619, 631; *Commons' Debates in 1621*, ed. W. Notestein, F. H. Relf and H. Simpson (New Haven, 1935), II, 27–8, 174, 360–1; III, 219–20, 236–7; BL, Harleian MS. 6383, fos. 135v–6.

37. *CJ*, I, 768.

38. *CJ*, I, 836a, 838a, 841a, 845a, 850a, 869a.

39. *CJ*, I, 874–5, 894a; *Lords' Debates in 1621, 1625 and 1628*, ed. F. H. Relf (Camden Soc., 3rd ser. XLII, 1929), 82–3; BL, Stowe MS. 366, fos. 147v, 159, 233v, 244v–5; Add. MS. 36825, fos. 463, 486.

40. *CJ*, I, 543a.

41. Murphy, *Lieutenancy Papers*, 110–11; McGurk, *op. cit.*, 209.

42. Murphy, *Lieutenancy Papers*, 116, 117, 126, 133; Norfolk RO, MSS. Martyn, bundles 18 and 49; 'Supplementary Stiffkey Papers', ed. F. W. Brooks, pp. 27, 29, 32, in *Camden Miscellany XVI* (Camden Soc., 3rd ser. LII, 1936); Boynton, *Militia*, 223–4; W. Rye, *Musters, beacons, shipmoney, etc. in Norfolk* (1907) (hereafter cited as Rye, *Musters*), 13.

43. Folger Library, MS. X.d.502, letter dated 14 Jan. 1617/18.

44. 4 and 5 Ph. and Mar. c. 3, clause 10. The relationship between the lieutenancy and corporate towns merits greater attention than it can be given here.

45. PRO, SP 14/78/46; Norfolk RO, MSS. Martyn, bundle 9, letters dated 23 Sept. and 27 Oct. 1616; Folger Library, MSS. X.d.502, letter dated 14 Jan. 1617/18; L.d.446; BL, Kings MS. 265, fos. 334–334v and 350–350v. *APC*, 1618–19, 119.

46. BL, Kings MS. 265, f.342v; Barnes, *Somerset*, 252; Rye, *Musters*, 144; PRO, SP 14/153/34; *CSPD*, 1623–5, 84.

47. PRO, SP 12/93, p. 196; *The musters returns*, ed. Bradfer-Lawrence, 59–113.

48. BL, Harleian MS. 168, f.63v.

49. Norfolk RO, MS. BL VIIb (2), letter dated 19 July 1599; Folger Library, MS. L.d.500.

50. 14 Eliz. c. 5; 35 Eliz. c. 4.

51. Coke, *Reports* (1727 ed.), v, 66–8; E. Cannan, *The history of local rates in England* (1896), 24–6, 70–7.

52. 39 Eliz. c. 3. My italics.

53. They instanced rates for purveyance, the setting forth of soldiers, and the muster-master's wages.

54. NRO, MSS. Bradfer-Lawrence, VIIb (2), letter dated 2 Dec. 1598; Wal XVII/1, fos. 40–1; Folger Library, MS. L.d.712.

55. See, for instance, *C J*, I, 543: speech by Sir Edward Coke.

56. 21 Jac. I. c. 28.

57. Rye, *Musters*, 5.

58. Murphy, *Lieutenancy Papers*, 145.

59. See, for instance, Norfolk RO, MSS. Norwich Assembly Book 1585–1613; King's Lynn Muniment Room, Congregation Books 5 and 6. York Corporation Records, House Books 30–33.

60. Murphy, *Lieutenancy Papers*, 61, 142; Folger Library, MS. X.d.502, letter dated 8 July 1611; Boynton, *Militia*, 229, 237; Norfolk RO, MS. WAL XVII/2, letter dated 18 Oct. 1617; Rye, *Musters*, 17–18.

61. Norfolk RO, MS. WAL XVII/2, letters dated 5 April. 1619 and 1 Oct. 1623.

62. Rye, *Musters*, 17; Folger Library, MS. L.d.926.

63. Rye, *Musters*, 141–2, 157.

64. Folger Library, MS. X.d.502, letter dated 8 July 1611.

65. BL, Kings MS. 265, fos. 310v and 336; Norfolk RO, MS. Ketton-Cremer 3/7/75, nos. 1/27 and 28; Boynton, *Militia*, 221; Rye, *Musters*, 100; *Calendar of Frere MSS: Hundred of Holt*, ed. B. Cozens-Hardy (Norfolk Rec. Soc., I, 1931), 7.

66. BL, Harleian MS. 168, f.62.

67. It is interesting, however, that purveyance rating appears to have continued on a parochial basis and ceased to be a source of friction.

68. *APC*, 1630–31, 44, 49–50, 208; 1629–30, 90, 273, 315–16, 322; 1628–9, 257; Norfolk RO, MSS. Bradfer-Lawrence VIIb (2), letters dated 2 Dec. 1598 and 29 June 1612; BL, Kings MS. 265, f.284v; Boynton, *Militia*, 94, 224, 227, 286, 289; Murphy, *Lieutenancy Papers*, 28, 175; Rye, *Musters*, 14, 77; PRO, SP 16/524/14; 14/5/71; Barnes, *Somerset*, 262, 264.

69. Folger Library, MS. L.d.497.

70. See above, pp. 103–4.

71. Norfolk RO, MS. Bradfer-Lawrence, VIIb (2), letter dated 2 Dec. 1598.

72. A. Everitt, *The Community of Kent and the Great Rebellion 1640–1660* (1966), 157.

73. *Acts and Ordinances of the Interregnum 1642–60*, ed. C. H. Firth and R. S. Rait (1911), I, 95–100.

74. J. S. Morrill, *The Revolt of the Provinces* (1976), 58–9.

75. 14 Car. II c. 3; 15 Car. II c. 14.

76. Fletcher, *op. cit.*, 188.

77. S. T. Bindoff, 'The making of the Statute of Artificers', in *Elizabethan Government and Society. Essays presented to Sir John Neale*, ed. S. T. Bindoff, J. Hurstfield and C. H. Williams (1961), 56–94.

78. G. R. Elton, *Reform and Renewal: Thomas Cromwell and the Common Weal*, (1973), 66–97.

79. Barnes, *Somerset*, 257; Murphy, *Lieutenancy Papers*, 107–8; *The parliamentary diary of Robert Bowyer*, ed. D. H. Willson, 130, 154–6; Rye, *Musters*, 17.

80. Above, p. 96. I hope to demonstrate this on another occasion.

6 CROWN, PARLIAMENT AND FINANCE: THE GREAT CONTRACT OF 1610

1. E. R. Foster (ed.), *Proceedings in Parliament 1610* (New Haven, 1966) (hereafter cited as Foster), I, 3–8; II, 9–27.
2. *Ibid.*, 24.
3. *Ibid.*, 358; S. R. Gardiner (ed.), *Parliamentary Debates in 1610* (Camden Soc. O.S. LXXXI, 1862) (hereafter cited as Gardiner), 10–12.
4. Foster, II, 32.
5. Gardiner, 15–16. On the conference as a whole see Foster, I, 13–16, 177–8; II, 34–6; Gardiner, 13–16.
6. Foster, II, 54.
7. For what follows see F. C. Dietz, *English Public Finance 1558–1641* (New York, 1932); W. R. Scott, *The Constitution and Finance of English Scottish and Irish Joint Stock Companies to 1720*, III (1911), 485–509; R. H. Tawney, *Business and Politics under James I* (1958), 134–42; R. Ashton, 'Deficit finance in the reign of James I', *EcHR*, N.S. X (1957–8), 15–29. On peace-time parliamentary taxation after 1534 see G. R. Elton, 'Taxation for war and peace in early Tudor England', in J. M. Winter (ed.), *War and Economic Development* (1975), 33–48.
8. A. G. R. Smith, *The Government of Elizabethan England* (1967), 8–9.
9. Ashton, *op. cit.*, 21–2; for the 1610 deficit, Dietz, *op. cit.*, 122 n. 41.
10. For the £80,000 valuation, Foster, II, 169.
11. On purveyance see A. Woodworth, 'Purveyance for the Royal Household in the reign of Queen Elizabeth', *Transactions of the American Philosophical Society*, XXXV (1945), 1–89. On the difficulties in Norfolk at the end of the reign see A. Hassell Smith, *Country and Court* (1974), 293–302.
12. Woodworth, 22–5; J. E. Neale, *Elizabeth I and her Parliaments, II, 1584–1601* (1957), 208–15.
13. *CJ*, I, 150–1.
14. See e.g. T. K. Rabb, 'Sir Edwin Sandys and the Parliament of 1604', *American Historical Review*, LXIX (1963–4), 647–8.
15. N. R. N. Tyacke, 'Wroth, Cecil and the parliamentary session of 1604', *BIHR*, L (1977), 120–5.
16. For Wroth, see *CJ*, I, 150–1, 231; for Hare, *ibid.*, 187, 190–3, 202, 207, 213–14, 223; for More, *ibid.*, 223, 226–8, 231; for Bacon, *ibid.*, 187, 190–3, 197, 204.
17. *Ibid.*, 160, 190–3.
18. *LJ*, II, 294–5.
19. *CJ*, I, 204–31.
20. *Ibid.*, 259–86; *LJ*, II, 406–14; D. H. Willson (ed.), *The Parliamentary Diary of Robert Bowyer 1606–7* (Minneapolis, 1931), 6–125. The government did take some action on purveyance in 1606. On 23 April, after its failure to reach agreement with the Commons on the subject, it issued a proclamation 'for prevention of further abuses' in the system: J. F. Larkin and P. L. Hughes (eds.), *Stuart Royal Proclamations*, I (1973), 136–42. It represented pious hopes.
21. On wardship see H. E. Bell, *An Introduction to the History and Records of the Court of Wards and Liveries* (1953); J. Hurstfield, *The Queen's Wards* (1958).

22. Hurstfield, *op. cit.*, 345–6.
23. For the working of the system in Essex at the end of Elizabeth's reign see A. G. R. Smith, *Servant of the Cecils* (1977), 116–18.
24. Neale, *op. cit.*, II, 91–4.
25. *CSPD*, 1598–1601, 110.
26. *C J*, I, 150–1.
27. *Ibid.*, 153–4, 155–6, 215–21; Tyacke, *op. cit.*
28. *C J*, I, 226–8.
29. *Ibid.*, 221.
30. *L J*, II, 309; *C J*, I, 230–1.
31. 'Journal of Sir Roger Wilbraham', *Camden Miscellany: X* (Camden Soc., 3rd ser. IV, 1902), 63.
32. Much the same line of argument is followed by Hurstfield, *op. cit.*, 316ff.
33. Foster, II, 66–7.
34. Gardiner, 147–52 (my italics).
35. See above, n. 10.
36. Foster, I, 80; II, 75–6.
37. *HMC*, Salisbury MSS., XXI, 217.
38. *L J*, II, 401.
39. Foster, II, 123.
40. *C J*, I, 441, 444; Foster, II, 168, 169.
41. *Ibid.*, 227.
42. Foster, I, 145–6; II, 283–4.
43. *L J*, II, 660–2.
44. PRO, SP 14/56/43.
45. *L J*, II, 662.
46. The problem of the levy is admirably discussed by Foster, I, xviii–ix; II, 290–1, n. 3.
47. *L J*, II, 662.
48. *Ibid.*
49. D. Hirst, *The Representative of the People?* (1975).
50. Foster, II, 75.
51. *Ibid.*, 292.
52. PRO, SP 14/57/32.
53. Foster, II, 76.
54. *Ibid.*, 138–9.
55. *Ibid.*, 318.
56. PRO, SP 14/57/62.
57. W. Notestein, *The House of Commons 1604–10* (New Haven, 1971), 394.
58. Foster, II, 301–2.
59. *Ibid.*, 297–302.
60. *Ibid.*, 300.
61. *Ibid.*, 296.
62. *Ibid.*, 309–10.
63. *Ibid.*, 305 n. 3, 311 n. 3.
64. *Ibid.*, 316.
65. *Ibid.*, 305.

66. *Ibid.*, 69–70, and 70 n. 1 (23 April).
67. *Ibid.*, 310.
68. *Ibid.*, 393–4.
69. *Ibid.*, 398.
70. Foster, I, 279; II, 71, 382.
71. *Ibid.*, 310–11.
72. *Ibid.*, 57 n. 1, 69.
73. *HMC*, Downshire MSS., II, 328.
74. Gardiner, 163–79. Caesar's memorandum is discussed by M. Prestwich, *Cranfield* (1966), 41–5. Mrs Prestwich is in general agreement with his analysis. It is not apparent if Caesar was acting simply on his own behalf or as the agent of others who were opposed to the Contract. The whole question of the relationship between court factions opposed to Salisbury and opposition to the Contract deserves detailed attention.
75. Foster, II, 313–6.
76. Dietz, *op. cit.*, 137.
77. For the House's somewhat stunned reaction to the message, Foster, II, 316–9.
78. *Ibid.*, 319.
79. *Ibid.*, 327, 340.
80. *Ibid.*, 316–17.
81. *HMC*, Salisbury MSS., XXI, 266.
82. For Salisbury's position during the last two years of his life see D. H. Willson, *King James VI and I* (1956), 268ff.; Hurstfield, *op. cit.*, 322–5. We await a detailed account of Salisbury's role in the Great Contract in Professor Hurstfield's forthcoming biography.
83. Gardiner, 11.
84. Prestwich, *op. cit.*, 40. Mrs Foster agrees; the basic reason for failure was 'lack of confidence in the Crown', I, xx.
85. This point is noted by Hurstfield, *op. cit.*, 321, who speaks of James's 'impossible demand'.
86. Dietz, *op. cit.*, 149, 271; Prestwich, *op. cit.*, 161 n. 5.
87. Bell, *op. cit.*, 49–50, 150–9.
88. G. E. Aylmer, 'The last years of purveyance, 1610–60', *EcHR*, n.s. X (1957–8), 81–93.
89. 12 Car. II c. xxiv.
90. Aylmer, *op. cit.*, 90–1; D. Ogg, *England in the Reign of Charles II*, I (1955), 159–61.
91. Foster, II, 327ff.
92. *HMC*, Salisbury MSS., XXI, 266.
93. On the union with Scotland and impositions see Notestein, *op. cit.*, esp. 211ff., 361ff.
94. See Hurstfield, *op. cit.*, 322–3; Prestwich, *op. cit.*, 43–4.

7 STAGING A PARLIAMENT IN EARLY STUART ENGLAND

The costs discussed in this article are chiefly drawn from the accounts at the Public Record Office and may be found in the various classes of records in the Exchequer, in the departments of the lord chamberlain of the king's Household, and of the lord steward of the Household. By their very nature, some accounts duplicate others; but this is helpful since often one series will supply the deficiencies in another.

Records in the Exchequer (King's Remembrancer) include the statements of particulars or *particule compoti* which officers brought with them in rendering their accounts. This class of documents therefore provided important details for the Wardrobe, the Household, and the King's Works. Accounts for the same departments may also be found in the declared accounts of the Exchequer (E 351, AO1 and AO3). Unexpectedly the stationers' accounts for the Long Parliament were discovered among the miscellaneous papers classified as AO3 (King's Works). Material concerning lords' diets, the king's barge, fees and annuities, was found in the Privy Seal Books (Auditor's) and the Imprest Books (Pells') of the Exchequer (E 403).

In the lord chamberlain's records, which include Wardrobe and Household, the accounts (LC9) were useful, also the copies of warrants and warrant books in the Wardrobe (LC5). In the lord steward's records, treatises and precedent books concerning the Household may be found (LS13). Fragments of accounts are among the Main Papers of the House of Lords (hereafter cited as HLRO, Main Papers, HL) and the Braye manuscripts at the House of Lords Record Office and in the Osborn collection at Yale University. Some material has been recovered from the State Papers Domestic (SP 14, SP 15, SP 16, SP 19) at the Public Record Office. I am grateful to Sir John Summerson, Professor G. E. Aylmer, Mr Maurice Bond, Mr H. S. Cobb, Mr J. C. Sainty and Ramona Livingston for valuable suggestions.

1.   This account is based on PRO, SP 15/40/56 (1614) and SP 16/471/11 (3 November 1640). See also *The Manner of Holding Parliaments in England . . . With The Stately and magnificent order, of proceeding to Parliament, of the most High and Mighty Prince, King Charles . . .* (1641), which gives details of the procession for both parliaments in 1640. Northumberland MSS., Alnwick 468 gives descriptions of Elizabethan processions. I have used the microfilms of the Northumberland MSS. and cite them here with the gracious permission of the Duke of Northumberland. In an Elizabethan procession, the bishops were said to wear Parliament robes: Thomas Milles, *The Catalogue of Honor* (1610, large paper edn) I, 65.

2.   The figure for 1610 is the sum of items for work done at the Parliament houses and the Court of Requests (PRO, E 351/3244). For other years, see E 351/3254; AO 1/2424 (56); E 351/3261; E 351/3262; AO 1/2429 (71).

3.   In 1601, the procession to Parliament was said to be so well-ordered that nobody received any hurt (Northumberland MSS., Alnwick 468). In 1621, several people were injured when scaffolds collapsed: N. E. McClure (ed.), *The Letters of John Chamberlain* (Philadelphia, 1939), II, 338.

4.   PRO, E 351/3248; E 351/3257; E 351/3261; AO 1/2424 (56); AO 1/2429 (71); LC 5/134, p. 386.

5.   PRO, E 351/3257.

6.   PRO, LC 5/134, p. 386.

7.   The phrase is borrowed from an order to Black Rod in November 1640 to keep New Palace Yard free of 'undecent and prejudicial' structures (PRO, LC 5/134, p. 422).

8.   PRO, E 351/3237; E 403/1718; AO 1/2424 (55); E 351/3260; E 351/3261;

AO 1/2429 (71). For paving in 1642 and 1644-5, see *L J*, VIII, 31; HLRO, Main Papers, HL, 2 Jan. 1642/3; 21 Oct. 1644; 9 Dec. 1645; PRO, E 351/3273.

9. HLRO, Main Papers, HL, 22 June 1643; *L J*, VI, 104. Best and his wife complained that they had been much molested by irate men and women. Wharfingers petitioned that passage might be permitted at certain times, but they were denied (HLRO, Main Papers, HL, 13 April, 27 Sept., 7 Oct. 1644; *L J*, V, 498; VII, 17, 69).

10. McClure (ed.), *op. cit.*, II, 337.

11. PRO, E 351/3237; E 351/3239; E 351/3242; HLRO, Main Papers, HL, 25 July 1645.

12. PRO, E 351/3239; E 351/3261.

13. For roof repairs, see PRO, AO 1/2417 (35), 1603; E 351/3239, 1603-4; E 351/3244, 1609-10; E 351/3248, 1613-14; E 351/3257, 1623-4; E 351/3261, 1627-8; E 351/3273, 1644-5; AO 1/2429 (73), 1645-6. For stealing lead, see PRO, AO 1/2429 (73). Lead had been stolen from Whitehall in 1607-9 (PRO, E 351/3243) and men were hired in 1604-5 to keep watch over the materials assembled for building repairs (E 351/3240).

14. PRO, E 351/3237; E 351/3239; E 351/3242; E 351/3257.

15. PRO, E 351/3237.

16. PRO, E 351/3242; E 351/3254; E 351/3257; PRO, AO 1/2429 (71).

17. PRO, E 351/3237; E 351/3242; AO 1/2429 (73); AO 1/2424 (56). In 1627-8, White was paid the same sum (E 351/3261).

18. PRO, E 351/3273.

19. PRO, E 351/3239.

20. J. E. Neale, *The Elizabethan House of Commons* (New Haven, 1950), 140; PRO, E 351/3239; *C J*, I, 141.

21. PRO, E 351/3254. This is interesting in view of the thesis advanced in 'Red and Green,' *Table*, XXXVII (1968), 33-40.

22. PRO, E 351/3242.

23. PRO, E 351/3261. In 1614, the Spanish ambassador attended Parliament. A crimson curtain was hung behind the chair of state, with holes cut in it so that he could see (PRO, SP 15/40/56).

24. PRO, E 351/3273.

25. There are references to the 'House of Records next the minster church' (which Sir John Summerson suggests is the chapter house) and to the 'House of Records over the Parliament House' in 1 *Jac.* I (PRO, E 351/3239). Once more I am grateful to Sir John Summerson who directed my attention to the statement that after the Restoration records were kept over the House of Commons: 'Westminster Palace in the Wren Period', 46-7, *Wren Society*, XI (1934). In the sixteenth and early seventeenth centuries, the House of Commons had no fixed place for its records: see J. E. Neale, 'The Commons Journals of the Tudor period', *TRHS*, 4th ser. III (1920), 153-7; William Hakewil, *The Manner How Statutes are enacted in Parliament by Passing of Bills* (1659), preface. During the years 1642-60, the journals of the Parliament were said to have been kept in presses in the Court of Wards, 'separate from the other journals (which were kept in the clerk's office)': O. C. Williams, *The Topography of the Old House of Commons* (1953), 5.

26. PRO, E 351/3254; A. J. Taylor, *The Jewel Tower* (1965), 14–15; E 351/3257; E 351/3260; AO 1/2429 (73).

27. PRO, E 351/3239; E 351/3242; AO 1/2424 (56); E 351/3273; AO 1/2429 (73).

28. PRO, E 351/3237; E 351/3239; E 351/3244; E 351/3257; AO 1/2424 (56); AO 1/2429 (71).

29. PRO, E 351/3239.

30. PRO, E 351/3237; E 351/3261. In 1624–5, the serjeant of the lower House also claimed 'one joined table of deal' in the Committee chamber and received 20s. as composition for this and his other table (PRO, AO 1/2424 (55)).

31. PRO, E 351/3244.

32. PRO, E 351/3257. In 1660, the clock in the upper House was said to be brass (HLRO, Main Papers, HL, 26 May 1660).

33. PRO, AO 1/2424 (56).

34. PRO, AO 1/2429 (71). In the Painted Chamber, there was a table with 'double forms round it': E. S. Cope (ed.), *Proceedings of the Short Parliament of 1640* (Camden Soc., 4th Ser., XIX, 1977), 201.

35. PRO, E 351/3273; AO 1/2429 (72) and (73). In March 1645, the Committee of Whitehall was ordered to 'take care to appoint some hangings out of the King's standing wardrobe at Whitehall . . . to be hung before the window of this House as Curtains, for the defending and preserving this Place against the injury of this bitter Weather' ('Red and Green', 38–9).

36. PRO, AO 1/2429 (71).

37. PRO, AO 1/2429 (73).

38. PRO, LC 5/38.

39. For this phrase, see HLRO, Main Papers, HL, 17 Dec. 1660.

40. PRO, LC 5/38. The term 'state' also may refer to the throne, but on this occasion it must apply only to the canopy and back cloth.

41. PRO, LC 5/38; SP 15/39/59; AO 3/1116; AO 3/1117; AO 3/1118; AO 3/1119; AO 3/1120; LC 9/96; LC 9/98; LC 5/132, p. 71; E 403/2565. Cf. *LP*, V, no. 470; VII, no. 53, where warrants for similar orders appear.

42. PRO, AO 3/1116; AO 3/1117; AO 3/1119; AO 3/1120; LC 9/103. The lord chamberlain's accounts for 1623–4 come to £137 18s. 6d. (LC 9/98). E 403/2568.

43. PRO, SP 25/78; HLRO, Main Papers, HL, 26 May 1660, 17 Dec. 1660; PRO, E 403/2569.

44. PRO, LC 9/98, f.6v; LC 5/38.

45. PRO, AO 3/1119; LC 9/98, fos. 6, 14; AO 1/2424 (56); E 351/3261; AO 3/1120.

46. PRO, LC 9/98, f.17; AO 3/1119; LC 5/134, p. 383; HLRO, Main Papers, HL, 26 May, 17 Dec. 1660.

47. PRO, LC 5/132, p. 2. In 1640, the cushions were to be long, of crimson or purple velvet, trimmed with tassels and short fringes of gold and silk (LC 5/134, p. 383). In an inventory of Cardinal Wolsey's household stuff (1530), a large Venetian 'window carpet' and a blue velvet cushion were noted to have been lost during the Parliament held at Blackfriars by fault of the gentlemen ushers (*LP*, IV, pt III, 2767). When Queen Elizabeth opened Parliament in 1601, she came to the north door and knelt on a small carpet (Northumberland MSS., Alnwick 468).

48. Sir Thomas Smith, *De Republica Anglorum*, ed. L. Alston (1906), 50–1; 'Red and

Green', 36; PRO, SP 15/40/56; J. T. Smith, *Antiquities of Westminster* (1807), 263. During the Commonwealth, the House of Commons, formerly wainscoted, may have been hung with tapestry. In the eighteenth century, a new set of tapestries was said to be provided for each Parliament, the housekeeper claiming the old as her fee (J. T. Smith, *op. cit.*, 144).

49. PRO, LC 5/132, p. 11.
50. PRO, LC 5/134, pp. 383, 385; LC 5/135.
51. PRO, LC 5/134, pp. 381, 387, 410.
52. Four suits of new tapestries for the rooms adjoining the Parliament chamber (SP 16/491/46); HLRO, Main Papers, HL, 12 Aug. 1644; *L J*, VI, 667.
53. PRO, LC 5/132, pp. 93, 96, 97, 120; SP 19/123/92.
54. HLRO, Main Papers, HL, 26 May, 17 Dec. 1660. The December bill probably included the earlier items for May, see HLRO, PO Paper 384.
55. PRO, LC 5/132, p. 121. The housekeeper was paid £4 11s. 3d. a quarter (PRO, SP 14/76/44).
56. PRO, LC 5/132, p. 130. These dates do not correspond with the days Parliament was in session. Crane also claimed an allowance of 3s. *per diem* for himself and servants, which is not considered here, but will be included later with officers' salaries.
57. PRO, LC 5/132, pp. 52, 131; see also p. 178. As above, n. 56, these dates do not correspond with the days Parliament was in session.
58. *Ibid.*, p. 121.
59. *Ibid.*, pp. 90, 96.
60. HLRO, Main Papers, HL, 13 April 1644.
61. PRO, E 351/3273.
62. HLRO, Main Papers, HL, 26 May, 17 Dec. 1660.
63. PRO, E 351/3262. Most, though possibly not all, would be chargeable to Parliament.
64. PRO, AO 1/2429 (73); E 351/3274.
65. HLRO, Main Papers, HL, 22 July 1646; *L J*, VIII, 439. In 1642, Fitchett and William Shallaker had considerable difficulty collecting £917 due them. In 1646, Fitchett still asserted that he had not been paid (*L J*, V, 508–9; HLRO, Main Papers, HL, 21 Dec. 1642, 21 Nov. 1646). Rushes and billets were usually taken in the 'back door' of the Parliament House near the Parliament stairs (PRO, SP 16/451/21).
66. Half the expense at Haberdashers' Hall of £200 for fire, candles, printing and messengers (Dec. 1642–Dec. 1643) was paid by the House of Commons (*L J*, VI, 398). 'Fire' for committees in the House of Commons during the Interregnum was provided by the messengers and doorkeepers who attended them. See the petition of 1654 (PRO, SP 18/70/59–60).
67. Osborn Collection, Yale University, Braye MSS. 112/41 (this manuscript is also available in photocopy at the House of Lords Record Office); PRO, SP 14/58, 3 Dec. 1610.
68. PRO, E 403/2561; E 403/1710; SP 14/54/22; SP 14/58, 3 Dec. 1610; Osborn Collection, Braye MSS. 112/33.
69. Osborn Collection, Braye MSS. 112/40, 112/90.
70. PRO, AO 3/1276, Part II; AO 3/1088(1).

71. Osborn Collection, Braye MSS. 112/40 and 41.

72. PRO, AO 3/1276, Part II (see also BL, Add. MS. 5756, fos. 5–6). There are several works by William Fulbecke which would satisfy this description: *A direction or preparative to the study of the lawe* (1600, 1620); *The pandects of the law of nations* (1602); *A parallele or conference of the civill law, the canon law, and the common law of England* (1601, 1602, 1620). I am grateful to Matthew Shaaber for information that *The French Academy* is a translation of a work by Pierre de La Primaudaye, available in several editions, 1586–1618, and that *Flores Doctorum* is an anthology of excerpts from patristic writings, compiled by Thomas Hibernicus; though never printed in England, there were many editions on the Continent. Thomas Wentworth, *The office and dutie of executors* (1641); John Kitchin, *Le court leete et courte baron* (various editions, 1580–1620); the complete works of Guillaume de Saluste Du Bartas, Huguenot poet, were published in France in 1579 and 1611; *Bartas: his devine weekes and workes*, translated by J. Sylvester, appeared in 1605 in England, followed by numerous other editions of individual pieces; *The souls solace* (1626, 1631); John Gerard, *The herball* (1597, 1633, 1636).

73. Coke's *Reports* were published in numerous editions beginning in 1600. The House of Commons, 12 May 1641, ordered that Coke's heir should publish 'The commentary on Magna Carta, the pleas of the crown, and the jurisdiction of the courts' (the second, third and fourth *Institutes*). A folio edition appeared in 1642. Separate editions of the third and fourth *Institutes* followed: *DNB*.

74. Possibly Desiderius Erasmus, *Seven dialogues both pithie and profitable* (1606). The description 'Dialogues' could apply to any of the numerous editions of Erasmus' *Colloquia*. The works of William Perkins on religious subjects were also available in many editions. I am grateful to John Spielman for recognizing 'Belzarke's Epistles' as the *Letters* of Jean Louis Guez, Sieur de Balzac (1634, 1638, 1639). Several English editions of the *Historie* of Phillip de Comines would have been available. Probably Baker was Sir Richard Baker who wrote a series of books entitled *Meditations and disquisitions* on the Lord's prayer and the penitential psalms. Thomas Milles, *The Catalogue of Honor* (1610). Thomas Brightman, *A revelation of the Apocalyps* (1611), reissued in 1615 as *A revelation of the revelation* and in 1616 as *The revelation of S. John*. George Hakewill, *An apologie or declaration of the power and providence of God* (1627, 1630, 1635). Probably the reference is to Joseph Hall, whose religious works were issued in various editions from 1625 onwards.

75. PRO, AO 3/1088(1). The clerk was supplied with a 'Mynion' Bible, probably a miniature, since 'Minion' is the name of a very small printer's type. A 32° Bible had been printed in Edinburgh in 1638, which was possibly the kind intended. Again I am grateful to Professor Shaaber. Clement Cotton compiled several concordances of the Bible. The reference is probably to *A complete concordance* (1631) or to *A large concordance* (1635). 'Mr. Roger's notes' is probably Thomas Rogers, *Faith, Doctrine and Religion, Professed and Protected in the Realm of England* (Cambridge, 1607 and later editions), which consists of 'notes' on the Thirty-Nine Articles; I am grateful to Nicholas Tyacke for this suggestion. *An harmony of the confessions of the faith of the Christian and reformed churches*, a reprint of the Cambridge edition of 1586, was published in London in 1643.

76. PRO, AO 3/1088 (1); AO 3/1276, Part II. 'Carnation' may mean flesh-colored, a light rosy pink, or occasionally crimson (*OED*). Elsewhere in these documents the tape purchased is referred to as 'red'.

77. For the commissioners for the Customs, the Crown Office, and the clerk of the parliaments, 1642, see PRO, AO 3/1088(1). For Mr Secretary Nicholas, Mr Secretary Vane, the commissioners of the Customs House, Lord Falkland, the Petty Bag Office, the Crown Office and the justices of Middlesex, 1640–2, see PRO, AO 3/1276, Pt II. For a later order to deliver various printed Acts and Declarations to the Fleet and elsewhere, see HLRO, Main Papers, HL, 15 May–16 Oct. 1649. In 1648, members of the House of Commons were responsible for distributing the Declaration of 17 April 1646 in their counties and towns (HLRO, Main Papers, HL, 20 Oct. 1648; see also PRO, SP 19/117/59–66). In 1625, members complained that books of the fast had not been sent into several dioceses and that excessive prices were demanded for them: S. R. Gardiner (ed.), *Debates of the House of Commons in 1625* (Camden Soc., n.s. VI, 1873), 72.

78. 2 April 1646 for the House of Commons; 6 Dec. 1647 for the House of Lords (PRO, AO 3/1088(1)).

79. PRO, AO 3/1276, Pt II; AO 3/1088(1).

80. For printing charges for Acts, subsidy books, and proclamations in the Elizabethan period and in 1605, see BL, Add. MS. 5756, fos. 135, 138, 139. The proclamations were not, of course, necessarily connected with Parliament. For an example of a printed form, see HLRO, Main Papers, HL, 28 June 1644, an order from the Committee for Advancement of Money.

81. PRO, SP 16/500/34. H. R. Plomer, 'The king's printing house under the Stuarts', *Library*, n.s. III (1901), 368–9. W. M. Clyde, 'Parliament and the Press, 1643–7', *Transactions of the Bibliographical Society*, 2nd ser. XIII (1933–4), 402–3.

82. PRO, SP 16/501/50; SP 16/498/8.

83. C. H. Firth and R. S. Rait, *Acts and Ordinances of the Interregnum, 1642–1660* (1911), III, vi. W. M. Clyde, *Transactions of the Bibliographical Society*, 2nd ser. XIV, 49. See 'The humble Petition and Information of John Hunscot Stationer, . . . to both Houses of Parliament', [1646], BL, Thomason Tract E. 340.15, 2.

84. HLRO, Main Papers, HL, 28 July 1642. He was to be paid from the money from the subsidy 21 *Jac.* I, still remaining in the hands of the Treasurers (*C J*, II, 698). *L J*, X, 181.

85. PRO, AO 3/1115. A robe made for Arthur Chichester, lord deputy of Ireland in 1612–13, cost £381 8s. 2d. (AO 3/1117).

86. PRO, AO 3/1117; LC 9/98, f. 9.

87. PRO, AO 3/1120.

88. For 1613–14, see PRO, LC 9/96; AO 3/1117; for 1614–15, see LC 9/97. For the period 1619–20, the charges for beating and airing and for the necessary 'coal' (probably charcoal) and wood came to £49 8s. annually. The brusher's salary was £10 (AO 3/1118). In 1622–3, £13 6s. 4d. was paid for airing (AO 3/1119). In 1623–4, £15 6s. went for perfuming, and £25 for beating, airing and for wood, 'coals', sweet powder and other necessaries (LC 9/98, fos. 13, 17v). In 1626–7, airing and beating came to £40 (AO 3/1120). In 1627–8, airing and the necessary materials came to £89 8s. and perfuming (for one-half year) to £16 (AO 3/1120; AO 3/909 (3)). In 1628, Robert Jossey was to be paid, as his predecessor was said

to have been paid, £40 per year for wood, charcoal, sweet powder and brushes for the airing and better keeping of His Majesty's 'crown robes' in the Tower of London (LC 5/132, p. 11). In 1628–9, perfuming cost £16, beating and airing £6 13s. 4d.: AO 3/909 (4). In 1630–31, beating and airing (by a furrier who also did some other work) again cost £6 13s. 4d. (AO 3/1120). Possibly the larger charges for salaries continued, though the account has not been found.

89. PRO, SP 16/3/62. *HMC*, Buccleuch and Queensberry MSS., III, 229. Northumberland MSS., Alnwick 468.

90. PRO, E 403/2562; AO 3/1118; LC 5/134, pp. 370, 375.

91. S. E. Lehmberg, *The Reformation Parliament 1529–1536* (1970), 213, n. 247.

92. E. R. Foster, *The Painful Labour of Mr. Elsyng* (Philadelphia, 1972), 10. BL, Add. MS. 5756, fos. 3–4. HLRO, Main Papers, HL, 27 July 1648. In the *Modus Tenendi Parliamentum* the clerk was to be paid daily, somewhat less if he was entitled to diet: M. V. Clarke, *Medieval Representation and Consent* (1936), 379, text of the English version of the *Modus*.

93. For this he sometimes compounded with the Office of Works, as in 1624–5, when he received 20s. and 1627–8 when he received 12s. for the desk left there since the last session: PRO, AO 1/2424 (55); E 351/3261.

94. Northumberland MSS., Alnwick 468; PRO, LC 5/132, pp. 51, 130–1; HLRO, Main Papers, HL, 31 July 1643. In August 1642, the House received an itemized bill of charges from the gentleman usher (*LJ*, V, 287). Perhaps such charges had earlier been met by the Crown.

95. PRO, E 351/3237. In Elizabeth's reign, he compounded for certain old pieces 'besides all the new stuff' for 53s. 4d. In 1603, he settled for 50s. The 'new stuff' in question cost the Crown £12 8s. 4d. to which 50s. payment must be added in reckoning total expenditure: E 351/3239. In 1604–5, he compounded for £6. The sum was actually delivered to the yeoman usher, but surely for Black Rod: PRO, AO 1/2424 (55).

96. PRO, LC 5/132, p. 73; LC 5/134, p. 386; E 351/3240.

97. Society of Antiquaries MSS. 40; PRO, LC 5/132, pp. 51, 130–1.

98. Neale, *Elizabethan House of Commons*, 332–3; BL, Add. MS. 36856, f.117v.

99. PRO, E 403/1736 (11 July 1625, 7 April 1626). O. C. Williams, *The Clerical Organization of the House of Commons* (1954), 18. In 1654–5, Scobell was voted £500 *per annum* for life, and in January 1657/8, Smith (who succeeded him) was voted £300 *per annum*: *Fourth Report of the Deputy Lord Keeper of the Public Record Office*, Appendix II, 191, 198.

100. PRO, E 403/1709, 23 July 1610; Neale, *Elizabethan House of Commons*, 334–5, 348. His perquisites were said to be high. For his disbursements, see Williams, *Clerical Organization*, 312. In 1654–5, he was voted an annual pension of £500 in addition to his daily fee (*Fourth Report of the Deputy Lord Keeper*, Appendix II, 195). PRO, E 351/3261.

101. BL, Add. MS. 5756, fos. 46, 49, 50, 54.

102. *Ibid.*, fos. 77, 84, 102, 105. For local payments to messengers on arrival, see P. L. Hughes and J. F. Larkin (eds.), *Stuart Royal Proclamations* (1973), I, *passim*.

103. BL, Add. MS. 5756, fos. 84, 109.

104. PRO, E 403/2561, fos. 13v, 305v.

105. PRO, E 101/602, no. 12. In James's reign, the lord steward complained that two

or three messes were provided for lords sitting at the Council table 'when most commonly there hath resorted thither but a very small number of lords to eat of it': PRO, LS 13/279.

106. PRO, E 403/2562; E 403/2563; E 101/437, no. 11; HLRO, Main Papers, HL, 5 March 1641/2.

107. PRO, E 101/602, no. 12 (for 68 days); E 101/627, no. 14; E 351/1823; E 351/1836 (for 14 days).

108. £1500 is probably not an exact figure (for 119 days). £918 5s. 7d. was spent from 20 March 1640/1 to 31 December 1641 (for 197 days) (HLRO, Main Papers, HL, 5 March 1641/2). PRO, E 101/440, no. 11. In December 1640, 'another screen', six yards long, was to be provided for the service of the lords at the lord steward's table: PRO, LC 5/134, p. 426.

109. £607 1d. for 30 days in July and August 1625 or £20 4s. 8d. per diem: PRO E 101/437, no. 11. 1625–6, £1244 8s. 5d. or £51 17s. per diem (for 24 days in February and June): E 351/1823. 1627–8, £1605 11s. 10d., or £19 16s. 5d. per diem (for 81 days): E 101/438, no. 2. For 57 days in 1640 (November and December), £380 8s. 2d. or about £6 13s. 6d. per diem. The charges for the lords in March 1641 for 9 days were intermingled with charges for the prince elector and the Scottish commissioners for a total of £254 8s. 3d., about £28 5s. 4d. per diem. In April 'etc.' and September 1641, the total was £304 1s. 8d.: E 101/440, no. 11. Diets for Star Chamber in 1604–5 ran from £21 5s. 8d. to £24 1s. 8d. per diem: Folger Library, MS. V.b.105, a reference I owe to Thomas G. Barnes, who also computed the per diem rates. The relation between the figures for diets for the Star Chamber and those for 'Lords in parliament time' suggests that only privy councillors were included in the phrase. I have omitted an item for diet for 58 knights of the Bath among the lords of Parliament during February 1625/6 (PRO, E 351/1823), for the Privy Seal Book (PRO, E 403/2563, p. 122) indicates that this payment was in fact for a feast.

110. E. R. Foster (ed.), *Proceedings in Parliament 1610* (New Haven, 1966), II, 19.

111. On this point, see G. E. Aylmer, *The King's Servants, 1625–1642* (New York, 1961), 246–9.

112. For election expenses, see Neale, *Elizabethan House of Commons*, 324–5. For the cost to lords, see Lehmberg, *op. cit.*, 58. In 1625/6, the Earl of Exeter asked licence to be absent from the coronation and from Parliament, protesting that he was not seeking to save 'the great charge' but that he was incapacitated with gout (PRO, SP 16/19/18). Glanville, speaking in the House of Commons in 1625, said 'he would not have it said the subject came hither, and spent 7,000li. a week only to grant 60 or 70,000li': Gardiner (ed.) *op. cit.*, *Debates of the House of Commons in 1625*, 114. For privilege, see *ibid.*, 55; HLRO, Main Papers, HL, 27 May 1641 (petition of the commonalty and citizens of London). V. Pearl, *London and the outbreak of the Puritan Revolution* (1964), 117.

113. Conrad Russell has recently suggested the potential cost of a Parliament to the Crown, in the threat to impositions (worth £70,000 a year) and the attack on patents and grants by which royal servants were rewarded: C. Russell, 'Parliamentary history in perspective, 1604–1629', *History*, LXI (1976), 14–16.

114. Nethersole wrote to Carleton on 2 June 1624 that bills of grace passed during the session were larger than all passed for 100 years and that the king sacrificed more

than the value of the subsidies. The king complained that part of his revenue had been taken away (pretermitted customs and the licence for wines): PRO, SP 14/167/10. R. E. Ruigh, *The Parliament of 1624* (1971), 395 n.

115. W. Notestein, F. H. Relf, H. Simpson, *Commons Debates 1621*, II (New Haven, 1935), 526. *Proceedings and Debates of the House of Commons in 1620 and 1621*, II (1766), 336–7. PRO, SP 14/158/59, 28 Jan. 1623/4.

116. Queen Elizabeth paid £1,097 6s. 1d. for the funeral of her relative, Lord Hunsdon (L. Stone, 'The anatomy of the Elizabethan aristocracy', *EcHR*, o.s. XVIII (1948), 13, a reference I owe to Myra Rifkin). For the cost of other funerals, see L. Stone, *The Crisis of the Aristocracy* (1965), Appendix XXV A. Examples in the first half of the seventeenth century run from £300 to £3,257.

8 THE PARLIAMENTARY CAREER OF JOHN PYM, 1621–9

I am grateful to the Central Research Fund of the University of London for grants for purchase of microfilms and other expenses, and to the Trustees of the Bedford Settled Estates, Sheffield University Library and Lord Delamere, The Trustees of the James M. Osborn Collection, Beineke Library, Yale University, and the Yale Center for Parliamentary History for permission to quote from copyright material in their possession.

1. Diary of John Hawarde, Wiltshire RO, Ailesbury MSS. (unnumbered and unfoliated), 27 Nov. 1621. *Commons' Debates in 1621* (hereafter cited as *1621 Debates*), ed. W. Notestein, F. H. Relf and H. Simpson (New Haven, 1935), III, 460; V, 215. Pym had been much irritated by a similar incident earlier in the session. He recorded that 'that interruption ceasing', the debate was resumed: *ibid.*, IV, 196–7.

2. *Ibid.*, III, 190; *C J*, I, 612.

3. Somerset RO, Pym MSS. no. 152. The document in question is a licence granted by Mompesson to an inn at Wingham in Kent. It is possible that Pym was named to the committee on the Masters in Chancery by his feoffee to uses Sir Edward Wardour. Some of the criticism of them arose from the case of Morgan *v.* Bowdler and Meggs, in which Wardour had a considerable personal interest.

4. R. P. Cust, 'A list of commissioners for the forced loan of 1626–7', *BIHR*, LI (1978), 202–8. Pym's nomination as a Forced Loan Commissioner was in Hampshire.

5. There is no known copy of Pym's will. Our knowledge that Rous was one of his executors is from Sheffield University Library, Hartlib MSS. 7/32 (Dury to Rous). For what may be a list of Pym's executors see Somerset RO, Pym MSS. no. 259. They are Oliver St John, Sir Benjamin Rudyerd, John Crew, Francis Rous, Anthony Nicoll and Alexander Pym.

6. PRO, PROB 11/70/f.293. I owe this reference to the late Miss Evelyn Gore.

7. *L J*, III, 615. *Letters of John Chamberlain*, ed. N. E. Mc.Clure (Philadelphia, 1939), II, 412. See also Clarendon's description of Pym, *History* (1732 edn), I, 185: 'always a man of business, being an officer in the Exchequer, and of a good reputation generally, though known to be inclined to the Puritan faction'.

8. *1621 Debates*, IV, 201; *C J*, I, 572; n. 2 above.

9. Somerset RO, Pym MSS. no.s 139–146; PRO, E 159/430, m.56. I am grateful to Mr David Thomas for this reference.

10. Clarendon, *History*, I, 183. Pym's letter in *CSPD*, 1637–8, 571, says he is about to return to the country 'where I have been the most part of these two years last past'. The dating of Pym's letters in Sheffield University Library, Hartlib MSS. 31/3, appears to show that 'the country' here means Northamptonshire. I am grateful to Dr Charles Webster for drawing my attention to these letters. On one of the rare occasions when Dorothy Pym gave an address in a letter to her brother Charles, she wrote from Fawsley. James M. Osborn Collection, Beineke Library, Yale University, Pym Box, Family Letters, no. 5. Some of the likely members of this gathering may be shown by the list of trustees chosen by Knightley when he converted his impropriations into a trust for John Dod, vicar of Preston Capes. They were Saye and Sele, Sir Nathaniel Rich, John Hampden, John Crew, John Pym and Christopher Sherland. On the deaths of Rich and Sherland, they were replaced by Edward Bagshaw and Sir Arthur Haselrig: Northamptonshire RO, Knightley MSS. no.s 36, 38, 40, 42, 45, 107. It was to Knightley's house that John Preston retired to die: P. S. Seaver. *The Puritan Lectureships* (Stanford, 1970), 265; Birmingham Reference Library, Coventry MSS., Commissions, no. 258, 16 Nov. 1639.

11. PRO, SP 14/134/90. I am grateful to Lynda Price for this reference.

12. *1621 Debates*, IV, 144–5.

13. BL, Add. MS. 40,629, f.128.

14. C. J. Sawyer and Co., Catalogue no. 155, no. 102, Francis Luttrell to Sir Charles Pym, March 15, 1660/1. I am grateful to Messrs Sawyer's for permission to quote from their sale catalogue. Many of the originals from this sale cannot now be found.

15. Yale University, Osborn Collection, Pym Box, Family Letters, no. 5 (undated: *c.* 1635–41). See Sawyer's Catalogue 155, no. 69 for another request to Charles Pym for virginals, this time from Pym's youngest daughter Katherine. Diary of Sir William Spring, 25 Feb. 1624: I am grateful to the Yale Center for Parliamentary History for allowing me to use a transcript of this diary. D. M. Hirst, *The Representative of the People?* (1975), 83, 198–9, 233, 234.

16. Diary of John Hawarde, Wilts. RO, Ailesbury MSS., 9 March 1624.

17. PRO, C 142/435/118.

18. BL, Add. MS. 26,637 (1621); Bedford MSS. 197 (1625). Add. MS. 26,639, though not annotated, consists of extracts from Pym's diary for 1624, and comes from a collection which appears to have once been in Bedford's possession.

19. *1621 Debates*, III, 331, II, 399–400, III, 353. In the case of Floyd, Pym's concern appears to have been to preserve the rights of the Commons as prosecutors, rather than as judges: IV, 361, III, 287–8.

20. *L J*, III, 514; Diary of Bulstrode Whitelocke, Cambridge University Library, MSS. Dd 12–20, 12–21 and 12–22 (hereafter cited as Whitelocke Diary); 12–20, fos. 51v, 46v; *Letters of John Chamberlain*, II, 629; BL, Add. MS. 40,089, fos. 38r–44v, 157v.

21. Whitelocke Diary, 12–22, f.12v; *L J*, III, 627; *Debates in the House of Lords 1624 and 1626*, ed. S. R. Gardiner (Camden Soc., n.s. XXIV, 1879), 196–200; *HMC*, Buccleuch MSS., III, 292.

22. Diary of Sir William Spring, 16 April 1624; Northants. RO, Finch-Hatton MS. 50, f.65r (Pym's diary); *C J*, I, 768. *Commons' Debates in 1628*, ed. R. C. Johnson, M. F. Keeler, M. J. Cole and W. B. Bidwell (New Haven, 1977) (hereafter cited as *1628 Debates*), III, 617. BL, Stowe MS. 366, f.276r; Bedford MSS. XI (i), 158–63. On the Manwaring case, Bedford was on the committee to take depositions, and copied part of Pym's speech into his commonplace book: *ibid.*, 1258; *L J*, III, 846.

23. Diary of Sir Richard Grosvenor, Trinity College Dublin MS. 612 (hereafter cited as Grosvenor MS. 1628), 10 June; PRO, PROB 11/154, fos. 37–8; *1628 Debates*, III, 10n.

24. Whitelocke Diary, 12–20, fos. 65v–64v; *Lords' Debates* (ed. Gardiner), 115; *HMC*, Buccleuch MSS., III, 272; Bedford MSS. XI (i), 56–8, 177.

25. Bedford MSS. 197, f.15r. Bedford's objection could be to the proposal to allow owners of impropriations to make them presentative by deed: his capitals are too large to allow precise statements about where he intended to place them. Bedford was equally unsympathetic to the pleas of Hoby and Rich for silenced ministers. On this issue also Pym appears to have been unhampered by his patron's objections. For Pym's further concern with impropriations, *1628 Debates*, III, 7–8, 10; *C J*, I, 924.

26. *Commons' Debates in 1625*, ed. S. R. Gardiner (Camden Soc., n.s. VI, 1873) (hereafter cited as *1625 Debates*), 20. The references to 'contagious and dangerous disease' should be read in the light of the fact that they were written during the 1625 plague. I am grateful to Mr P. D. Lake and Mr R. I. Moore for discussions of these points.

27. *1621 Debates*, IV, 62–5, V, 499–502. For Shepherd's reputation as a papist, see W. R. Prest, *The Inns of Court under Elizabeth I and the Early Stuarts* (1972), 184.

28. Bodl., Tanner MS. 392, fos. 40v, 50v, 77v; BL, Add. MS. 18, 597, f.109v.

29. *C J*, I, 853; Grosvenor MS. (1626), 3 May. Grosvenor establishes Pym's personal responsibility, and gives a figure of only two servants.

30. *1621 Debates*, IV, 110–1, V, 260; *C J*, I, 530.

31. PRO, C 65/185. This declaration was the work of Hakewill, Clement Coke and Pym. Pym's diary (*1621 Debates*, IV, 140) describes it as a declaration in writing made by Mr Hakewill, but does not say whether it was the declaration or the writing that was made by Mr Hakewill.

32. Whitelocke Diary, 12–20, f.53v; Grosvenor MS. (1626), 1 May; *L J*, III, 615.

33. Grosvenor MS. (1626), 3 May; *1628 Debates*, II, 570: Whitelocke Diary, 12–21, f.129v.

34. E. Nicholas, *Proceedings and Debates in the House of Commons in 1620 and 1621* (1766) (hereafter cited as Nicholas), II, 235.

35. Nicholas, II, 238. It must be stressed that this is an *ex parte* text, as the reference to 'your' Majesty illustrates. It was written out by Pym for submission to the king. However, Pym left in the most offensive matter, including the reference to the king's 'wariness of his own person'. The passage quoted here has a close enough resemblance to the texts in *1621 Debates*, II, 463, V, 222 and VI, 327 to suggest that it is not dramatically different from what he delivered in the House. Diarists frequently skipped divine right imagery, treating it as so much padding.

36. M. Judson, *The Crisis of the Constitution* (Rutgers, 1949), 18; Nicholas, II, 234.

37. Nicholas, II, 219; *1621 Debates*, IV, 442.

38. *L J*, III, 614.
39. Spring Diary, 19 March 1624: also BL, Harleian MS. 6383, f.105r; PRO, SP 14/166, f.92r; Cumberland RO, diary of Sir John Lowther, 19 March 1624. I am grateful to Professor Robert E. Ruigh for drawing my attention to this diary.
40. Bodl., Tanner MS. 392, f.19r; Wilts. RO, Hawarde Diary, 2 March 1624.
41. *1621 Debates*, II, 463; Nicholas, II, 264; *1625 Debates*, 19. By 1625, the last clause no longer referred to the subversion of the true religion, but to 'the extermination both of us and our religion'. The 1625 petition, drafted by Pym and Sandys, also repeated Pym's charges of 1621 about the 'popularity' of papists. The same phrases were repeated by Sir Robert Grosvenor in his charge to the Cheshire electors in 1624. It is not clear whether Grosvenor is quoting from Pym or from the petition quoting from Pym (Cheshire RO, Grosvenor MS., 2 Feb. 1623/4). I am grateful to Richard Cust for this reference.
42. *1621 Debates*, IV, 448 (Pym's diary). The fact that Pym's diary comes to a sudden halt at this point could be held to indicate a fear that his labours to 'win the King' were proving unsuccessful.
43. Nicholas, II, 297; *1621 Debates*, VI, 244. For a sharply different version of the speech of 7 Dec. see *1621 Debates*, VI, 229.
44. The conclusion of Pym's speech of 27 Nov. was that they should vote additional supply 'without any mention of the war' and go back to bills: *1621 Debates*, IV, 441, 439, 443.
45. Northants. RO, Finch-Hatton MS. 50, f.8v.
46. *1621 Debates*, III, 44. Pym said the proclamation which took it away was good, 'which was not denied, all the house saith'.
47. Nicholas, I, 344.
48. Grosvenor MS. (1626), 8 June; *1628 Debates*, II, 403. See also the instructive case of Sir Simeon Steward, *ibid.*, III, 136.
49. BL, Add. MS. 36, 825, fos. 414r, 416r; Grosvenor MS. (1628), 30 May.
50. It is interesting to contrast the reports of Pym and Barrington for 28 May–4 June 1621, and of Pym and Dyott for 11 Aug. 1625. See also the comments on Coke and Seymour, *1625 Debates*, 71, 121.
51. Wilts. RO, Hawarde Diary, 23 Feb. 1624; *C J*, I, 716.
52. C. Russell, 'The examination of Mr Mallory after the Parliament of 1621', *BIHR*, XLX (1977), 125–32. The issue is discussed further in my article, 'The foreign policy debate in the House of Commons', *Historical Journal*, XX (1977), 289–309, and in my forthcoming book, *Parliaments and English Politics 1621–9*, chapter II.
53. Pym had been given a warning before his speech of 28 Nov. (*1621 Debates*, IV, 448). The only possible occasions for this warning are his speech of 27 Nov., in which he proposed to vote supply unconditionally and go back to bills, and his speech on Lepton and Goldsmith on 24 Nov. See *1621 Debates*, III, 462, II, 464, VI, 206–7; Nicholas, II, 219, 236.
54. *Letters of John Chamberlain*, II, 412.
55. *1621 Debates*, III, 439. There is a significantly full text in Nicholas, II, 201, which would have been available to the Duke.
56. National Register of Archives, Sackville MSS. ON 8746, 867 and 277: I am grateful to Professor Roy Schreiber for these references. See also *HMC*, 4th Report

App., 312–3. Bedford was Cranfield's sponsor when he took his seat in the Lords in November 1621: *L J*, III, 163.

57. *1621 Debates*, III, 264, 287–8, IV, 361 and other references; C. G. C. Tite, *Impeachment and Parliamentary Judicature in Early Stuart England* (1974), 51, 175–6 and other refs. On the impeachment of Manwaring, *L J*, III, 847; *Debates in the House of Lords*, ed. F. H. Relf (Camden Soc., 3rd ser. XLII, 1929), 219. The key point in control of an impeachment prosecution was control over the production of witnesses. Pym achieved this in part by selecting witnesses some of whom were members of the Commons: House of Lords RO, Braye MS. I, f.67.

58. *1621 Debates*, III, 30, II, 303.

59. In some of these cases, notably those of Aleyn and Lambert, Pym's interventions were procedural, and their tactical object is not certain.

60. N. R. N. Tyacke, in C. Russell (ed.), *The Origins of the English Civil War* (1973), 121, 135.

61. John Preston, *A Funeral Sermon on Mr. A. Upton* (1619), dedicated to Pym.

62. BL, Add. MS. 36,825, fos. 470r–471v. See also his explicit contrast between Arminianism and 'our religion', *Commons' Debates in 1629*, ed. W. Notestein and F. H. Relf (Minneapolis, 1921) (hereafter cited as *1629 Debates*), 112. Dr Tyacke remarks: 'for many people in the early seventeenth century the basic issue between Protestantism and Catholicism was that of divine determinism versus human free will': Russell, *Origins*, 128. See also C. Russell, *The Crisis of Parliaments* (1971), 216–7. Pym appears to have been uncertain whether the Arminians actually were papists: in 1643, he accused the bishops of introducing 'Arminian or papistical ceremonies, whether you please to term them, there is not much difference': *A Declaration or Vindication of John Pym, Esq.* (1643), 5.

63. E.g. PRO, PROB 11/116/f.199 (William Pym); PROB 11/137/f.508 (Anthony Rous) and PROB 11/181/f.386 (Richard Knightley). The only exception is Pym's mother, who seems to have believed she was predestined to damnation: C. Russell, 'The wardship of John Pym', *EHR*, LXXXIV (1969), 307 and n.; also 315–16 and n.

64. *1625 Debates*, 49; BL, Add. MS. 36,825, f.471r. See also Francis Rous, *Testis Verilatis* (1626), 105–7. Contrast the lack of any immediate fear of idolatry in Francis Rous, *Oil of Scorpions* (1623), 108–10.

65. *1625 Debates*, 46, 47, also his significant seconding of Fleetwood's motion of 8 Aug., *ibid.*, 140–1.

66. The correct order of speeches was established by Tite, *op. cit.*, 198n., and the correct division between the speeches is according to *L J*, III, 610–6.

67. Grosvenor MS. (1626) 3 June; Whitelocke Diary, 12–22, f.33r.

68. J. H. Hexter, *The Reign of King Pym* (Cambridge, Mass., 1941), 194–5. See also his clash with Selden in 1629 about whether the Lambeth Articles and other formulations not confirmed by law could properly be regarded as 'public acts of the church'. *HMC*, 13th Report App VII, 64, 68; *1629 Debates*, 119–20.

69. *1628 Debates*, III, 77, II, 106. On most topics, the body of explicit political ideas material in parliamentary debates before 1628 is small. After 1628, these debates circulated in numerous manuscript copies and some printed extracts.

70. BL, Add. MS. 36,825, f.495r. Also fos. 493v–494r, 506r–v.

71. *Ibid.*, f.498v. It is impossible to be certain that Pym taxed the Lords' patience

with the whole of this script. Yet the report to the Lords by Coventry seems to be an accurate précis of the whole speech: House of Lords RO, Braye MS. I, fos. 60–67. See also *C J*, I, 919.

72. *1628 Debates*, III, 102, 156–7, 162.
73. *1628 Debates*, III, 102 (also 97, 107).
74. *Ibid.*, II, 367.
75. *Ibid.*, III, 281–2. See also 276, 286: 'the King's word can add no obligation to the oath he took at his coronation'.
76. BL, Stowe MS. 366, f.276r; *1629 Debates*, 156–7, 222–3.
77. *L J*, III, 615. In this speech, and in his attack on Manwaring, Pym feared what Locke, in the last chapter of his *Second Treatise*, called 'the dissolution of government'. The loss of religious unity threatened 'the dissolution of society', which was the more irreparable fate of the two. See C. Russell, 'Arguments for religious unity in England 1530–1650', *Journal of Ecclesiastical History*, XVIII (1967), 203–11, 217–22.
78. There is no evidence that Manwaring was an Arminian. The speech in *1628 Debates*, II, 92, if it is Pym's, suggests that Pym believed him to be one.
79. BL, Add. MS. 36,825, fos. 490v–510r *passim*. See also C. Russell, 'The theory of treason in the trial of Strafford', *EHR*, LXXX (1965), 33–4, 42–4, 46–8.
80. *1628 Debates*, III, 410 (Pym's report to the Commons of 14 May. This passage was delivered to the Lords by Pym's assistant Francis Rous.
81. BL, Stowe MS. 366, f.218v; J. Rushworth, *Historical Collections* (1659), I, 609–10; BL: Stowe MS. 366, f.223r; Add. MS. 36,825, f.450r and also 451r.
82. BL, Add. MS. 31,116, f.99v. I am grateful to Professor V. Pearl for this reference. It is worth remembering that in 1643, Pym claimed to be defending 'the orthodox doctrine of the church of England': *A Declaration or Vindication* (1643), 4.
83. See Pym's speech on the subscription bill, *1628 Debates*, III, 515, 519, 520, 522 (text of bill, *ibid.*, 459). Also BL, Add. MS. 36,825, f.470r–v.
84. *1625 Debates*, 179 (Report of 17 April 1626); W. Laud, *A Sermon Preached on Monday the Sixt of February* (1625), 40, 9. Cf. R. C. Richardson, *Puritanism in North-West England* (1972), 174–6.
85. Tyacke, in Russell, *Origins*, 143.
86. Clarendon, *History*, I, 3; S. R. Gardiner (ed.), *Constitutional Documents of the Puritan Revolution* (1906), 206–9.
87. *1625 Debates*, 183; BL, Add. Ms. 36,825, fos. 506r, 509v, 472v; *1629 Debates*, 20.

9 'THE RAMOTH-GILEAD OF THE GOOD': URBAN CHANGE AND POLITICAL RADICALISM AT GLOUCESTER 1540–1640

1. Research for this paper has been generously supported by the Social Science Research Council and the Open University Research Board. I am indebted to Dr P. Morgan and Dr A. Foster for their research help and to Dr P. Corfield for her comments on an early version of this paper. The scriptural parallel in the title first appeared in verses by the city puritan Samuel Kenrick which prefaced J. Dorney's *Certain Speeches Made upon the day of the Yearly Election of Officers in the City of Gloucester* (1653).

2. Clarendon, Edward, Earl of, *The History of the Rebellion and Civil Wars in England* (ed. W. D. Macray, 1888), II, 470; *Mr Thomas Pvry Alderman of Glocester his Speech* (1641); for Pury see M. F. Keeler, *The Long Parliament 1640–41* (Philadelphia, 1954), 316–17.

3. F. A. Hyett, *Gloucester in National History* (1896), 100–24; S. Rudder, *The History and Antiquities of Gloucester* (1781), 120–1; Gloucestershire RO (hereafter GRO), GBR 1470, fos. 4–19.

4. P. Clark and P. Slack, *English Towns in Transition* (1976), esp. 158–9.

5. M. D. Lobel (ed.), *Historic Towns: I* (1969), pt iv, 1–2; W. H. Stevenson, *Calendar of the Records of the Corporation of Gloucester* (1893), 16–19; L. T. Smith (ed.), *The Itinerary of John Leland 1535–1543: Parts IV and V* (1908), 57–8.

6. A. Everitt, 'The market town' in J. Thirsk (ed.), *The Agrarian History of England and Wales: IV* (1967), 471.

7. P. Ripley, 'Parish register evidence for the population of Gloucester 1562–1641', *Bristol and Gloucestershire Archaeological Society Transactions* (hereafter *BGAS*), XCI (1972), 203–4; GRO, GBR 1376/1451, fos. 58v and 143v; PRO, St Ch 8/4/9; *HMC*, 12th Report App. IX, 476, 490.

8. Ripley, *op. cit.*, 203. The data is derived from diocesan deposition books, GRO, GDR 79 *et passim*; for some of the problems in exploiting this kind of material see P. Clark, 'The migrant in Kentish towns 1580–1640', in P. Clark and P. Slack (eds.), *Crisis and Order in English Towns 1500–1700* (1972), 119–21.

9. *Ibid.*, 134 *et seq.* The apprenticeship evidence is taken from GRO, GBR 1458. I intend to discuss the general limitations of apprenticeship data on another occasion.

10. For pauper immigration to other towns see P. Slack, 'Vagrants and vagrancy in England 1598–1664', *EcHR*, n.s. XXVII (1974), 360–79. GRO, GBR 1453/1542, fos. 34, 117; 1453–4/1542–3, *passim*.

11. PRO, SP 12/114/32; J. Thirsk, 'Projects for gentlemen, jobs for the poor: mutual aid in the Vale of Tewkesbury 1600–1630', in P. McGrath and J. Cannon (eds.), *Essays in Bristol and Gloucestershire History* (1976), 148–9; GRO, GDR 89 (Robertes *v*. Darston).

12. Gloucester City Reference Library (hereafter GCL), MS. 16,526, f.99; W. B. Willcox, *Gloucestershire: A Study in Local Government 1590–1640* (New Haven, 1940), 156, 157n.

13. Lobel, *op. cit.*, 9–10; R. Perry, 'The Gloucestershire woollen industry 1100–1690', *BGAS*, LXVI (1945), 58–9; J. Langton, 'Late medieval Gloucester: some data from a rental of 1455', *Transactions of Institute of British Geographers*, n.s. II (1977), 272–5.

14. *HMC*, 12th Report App. IX, 406–7. The complaint prefaced a petition for a reduction in the city fee-farm; there is no evidence the Crown granted this. *Statutes of the Realm* (ed. A. Luders, T. E. Tomlins *et al.*, 1810–28), III, 531 (Gloucester was not included in subsequent Henrician legislation for towns); C. Phythian-Adams, 'Urban decay in late medieval England', in P. Abrams and E. A. Wrigley (eds.), *Towns in Societies* (1978), 159–85; GRO, GBR 1300/1355; see also Perry, *op. cit.*, 112.

15. PRO, E 134/25 Elizabeth/H3; J. Vanes (ed.), *The Ledger of John Smythe 1538–1550* (1974), 7, 36, 49 *et passim*; *idem*, 'The overseas trade of Bristol in the sixteenth

century' (unpublished Ph.D. thesis, University of London, 1975), 390; *VCH*, Gloucestershire, II, 26.

16. GRO, GBR 1375/1450, f.103v. The first and third sets of data are taken from freeman registrations in GRO, GBR 1300/1355, 1466B. The 1608 material is derived from the fairly comprehensive muster returns printed in *Men and Armour for Gloucestershire in 1608* (1902), 1–10. To assist comparison of data those persons engaged in unskilled or semi-skilled work (particularly numerous in the 1608 listing) have been omitted from the analysis, as also those whose occupations are unspecified. The freemen evidence is probably biased towards respectable trades; the muster return is (nominally) limited to men aged 16–60. The 1653–72 data may also be affected by the growing fluidity of occupational styles at that time. For a general discussion of the problems of occupational classification in this period see J. Patten, 'Urban occupations in pre-industrial England', *Transactions of Institute of British Geographers*, n.s. 11 (1977), 296–311.

17. PRO, E 134/11 Charles I/M45; 25 Elizabeth/H3.

18. For the general trend: Clark and Slack (eds.), *op. cit.*, 11; *Statutes of the Realm*, IV, 323–6. Worcester's textile industry which continued to flourish into the late sixteenth century had special legislative protection from rural competition after 1533: A. D. Dyer, *The City of Worcester in the Sixteenth Century* (1973), 117.

19. G. D. Ramsay, *The Wiltshire Woollen Industry in the Sixteenth and Seventeenth Centuries* (1943), 131 *et seq.*; G. Unwin, *Industrial Organization in the Sixteenth and Seventeenth Centuries* (2nd edn, 1957), 71–2; for attempts to establish substitute industries see: GRO, GBR 1394/1500, f.241 *et seq.*; *VCH*, Gloucestershire, II, 190; Willcox, *op. cit.*, 256n.

20. H. B. Walters, 'The church bells of Gloucestershire', *BGAS*, XVIII (1893–4), 238, 243; Willcox, *op. cit.*, 254–5; C. Phythian-Adams, 'Urban crisis or urban change?', in *The Traditional Community under Stress* (Open University course A 322, 1977), 20; PRO, E 134/4 Charles I/E3.

21. For data on other towns see Clark and Slack, *op. cit.*, 102–3; in 1605 the city acquired a third fair (Stevenson, *op. cit.*, 39).

22. PRO, E 134/22 James I/M13; Bodl., MS. Engl. Misc. E.6, f.39v *et passim*; GRO, GDR 114 (Dorney *v.* Haselton); GBR 1422/1544.

23. PRO, E 134/25 Elizabeth/H3; 22 James I/M31; REQ 2/275/13. In 1609 William Woodwall condemned the 'flaunting in fashions . . . nowadays used of many' in the area south of the city: *A Sermon Vpon the xii. xiii and xiiii verses . . .* (1609), 22. J. Taylor, *The Carriers Cosmographie* (1637), sig.B 2v; Bodl., MS. Engl. Misc. E.6, *passim*; P. McGrath (ed.), *Merchants and merchandise in seventeenth century Bristol* (Bristol Rec. Soc., XIX, 1955).

24. GRO, GBR 1375/1450, f.91v; E. Kerridge, *The Agricultural Revolution* (1967), 113–4, 126–7; eg. PRO, St Ch 8/220/1; E 134/25 Elizabeth/H3; E 190/1241/1, 3, 5–6 *et passim*; Vanes, thesis, 46, 391–2. For more on the active trade with Camarthen and other Welsh ports see E. A. Lewis (ed.), *The Welsh Port Books (1550–1603)* (Cymmrodorion Rec. Series, XII, 1927), xxxii, xxxv. Gloucester was also a major transhipment centre up the Severn: e.g. PRO, E 134/4 Charles I/E3, T9.

25. GRO, GBR 1375/1450, f.86; cf. F. S. Hockaday, 'The Consistory Court of the diocese of Gloucester', *BGAS*, XLVI (1924), 195–287; BL, Harleian MS. 4,131, fos.

478–569v; for the growing importance of county quarter sessions in this period see J. Hurstfield, 'County Government c. 1530–c. 1660', in *VCH*, Wiltshire, V, esp. 92 *et seq.*; GRO, GBR 1889B, f.63.

26. GRO, 1696/1885; GDR 114 (Boyle *v.* Messenger); GBR 1376/1451, f.449. For a valuable account of the growing socio-economic importance of inns see A. Everitt, 'The English urban inn', in *idem* (ed.), *Perspectives in English Urban History* (1973), 91–137; for the splendid Gloucester New Inn see W. A. Pantin, 'Medieval inns', in E. M. Jope (ed.), *Studies in Building History* (1961), 169–73.

27. Number of lawyers based on examination of GRO, GBR and GDR records; for Gloucester doctors see J. H. Raach, *A Directory of English Country Physicians* (1962), 103; also GDR 79 (White *v.* Thair); J. Bruce (ed.), *Letters and Papers of the Verney Family* (Camden Soc., 1st ser. LVI, 1853), 156, 160; Rudder, *op. cit.*, 396; GDR 159 (Blomer *v.* Estcourt); PRO, SP 14/181/35(1); see also A. Everitt, *Change in the Provinces: the Seventeenth Century* (Dept. of English Local History, University of Leicester, Occasional Papers in English Local History, 2nd ser. I, 1972), 44–5.

28. GRO, GBR 1377/1452, f.105; PRO, REQ 2/163/90; *APC*, 1586–7, 71–2; GBR 1375/1450, f.92; 1420/1540, fos. 131–2; *HMC*, 12th Report App. IX, 476–7; W. B. Stephens, 'Trade trends at Bristol, 1600–1700', *BGAS*, XCIII (1974), 157; *idem*, 'The West-Country ports and the struggle for the Newfoundland fisheries in the seventeenth century', *Transactions of the Devon Ass.*, LXXXVIII (1956), 91–3.

29. PRO, E 179/113/189; GRO, D383, part ii.

30. Eg., GRO, 1376/1451, f.27; PRO, E 134/40 Elizabeth/H9. The inventories used in this analysis are in Kent AO, PRC: 10/1–72; 11/1–7; 27/1–8; 28/1–20. J. MacLean and W. C. Heane (eds.), *Visitation of the County of Gloucester . . . 1623* (Harleian Soc., XXI, 1885), 96, 100–1, 106–7; GRO, City Map of 1624.

31. GRO, P154/6, OV1/1–14; in 1624 the magistrates noted the 'great want and misery' of the city poor; GBR, 1376/1451, f.496v; 1453/1542, f.62v *et passim*; PRO, SP 16/194/11(I). See the acute situation elsewhere in J. F. Pound (ed.), *The Norwich Census of the Poor 1570* (Norfolk Rec. Soc., XL, 1971), 7–21; P. Clark, *English Provincial Society from the Reformation to the Revolution: Religion, Politics and Society in Kent 1500–1640* (1977), 239–41.

32. The physical polarization was mirrored in the pattern of rental values: P. Ripley, 'The trade and social structure of Gloucester 1600–1640', *BGAS*, XCIV (1976), 119–20. GRO, GBR 1444/1566, fos. 147v–8; Ripley, 'Parish register evidence', 203.

33. GRO, GBR: 1450/1572; 1376/1451, fos. 529–31; 1453/1542, f.113; 1450/1572, fos. 483 and 484; for more on alehouses see P. Clark, 'The alehouse and the alternative society', in D. Pennington and K. Thomas (eds.), *Puritans and Revolutionaries* (1978), 47–72. The Gloucester puritan William Loe complained that 'the rude people . . . seldom or never think of' Christ: *The Blisse of Brightest Beavtie* (1614), 15.

34. Eg., GRO, GBR: 1444/1566, f.72v; 1454/1543, f.13; 1376/1451, fos. 17v, 18v, 84, 98v; *HMC*, 12th Report App. IX, 458–9; PRO, SP 12/188/47; St Ch 8/4/9; GBR, 1444/1566, f.162v.

35. Cf. E. M. Leonard, *The Early History of English Poor Relief* (1900), 23–45; one of the few early measures at Gloucester was the registration of local beggars (*HMC*, 12th Report App. IX, 436–8). GRO, GBR 1349–61/1403–15; 1375/1450, f.79;

1376/1451, f.69; 1453/1542, f.125; 1394/1500, f.241 *et seq.*

36. GRO, GBR 1394/1500, f.269 *et seq*; 1376/1451, fos. 122v, 143v, 144v, 167; BL, Lansdowne MS. 76, f.101; *HMC*, 12th Report App. IX, 459; *APC*, 1597, 119.

37. GRO, GBR 1324/1378; *VCH*, Gloucestershire, II, 121–22; *Civitas, Glouc. Ordinances statutes and rules made . . . for the good government of the several hospitals . . .* (n.d.); GRO, GBR 1701, f.82 *et seq.*; P. Slack, 'Poverty and politics in Salisbury 1597–1666', in Clark and Slack (eds.), *op. cit.*, 180–94; Leonard, *op. cit.*, 311–15.

38. GRO, GBR 1453–4/1542–3; *HMC*, 12th Report App. IX, 445–7; GRO, GBR 1376/1451, fos. 39–40, 529–31; in 1639–43 the largest number of indictments at city quarter sessions involved alehouse-keeping. For action in other puritan towns see: Colchester, Assembly Book 1576–99, f.149 *et seq.*; J. C. Cox (ed.), *The Records of the Borough of Northampton: II* (1898), 304–5.

39. *Civitas, Glouc., op. cit.*, 16, 18–20, 26–7; GRO, GBR 1376/1451, fos. 560–2.

40. GRO, GBR: 1394/1500, *passim*; 1376/1451, fos. 67v *et seq.*, 86v *et seq.*; PRO: St Ch 8/4/8; E 134/3 James I/M3. Civic insolvency was increasingly common at this time; for more examples see A. B. Rosen, 'Economic and social aspects of the history of Winchester 1520–1670' (unpublished D.Phil. thesis, University of Oxford, 1975), 99, 101; *VCH*, Warwickshire, VIII, 266 (Coventry).

41. GRO, GBR: 1878; 1376/1451, fos. 187v–8, 251v, 506v; PRO, E 134/3 James I/M3. The average age at entry to the council in the last part of Elizabeth's reign was 39.

42. Of the 20 wealthiest inhabitants assessed in 1594 13 were acting or future aldermen and two more connected to the bench by high legal office (PRO, E 179/115/430). J. Browne senior, a mercer, died worth about £2,000 in goods in 1593; Thomas Machin, another mercer, died in 1614 with an estate in lands, sheep and goods estimated at £5-6,000 (PRO, REQ 2/118/59; St Ch 8/4/9). See also Ripley, 'Trade and social structure', 122. Comparative data on urban wealth is detailed in R. Grassby, 'The personal wealth of the business community in seventeenth-century England', *EcHR*, n.s. XXIII (1970), 230–3. For the property holdings of the Norwich aldermanic bench see B. H. Allen, 'The administrative and social history of the Norwich merchant class 1485–1660' (unpublished Ph.D. thesis, Harvard University, 1951), 340, 351, 356.

43. PRO: St Ch 8/220/1; E 134/30, 31 Elizabeth/M4; C 3/324/55; for the gerontocratic bias in society as a whole see K. Thomas, 'Age and Authority in Early Modern England', *Proceedings of the British Academy*, LXII (1976), 5–10; GRO, GBR 1416/1535 (reversed); *HMC*, 12th Report App. IX, 523; Stevenson, *op. cit.*, 38; W. R. Williams, *The Parliamentary History of the County of Gloucester . . . 1213–1898* (1898), 190–4.

44. Stevenson, *op. cit.*, 18, 37, 41; GRO, GBR: 1396/1501, f.424 *et seq.*; 1376/1451, f.188; PRO, St Ch 8/A 20/11; A 1/15. The more open, consensus politics in the late medieval town is discussed by S. Reynolds, *An Introduction to the History of English Medieval Towns* (1977), ch. 6.

45. GRO, GBR: 1376/1451; 1878; PRO, St Ch: 8/4/9; 5/A 20/11; 8/228/30; J. E. Neale offers a useful account of the city's Tudor elections in *The Elizabethan House of Commons* (1949), 260–9.

46. *HMC*, 12th Report App. IX, 431, 529; GRO, GBR: 1394/1500, f.19 *et seq.*; 1376/1451, f.188; 1396/1501, f.464v.

47. *HMC*, 12th Report App. IX, 457; for an analysis of the general growth of urban oligarchy at this time see Clark and Slack, *op. cit.*, 128–32.

48. PRO, St Ch 8/254/23; 8/4/9; GRO, GBR: 1376/1451, f.174v; 1453/1542, f.16; PRO, St Ch 8/4/8–9; 228/30; GRO, GBR 1376/1451, f.92–v.

49. PRO, St Ch 8/228/30; 207/25; eg. Clark, *English Provincial Society*, 340–1; *HMC*, 13th Report App. I V, 164 (Winchilsea).

50. GRO, GBR: 1375/1450, fos. 115v and 116; 1376/1451, f.86; PRO, SP 12/171/24; the city continued to dominate the close liberties after the Restoration: R. Beddard, 'The Privileges of Christchurch, Canterbury: Archbishop Sheldon's Enquiries of 1671', *Archaeologia Cantiana*, LXXXVII (1972), 93–100.

51. GRO, GBR 1889B, f.16; PRO, St Ch 5/A 20/11; GBR 1878; PRO, PC 2/45, p.209; Lobel, *op. cit.*, 13.

52. GRO, GBR: 1452/1574, f.59 *et seq.*; 1889B, fos. 3 and 79v; for another dispute with the county justices: *ibid.*, f.56.

53. GRO, GBR, 1376/1451, fos. 167v, 170, 172v, 203v *et seq.* Interestingly, the city never took a prominent part in the onslaught on Council jurisdiction from the 1590s (Willcox, *op. cit.*, 26–7).

54. Eg., *APC*, 1595–6, 327–8; 1596–7, 154, 277–8; parallel developments in other towns are noted by J. W. F. Hill, *Tudor and Stuart Lincoln* (1956), 77–n; GRO, GBR 1376/1451, f.108; *HMC*, 12th Report App. IX, 457–8.

55. GRO, GBR 1889B, f.3; PRO, SP 14/63/45, 68; *HMC*, Salisbury MSS., XVII, 353; XXIII, 125; GRO, GBR 1376/1451, f.66v.

56. PRO, SP 16/56/8; 77/30, 30(I); 94/57; *HMC*, 12th Report App. IX, 478–9, 482, 486; GRO, GBR 1453/1542, f.117v.

57. GRO, GBR: 1878; 1452/1574 (at end); W. Notestein and F. H. Relf (eds.), *Commons Debates for 1629* (Minneapolis, 1921), 201, 231.

58. *LP*, X, 463; XII(1), 139–40, 313; XII(2), 484; also K. G. Powell, 'The social background to the Reformation in Gloucestershire', *BGAS*, XCII (1973), 115–117.

59. GCL, MS. 29, 334; GRO, GBR 1376/1451, fos. 176v–7; *HMC*, Salisbury MSS., V, 207; R. Willis, *Mount Tabor or Private Exercises of a Penitent Sinner* (1639), 105; GRO: GBR 1376/1451, fos. 71v and 72; GDR 89 (at front); B. Taylor, 'William Laud dean of Gloucester 1616–1621', *BGAS*, LXXVII (1958), 89.

60. W. J. Sheils (ed.), 'A survey of the diocese of Gloucester 1603', in *An Ecclesiastical Miscellany* (Bristol and Gloucestershire Archaeological Soc., Records Section, XI, 1976), 68–9. In 1583–4 we hear: 'all the townsmen clergy [are] very poor' (Lambeth Palace Library, Cartae Misc. XII/7); in 1641 there was a petition against 'the promoting of many lewd, worthless and ignorant persons into the ministry, especially in the city, where singing men of the cathedral are made ministers, and set over most of the parishes in the city, being known to be grossly ignorant and very scandalous for their lives' (GCL, MS. JF.4.13). F. D. Price, 'Bishop Bullingham and Chancellor Blackleech: a diocese divided', *BGAS*, XCI (1972), 175–98; PRO, REQ 2/165/182; *DNB*, Bullingham, John; P. Heylyn, *Cyprianus Anglicus* (Dublin, 1719), pt i, 44.

61. Eg., GRO, GDR: 55 (unfol.); 89 (Hallowes *v.* Trotman); D 326, Z1; R. Austin, *The Crypt School, Gloucester* (1939), 47 *et seq.*; *VCH*, Gloucestershire, II, 321–6; the city not only financed the Crypt School, but from the 1620s augmented the stipend of the cathedral schoolmaster (GRO, GBR 1376/1451, f.521).

62. Data in tables 6–7 derived from deposition books, GRO, GDR 79 *et passim.*
63. BL, Sloan MS. 1199, fos. 92v and 93; S. M. Eward (ed.), *A Catalogue of Gloucester Cathedral Library* (1972), vii–viii; GRO: P154/6, CW 1/10a; P154/14, C1/41; Ripley, 'Trade and social structure', 118; for more urban evidence see P. Clark, 'The ownership of books in England, 1560–1640: the example of some Kentish townsfolk', in L. Stone (ed.), *Schooling and Society* (1976), 95–109; BL, Harleian MS. 425, f.121; Deighton's books are listed in GRO, D381.
64. J. Latimer, *Annals of Bristol: Seventeenth Century* (1900), 58, 145, 148–9; J. R. Chanter and T. Wainwright, *Reprint of the Barnstaple Records* (1900), II, 13, 100; D. Underdown, *Somerset in the Civil War and Interregnum* (1973), 22; G. Davies (ed.), *Autobiography of Thomas Raymond and Memoirs of the Family of Guise* ... (Camden Soc., 3rd ser. XXVIII, 1917), 113; G. A. Harrison, 'Royalist organization in Gloucestershire and Bristol 1642–5' (unpublished M.A. thesis, University of Manchester, 1961), 16; *DNB*, Rudd, Anthony; BL, Stowe MS. 76, f.249; Heylyn, *op. cit.*, 44; Rudder, *op. cit.*, 351.
65. GRO, GBR 1376/1451, fos. 176v–7, 236, 466–7; Taylor, *op. cit.*, 89.
66. PRO, St Ch 8/4/8; 207/25; Taylor, *op. cit.*, 89; BL, Royal MS. 12.A.LXX, f.9v *et seq.*
67. *HMC*, Salisbury MSS., XIV, 149; XV, 47–8; *CSPD*, 1635, xli; T. Fuller, *The Worthies of England* (ed. P. A. Nuttall, 1840), I, 563–4; Hyett, *op. cit.*, 98. The idea of the godly citadel was a recurrent theme in the addresses of John Dorney, the town clerk, to the magistrates in the 1640s (Dorney, *op. cit.*).
68. See above, p. 173; Willcox, *op. cit.*, 177n; PRO, E 134/11 Charles I/M 45; J. Taylor, 'John Taylors last Voyage (1641)' in *Works: II* (Spenser Soc., 1873), 3, 25, 29–30.
69. GRO, GBR 1420/1540, fos. 166–7, 231; *Privy Council Registers*, IV, 423–4; GRO, P 154/6, OV1/14; GBR 1396/1501, f.141; 1454/1543, f.13.
70. GRO, GBR 1377/1452, p. 86; *Privy Council Registers*, V, 205; *CSPD*, 1635, 470; 1636–7, 109; PRO, PC 2/44, pp. 265–6; PC 2/45, pp. 169, 209.
71. For a general discussion see N. Tyacke, 'Puritanism, Arminianism and counter-revolution' in C. Russell (ed.), *The Origins of the English Civil War* (1973), 132–43; GRO, GDR 190; PRO, SP 16/308/22; H. C. Dancey, 'The high cross at Gloucester', *BGAS*, XXIV (1901) 299, 302; GRO, GBR 1377/1452, p. 76; GDR 201 (Sept. 1639).
72. GRO, GBR 1376/1451, f.508; J. N. Langston, 'J. Workman, Puritan Lecturer in Gloucester', *BGAS*, LXVI (1945), 219–31; *HMC*, House of Lords MSS., n.s. XI, 418–19; GRO, GBR 1377/1452, pp.18, 23, 121.
73. *CSPD*, 1637–8, 285–7; PRO, SP 16/379/88; GRO, GBR 1377/1452, p.132; J. Bird, *Grounds of Grammer Penned and Pvblished* (1639), sig. A2v–3; *CSPD*, 1635, xl.
74. *Privy Council Registers*, VII, 629; VIII, 46; X, 509; *CSPD*, 1639, 519–21; J. Washbourn, *Bibliotheca Gloucestrensis* (1825), 6–7.
75. A. M. Johnson, 'Politics in Chester during the Civil War and the Interregnum 1640–62', in Clark and Slack (eds.), *op. cit.*, 204 *et seq.*; Rosen, *op. cit.*, 237–44.
76. Clark, *English Provincial Society*, 340–1, 381–2 *et passim; idem*, 'Thomas Scott and the growth of urban opposition to the early Stuart regime', *Historical Journal*, XXI (1978), 1–26; A. Fletcher, *A County Community in Peace and War: Sussex 1600–1660* (1975), 234–9 *et passim*; P. Zagorin, *The Court and the Country* (1970),

149–54; *VCH*, Leicestershire, IV, 66–8, 74–5; D. Hirst, *The Representative of the People? Voters and Voting in England under the Early Stuarts* (1975), 46–64. There is virtually no evidence of sectarianism in Gloucester before 1640; for activity after 1640 and concerted magisterial opposition see R. Bacon, *The Spirit of Prelacie Yet Working . . .* (1646), 1–5.

77. Northampton: Northamptonshire RO, Northampton Assembly Book, 1547–1627, fos. 422, 426; 1627–1744, fos. 14, 42, 45, 62; see also Cox, *op. cit.*, 179–80 *et passim*. Salisbury: P. Slack, 'Religious protest and urban authority: the case of Henry Sherfield iconoclast, 1633' in D. Baker (ed.), *Studies in Church History* IX (1972), 295–302; Clark and Slack (eds.), *op. cit.*, 164–94; P. Slack, 'An election to the Short Parliament', *BIHR*, XLVI (1973), 108–114 (Salisbury's puritan magnates, on the defensive in the 1630s, had recovered power by 1640). Barnstaple: R. W. Cotton, *Barnstaple and the Northern Part of Devonshire during the Great Civil War 1642–6* (1889), 13 *et passim*; Chanter and Wainwright, *op. cit.*, 65 *et passim*; Stephens, 'West Country ports', 92–3. Taunton: Underdown, *op. cit.*, 22, 41, 80; J. Toulmin and J. Savage, *The History of Taunton* (1822), 410 *et seq.*; *CSPD*, 1634–5, 32. Colchester: T. Cromwell, *History and Description of the Ancient Town and Borough of Colchester* (1825), I, 88 *et seq.*; *APC*, 1626, 103–4; 1630–1, 358–9. Coventry: *VCH*, Warwickshire, VIII, 163, 218–19, 265–6.

78. Birmingham: C. Gill, *History of Birmingham: I* (1952), esp. 48–54; S. C. Ratcliff and H. C. Johnson (eds.), *Warwick County Records: II* (1936), 3, 4, 6 *et passim*. Manchester: J. P. Earwaker (ed.), *The Court Leet Records of the Manor of Manchester: II* (1885), 239–40, 288–9; *III* (1886), 122, 163, 268; F. A. Bruton, *A Short History of Manchester and Salford* (1924), 111–14, 118–20; A. P. Wadsworth and J. De Lacy Mann, *The Cotton Trade and Industrial Lancashire* (1931), 33–5, 42–3, 68.

10 PALATINE PERFORMANCE IN THE SEVENTEENTH CENTURY

1. P. Williams, *The Council in the Marches of Wales under Elizabeth I* (1958), 205.
2. J. E. Neale, *The Elizabethan House of Commons* (1949), 21.
3. 5 Eliz. c. 26.
4. *The Letters and the Life of Francis Bacon,* ed. J. Spedding (1861–74), III, 220–1.
5. At Chester this court was known as the Exchequer. In providing references the simplest method has been adopted according to the circumstances. Some books are foliated, others are paginated, many are damaged (a date is thus the best indication), and several are lost although individual draft orders survive.
6. *VCH*, Wiltshire, V, 80, 104, 110.
7. (1627).
8. PRO, E 124/1, fos. 62v, 63; E 126/2, f.91.
9. Henry E. Huntington Library, Bridgewater and Ellesmere MS. 2623.
10. E. Coke, preface, *The Fourth Part of the Institutes of the Lawes of England* (1669).
11. *Letters and Life*, VI, 36.
12. *Continuation of the Court Leet Records of the Manor of Manchester, 1586–1602,* ed. J. Harland (Chetham Soc., LXV, 1865), 33. See generally A. Redford, *The History of Local Government in Manchester,* I (1939).

13. D. J. Butler, *Quarter Sessions and the Justices of the Peace in West Sussex* (1972), 1; J. E. Neale, *Essays in Elizabethan History* (1958), 204.

14. P. Williams, 'The Welsh Border land under Queen Elizabeth', *Welsh History Review*, I (1960), 30.

15. T. F. T. Plucknett, *A Concise History of the Common Law* (1956), 676.

16. 12 Co. Rep. 54 (*English Reports*, 77); Huntington Library, Bridgewater and Ellesmere MSS. 7526, 7564–7601; P. Williams, 'The activity of the Council in the Marches under the early Stuarts', *Welsh History Review*, I (1961), 133–60; *VCH*, Yorkshire: The City of York, 137; R. R. Reid, *The King's Council of the North* (1921), 371; F. W. Brooks, *The Council of the North* (1966), 21; PRO: Durham 5/12, 5/13; Durham 4/1; Chester 14/7, fos. 52v–83; Chester 14/6, fos. 78v–83; Chester 14/5, 14/15. There was more than one series of entry book at Chester. W. H. Bryson, *The Equity Side of the Exchequer* (1975), 168. *Ducatus Lancastriae: Calendar to the Pleadings*, III, pt 4.

17. Flint, although part of the palatine, may have provided a majority of its equity cases to the Great Sessions.

18. 27 H.VIII c. 24; 32 H.VIII c. 43; J. S. Morrill, *Cheshire 1630–1660* (1974), 1–2; W. J. Jones, 'The Exchequer of Chester in the last years of Elizabeth I', in *Tudor Men and Institutions*, ed. A. J. Slavin (Baton Rouge, 1972), 123–70; 'The rights and jurisdiction of the County Palatine of Chester', ed. J. B. Yates, *Chetham Miscellanies: II* (Chetham Soc., 1st ser. XXXVII, 1854), 25.

19. PRO, DL 5/33, fos. 479v, 507, 511v; *Ducatus Lancastriae: Calendar of Pleadings*, III, pt 4, 184, 198, 280, 486; R. Somerville, 'The seals of the Duchy and County Palatine of Lancaster', *Archives*, X (1972), 146.

20. M. James, *Family, Lineage, and Civil Society* (1974), 2; G. T. Lapsley, *The County Palatine of Durham* (Cambridge, Mass., 1900), 190, 300. *Reports of the deputy keeper of the public records*, 16, App. 4, 44–95.

21. 27 H.VIII c. 24; Lapsley, 259, 263; Reid, *op. cit.*, 154, 245, 259, 263, 321; *Calendar of State Papers, Foreign*, 1559–60, no. 850; *APC*, 1575–77, 140–2, 169–70, 291–2, 313; *HMC*, Salisbury MSS., II, 642; BL, Harleian MS. 6992, f.131.

22. F. W. Brooks, *York and the Council of the North* (1954), 15; Reid, 321–2; PRO, SP 12/259, no. 100; *Depositions from the Castle of York* (Surtees Soc., XL, 1861), viii–x.

23. R. Somerville, *Office-Holders in the Duchy and County Palatine of Lancaster from 1603* (1972), 94; PRO, Chester 14/9, fos. 25v–26, 106v, 107; *APC*, 1613–14, 551–2, 640–1.

24. Lapsley, 198; *VCH*, York, 181; PRO, Durham 5/6, fos. 125, 126–7; Durham 5/7, fos. 51–2, 65–6; W. S. Holdsworth, *A History of English Law*, I (1956 edn), 111.

25. *Letters and Life*, VI, 65.

26. T. Powell, *The Attourneys Academy* (1623), 91.

27. Brooks, *York and the Council of the North*, 6; PRO: Durham 5/13, no. 32; Chester 14/5, 890–1.

28. PRO: PL 11/7, 22 Dec. 1625, 16 Jan. 1626; PL 11/8, 7 Aug. 1628; PL 11/6, 30 July 1625; Durham 5/9, f.40; Durham 5/1, f.10; Durham 5/3, fos. 40–1, 54–5; Durham 5/11, no. 7.

29. PRO, Chester 14/6, f.73; Chester 14/8, fos. 99–100, 102v–103, 161.

30. *The Practice of the Court of Chancery of the County Palatine of Durham* (1807), 30;

PRO, Durham 5/6, fos. 1–2; Durham 5/9, f.29; 'List of Documents relating to Legal Proceedings . . . Durham', compiled N. M. Million (September 1960), 3–6, 7–8, 9.

31. Williams, 'Activity', 142.

32. PRO: Chester 14/9, fos. 201, 208v–209v; Durham 5/7, fos. 100–4.

33. Reid, *op. cit.*, 317, 327–32; PRO SP 12/259, no. 100; Brooks, *York and the Council of the North*, 12, 15–16; *VCH*, York, 197–8.

34. R. Howell, *Newcastle-upon-Tyne and the Puritan Revolution* (1967), 42–3; *The Royal Charters of Grantham*, ed. G. H. Martin (1963), 9, 14–15.

35. G. Chandler, *Liverpool under Charles I* (1965), 37; *The Rolls of the Burgesses of the Guild Merchant of the Borough of Preston* (Lancashire and Cheshire Rec. Soc., IX, 1884), xxxiii; W. A. Abram, *Memorials of Preston Guilds* (1882), 32, 39; *Calendar of Chester City Council Minutes, 1603–1642*, ed. M. J. Groombridge (Lancashire and Cheshire Rec. Soc., CVI, 1956), 18, 36; R. Muir and E. M. Platt, *A History of Municipal Government in Liverpool* (1906), 89.

36. PRO, PL 11/3, 23 Feb. 1613; PL 11/4, 25 March 1617; Muir and Platt, *op. cit.*, 69–70, 72, 77–8, 89, 188; *Liverpool Town Books, 1571–1603*, ed. J. A. Twemlow (1935), 102–111, 272, 1063–64.

37. Groombridge, ii–iii, xix, xx, xxv, xxxv, 36, 49 n. 1; J. S. Morrill, *The Revolt of the Provinces* (1976), 26–7; PRO, Chester 14/7, f. 60.

38. Groombridge (ed.), *op. cit.*, xiv, 36–7, 185; PRO, Chester 14/5, pp. 1062–3; Chester 14/6, fos. 11–12, 55, 83, 205v; BL, Harleian MS. 2091, fos. 15, 138v–139, 202, 202v; Chandler, *op. cit.*, 37, 48, 219–20, 232, 233, 235, 254; Muir and Platt (eds.), *op. cit.*, 79–85, 88, 92.

39. *VCH*, Durham, II, 238; III, 30–7; List, compiled Million (September 1960), 8.

40. Redford, *op. cit.*, I, 58, 73.

41. PRO, PL 11/3, 8 March 1615.

42. PRO, Chester 14/9, fos. 157–158v.

43. *CSPD*, 1603–10, 198; PRO, Chester 14/8, fos. 132–3; Chester 14/9, fos. 73, 161v–62, 205, 215, 245.

44. *Reports of Deputy Keeper*, 37, App. I, 116–121, etc.; *Practice . . . of Durham*, 14–15. A number of sixteenth-century statutes provided rules for exigent and other matters.

45. PRO, Chester 14/8, fos. 92, 95; Chester 14/9, fos. 177v–178, 181v.

46. PRO, PL 11/2, 22 August 1608; PL 11/9, f. 348v; Lapsley, *op. cit.*, 200–1, 317–26; *CSPD*, 1635, 370, 371, 407; *Durham Civic Memorials*, ed. C. E. Whiting (Surtees Soc., CLX, 1952), xiii; *Reports of Deputy Keeper*, 37, App. I; 44, App.; J. Hurstfield, *The Queen's Wards* (1958), 102; 18 Eliz. c. 13; 'List', compiled Million (September, 1960), 1, 2.

47. PRO, E 126/2, fos. 72v–77v; E 126/3, fos. 117v–118.

48. James, *op. cit.*, 84–5. BL, Lansdowne MS. 163, fos. 9–10; *LJ*, III, 710, 831; T. S. Willan, *River Navigation in England* (1964), 18–21.

49. Bryson, *op. cit.*, 30; C. Monro, *Acta Cancellaria* (1847), 67, 285; 'Rights and jurisdiction of Chester', 26–7. *HMC*, Salisbury MSS., XVII, 466; XX, 17–18; Hutton 59 (*English Reports*, 123). Some practical limitations of palatine jurisdiction, with particular reference to Chester, were illustrated in a case of 1614: Coke, *op. cit.*, 213–14.

50. Brooks, *York and the Council of the North*, 7, 11, 16. In 1654, Duchy Chamber was revived for pending cases: *Acts and Ordinances of the Interregnum 1642–60*, ed. C. H. Firth and R. S. Rait (1911), II, 916, 1137.

51. 1 Wm and Mary c. 27; Huntington Library, Bridgewater and Ellesmere MSS. 8563, 8564; Chester RO, DDX 15, Umfreville MSS., no. 19, 'A short essay on the Exchequer at Chester', 152; Lapsley, *op. cit.*, 202–4, 207; Holdsworth, *op. cit.*, I, 117; Bryson, *op. cit.*, 168.

52. J. S. Cockburn, *A History of English Assizes, 1558–1714* (1972), 138–9; Holdsworth, *op. cit.*, I, 131; *A Calendar of the White and Black Books of the Cinque Ports, 1432–1955*, ed. F. Hull (*HMC*, 1966), xvi; Redford, *op. cit.*, I, 43; J. P. Dawson, *A History of Lay Judges* (Cambridge, Mass., 1960), 229, 232–4; C. Carlton, *The Court of Orphans* (1974), 89–91.

53. Plucknett, *op. cit.*, 677.

54. Holdsworth, *op. cit.*, I, 188.

INDEX